Gender, Race,

*Journal of the European Society of Women
in Theological Research*

*Revista de la asociación europea de mujeres
en la investigación teológica*

*Jahrbuch der Europäischen Gesellschaft
für theologische Forschung von Frauen*

Volume 28

ESWTR

**Bibliographical information and books for review
in the Journal should be sent to:**
Prof. Dr. Agnethe Siquans,
Universität Wien, Schenkenstraße 8-10, 1010 Wien, Austria

**Articles for consideration for the Journal
should be sent to:**
Prof. Dr. Agnethe Siquans,
Universität Wien, Schenkenstraße 8-10, 1010 Wien, Austria

Gender, Race, Religion

De/constructing Regimes of In/visibility

Editors:
*Agnethe Siquans, Anne-Claire Mulder,
Clara Carbonell Ortiz*

PEETERS
LEUVEN – PARIS – BRISTOL, CT
2020

Journal of the European Society of Women
in Theological Research, 28

A catalogue record for this book is available from the Library of Congress.

© 2020, Peeters Publishers, Leuven / Belgium
ISBN 978-90-429-4329-2
ISSN 1783-2454
eISSN 1783-2446
D/2020/0602/113
Cover design by Margret Omlin-Küchler

All rights reserved. No part to this publication may be reproduced, stored in a retrieval system, or transmitted, in any form of by any means, electronic, mechanical, photocopying, recording or otherwise, without the prior permission of the publisher.

CONTENTS – INHALT – ÍNDICE

Editorial 1

Theme – Thema – Tema

Annemie Dillen & Judith Gruber
Gender, Race, Religion: De/constructing Regimes of In/visibility   25

Kristine Suna-Koro
Revisiting the Sacrament of the Stranger: Reflections on Migration, Invisibility, and Postcolonial Imagination   37

Silvia Martínez Cano
Claves teológicas para la construcción de un imaginario a favor del reconocimiento del otro   65

Bess Brooks
She Who Is [...] Invisible? A Glimpse of the Mothering God in the Church of England's Eucharistic Prayers   85

Jadranka Rebeka Anić & Ana Thea Filipović
Gehört die Ausbeutung zum System? Kirche und die (Ordens)frauen   109

Sylvia Hübel
Herstory of Epistemic Injustice: Wo/men's Silencing in the Catholic Church   127

Monica Ruset Oanca
Julian of Norwich: The Visible Writings of an Invisible Recluse   153

Aleksandra Michalska
Reverend Stoyna: The Blind Seeing With (de)Constructing Power   167

Zilya Khabibullina
The Image of a Muslim Woman in the Russian Mass Media: Trying to Overcome Stereotypes in Islamic Media Space   183

Karin Hügel
Queere Auslegungen der Liebesgebote aus Levitikus 201

Forum
Eleonore Lappin-Eppel
Bet Debora – Frauenperspektiven im Judentum 237

Ulrike Sallandt
Pentekostalismus und Körper: Religionsästhetische Impulse für die Untersuchung von Körperpraktiken pentekostaler Frömmigkeit 253

Book Review
Trees van Montfoort
Green theology: The (in)visibility of the non-human world 279

List of Advisory Board Journal ESWTR 285

List of Board members ESWTR 286

Editorial

Theme
At the moment of writing this introduction – May 2020 – the world is in the grip of an invisible threat; a threat which is countered in a number of ways, especially through the disciplining the behaviour of all both inside the house as in the public space: a lockdown – a (more or less strict) prohibition to freely leave the house and an admonition to wash hands thoroughly when having done so, a prohibition to gather with more than two persons, a directive to keep physical distance in the public space, a directive to wear mouth caps, a prohibition to gather with others…Taken together these directives construct a regime of visibility, by disciplining our behaviour they also ensure that we are made aware of the reigning value system: health over freedom of mobility and of gathering. On the other hand, this crisis also deconstructs the regimes by which the value of a physical gesture of affection, or of care and of the work of care-taking remained invisible and thereby undervalued.

Thus, the Covid-19 or Corona crisis offers the possibility of an experiential entry to the theme of this issue – "Gender, Race, Religion. De/constructing regimes of in/visibility". This theme is derived from that of the 2019 conference of the "European Society of Women in Theological Research" in Leuven, Belgium. At this lively conference, the regimes of in/visibility constructed by the intersection of gender, race and religion were addressed in the key-note lectures and in their responses and in some papers offered at the conference. However, the majority of the papers in the paper-sessions and in this issue of the journal addressed the different regimes of in/visibility at play in the relation between gender and religion/ theology only. This illuminates both the agenda-setting character of the theme of this conference as well as the time it takes to address issues that are so interwoven with the way in which 'we' deal with Europe's colonial past and with its contemporary reaction to migration.

This issue is opened by a text by the organizers of the conference, *Annemie Dillen* and *Judith Gruber*, in which they offer an introduction to the theme of this issue and of the conference by showing the complex intersection and intertwining of gender, race, and religion. Their intention is to stimulate the reflection within the ESWTR on the theme of the conference – the intersection of gender, race, religion, and the regimes of visibility and invisibility that govern these intersections. In their reflections, they use ordinary experiences and controversies in everyday life as starting point or illustration, thus sparking the memories/ experiences of the reader. In the analysis of these experiences and controversies they indicate the processes of power, the processes of 'othering', at work in these situations, and illuminate the process-oriented character of regimes of genderisation, racialisation and religionization. The article closes with a number of important theological issues which are urgently waiting theological reflection. This introduction is followed by the opening lecture of the conference by Kristine Suna-Koro and the text of the response by Silvia Martínez Cano. In her article *Revisiting the sacrament of the stranger*, Kristine Suna-Koro presents a theological interpretation of the current world wide migration crisis due to war and climate change, rooted in the conviction that a theological reinterpretation of what it means to be human is more than ever necessary. She interprets the migration crisis as a supreme challenge to the world's religions, as a *locus theologicus* and the migrant as symbol of all those rejected by today's globalized society. This means that 'migrants' should not be considered a separate issue, but rather as part of a whole range of global issues which asks for a theopoetics and -politics of affinity or kinship rather than for a theopoetics and -politics of provincialisation. She proceeds to sketch the direction of a theological anthropology that starts with the figure of the stranger. What theological answers could be given to those who answer the question: "Is being human enough for survival, let alone leading or aspiring to flourishing life?" in the negative. Suna-Koro explores three directions to come up with a positive answer to this question. First, she shows that from a Christian perspective abundant life is what creation, incarnation and salvation are all about, and not only for humans but for all creation. Her second step is an exploration of the *imago Dei* trope, arguing that this is a unique and utterly democratic human entanglement with God. Thirdly, she explores the possibilities of the word likeness, *similitude,* to think through that human beings are different yet similar and in the image of God, even the strangest stranger. But to acknowledge the strangest stranger demands hard and courageous work; the work of love. If this work would have anything to do with God, it would appear in the place of the other, in the encounter with the hungry, the thirsty (Matt 25), what Suna-Koro calls after Hans Urs von Balthasar the sacrament of the stranger; an encounter, a sacrament which has revelatory power, indicating that divine love is without borders.

Editorial

In a rich response *Silvia Martínez Cano* elaborates upon the ideas of Kristine Suna-Koro, also turning to the idea that the theological anthropology needs to be revised, revisioned, reshaped in order to find (some) answers on the three crises of our times – migration, the ecological crisis and neoliberalism. Presupposition of such a theological anthropology is that it would not repeat the opposition between humans and nature, but rather that it would be biocentric – in the sense that the *imago Dei* would be imagined as relating to God's body, i.e God's creation, through their own body. She moreover suggests that narratives in which corporeality, relationality, justice and solidarity would be important keys in the development of this anthropology. Looking for narratives from which this anthropology could be developed she turns to narratives of the displaced, the migrant women. Their narratives tell a story of what it means to be human – to suffer and to resist. They are invisible, oriented towards survival, which prevents them of rebelling against their situation. Martínez Cano interprets their brokenness expressive of the broken body of Christ and suggests that the sacrament of the stranger, Kristine Suna-Koro talks about, is a sacrament of migrant women. This sacrament forces us to fight against their situation. This brings her to a theological anthropology in an eschatological key – 'in which we discover the wisdom with which God sustains our lives and the life of creation'.

As indicated in the above, the other texts focus on the intersection of gender and religion/theology in their discussion of the de/constructing of regimes of in/visibility. *Bess Brooks* describes the genealogy of the insertion of the only Eucharistic Prayer in the *Book of Common Worship* of the Church of England with a female image of God as the effect of a process of defeminisation. She has borrowed this concept from biology to describe the regimes that have brought about the invisibility of the female in this process. She identifies, first, the dominance of the father metaphor in the Christian tradition; secondly, the bypassing of this scholarship in the process of the debate about this one prayer, and the passing off of their discussions as their own as becomes apparent in the pronouncement that the mother metaphor could not be attributed to 'strident' feminism as the metaphor has been in the Bible all along. And lastly, she points out that the metaphor itself is deeply lacking because it does not portray the mothering God as feeding her chicks but only as protecting them. In her conclusion she clarifies that this defeminisation of the Eucharistic Prayers affects the way she and other women relate to this liturgy: they have difficulty in feeling included and in affirming it.

This article is followed by two texts which deal in different ways with the gendered construction of regimes of invisibility in the church, especially in the Roman Catholic Church. It is interesting that these regimes of invisibility

Editorial

appear to be regimes of silence and silencing, of preventing the abuse of women to be revealed and thereby made visible. *Jadranka Rebeka Anić* and *Ana Thea Filipović* give an elaborate description of the world-wide exploitation of female monastics through labour and sexual services as well as of the different means used to silence these nuns. In their analysis of the causes of this exploitation, they point to the hierarchical and clerical structure of the Roman Catholic Church, the secondary status of women which is also expressed in a heteronomous spiritual tradition. They advocate in the first place that the church recognizes the suffering of the victims of the exploitation and takes care of these female monastics in multiple ways. In the second place they point out that to change the structures which enable exploitation, the church has to change its structures in the direction of an egalitarian and inclusive community of the faithful.

Three concrete examples of the silencing of women in the Roman Catholic Church form the point of departure for *Sylvia Hübel*'s text on wo/men's silencing in this church. She uses the concept of epistemic injustice to analyse the manners in which the production of knowledge by women and its recognition as trustworthy are prevented in the Church. She derives the concept 'epistemic injustice' from the work of Miranda Frick, who defines this as wronging someone in their capacity of knower, informant or participant in the community's production or sharing of knowledge. She charts this process of marginalization of women in the Church and its traditions by describing five different sources of epistemic injustice, ranging from negative stereotyping to epistemic smothering and the culture of cover-up. In her final paragraph she turns to the achievements of feminist theology in the production of knowledge which counter this epistemic injustice. And like Jadranka Rebeka Anić and Ana Thea Filipović, Sylvia Hübel points to the growing number of initiatives who use the crisis brought about by the sexual abuse scandal to advocate a transformation of the church in the direction of a discipleship of equals.

Monica Ruset Oanca and Aleksandra Michalska use a different perspective again on the idea of de/construction of regimes of in/visibility. They show these regimes as dynamic ones of seeing and being seen, of seeing the invisible and being invisible to the seeing, in and through the life stories of two female anchorites, namely the fourteenth century mystic Julian of Norwich and the Bulgarian prophetess prepodobna Stoyna, who lived around the turn of the nineteenth to the twentieth century. In her text on Julian of Norwich *Monica Oanca* argues that the current scholarly focus in Medieval studies on making visible the unknown, invisible lives of female mystics may lead to bypassing the theological relevance of their visions. She aims to present the relevance of the visions of Julian of Norwich for contemporary theological reflections. She describes Julian of Norwich as someone who chose to become an anchoress, living in an enclosed space close to the church, in order to concentrate on her relation with God. Being physically invisible for others enabled Julian of Norwich to focus all her attention and devotion upon the invisible God, whom she saw in her visions; visions she meticulously described so that the reader can see what she saw. In a careful description of what is known of her life and of her work Monica Oanca renders visible Julian's theology of joy and her faith in God's love for humankind and emphasises its relevance for today.

Aleksandra Michalska's text on the life of prepodobna Stoyna approaches the dynamic of visibility and invisiblity from the perspective of the power to construct or deconstruct a religious phenomenon, in this case the growing cult around prepodobna Stoyna. She was a blind woman who led the life of an anchoress in a church in Bulgaria, and was seen as a clairvoyant and prophetess, and as a saint by the people, because of her powers of seeing and healing. Although, it was only from the 1980s onwards that her reputation grew, the result is that the veneration of prepodobna Stoyna has grown into a cult, with thousands of people visiting this church and her old room in pilgrimage and in the hope of a miracle. This development is met with ambivalence by the Bulgarian orthodox church, however, who on the one hand consider it idolatry and on the other hand do not want to dissuade people from visiting this church. Aleksandra Michalska shows, though, that the answer to the question whether she is a saint or not depends not only on the question who defines saintliness, but also on how to understand this form of folk religion and its authority for the lived religion of her followers.

Zilya Khabibullina analyses in her article the regimes of in/visibility that govern the image of Muslim women in Russian media. Situating her analysis both in the changing Russian media landscape and political situation she shows, that nowadays most information on Islam and on Muslims is found on the internet, in Islamic internet sites and -fora. Before 1990 however, information about and attention to Islam were given via the official mass media, in television programs. After the 1990, these channels were closed and Internet became the most important source of information on Islam and Muslims, both for Russian as for Muslim persons. Khabibullina explains that just as in the West, in Russian media Muslim women are portrayed as submissive, oppressed and clad in black and in hijab. She also shows that Muslim women bloggers, who often have acquired a large following, counter this image in a variety of ways, for instance by advocating a colourful dress-style. On the other hand, the internet also seems to stimulate a competition among women about excelling in devotion. Thus Khabibullina manages to paint the complexity of and the many influences on the representation of Muslim women in and through the Internet in Russia.

The last text of this section of this issue on de/constructing regimes of in/visibility is by *Karin Hügel*, who presents a queer reading of the commandments of love in Leviticus. In a detailed analysis of the two commandments, the first in Lev 19:18 about the love of neighbour, the second in Lev 19:34 about the love for the stranger, Hügel shows that these commandments can be read in such a way that they can counter the injunctions against homosexuality in Lev 18. For these commandments can be interpreted as advocating love of self and implicitly as advocating a culture that promotes the love of self of all individuals. They can moreover be interpreted as pointing to the fact that the other is a human being like the subject and thirdly she offers an interpretation in which love of neighbour is another formulation of the golden rule. Her analysis shows that by using a queer hermeneutics it is possible to construct a regime that makes visible the various forms of love of self and love of others of self-identified queer persons.

Forum

In the *Forum* section of this volume we publish two articles that do not strictly fit the theme of this volume, but that discuss issues of visibility/ invisibility in a roundabout way. This section opens with an article by *Eleonore Lappin-Eppel* about *Bet-Debora,* making visible the existence of a European scholarly network of Jewish women – female Rabbis and Cantrices, women and women activists of Jewish faith communities, academics and others – as well as a local house of study in Berlin for women, which organizes small events. Founded in 1998, nine years after the Fall of the Wall – which brought about a huge change in the Jewish communities in Europe – the founders of *Bet-Debora* wanted to develop a house of study or Lehrhaus, in the tradition of studying together within the Jewish community. But this Lehrhaus ought to be one devoted to developing a Jewish tradition that would be more attractive and/or (by being) more just to women. Eleonore Lappin-Eppel shows that *Bet-Debora* realizes this goal in the first place by organizing international conferences every two to three years in different countries of Europe, often together with local Jewish communities. By giving a succinct description of the themes, the local context of the different conference venues and of the participants – she offers a picture of the continuous and continuing reflection upon the question what a more just tradition would look like.

The second article in this section by *Ulrike Sallandt* departs from the idea that in order to do justice to Pentecostalism, especially to its different styles of piety – experiential and embodied – it is necessary to use a methodology and a frame of interpretation that does justice to this embodied, experiential mode of faith. Sallandt turns therefore to the disciplines of the esthetics of religion and of corporeal knowledge to develop and elaborate a theoretical framework of embodied cognition – of a knowledge of and in the body which is not easily communicated in words – to interpret the experiences of participants of Pentecostal religious services. This article deals in a highly theoretical way with issues of visibility and invisibility in epistemology, and reveals the underlying regime or norm that knowledge generation means research in the stories of experiences. When a phenomenon resists such an approach, it remains to a certain extent 'invisible'.

Books – book reviews – book presentations
This issue's last section is traditionally devoted to new books and book reviews. This time we have a book presentation by the author. For *Trees van Montfoort* presents some key notions from her book *Groene Theologie. (Green Theology)*, which won the prize for Best Theological Book in 2019 in the Netherlands. In this book on eco-theology van Montfoort departs from the thesis that eco-theology is not a subdiscipline of theology but rediscovery of theology as such. She substantiates this thesis in a presentation of her reading of the Bible from an ecofeminist point of view and develops a constructive ecofeminist theological position in and through a reading of the work of Sallie McFague, Ivone Gebara, Catherine Keller, and Elisabeth Theokritoff.

We would like to thank Judith Gruber and Annemie Dillen, the organizers of the conference, for their collaboration in the publication of this volume.

We thank Katharina Rötzer and Lydia Steininger in Vienna for their support with the editorial work on this volume.

Anne-Claire Mulder is associate professor for Women's and Genderstudies as well as supervisor of the internships for the ministry at the Protestant Theological University (Groningen). acmulder@pthu.nl

Agnethe Siquans is professor for Old Testament Studies at the faculty of Catholic Theology at the University of Vienna. agnethe.siquans@univie.ac.at

Clara Carbonell Ortiz is a PhD candidate at Universidad Complutense de Madrid, whose thesis targets the expression of sexual intercourse in biblical Hebrew. clarcarb@ucm.es

Editorial

Tema
En el momento que se escribe esta introducción, mayo de 2020, el mundo se encuentra afligido por una amenaza invisible; una amenaza que está siendo contraatacada de distintas maneras, pero especialmente a través de control del comportamiento de todas las personas, tanto dentro de casa como en el espacio público. Un confinamiento. Una prohibición, más o menos estricta, de abandonar libremente el hogar y una advertencia de lavarse meticulosamente las manos en caso de haber salido. Una orden de mantener la distancia física en el espacio público. Una orden de llevar mascarillas. Una prohibición de reunirnos con otras personas. Tomadas en su conjunto, estas directrices construyen un régimen de visibilidad. Al disciplinar nuestro comportamiento, también se aseguran de que nos concienciamos del sistema de valores imperante: la salud sobre la libertad de movimiento y la libertad de reunión. Por otro lado, esta crisis también deconstruye los regímenes por los cuales el valor de un gesto de afecto o cariño o el trabajo de cuidados han permanecido invisibles y, por ende, infravalorados.

Así, la COVID-19 o crisis del coronavirus ofrece la posibilidad de adentrarnos desde la experiencia en este número: "Género, raza, religión. De/construyendo regímenes de in/visibilidad". Este tema se deriva del congreso de 2019 en Lovaina, Bélgica. En este congreso, los regímenes de in/visibilidad construidos a partir de la intersección entre género, raza y religión se abordaron en una serie de conferencias magistrales y sus respuestas, aparte de sesiones de ponencias. No obstante, la mayoría de las ponencias, en las sesiones y en este número de la revista, tratan exclusivamente de distintos regímenes de in/visibilidad con relación al género y la religión/teología. Esto ilustra tanto el carácter de *agenda-setting* del tema del congreso como el tiempo que lleva abordar temas que se encuentran tan entrelazados con la manera en que nos relacionamos con el pasado colonial de Europa y nuestra reacción contemporánea a la migración.

Este número se abre con un texto de las organizadoras del congreso, *Annemie Dillen* y *Judith Gruber*, donde ofrecen una introducción a este tema reflexionando sobre el congreso y donde se muestra la compleja intersección y entrecruzamiento entre género, raza y religión. Su intención es estimular la reflexión con la ESWTR acerca del tema del congreso: dicha intersección y los regímenes de visibilidad e invisibilidad que las gobiernan. En sus reflexiones, usan experiencias ordinarias y controversias de la vida cotidiana como punto de inicio o como ilustración, activando así la memoria de la lectora o lector. En el análisis de estas experiencias y controversias, indican los procesos de poder, los procesos de la otredad, que operan en estas situaciones, y ejemplifican el carácter de regímenes de generización, racialización y religionización. Este artículo cierra con un número de importantes cuestiones que esperan, urgentemente, una reflexión teológica.

A dicha introducción le sigue el discurso inaugural de Kristine Suna-Koro y el artículo de Silvia Martínez Cano. En su artículo "Revisiting the sacrament of the stranger", *Kristine Suna-Koro* hace una interpretación teológica de la actual crisis de migración global debido a la guerra y el cambio climático, enraizada en la convicción de que una reinterpretación teológica de qué significa ser humano es, ahora más que nunca, necesaria. Interpreta la crisis migratoria como un enorme reto para las religiones mundiales, como *locus theologicus* y como la persona migrante en tanto en cuanto símbolo de todas aquellas rechazadas por la sociedad globalizada de hoy en día. Esto significa que las personas "migrantes" no deberían considerarse aparte, sino como parte de un espectro de cuestiones globales que demanda una teopoética y una teopolítica de afinidad o parentesco más que una teopoética o teopolítica de provincialización. Continúa trazando la dirección de una antropología teológica que comienza con la figura del extranjero. Qué respuestas teológicas podrían darse a quienes se plantean la pregunta: ¿es suficiente ser humano para sobrevivir, por no hablar de liderar o aspirar a una vida floreciente? Suna-Koro explora tres direcciones para proponer una respuesta a esta pregunta. Primero, muestra que, desde una perspectiva cristiana, la vida abundante es lo que la creación, encarnación y salvación tratan, y no solo para los seres humanos sino para toda creación en su conjunto. Su segundo paso es explorar la figura de *imago Dei*, argumentando que este es una implicación humana única y absolutamente democrática. En tercer lugar, explora las posibilidades de la palabra "semejanza", *similitude*, para pensar que los seres humanos son diferentes pero similares a y en la imagen de Dios, incluso el más extranjero. Pero para reconocer al más extranjero, hace falta un duro y valiente trabajo: el trabajo del amor. Si este trabajo tuviera algo que ver con Dios, aparecería en el lugar del otro, al encuentro del hambriento y el sediento (Mat 25); lo que Suna-Koro denomina, siguiendo a Han Urs von Balthasar, el sacramento del extranjero: un encuentro, un sacramento que alberga un poder revelador, enseñando que el amor divino no tiene fronteras.

La copiosa respuesta de *Silvia Martínez Cano* elabora las ideas de Kristine Suna-Koro, al mismo tiempo que regresa a la idea de que la antropología teológica necesita ser revisada, corregida, remoldeada... para encontrar (algunas) respuestas a las tres crisis de nuestros tiempos: la migración, la crisis ecológica y el neoliberalismo. La presuposición de la antropología teológica es que no repetiría la oposición entre humanos y naturaleza, sino que sería, más bien, biocéntrica, en el sentido de que la *imago Dei* se imaginaría en relación con el cuerpo de Dios, *i.e.*, con la creación de Dios, a través de su propio cuerpo. Ella, además, sugiere que las narrativas en las que la corporalidad, relacionalidad, justicia y solidaridad serían claves en el desarrollo de esta antropología. Buscando narrativas desde las que esta antropología pudiera desarrollarse, vuelve a las narraciones de la persona desplazada, las mujeres migrantes. Sus narrativas cuentan la historia de qué significa ser humano: sufrir y resistir. Son invisibles y están orientadas hacia la supervivencia, lo cual las impide rebelarse ante su situación. Martínez Cano interpreta la rotura del cuerpo de Cristo y sugiere que un sacramento del extranjero, del que Kristine Suna-Koro habla, es un sacramento de la mujer migrante. Este sacramento nos urge a luchar contra su situación. Ello le lleva a una antropología teológica escatológica, en la que descubrimos la sabiduría con la que Dios sustenta nuestras vidas y la vida de la creación.

Tal y como se indica arriba, los otros textos se centran en la intersección de género y religión/teología en su discusión sobre la de/construcción de regímenes de in/visibilidad. *Bess Brooks* describe la genealogía de la inserción de la oración eucarística en el *Book of Common Worship* ('Libro de la Adoración Común') de la Iglesia de Inglaterra, junto con la de una imagen femenina de Dios, como el efecto de un proceso de defeminización. Ha tomado prestado el concepto de la biología para describir regímenes que han ocasionado, en su transcurso, la invisibilidad de lo femenino. Primero, identifica el dominio de la metáfora del padre en la tradición cristiana. En segundo lugar, procede con la elisión de la genealogía de esta inserción, que culmina con que la metáfora de la madre no podría ser atribuida a un feminismo estridente porque dicha metáfora ha estado ahí todo este tiempo. En última instancia, señala que la propia metáfora es profundamente deficiente porque no retrata la maternidad de Dios en su faceta de alimentar a los polluelos, sino describiendo su mera protección. En su conclusión, clarifica que esta defeminización de las oraciones eucarísticas afecta a la manera en la que ella y otras mujeres se sienten incluidas en esta liturgia: experimentan dificultad al sentirse integradas y al afirmarlo.

A continuación, se encuentran dos artículos que se enfrentan, de modo distinto, a la construcción basada en el género de los regímenes de invisibilidad en la Iglesia, en especial en la Iglesia Católica Romana. Es interesante que estos

Editorial

regímenes de invisibilidad resultan ser regímenes de silencio y silenciamiento, de obstaculizar que se pongan en descubrimiento los abusos a las mujeres, haciéndolos, así, visibles. *Jadranka Rebeka Anić* y *Ana Thea Filipović* proporcionan una elaborada descripción de la explotación, a nivel mundial, de las monjas a través del trabajo y los servicios sexuales así como de los distintos procedimientos empleados para silenciar a estas religiosas. En su análisis de las causas de esta explotación, señalan a la estructura jerárquica clerical de la Iglesia Católica Romana y el estatus secundario de las mujeres, expresado también en una tradición espiritual heterónoma. Abogan, en primer lugar, por que la Iglesia reconozca el sufrimiento de estas monjas como víctimas de explotación y las cuide, en distintos ámbitos. Además, señalan que, para cambiar esas estructuras que permiten la explotación, la Iglesia ha de modificar sus estructuras en pos de una comunidad igualitaria e inclusiva de los y las fieles.

Tres ejemplos concretos del silenciamiento de mujeres en la Iglesia Católica Romana constituyen el punto de partida del texto de *Sylvia Hübel*. Esta autora usa el concepto de injusticia epistemológica para analizar los modos en los que la Iglesia evita la producción de todo conocimiento generado por mujeres, así como el hecho de que este sea reconocido como digno de confianza. Extrae este concepto de "injusticia epistemológica" de la obra de Miranda Frick, quien la define como el daño hecho a alquien en calidad de sujeto conocedor, informante o participante en la producción o reparto de conocimiento en la comunidad. La autora representa este proceso de marginalización de las mujeres en la Iglesia junto con sus tradiciones mediante la descripción de cinco fuentes diversas de injusticia epistemológica, que van desde la estereotipación negativa, a la asfixia epistemológica o la cultura de la cortina de humo. En su último párrafo, retorna a los logros de la teología feminista en la producción de conocimiento con el que reta a esta injusticia epistemológica. Y, como Jadranka Rebeka Anić y Ana Thea Filipović, apunta al número creciente de iniciativas que hacen uso de la crisis generada por los escándalos de abusos sexuales para propugnar una transformación de la Iglesia en pos de un discipulado de iguales.

Monica Oanca y Aleksandra Michalska emplean una perspectiva distinta acerca, de nuevo, de la idea de de/construcción de regímenes de in/visibilidad. Muestran que estos regímenes son dinámicos a la hora de ver y manifestarse (de ver al invisible y manifestarse como invisibles) a través de las historias vitales de dos anacoretas, a saber, la mística del siglo xiv Juliana de Norwich y la profetisa búlgara *prepodobna* Stoyna, quien vivió entre los siglos xix y xx. En su texto sobre Juliana de Norwich, *Monica Oanca* argumenta que el foco académico actual en Estudios Medievales que hace visible las vidas desconocidas (por invisibles) de místicas puede acabar ignorando la relevancia de sus visiones. Pretende mostrar la importancia de las visiones de Juliana de Norwich para reflexiones teológicas contemporáneas. Describe a Juliana de Norwich como alguien que eligió hacerse anacoreta, viviendo en un espacio cerrado cerca de una iglesia, con el objetivo de concentrarse en Dios. Ser físicamente invisible para otros sujetos permitió a Juliana de Norwich centrar toda su atención y devoción en el Dios invisible, a quien veía en sus visiones; unas visiones que describió de manera detallada para que el lector pudiera ver lo que ella veía. En una cuidadosa descripción de qué se conoce de su vida y obra, Monica Oanca hace visible la teología de la alegría de Juliana y su fe en el amor de Dios hacia la humanidad, enfatizando su relevancia hoy en día.

El texto de *Aleksandra Michalska* sobre la vida de *prepodobna* Stoyna se aproxima a las dinámicas de in/visibilidad desde la perspectiva del poder de de/construir un fenómeno religioso, en este caso el creciente culto a *prepodobna* Stoyna. Ella era una mujer ciega que mantuvo una vida de anacoreta en una iglesia en Bulgaria y fue considerada clarividente y profetisa, así como santa, por el pueblo, debido a sus poderes de visión y curación. A pesar de que solo a partir de los años 80 en adelante crecía su reputación, el resultado es que la veneración de *prepodobna* Stoyna ha crecido hasta ser un culto en el que miles de personas visitan su iglesia y su antigua habitación en peregrinación, esperando un milagro. La Iglesia Ortodoxa Búlgara, sin embargo, se enfrenta a este desarrollo desde la ambivalencia, considerándolo, por un lado, idolatría, y por otro, no queriendo disuadir a la gente de visitar esta iglesia. Aleksandra Michalska muestra, no obstante, que la respuesta a la pregunta de si es una santa o no depende no solo de la pregunta "quién define la santidad", sino también de cómo se entiende este tipo de religión popular y su autoridad por parte de sus seguidores y seguidoras.

En su artículo, *Zilya Khabibullina* analiza los regímenes de in/visibilidad que gobiernan la imagen de las mujeres musulmanas en los medios de comunicación rusos. Situando su análisis tanto en el panorama cambiante de los medios rusos como en la situación política, muestra que, hoy en día, la mayor parte de la información sobre el islam y las personas musulmanas se encuentra en Internet, páginas y fórums islámicos. Antes de 1990, sin embargo, se daba información, y prestaba atención, al islam en los medios de comunicación oficiales, como en programas de televisión. Después de 1990, estos canales cerraron e Internet se convirtió en la fuente de información más importante sobre este tema, tanto para las personas rusas como musulmanas. Khabibulina explica que, de la misma manera que en Occidente, las mujeres musulmanas son retratadas como sumisas por los medios rusos, como oprimidas y ataviadas de negro y en un hiyab. También muestra que las blogueras musulmanas, quienes a menudo han logrado muchos seguidores, contrarrestan esta imagen de varias maneras, por ejemplo, con ropas coloridas. Por otro lado, Internet también parece estimular una competición entre mujeres sobre quién es la más devota. Así, Khabibulina logra reflejar la complejidad y las muchas influencias de la representación de mujeres musulmanas a través de Internet en Rusia.

El último texto de esta sección del volumen de de/construir regímenes de in/visibilidad es el de *Karin Hügel*, quien presenta una lectura queer de los mandamientos de amar en Levítico. En un detallado análisis de los dos mandamientos, primero de Lev 19,18, sobre el amor al prójimo, y después de Lev 19,34, sobre el amor al extranjero, Hügel muestra cómo estos mandamientos pueden leerse de tal manera que contrarrestan la condena de la homosexualidad en Lev 18. La razón es que estos mandamientos pueden interpretarse como la defensa del amor propio e, implícitamente, como la defensa de una cultura que fomenta el amor propio de todos los individuos. Pueden, además, tomarse como una advertencia de que "el o la otra" es un ser humano como uno o una misma. En tercer lugar, la autora ofrece una interpretación en la que el amor al prójimo es otra formulación de la regla de oro. Su análisis muestra que, usando una hermenéutica queer, es posible construir un régimen que haga visible las varias formas de amor propio y amor a otras personas que se identifican como queer.

Foro

En la sección de *Foro* de este volumen, publicamos tres artículos que no encajan estrictamente con el tema del mismo, pero que discuten indirectamente aspectos de la in/visibilidad. Esta sección se abre con un artículo de *Eleonore Lappin-Eppel* sobre Bet Débora, haciendo visible la existencia de una red académica europea de mujeres judías (rabinas, cantoras, mujeres activistas en comunidades judías, académicas y otras) así como una casa local de estudio para mujeres en Berlín, que organiza pequeños eventos. Fundada en 1998, nueve años después de la caída del Muro que trajo consigo un enorme cambio en las comunidades judías de Europa, las fundadoras de Bet Débora quisieron ayudar a construir una casa de estudio, o *Lehrhouse*, siguiendo la tradición judía de estudiar en compañía. Pero esta *Lehrhouse* debía ser una destinada a desarrollar la tradición judía que resulte más atractiva y justa para las mujeres. Eleonore Lappin-Eppel muestra que Bet Débora lleva a cabo este cometido

Editorial

organizando, en primer lugar, congresos internacionales cada dos o tres años en distintos países de Europa, a menudo junto con una comunidad judía local. Ofreciéndonos una sucinta descripción de los temas, el contexto local de los diferentes emplazamientos de congresos y de los participantes, retrata la continua y constante reflexión sobre la cuestión de cómo sería una tradición más justa.

El segundo artículo de esta sección pertenece a *Ulrike Sallandt* y parte de la idea de que, con el objetivo de hacer justicia al pentecostalismo, en particular a sus diferentes estilos de piedad, empírica y encarnada, es necesario usar una metodología y un marco de interpretación que hagan justicia a ese modo de fe encarnado y empírico. De esta forma, Sallandt vuelve a las disciplinas de estética de la religión y conocimiento corpóreo para elaborar un marco teórico de la cognición encarnada (del conocimiento de y en el cuerpo que no es fácilmente comunicable con palabras) para interpretar las experiencias de las personas participantes en los serivicios pentecostales. Este artículo aborda, de manera teórica, cuestiones de in/visibilidad en la epistemología, y revela el régimen o la norma subyacentes de que el conocimiento generacional significa investigación en las historias de las experiencias. Cuando un fenómeno se resiste a tal aproximación, permanece, de cierto modo, invisible.

Libros – reseñas de libros – presentaciones de libro
Esta sección está tradicionalmente consagrada a nuevos libros y reseñas de libros. En esta ocasión, contamos con una presentación por su autora: *Trees van Montfoort* introduce cuestiones claves de su libro *Groene Theologie* ('Teología verde'), que ganó el premio al Mejor Libro Teológico en 2019 en Los Países Bajos. En este libro sobre ecoteología, van Montfoort parte de la tesis de que la ecoteología no es una subdisciplina de la teología, sino un redescubrimiento de la misma como tal. Cimienta su tesis en la presentación de su lectura de la Biblia desde una perspectiva ecofeminista y desarrolla una posición teológica ecofeminista constructiva a través de la lectura de la obra de Sallie McFague, Ivone Gebara, Catherine Keller y Elisabeth Theokritoff.

Querríamos agradecer a Judith Gruber y Annemie Dillen, organizadoras del congreso, por colaborar con la publicación de este volumen.

Agradecemos a Katharina Rötzer y Lydia Steininger, en Viena, por su ayuda con el trabajo editorial de este volumen.

Anne-Claire Mulder es profesora asociada de Estudios de Género y de la Mujer, así como supervisora de prácticas de ministerio en la Protestant Theological University (Groningen). acmulder@pthu.nl

Agnethe Siquans es profesora de Estudios de Antiguo Testamento en la Facultad de Teología Católica en la Universidad de Viena. agnethe.siquans@univie.ac.at

Clara Carbonell Ortiz es doctoranda en la Universidad Complutense de Madrid, en cuya tesis investiga la expresión de las relaciones sexuales en hebreo bíblico. clarcarb@ucm.es

Editorial

Thema
In dem Moment, als wir diese Einleitung verfassen, – im Mai 2020 – wird die Welt von einer unsichtbaren Bedrohung im Griff gehalten, einer Bedrohung, der auf vielfältige Weise begegnet wird, insbesondere aber durch die Disziplinierung des Verhaltens aller sowohl zuhause als auch im öffentlichen Raum: ein Lockdown – das (mehr oder weniger strikte) Verbot, das Haus frei zu verlassen, und die Ermahnung, uns, falls wir es doch tun, danach gründlich die Hände zu waschen, das Verbot, sich mit mehreren Personen zu treffen, die Anordnung, physischen Abstand im öffentlichen Raum zu halten, die Anordnung, einen Mund-Nasen-Schutz zu tragen, das Verbot, sich mit anderen zu treffen. Zusammen genommen konstruieren diese Anordnungen eine Ordnung von Sichtbarkeit. Durch die Disziplinierung unseres Verhaltens gewährleisten sie auch, dass wir auf das herrschende Wertsystem aufmerksam gemacht werden: Gesundheit vor Bewegungsfreiheit und Versammlungsfreiheit. Auf der anderen Seite dekonstruiert diese Krise auch die Ordnungen, durch die der Wert physischer Gesten der Zuneigung, der Pflege und die Pflegearbeit unsichtbar und daher unterbewertet blieben.

Daher eröffnet die Covid-10- oder Corona-Krise die Möglichkeit eines erfahrungsorientierten Zugangs zum Thema dieser Ausgabe: „Gender, Rasse, Religion: De-/Konstruktion von Ordnungen der Un-/Sichtbarkeit". Dieses Thema leitet sich vom Thema der Konferenz der „Europäischen Gesellschaft für theologische Forschung von Frauen" 2019 in Leuven, Belgien, her. Bei dieser lebendigen Konferenz wurden die Ordnungen von Un-/Sichtbarkeit aufgrund der Überschneidung von Gender, Rasse und Religion in den Hauptvorträgen und den Responsen darauf sowie in einigen weiteren Vorträgen angesprochen. Die Mehrheit der Vorträge in den thematischen Gruppen und in dieser Ausgabe des Jahrbuchs sprechen jedoch die unterschiedlichen Ordnungen von Un-/Sichtbarkeit nur in der Beziehung zwischen Gender und Religion/Theologie an. Das zeigt sowohl den zukunftsweisenden Charakter des Themas der Konferenz an, wie es auch deutlich macht, dass es Zeit braucht, um Themen anzusprechen, die mit der Art, wie „wir" mit der kolonialen Vergangenheit Europas und mit seiner gegenwärtigen Reaktion auf die Migration umgehen, eng verknüpft sind.

Die Ausgabe wird von einem Text der Organisatorinnen der Konferenz, *Annemie Dillen* und *Judith Gruber*, eröffnet, in dem sie eine Einführung ins das Thema dieser Ausgabe und der Konferenz bieten und die komplexe Überschneidung und Verknüpfung von Gender, Rasse und Religion zeigen. Ihre Absicht ist es, die Reflexion der ESWTR über das Thema der Konferenz – die Überschneidung von Gender, Rasse, Religion und die Ordnungen von Sichtbarkeit und Unsichtbarkeit, die diese Überschneidung beherrschen – weiter anzuregen. In ihren Überlegungen verwenden sie gewöhnliche Erfahrungen und Kontroversen des alltäglichen Lebens als Ausgangspunkt oder Illustration, um so die Erinnerungen und Erfahrungen der Leser*innen zu entfachen. In der Analyse dieser Erfahrungen und Kontroversen zeigen sie die Prozesse von Macht und „Othering", die in diesen Situationen am Werk sind, und beleuchten den prozessorientierten Charakter der Ordnungen von Gender, Rasse und Religion („genderisation, racialisation, religionisation"). Der Artikel schließt mit der Nennung einer Reihe von wichtigen theologischen Themen, die dringend einer theologischen Reflexion bedürfen.

Diese Einleitung wird gefolgt vom Eröffnungsvortrag der Konferenz von *Kristine Suna-Koro* and dem Text der Response durch Silvia Martínez Cano. In ihrem Artikel *Revisiting the Sacrament of the Stranger* präsentiert Kristine Suna-Koro eine theologische Interpretation der gegenwärtigen weltweiten Migrationskrise aufgrund von Krieg und Klimawandel, die in der Überzeugung wurzelt, dass eine theologische Re-Interpretation dessen, was es bedeutet, menschlich zu sein, mehr als notwendig ist. Sie deutet die Migrationskrise als höchste Herausforderung für die Religionen der Welt, als einen *locus theologicus*, und die Migrant*innen als Symbol für alle, die durch die heutige globalisierte Gesellschaft zurückgewiesen werden. Das heißt, dass Migrant*innen nicht als eigenes Thema bedacht werden sollen, sondern vielmehr als Teil einer ganzen Reihe von globalen Themen, was nach einer Theopoetik und Theopolitik der Nähe oder Verwandtschaft eher verlangt, als nach einer Theopoetik und Theopolitik der Provinzialisierung. Im Folgenden skizziert sie die Richtung einer theologischen Antropologie, die mit der Figur des/der Fremden beginnt. Welche theologischen Antworten können denen gegeben werden, die die Frage negativ beantworten, ob menschlich zu sein genug ist, um zu überleben oder gar um ein blühendes Leben zu führen oder anzustreben? Suna-Koro ergründet drei Richtungen für eine positive Antwort auf diese Frage. Zuerst zeigt sie, dass aus einer christlichen Perspektive überbordendes Leben das ist, worum es in Schöpfung, Inkarnation und Erlösung geht, und zwar nicht nur für die Menschen, sondern für die ganze Schöpfung. Ihr zweiter Schritt ist eine Erkundung des Bildes der *imago Dei*. Sie argumentiert, dass dieses eine einmalige und äußerst demokratische menschliche Verbindung mit Gott ist. Drittens untersucht sie die Möglichkeiten des Wortes Ebenbild, Ähnlichkeit, um durchzudenken, dass Menschen verschieden, aber dennoch ähnlich und im Bild Gottes sind, selbst der/die fremdeste Fremde. Aber den/die fremdeste/n Fremde/n anzuerkennen verlangt harte und mutige Arbeit, die Arbeit der Liebe. Wenn diese Liebe etwas mit Gott zu tun hat, dann erscheint sie am Ort des/der anderen, in der Begegnung mit den Hungrigen, den Durstigen (Mt 25), was Suna-Koro nach Hans Urs von Balthasar das Sakrament des/der Fremden nennt, eine Begegnung, ein Sakrament, das offenbarende Macht hat, die anzeigt, dass göttliche Liebe grenzenlos ist.

In ihrer facettenreichen Antwort baut *Silvia Martínez Cano* auf den Gedanken von Kristine Suna-Koro auf und wendet sich ebenso der Überlegung zu, dass die theologische Anthropologie revidiert, überholt und neu geformt werden muss, um (einige) Antworten auf die drei Krisen unserer Zeit zu finden – Migration, ökologische Krise und Neoliberalismus. Voraussetzung einer solchen theologischen Anthropologie ist es, dass sie nicht die Entgegensetzung von Menschen und Natur wiederholt, sondern vielmehr biozentrisch ist – in dem Sinne, dass die *imago Dei* vorgestellt wird als in Bezug stehend zu Gottes Körper, d.h. Gottes Schöpfung, durch den eigenen Körper. Sie legt außerdem nahe, dass Erzählungen, in denen Körperlichkeit, Relationalität, Gerechtigkeit und Solidarität eine Rolle spielen, wichtige Schlüssel für die Entwicklung dieser Anthropologie sind. Auf der Suche nach Erzählungen, von denen aus diese Anthropologie entwickelt werden könnte, wendet sie sich den Erzählungen der Vertriebenen, der Migrantinnen, zu. Diese erzählen eine Geschichte davon, was es heißt, menschlich zu sein – zu leiden und Widerstand zu leisten. Sie sind unsichtbar und auf das Überleben orientiert, was sie daran hindert, gegen ihre Situation zu rebellieren. Martínez Cano interpretiert ihre Gebrochenheit als Ausdruck des gebrochenen Körpers Christi und schlägt vor, dass das „Sakrament des/der Fremden", über das Kristine Suna-Koro

Editorial

spricht, das Sakrament der Migrantinnen ist. Dieses Sakrament zwingt uns, gegen ihre Situation zu kämpfen. Das führt sie zu einer theologischen Anthropologie mit einer eschatologischen Perspektive – „in der wir die Weisheit entdecken, mit der Gott unser Leben und das Leben der Schöpfung erhält".

Wie bereits erwähnt, konzentrieren sich die anderen Texte in ihrer Diskussion der De-/Konstruktion von Ordnungen der Un-/Sichtbarkeit auf die Überschneidung von Gender und Religion/Theologie. *Bess Brooks* beschreibt die Entstehung der Einfügung des einzigen eucharistischen Gebets in das „Book of Common Worship" der Kirche von England, das ein weibliches Bild Gottes enthält, als Auswirkung eines Prozesses der Entweiblichung (*defeminisation*). Sie hat dieses Konzept der Biologie entlehnt, um die Ordnungen zu beschreiben, die die Unsichtbarkeit des Weiblichen in diesem Prozess hervorbrachten. Sie identifiziert zuerst die Dominanz der Vater-Metapher in der christlichen Tradition. Zweitens wird diese Wissenschaft im Prozess der Debatte über dieses eine Gebet übergangen und ihre Diskussion wird als deren eigene ausgegeben, was in der Aussage gipfelt, dass die Mutter-Metapher nicht einem „scharfen" Feminismus zugeschrieben werden kann, weil die Metapher schon immer in der Bibel da war. Zuletzt betont sie, dass die Metapher selbst zutiefst mangelhaft ist, weil sie den mütterlichen Gott nicht als einen darstellt, der seine Küken füttert, sondern nur als einen, der sie beschützt. In ihrer Schlussfolgerung macht sie klar, dass diese Entweiblichung der eucharistischen Gebete sich auf die Weise auswirkt, auf die sie und andere Frauen sich zu dieser Liturgie in Beziehung setzen – sie haben Schwierigkeiten, sich eingeschlossen zu fühlen und sie zu bejahen.

Diesem Artikel folgen zwei Texte, die sich in unterschiedlicher Weise mit der gegenderten Konstruktion von Ordnungen der Unsichtbarkeit in der Kirche, speziell in der römisch-katholischen Kirche, beschäftigen. Es ist auffällig, dass diese Ordnungen der Unsichtbarkeit offensichtlich Ordnungen von Schweigen und Zum-Schweigen-Bringen sind, um zu verhindern, dass Missbrauch von Frauen aufgedeckt und so sichtbar gemacht wird. *Jadranka Rebeka Anić* und *Ana Thea Filipović* bieten eine ausführliche Beschreibung der weltweiten Ausbeutung von weiblichen Ordensangehörigen durch Arbeit und sexuelle Dienste sowie der verschiedenen Methoden, die verwendet werden, um diese Nonnen zum Schweigen zu bringen. In ihrer Analyse der Gründe für die Ausbeutung verweisen sie auf die hierarchische und klerikale Struktur der römisch-katholischen Kirche, den sekundären Status von Frauen, der sich auch in einer fremdbestimmten spirituellen Tradition ausdrückt. Sie befürworten zuallererst, dass die Kirche das Leiden der Opfer der Ausbeutung von weiblichen Ordensangehörigen (an)erkennt und für sie in vielfältiger Weise Sorge trägt. In zweiter Linie betonen sie, dass die Kirche, um die Strukturen zu ändern, die Ausbeutung ermöglichen, diese in Richtung einer egalitären und inklusiven Gemeinschaft von Gläubigen ändern muss.

Drei konkrete Beispiele für das Zum-Schweigen-Bringen von Frauen in der römisch-katholischen Kirche stellen den Ausgangspunkt für *Sylvia Hübels* Text über das Zum-Schweigen-Bringen von Frauen/Männern in dieser Kirche dar. Sie verwendet das Konzept der epistemischen Ungerechtigkeit, um die Formen zu analysieren, in denen die Produktion von Wissen durch Frauen und ihre Anerkennung als vertrauenswürdig in der Kirche verhindert werden. Sie entlehnt das Konzept der „epistemischen Ungerechtigkeit" aus dem Werk von Miranda Frick, die es definiert als die ungerechte Behandlung von jemandem in seiner/ihrer Kapazität als Wissende/r, Informant*in oder Teilnehmer*in an der Produktion oder am Teilen von Wissen der Gemeinschaft. Sie zeichnet den Prozess der Marginalisierung von Frauen in der Kirche und ihren Tradition nach, indem sie fünf verschiedene Quellen epistemischer Ungerechtigkeit beschreibt, die von negativen Stereotypen bis zu epistemischem Unterdrücken und einer Kultur der Vertuschung reichen. In ihrem letzten Abschnitt wendet sie sich den Errungenschaften der feministischen Theologie in der Produktion von Wissen zu, das epistemischer Ungerechtigkeit entgegenwirkt. Wie Jadranka Rebeka Anić und Ana Thea Filipović weist sie auf die wachsende Anzahl von Initiativen hin, die die Krise, die durch den Skandal des sexuellen Missbrauchs ausgelöst wurde, nutzen, um für eine Transformation der Kirche in Richtung einer Jüngerschaft von Gleichwertigen einzutreten.

Monica Oanca und Aleksandra Michalska haben wiederum eine andere Perspektive auf die Idee der De-/Konstruktion von Ordnungen der Un-/Sichtbarkeit. Sie zeigen diese Ordnungen als dynamische Ordnungen von Sehen und Gesehen-Werden, Sehen des Unsichtbaren und unsichtbar Sein für das Sehen, in und durch die Lebensgeschichten von zwei Einsiedlerinnen, nämlich Juliana von Norwich, einer Mystikerin des 14. Jahrhunderts, und Prepodobna Stoyna, einer bulgarischen Prophetin, die um die Wende vom 19. zum 20. Jahrhundert lebte. In ihrem Text über Juliana von Norwich argumentiert *Monica Oanca*, dass sich der gegenwärtige Fokus der Mittelalterforschung auf die Sichtbarmachung des unbekannten, unsichtbaren Lebens von Mystikerinnen dazu führen kann, die theologische Relevanz ihrer Visionen zu übergehen. Ihr Ziel ist es, die Bedeutung der Visionen von Juliana von Norwich für gegenwärtige theologische Reflexionen darzustellen. Sie beschreibt Juliana von Norwich als eine, die sich entschied, Einsiedlerin zu werden und in einem abgeschlossenen

Editorial

Raum in der Nähe der Kirche zu leben, um sich ganz auf ihre Beziehung zu Gott zu konzentrieren. Die physische Unsichtbarkeit für andere ermöglichte es Juliana von Norwich, all ihre Aufmerksamkeit und Hingabe auf den unsichtbaren Gott zu richten, den sie in ihren Visionen sah, Visionen, die sie akribisch beschrieb, sodass die Leser*innen sehen konnten, was sie sah. In einer sorgfältigen Beschreibung dessen, was von ihrem Leben und Werk bekannt ist, macht Monica Oanca Julianas Theologie der Freude und ihren Glauben an Gottes Liebe zu den Menschen sichtbar und betont ihre Relevanz für heute.

Aleksandra Michalskas Text über das Leben von *Prebodobna Stoyna* nähert sich der Dynamik von Sichtbarkeit und Unsichtbarkeit aus der Perspektive der Macht, ein religiöses Phänomen zu konstruieren oder zu dekonstruieren, in diesem Fall den wachsenden Kult um *Prebodobna Stoyna*. Sie war eine blinde Frau, die ein Leben als Einsiedlerin in einer Kirche in Bulgarien führte und von den Leuten wegen ihrer Kräfte des Sehens und Heilens als Hellseherin und Prophetin und als Heilige angesehen wurde. Obwohl ihr Ruf erst seit den 1980er Jahren größer wurde, ist die Verehrung von *Prebodobna Stoyna* zu einem Kult angewachsen, mit tausenden Menschen, die die Kirche und ihr altes Zimmer in Wallfahrten besuchen und auf ein Wunder hoffen. Diese Entwicklung wird jedoch von der orthodoxen Kirche in Bulgarien ambivalent aufgenommen, die sie auf der einen Seite als Idolatrie ansieht, aber auf der anderen Seite die Menschen nicht vom Besuch dieser Kirche abhalten will. Aleksandra Michalska zeigt, dass die Antwort auf die Frage, ob sie eine Heilige ist oder nicht, nicht nur davon abhängt, wer Heiligkeit definiert, sondern auch wie diese Form der Volksreligion und ihre Autorität für die gelebte Religion ihrer Anhänger*innen zu verstehen ist.

Zilya Khabibullina analysiert in ihrem Artikel die Ordnungen der Un-/Sichtbarkeit, die das Bild muslimischer Frauen in russischen Medien prägen. Indem sie ihre Analyse sowohl innerhalb der sich verändernden russischen Medienlandschaft als auch in der politischen Situation verortet, zeigt sie, dass heutzutage der Großteil der Information über den Islam und die Muslime im Internet, in muslimischen Internetseiten und -foren zu finden ist. Vor 1990 wurde Information über und Aufmerksamkeit gegenüber dem Islam über die offiziellen Massenmedien, in Fernsehprogrammen, gegeben. Nach 1990 wurden die Kanäle geschlossen und das Internet wurde die wichtigste Informationsquelle über den Islam und die Muslime, für Russ*innen sowie für Muslim*innen. Khabibullina erklärt, dass, ebenso wie im Westen, in russischen Medien muslimische Frauen als unterwürfig, unterdrückt und gekleidet in Schwarz und mit Hijab dargestellt werden. Sie zeigt ebenso, dass muslimischen Bloggerinnen,

Editorial

die oft eine große Gefolgschaft haben, diesem Bild in verschiedener Weise entgegentreten, zum Beispiel indem sie einen farbigen Kleidungsstil propagieren. Auf der anderen Seite scheint das Internet auch einen Wettbewerb unter Frauen zu fördern, sich gegenseitig in Devotion zu übertreffen. So gelingt es Khabibullina, die Komplexität und den vielfältigen Einfluss auf die Repräsentation muslimischer Frauen im und durch das Internet in Russland zu zeichnen.

Der letzte Text des thematischen Teils der Ausgabe über die De-/Konstruktion von Ordnungen der Un-/Sichtbarkeit stammt von *Karin Hügel*, die eine queere Lesart der Liebesgebote in Levitikus präsentiert. In einer detaillierten Analyse der beiden Gebote, des ersten in Lev 19,18 über die Nächstenliebe und des zweiten in Lev 19,34 über die Liebe zu dem/der Fremden, zeigt Hügel, dass diese Gebote so gelesen werden können, dass sie den Vorschriften gegen Homosexualität in Lev 18 entgegentreten. Denn diese Gebote können so interpretiert werden, dass sie sich für Selbstliebe und implizit für eine Kultur der Unterstützung der Selbstliebe aller Individuen einsetzen. Sie können außerdem als Hinweis auf die Tatsache gedeutet werden, dass der/die andere ein Mensch wie das Subjekt ist. Drittens bietet sie eine Interpretation an, in der Nächstenliebe eine andere Formulierung der Goldenen Regel ist. Ihre Analyse zeigt, dass es durch die Verwendung einer queeren Hermeneutik möglich ist, eine Ordnung zu konstruieren, die die verschiedenen Formen der Selbstliebe und der Liebe zu anderen Menschen, die sich selbst als queer identifizieren, sichtbar macht.

Forum

Im Forum-Teil dieser Ausgabe veröffentlichen wir zwei Artikel, die nicht strikt in das Thema dieses Heftes passen, die aber Themen von Sichtbarkeit/Unsichtbarkeit in einem weiteren Sinn diskutieren. Der Teil beginnt mit einem Artikel von *Eleonore Lappin-Eppel* über *Bet Debora*, der die Existenz eines europäischen wissenschaftlichen Netzwerks jüdischer Frauen – Rabbinerinnen, Kantorinnen, Frauen and Aktivistinnen in jüdischen Gemeinden, Akademikerinnen und andere – sichtbar macht sowie über ein Lehrhaus in Berlin für Frauen, das kleinere Veranstaltungen organisiert. Gegründet 1998, neun Jahre nach dem Fall der Mauer, der eine enorme Veränderung für die jüdischen Gemeinden in Europa mit sich brachte, wollten die Gründerinnen von *Bet Debora* ein Lehrhaus entwickeln, in der Tradition des gemeinsamen Lernens in der jüdischen Gemeinschaft. Aber dieses Lehrhaus sollte sich der Entwicklung einer jüdischen Tradition widmen, die attraktiver und gerechter gegenüber Frauen ist. Eleonore Lappin-Eppel zeigt, dass *Bet Debora* dieses

Ziel vor allem durch die Organisation internationaler Konferenzen alle zwei bis drei Jahre in verschiedenen Ländern Europas verfolgt, oft zusammen mit der örtlichen jüdischen Gemeinde. Durch die prägnante Beschreibung der Themen, lokalen Kontexte der verschiedenen Konferenzorte und der Teilnehmerinnen bietet sie das Bild einer andauernden Reflexion über die Fragen, wie eine gerechtere Tradition aussehen könnte.

Der zweite Artikel in diesem Teil von *Ulrike Sallandt* geht von der Idee aus, dass, um dem Pentekostalismus, insbesondere seinen verschiedenen Frömmigkeitsformen, die erfahrungs- und körperbezogen sind, gerecht zu werden, es notwendig ist, eine Methodologie und einen Interpretationsrahmen zu verwenden, die dieser körperlichen, erfahrungsbezogenen Form des Glaubens gerecht werden. Sallandt wendet sich daher den Disziplinen der Religionsästhetik und des Körperwissens zu, um einen theoretischen Rahmen für verkörperte Erkenntnis – ein Wissen des Körpers und im Körper, das nicht leicht in Worten kommuniziert werden kann – zu entwickeln und auszuarbeiten, um die Erfahrungen der Teilnehmer*innen an pentekostalen Gottesdiensten zu interpretieren. Der Artikel behandelt auf hochtheoretische Weise die Themen von Sichtbarkeit und Unsichtbarkeit in der Epistemologie und deckt die zugrundeliegende Ordnung oder Norm auf, dass die Generierung von Wissen Forschung über die Geschichten von Erfahrungen bedeutet. Wenn ein Phänomen so einem Zugang widersteht, bleibt es bei zu einem gewissen Grad „unsichtbar".

Bücher – Rezensionen – Buchpräsentationen

Der letzte Teil dieser Ausgabe ist traditionell neuen Büchern und Rezensionen gewidmet. Dieses Mal haben wir eine Buchpräsentation durch die Autorin. *Trees van Montfoort* präsentiert einige Grundideen ihres Buches *Groene Theologie (Grüne Theologie)*, das in den Niederlanden den Preis für das beste theologische Buch 2019 gewonnen hat. In diesem Buch über Öko-Theologie geht van Montfoort von der These aus, dass Öko-Theologie nicht eine Subdisziplin der Theologie ist, sondern eine Wiederentdeckung der Theologie als solche. Sie untermauert diese These durch eine Darstellung ihrer Lesart der Bibel aus einer öko-feministischen Perspektive und entwickelt eine konstruktive öko-feministische theologische Position in und durch die Lektüre der Werke von Sallie McFague, Ivone Gebara, Catherine Keller und Elisabeth Theokritoff.

Wir möchten uns bei Judith Gruber und Annemie Dillen, den Organisatorinnen der Konferenz, für ihre Kooperation bei der Publikation dieser Ausgabe bedanken.

Wir danken Katharina Rötzer und Lydia Steininger in Wien für ihre Unterstützung bei der editorischen Arbeit an diesem Band.

Anne-Claire Mulder ist assoziierte Professorin für Frauen- und Genderstudien und Betreuerin des Praktikums für angehende Pfarrer*innen an der Protestantischen Theologischen Universität (Groningen). acmulder@pthu.nl

Agnethe Siquans ist Professorin für Alttestamentliche Bibelwissenschaft an der katholisch-theologischen Fakultät der Universität Wien. agnethe.siquans@univie.ac.at

Clara Carbonell Ortiz ist Dissertantin an der Universität Complutense Madrid. Ihre Dissertation befasst sich mit dem Ausdruck von Geschlechtsverkehr im biblischen Hebräisch. clarcarb@ucm.es

Annemie Dillen and Judith Gruber

Gender, Race, Religion: De/constructing Regimes of In/visibility

Abstract
This contribution introduces the theme "Gender, Race, Religion: De/constructing Regimes of In/visibility" of the 2019 conference of the European Society for Women in Theological Research. It outlines the societal and theological relevance of this theme, clarifies the key terms and indicates some of the research questions that emerge in the intersectional field of gender, race and religion, with a particular focus on how these categories intersect in productions of social in/visibility.

Keywords: Gender; race; religion; invisibility; feminist theology.

Resumen
Esta contribución introduce el tema "Género, raza, religión: de/construyendo regímenes de in/visibilidad", del congreso del año 2019 de Asociación Europea de Mujeres para la Investigación Teológica. En esta introducción, se resume la relevancia social y teológica del presente volumen, se clarifican los términos clave y se indican algunas de las cuestiones académicas que emergen en el campo interseccional de género, raza y religión, poniendo especial atención en cómo estas categorías intersectan con la producción de la in/visibilidad social.

Palabras clave: género; raza; religión; invisibilidad; teología feminista.

Zusammenfassung
Dieser Beitrag führt in das Thema „Gender, Rasse, Religion: De-/Konstruktion von Ordnungen der Un-/Sichtbarkeit" der Konferenz der Europäischen Gesellschaft für theologische Forschung von Frauen 2019 ein. Er skizziert die gesellschaftliche und theologische Relevanz dieses Themas, klärt die Schlüsselbegriffe und weist auf die Forschungsfragen hin, die im intersektionalen Feld von Gender, Rasse und Religion auftauchen, mit einem besonderen Fokus auf der Frage, wie diese Kategorien sich in der Produktion sozialer Un-/Sichtbarkeit überschneiden.

Schlagwörter: Gender; Rasse; Religion; Unsichtbarkeit; feministische Theologie.

Annemie Dillen, Judith Gruber
Gender, Race, Religion: De/constructing Regimes of In/visibility

Introduction: gender, race and religion

Women and religion, or women in the Church – for theologians, these have been common topics for a few decades. There is, of course, much to say, and the debates continue. Contemporary feminist thinking shows us that an intersectional approach is important to understand issues.[1] This means that gender issues, and gender and religion issues, should not be discussed as stand-alone topics, for they interact largely with various other social issues, such as socio-economic status or education. One of the other axes, besides gender, on which power is exercised and privileges and domination are experienced, is "race."

For the 2019 ESWTR conference, we have chosen to deepen our reflection on the relationship between these three complex fields: "gender, race, and religion." In this contribution, we will explain the relevance of this topic, and explore some aspects of the triad "gender, race, religion." We do not want to present a report of the conference or summarize the main insights. We refer to some aspects discussed during the conference in order to highlight the meaning of the topic and the title "Gender, Race, Religion: De/constructing Regimes of In/visibility." We will also raise questions, without pretending to have clear answers. This article should be considered as a programmatic text, which might stimulate others to continue the reflection and to start with more research and discussion in this area.

By discussing these three concepts in relationship to each other, we want to show how underlying patterns in society function in favor of specific groups of people and oppress others. The question here is how theologians can help to make these patterns more visible in order to contribute to the flourishing of everyone and to more justice in society.

Our first associations with the triad "gender, race, and religion" lead us to societal debates on the veiling of women. Why is covering a female head so often considered as a problem when these women identify as Muslim, and so rarely when they are Christian, e.g. nuns? Religion becomes "racialized" and people might feel oppressed because of their religion/race. On the other hand, societies are confronted with many forms of discrimination or oppression of women in the name of a particular religion, and with the legitimization of racist actions in the name of religion or in the name of the so called "liberation of women." The discussion about the veil illustrates this last point again:[2] in

---

[1] Kimberle Crenshaw, "Mapping the Margins: Intersectionality, Identity Politics, and Violence against Women of Color," in: *Stanford Law Review* 43/6 (1991) 1241-1299.

[2] Joan W. Scott, *The Politics of the Veil* (Princeton University Press: Princeton, NJ 2007).

various countries in Europe, people argue that Muslim women, often with Arabic roots, wearing a veil are oppressed and thus have to be liberated by a ban on wearing veils in public spaces. Others stand up to protest: this so-called feminism, which aims at liberating others by taking away their freedom of expression and religion, by limiting their own rights of self-determination in terms of choosing what to wear, is certainly not what is wanted by many feminist theologians and scholars in religion. Thus, the question of "covered women" illustrates the complexity of debates around gender, race, and religion. At the same time, however, many Muslim women experience a kind of "fatigue" when they are repeatedly confronted with this question, as Schirin Amir-Moazami outlined in her keynote lecture given at the ESWTR conference.[3] Jewish women too are often oppressed in name of a racialized religion, where certain Christian groups distance themselves from Jewish groups in order to cultivate a sense of nationalism and belonging.[4] This dualistic thinking is often particularly difficult for women who are in many other ways also in underprivileged situations.

As indicated, we wanted to focus on "race" during the conference. Some prefer to speak about ethnicity, as "race" reminds some people about practices and theories as we know them from the second World War and the period before.[5] However, especially in contemporary contexts and in the English speaking world, the term "race" is not an outdated term which should not to be used anymore, but refers to a living and often painful reality for many people who are, even today, oppressed in name of their "race." What is needed, is a critical theory of race.[6] This is developed within various disciplines, also within theology.[7] A critical concept of race is important to address racist structures in societies.

---

[3] Schirin Amir-Moazami (ed.), *Der inspizierte Muslim: Zur Politisierung der Islamforschung in Europa* (Transcript Verlag: Bielefeld 2018).

[4] See, for example, the situation in Poland, Marek Kucia, Marta Duch-Dyngosz, Mateusz Magierowski, "Anti-Semitism in Poland: Survey results and a qualitative study of Catholic communities," in: *Nationalities Papers,* 42/1 (2014), 8-36; See also Piotr Żuk, "Anti-Semitism in Poland, yesterday and today," in: *Race & Class* 58/3 (2017), 81-86.

[5] For recent shifts in the German-speaking world around the taboo of using "Rasse," cf. Mithu Sanyal, "Suddenly, it's OK to be German and to talk about race," in: *The Guardian* (18 September 2019).

[6] Richard Delgado and Jean Stefancic (eds.), *Critical Race Theory: The Cutting Edge* (Temple University Press: Philadelphia 1995); Adrien K. Wing (eds.), *Critical Race Feminism: A Reader* (New York University Press: New York 2003), Critical America.

[7] Within feminist theology, a critical discussion around race has played an important role from an early stage onwards, as womanist theologians highlighted how the experiences of oppression and desires for liberation of black women differ in significant ways from those of white women.

Recently, we learned about the experience of a highly-educated Muslim woman with Moroccan roots for whom it was difficult to find a house to rent in a country such as the Netherlands, even though she had a stable income. This is not a one-off example, as we learned from someone working in a rental office. In Belgium, Unia, the "independent institution that combats discrimination" advocates strongly against racial discrimination on the rental market.[8] The example of the women with Moroccan roots is only one of many examples of how structural racism and discrimination on the basis of gender and religion, are often intertwined.

De/constructing regimes of In/visibility

The concepts "gender, race, and religion" are not static ideas. We use them here in reference to processes in society, which we call "genderisation," "racialization" and "religionisation."[9] These neologisms indicate that gender, race and religion are not "just there," but are constructed in a society, in social interaction, through discourses and practices. This means their meaning can also be deconstructed. In other words, one can show how the terms "gender," "race" and "religion" can take on different meanings and interpretations, or how they are used in unjust ways. One example can illustrate this. Geert Mak, a Dutch author, writes in his most recent book *Grote verwachtingen* (*Big expectations*):

> After 9/11, children did not call each other immigrant any more. They no longer looked at their ethnic origin, but only called themselves and each other Muslims. No Pakistani, no Iranian, no Iraqui, no: we are Muslims. In a certain way, this brought about unity: we share the same faith. On the other hand, it also brought about stricter social control: what do you eat, what do you drink, who do you go out with?[10]

This is an example of "religionisation." The religion becomes suddenly much more visible than before, as a clear result of specific discourses and patterns of social interaction. After 9/11 the category "Muslim" is constructed as the negative counterpart of what many consider as the "West" and of what is

---

[8] https://www.unia.be/nl/actiedomeinen/huisvesting, 7 May 2020.
[9] For intersections between racialisation and religionisation, cf. Anya Topolski, "The Race-Religion Constellation: A European Contribution to the Critical Philosophy of Race," in: *Critical Philosophy of Race* 6/1 (2018), 58-81.
[10] Geert Mak, *Grote verwachtingen: In Europa, 1999-2019* (Atlas Contact: Amsterdam 2019), 76.

good. For some Muslim persons, this dualistic worldview increases their self-awareness as "Muslims," which leads in turn to a search for what is "a good Muslim."

Many identitarian movements in Europe use religion as a way to express their specific identity. This is also true for the reference to the so-called "Judeo-Christian" tradition. The combination of Jewish and Christian does not necessarily refer to an inherent connection between these two religions, but is often used by Christians as a way to distance oneself from Muslims. The term "Judeo-Christian" often means "non-Muslim," even for those who do not consider themselves a believer or faithful.[11] The religious reference functions to express one's own particular identity.

Genderisation refers, among others, to the increased visibility of gender norms, which often go together with the two other processes of racialisation and religionisation. An example given by Schirin Amir-Moazami in her keynote lecture "Regimes of in/visibility, Secular Embodiments and the Coupling of Gender, Race and Religion in Public Controversies on Muslim Bodily Practices in Europe" can illustrate this. Referring to an increased attention for covered female bodies, she argued that the prohibition to wear burkinis in many swimming pools evidences this genderisation that goes together with religionisation and racialisation. For this prohibition is mainly a means to exclude those who are considered "others," in this case, Muslim women from swimming, whereby "Muslim" often refers not only to religion but also to "race." On the other hand, non-covered female bodies are allowed to be shown, but are at the same time much less visible because they get considerably less attention in public discourse. The same is true for the pictures of half-naked women in advertisements, movies, and clips, which are mostly tolerated. This distinction between what is and what is not discussed about the covering of the female body explains how what is tolerated and what is not, is the result of "regimes" – structured social discourses – and of (often implicit) rules.

An experience of one of our students can function as another illustration of the manner in which these processes are diffused with power. A dentistry student, who was born in Armenia and identifies as Christian, told the story of how she was looking for an internship and was asked on the phone whether she was wearing a veil. She answered in Dutch that she was not as she was a

---

[11] For a nuanced exploration of these dynamics, cf. the contributions in Emmanuel Nathan and Anya Topolski (eds.), *Is there a Judeo-Christian Tradition?: A European Perspective* (De Gruyter: Berlin 2016) Perspectives on Jewish texts and contexts 4.

Christian. Then, there was no problem. This question shows how a foreign name, in combination with a non-native pronunciation of Dutch, immediately leads to an association with a particular group and, then again, to a specific interpretation of it. The logic behind this question is: "Foreign women are Muslims and Muslim women wear veils, and that is problematic." This is, however, very often considered more problematic for women in higher positions than for those in cleaning jobs, for it seems that society has less problems with women in cleaning jobs who wear a veil. Probably because women in higher positions are more often (already) considered a "threat" to those who have more power and privileges. This particular example does not stand alone: it illustrates many similar practices or comments, which are the consequences of constructed ideas about gender, race, and religion.

This construction is the result of power processes. What is considered as adequate for a particular gender, specific religion, or people of a specific race is often constructed by people in power positions. Politicians decide about what is considered as an appropriate way to express one's religion, what can be visible and what not, but very often the processes of "religionization" and "racialization" remain hidden and are covered up by so called good intentions: "liberating women" or "protecting the freedom of choice" (Schirin Amir-Moazami). The process of "religionization" refers to the process where the religion of people is considered as something that matters for making distinctions between themselves and the others, although precisely making these distinctions is also very often oppressed, when certain forms of religious expression are considered as dangerous by those in power. They confront people with "otherness." In broad terms, this is often called "othering."

This construction is the result of power processes: processes which are often called othering, because they are the effect of the confrontation with "otherness." This implies that what is considered as adequate for a particular gender, specific religion, or people of a specific race is often constructed by people in power positions. "Religionisation" refers to the process where the religion of people is considered as something that matters for making distinctions between oneself and others as well as of the oppression of these distinctions when they are considered as dangerous by those in power. Thus, politicians decide what is considered as an appropriate way to express one's religion, what can be visible and what not, but very often these processes of "religionization" and "racialization" remain hidden and are covered up by so called good intentions: "liberating women" or "protecting the freedom of choice" (Schirin Amir-Moazami).

In whose interests?

What is made visible and invisible is the result of choices that serve particular interests. It is a clear characteristic of feminist theology to ask this critical question: "in whose interests are we speaking/acting?" The processes described so far are the products of the interests of people and institutions who try to achieve power. The question at stake here is: who profits from processes where certain views on gender, race, and religion are used as means to claim one's identity, and who does not benefit from these processes? Racism is a mechanism that helps people to claim their own superiority and to help them feel self-confident.[12] Remarks to a woman of color such as "but you are different (than all the other persons of your religion/race/gender), you are one of us," are an example of a racism that remains almost invisible. These comments start from a general negative idea about these women as a group, and then make an exception for this particular woman. A clear way of binary thinking in order to stimulate the sense of group identity ("we") lies behind these kinds of expressions. They are very common in today's society.

Other forms of racism are more visible, and much less tolerated nowadays. The renovation of the Africa-museum in Tervuren (Brussels) might function here as a case in point. The participants to the ESWTR conference visited this museum, that reopened in 2019 after five years of renovation and intensive reorganisation in order to deal with its colonial heritage. The original museum showed many objects and pictures, often taken away from Congo, the former colony of Belgium, and presented them without much critical reflection. The renewed museum wants to make visitors aware of the inherent racism and colonial supremacy of many of the old objects. Some objects were removed, as they were clearly not tolerable in a postcolonial society. The museum also shows movies of men and women in Africa today, and focuses on the flourishing of people in Africa, on the beauty and the treasures in their culture and way of living. One can however ask critically why there is not much more focus on the dangers of racism and colonialism and why the wounds of the colonization are so easily covered by a story of healing.[13] It seems as if the museum wants to cover up the negative aspects of the past in order to step

---

[12] Peggy McIntosh, "Unpacking the Invisible Knapsack," in: Maxine B. Zinn, Pierrette Hondagneu-Sotelo and Michael Messner (eds.), *Gender through the Prism of Difference* (Oxford University Press: New York 1988), 235-238.

[13] Judith Gruber, "Doing Theology with Cultural Studies: Rewriting History – Reimagining Salvation – Decolonizing Theology," in: *Louvain Studies* 42/2 (2019), 103-123.

quickly to a new, resilient future. Is the pain really recognized? Or in Christian terms, is this not too easily a step from Good Friday to Easter, without recognizing the despair, the suffering, and the silence of Holy Saturday?[14] Dealing with traumas from the past seems to be very difficult. In her keynote lecture at the ESWTR conference, Anya Topolski also pointed this out when she referred to the massive killing of witches in the past, women who were killed because they did not have the "right" gender and religion. But this part of history is rarely told and easily forgotten. For people tend to switch easily to positive stories, as in the case of their colonial history.

However, it would be a very constructive and positive step forwards, when people would accept the value of recognizing the wounds, the scars, the injustice done to others without covering it up in positive stories of healing and resilience. The difficultly of this process becomes clear, if we compare it to the strategies commonly used by people when others express their pain or suffering. We can ignore the pain of others, and just behave as if nothing happened, only focusing at what has to be done next, or we can hear the pain, but come up with easy solutions. This kind of reaction fits what is often called a "reparation strategy": when a hospitalized patient expresses her despair, a nurse might easily say something as "this happened to me too," "keep up your courage, you have plenty other possibilities," "it will be all right" or "you can't help this, it is not your fault." All these sentences do not really acknowledge the pain and the feelings of the patient. People tend to be very hesitant to really listen to feelings of pain, also in daily life. It often confronts them with their own insecurity, pain, and doubts.

Real, active listening to the other and showing empathy, giving space for expressing the negative feelings is very important, but not easy. From the perspective of those who are in a privileged position, however, that is the only – but very complex – way to show real solidarity with the other. Recognising how difficult it is, and perhaps expressing the complexity of one's own position (as being in a privileged situation),[15] would help those who survived serious forms of oppression due to patriarchy, colonialism, racism, sexism, etc. Acknowledging that what happened in the past was wrong and making the wounds visible would help survivors to get recognition. It would also help to

---

[14] Anne Vandenhoeck, "Stille zaterdag in de zorg voor mensen met dementie. Een 'en toch' vanuit pastoraaltheologisch perspectief", in: *Collationes* 39/4 (2009), 401-411.
[15] Claudia Brunner, "Von Selbstreflexion zu Hegemonieselbstkritik," in: *S&F Sicherheit und Frieden* 35/4 (2014), 196-201.

make these forms of evil more visible. In the Africa Museum, something more could still be done in this respect. The same is true for many other museums – such as e.g. also in Belgium the Suske and Wiske museum.[16] This recently renovated museum offers lots of experiences about how comics are made, in an all in all very positive story, focused on the future. However, any reference to or excuse about the manner in which these particular comics have used racist and stereotypical ways of presenting African people and women is absent.

Many other examples can be given, especially about the Church. Although victims of sexual child abuse in the Church are increasingly recognised as such, for some theologians and church leaders it does not seem evident to openly confess that many people in the world, especially women, have suffered from the Church and actions by clerics and pastoral ministers.[17] It seems to be very difficult to openly speak about the scars of the past, the wounds made by specific institutions, groups or cultural practices/products.

Another example illustrates how gender, race, and religion are often used in a way that oppresses certain groups of people and gives privileges to others. In Belgium and Austria, you have to be recognizable when you are in public space. It is forbidden to cover your face, except when it is carnival. This rule is especially directed at preventing Muslim women to cover their faces on the street. It is an example of a "regime," stating what the right form of dressing and expressing one's religion and gender is. A recent visit to the Philippines functioned as an eye-opener to the different ways in which norms about covering faces are constructed: many men and women were driving bicycles or motorbikes with their faces totally covered, in order to protect themselves against the air pollution. A local colleague did not understand how this could be forbidden in Belgium. The recent corona-crisis, asking many people to wear a mouth mask for health reasons, again confronted the Belgian society with a paradox. The letter of the law would forbid people to wear mouth masks on the street. Again, it was clear that this law was only directed at Muslim women. A similar example about refers to Judaism. When a Chassidic Jew in Antwerp told a newspaper that he would refuse to shake hands with a woman, this was considered as very problematic. This person could not be put on the list of a political party, a Belgian political party decided. Shaking hands was considered as the ultimate form of respect, and this was a form of discrimination of

---

[16] https://www.suskeenwiskemuseum.be/, 11 May 2020.
[17] Doris Wagner, *Nicht mehr ich. Die wahre Geschichte einer jungen Ordensfrau* (Edition a: Wien 2014).

women in name of the religion. However, in 2020, someone who wants to shake hands is diabolized. Shaking hands is absolutely forbidden for health reasons. Of course, these are totally different situations and there are very good (health) reasons why covering one's face or not shaking hands is now tolerated. Nevertheless, both examples show how norms are constructed and how religion, race and gender often intersect when societal norms are expressed.

The role of theology
The processes of genderisation, racialisation, and religionisation can be illustrated by many more examples. In daily life situations, maleness and whiteness are often considered as the (implicit) norm, very often combined with a presumption that persons are (cultural) Christians.[18] If people are confronted with people of color, women, Muslims, Jews or people of other religions, then the focus is very often concentrated on only or mainly this particular point of one's identity. In many cases, the "otherness" (such as a black skin, a veil, a turban, ...) becomes very visible, and not seldom functions as a basis for discrimination. The German theologian Eske Wollrad explained this clearly in her keynote lecture "White Families: Christianity and the Art of Transgression". The next question is then: what is the role of theology in this situation?

Wollrad showed that, although black theologies and feminist theologies have grown extensively and in various forms during the last decades, there is a long way to go for theologies that deal with maleness or with whiteness. Theologies from the perspective of those who are often considered as the "oppressed," are developed partly in line with liberation theologies. The question, however, is what it means to develop a theology that not only speaks about "the option for the poor" (as in Catholic social teaching) or about "solidarity" with people who are discriminated, but which also critically reflects on its own presuppositions. What would a theology that critically reflects on its implicit norms look like? It is important that theology is not just "inclusive" or "open for diversity" and does allow for "others" next to the centre with clear norms, but also that it reflects critically on this centre, on the norms, which are often made invisible.[19]

---

[18] Adil Khan and Michael Cowan, "Why Christian-Muslim 'Dialogue' is not always Dialogical," in: *Studies in Interreligious Dialogue* 28/2 (2018), 23-48; Mara Brecht, "Soteriological Privilege," in: Mara Brecht and Reid B. Locklin (eds.) *Comparative Theology in the Millennial Classroom: Hybrid Identities, Negotiated Boundaries* (Routledge: New York 2016), 85-98.

[19] See also Stefan Gärtner and Annemie Dillen (eds.), *Discovering Practical Theology: Exploring boundaries* (Peeters: Leuven 2020).

Eske Wollrad showed how whiteness is only rarely thematised in Christian theology – but very often presumed. Blackness is associated with darkness and sin in many Christian sources, and whiteness is often associated with light and God.[20] She also explained how the Christian history of colonisation (especially from a protestant German perspective) was an example of how white women dominated black women, because the wives of the (protestant) missionaries did have the "power to define." This means that they were able to decide what was the proper belief, civilisation, and purity. These norms were not set by black women. This raises the question whether it is possible for white feminist theologians to speak critically about racism, if one belongs historically to the camp of the perpetrators? According to Wollrad, one important condition to develop an adequate theology which critically deals with whiteness is to avoid essentialism. Whiteness is part of many theologians' positionality, including ours. It is however something constructed and dynamic, which can change and does not have to be considered as an essential part of one's identity.

Critical whiteness studies often speak about white supremacy as a problem. Masculinity studies nowadays try to reconsider "masculinity" in a such way that it is not "toxic," but interpreted in a positive way in solidarity with women. Wollrad suggests that this more complex interpretation might also be possible for whiteness. This is one step towards a theology that takes the complex interactions of gender, race, and religion seriously. Much more has to be done.

We hope this article might function as an eye-opener for this topic of the interrelatedness of gender, race and religion on the one hand and the constructed character of the norms and power aspects related to these concepts on the other hand. In malestream theology this is a blind spot. However, there are a lot of theological themes at stake here. Without being able to give answers or to have clear solutions, we at least name a few of them and hope that these questions will stimulate more research and teaching in this field.

From a theological perspective, one could question how the creation stories can be interpreted in such a way that binary thinking, with a focus on essentialist identities, can be deconstructed. Or one can critically reflect on ways in which God or the trinity is presented during history and in contemporary systematic theology. How are "gender and race" intertwined in classical perceptions, and how is a constructive theology that goes beyond classical presentations of God as male or female, or white or black possible? Theological

---

[20] Cf. also Willie J. Jennings, *The Christian Imagination: Theology and the Origins of Race* (Yale University Press: New Haven 2010).

imagination has the task to stimulate people to dare to walk in the shoes of the other, to critically reflect on one's own privileges and positionality. We sincerely hope the ESWTR congress of 2019 has contributed to stimulating this reflection.

Annemie Dillen is Professor at the Faculty of Theology and Religious Studies, KU Leuven, Belgium and Extraordinary Researcher at North-West University, South-Africa. Her research is focused on spirituality, lived religion, practical and empirical theology. annemie.dillen@kuleuven.be

Judith Gruber is a research professor and director of the Centre for Liberation Theologies at KU Leuven, Belgium. Her research brings Catholic theology into conversation with critical cultural theories. She has published on intercultural theology, global Christianities, postcolonial theology, and trauma. judith.gruber@kuleuven.be

Kristine Suna-Koro

Revisiting the Sacrament of the Stranger: Reflections on Migration, Invisibility, and Postcolonial Imagination

Abstract
The article invites reflection on the theological, ethical, and theopolitical challenges that global migration presents to contemporary Euro-Atlantic theological inquiry in dialogue with feminist critiques as well as postcolonial and decolonial imaginaries from a diasporic perspective. Engaging the current ethical and theological exigencies of forced migration and displacement in the context of both Europe and North America, the article reflects on the erosion of human rights, racism, and intensifying invisibility of migrants and refugees as bearers of *imago dei*. This situation calls for novel postcolonial approaches to theological anthropology. The constructive reflections suggest that instead of unbridled glorification of sheer postmodern difference, the current situation rather invites a search for renewed "spiritual senses" to foster intervisibility and a new poetics of creaturehood. A postcolonial poetics of creaturehood, as inspired by ideas of Rabbi Jonathan Sacks, Achille Mbembe, Gloria Anzaldua, Kelly Oliver, Shawn Copeland, and Hans Urs von Balthasar, can be envisioned in terms of a poetics and a theopolitics of similitude that manifests through paradoxical encounters with the Divine through the sacrament of the stranger.

Keywords: Global migration; postcolonial imaginary; poetics of creaturehood; *imago dei*; poetics of similitude, sacrament of stranger.

Resumen
Este artículo invita a reflexionar acerca de los retos teológicos, éticos y teopolíticos que la migración global presenta para la investigación teológica euro-atlántica en diálogo con una crítica feminista así como con imaginarios poscoloniales y decolonialistas desde una perspectiva diaspórica. Engranando las actuales exigencias éticas y teológicas de la migración forzada y del desplazamiento en el contexto tanto europeo como norteamericano, el artículo reflexiona sobre la erosión de los derechos humanos, el racismo y la creciente invisibilidad de personas migrantes y refugiadas como portadores de *imago dei*. La situación demanda nuevas aproximaciones poscoloniales en la antropología teológica. Las reflexiones constructivas sugieren que, en lugar de una

desatada glorificación de la diferencia posmoderna, la situación actual invite, por el contrario, a buscar "sentidos espirituales" renovados para fomentar la intervisibilidad y una nueva poética de la condición de ser criaturas. Una poética poscolonial de esta condición, como aquella inspirada por las ideas del rabino Jonathan Sacks, Achille Mbembe, Gloria Anzaldua, Kelly Oliver, Shawn Copeland y Hans Urs von Balthasar pueden concebirse en términos de una poética y una teopolítica de la similitud que se manifiesta a través de encuentros paradójicos con lo Divino mediante el sacramento de la persona extranjera.

Palabras clave: migración global; imaginario poscolonial; poética de la condición de criaturas; *imago dei*; poética de la similitud; sacramento de la persona extranjera.

Zusammenfassung
Der Artikel lädt zur Reflexion über theologische, ethische und theopolitische Herausforderungen ein, die die globale Migration an die euro-atlantische theologische Forschung in Dialog mit feministischer Kritik sowie postkolonialen und dekolonialen Vorstellungen aus einer Diasporaperspektive darstellt. Unter Einbeziehung der gegenwärtigen ethischen und theologischen Erfordernisse durch erzwungene Migration und Vertreibung im Kontext von Europa und Nordamerika reflektiert der Artikel über die Erosion der Menschenrechte, Rassismus und sich verschärfende Unsichtbarkeit von Migrant*innen und Flüchtlingen als Träger der *imago dei*. Die Situation ruft nach neuen postkolonialen Zugängen zur theologischen Anthropologie. Die konstruktiven Reflexionen legen nahe, dass die gegenwärtige Situation anstelle grenzenloser Glorifizierung der bloßen postmodernen Differenz vielmehr eine Suche nach erneuerten „spirituellen Sinnen" einlädt, um Sichtkontakt und eine neue Poetik der Kreatürlichkeit zu fördern. Eine postkoloniale Poetik der Kreatürlichkeit, wie sie durch Ideen von Rabbi Jonathan Sacks, Achille Mbembe, Gloria Anzaldua, Kelly Oliver, Shawn Copeland und Hans Urs von Balthasar inspiriert ist, kann in Form einer Poetik und einer Theopolitik der Ähnlichkeit in den Blick kommen, die sich durch paradoxe Begegnungen mit dem Göttlichen durch das Sakrament des/der Fremden manifestiert.

Schlagwörter: globale Migration; postkoloniale Imagination; Poetik der Kreatürlichkeit; *imago Dei*; Poetik der Ähnlichkeit; Sakrament des/der Fremden.

In the era of building walls, the old – and yet so new and so consequential – conundrum of how to deal with strangers acquires a new sense of urgency. The current surge of global migration is increasingly registering in our Euro-Atlantic awareness as a protracted quandary with immense political, economic, cultural, and religious implications. Some even talk about the steadily increasing numbers of people on the move as the "new normal" state of affairs in the

21st century. From a theological point of view, it is becoming much harder to avoid noticing that as Chief Rabbi emeritus of the United Hebrew Congregations of the Commonwealth Jonathan Sacks put it, "hatred of foreigner is the oldest of passions" – the "dislike of the unlike is as old as [hu]mankind."[1] Our Euro-Atlantic lifeworlds are currently at risk of becoming ever more treacherously polarized by fear, inequality, and resentment. Often the inequality is blamed on the undeserving outsider "others." Even more often, the fear and resentment toward "strangers" is manipulated to distract from the underlying structural causes of injustice and hopelessness to sow acrimony and distrust. In the present Covid-19 pandemic crisis, it is migrants and refugees (rather than cruise ship passengers, jet-setting tourists, and ubiquitous business travelers) who are often and without factual proof accused of spreading the virus. Such scapegoating comes in handy to suspend processing asylum claims and enacting even tighter border closures in Europe and the United States. Meanwhile migrant workers, both documented and undocumented, perform hazardous responsibilities now deemed "essential" in agriculture, food processing, healthcare, and service industries. In this context, I submit, the realities and experiences of migration constitute a unique crucible for theological and ethical imagination in our moment in history.

The following reflections on the significance of migration for Euro-Atlantic theological (including feminist) imagination and practice were initially presented as a keynote address at the 2019 bi-annual conference "Gender, Race, Religion: De/Constructing Regimes of In/Visibility" of the European Society of Women in Theological Research (ESWTR) in Leuven, Belgium. The overarching purpose of my reflections was – and is – to invite further conversations among theologians working from a broad spectrum of perspectives, including feminist discourses, to discern how the urgent summons through the real and often very challenging presence of contemporary racial, cultural, religious, and linguistic migrants and refugees in our midst is also a summons toward rekindled and meaningful theological anthropologies as well as theo-ontologies of creaturehood. Just to clarify: by "our midst" I mean the Euro-Atlantic theopolitical and socio-cultural milieu where most ESWTR members live, work, pray, love, and go about their daily lives interacting with others in their communities.

---

[1] Jonathan Sacks, *Mishpatim (5779) – Loving the Stranger* (http://rabbisacks.org/loving-the-stranger-mishpatim-5779/, 5 September 2019).

The real presence of migrants and refugees in our midst is a revelatory sign of the time, indeed, a *locus theologicus*, which today compels a renewed attention to the ancient imaginary of hospitality: first, to the divine welcome of the created world into existence as well as what Richard Kearney and James Taylor have called "the sacred commitment to hosting the stranger" which is prominent in most major wisdom traditions.[2] They insist – rightfully so – that "interreligious hospitality is a primary task of our time."[3] Hospitality itself, they discern, is "a central and inaugural event in the world's great wisdom traditions" since "it marks that moment when the self opens to the stranger and welcomes what is foreign and unfamiliar into its home" even as "hosting a stranger is always a risk, never a fait accompli."[4] In light of the ongoing controversies in many Euro-Atlantic societies and communities of faith, it is hard to disagree that welcoming the other is nothing less than "an act of daring and trust, of bold compassion and justice, never a matter of cheap grace or easy virtue."[5]

My itinerary for these reflections goes as follows: 1) to explore the regimes of visibility/invisibility through the lens of migratory experience toward 2) re-envisioning some exasperating aspects of theological anthropology with 3) a brief constructive focus on the notions of creation, *imago dei*, similitude, and the stranger as a sacrament – and to do it all 4) from a postcolonial perspective.

Context, Intersectionality, and the Oldest of Passions

To explore the regimes of visibility and invisibility I will proceed as a Christian theologian who sees theological endeavor as being rooted in the revelation of the Word and Wisdom of God incarnate, crucified, and risen in history. At the same time, my reflections are always already inflected by the lived experience of migration. While I am a Lutheran theologian and pastor, I am also a diasporic Latvian-American and a migrant. Hence I am compelled to underscore that Christian theology is lifeless at the least, and perhaps even blasphemous at the worst, if it proceeds as if the routinely suppressed and devalued

---

[2] Richard Kearney and James Taylor, "Introduction," in: Richard Kearney and James Taylor (eds.), *Hosting the Stranger: Between Religions* (Continuum: New York and London 2011), 1-8, here 1.
[3] Kearney and Taylor, "Introduction," 1.
[4] Kearney and Taylor, "Introduction," 1.
[5] Kearney and Taylor, "Introduction," 1.

histories of those sinned-against and vanquished (still) simply do not matter in theological reflection.

From my perspective as a Latvian-American diasporic theologian working from postcolonial perspectives, I share the sense of urgency that migration presents precisely on a *theological* level. Ethnographic vignettes in terms of how to "apply" or "illustrate" methods and doctrinal insights generated in the metropolitan centres will no longer suffice for theological authenticity as ambiguous and as hybrid as such authenticity is for those of us who live betwixt and between cultures, languages, nationalities, and political allegiances. Fortunately, the current "turn to context," or the turn to experiential histories as sources *of* and challenges *for* theological inquiry, entail a praiseworthy shift toward more attentive engagements with the ethical and existential exigencies of life precisely if we allow them to shape the methods, doctrines, and paradigms of theological creativity and not just their local "applications," "inculturations," "contextualizations" and "adaptations."

Among such theological engagements, feminist theological inquiries have often served as trailblazers. Amid the exceedingly convoluted processes of postcolonial – and some would say, neocolonial – globalization, we are seeing the emergence of an uncertain and volatile multipolar world under the widening shadow of an overarching ecological degradation. In this emerging world of Anthropocene, Christianity, let alone North-Atlantic Christianity or Western Christianity or even more narrowly, the European type of Western Christianity, offers only *one* cosmovision or only *one* ontology, or only *one* epistemological imaginary – *among* others. In this context, it is no secret that the emergence of womanist, Mujerista, postcolonial, decolonial, and a whole spectrum of indigenous feminisms from the Global South has, in turn, called into question the theories, methods, and values of Euro-Atlantic feminisms and their unease around the issues of race. These emerging discourses highlight a continued scarcity of attention to the coloniality of gender.[6] As the Arab feminist thinker from Australia, Ruby Hamad, has just reminded everyone in her new book *White Tears/Brown Scars*, "white women were not bystanders to the

---

[6] For a good overview of this debate, see, for example: Raewyn Connell, "Meeting at the Edge of Fear: Theory on the World Scale," in: Bernd Reiter (ed.), *Constructing the Pluriverse: The Geopolitics of Knowledge* (Duke University Press: Durham and London 2018), 19-38 as well as the essay collection by Margaret A. McLaren (ed.), *Decolonizing Feminism: Transnational Feminism and Globalization* (Rowman & Littlefield: London and New York 2017) among other publications.

global colonial project;" hence a lot more careful attention should be paid to "the legacy of both confounding and collaborating" of European colonialist women within colonial designs.[7]

The stream of postcolonial refugees, migrants, and asylum seekers in Euro-Atlantic societies highlights the intersections of gender and race ever more intensely. Yet these intersections remain in need of deeper theological interrogation especially in some European milieus, including feminist discourses, where the issues of race, even in relation to the undeniable problems of racism, are still often avoided since they are seen (perhaps too conveniently?) as exclusively tied to the histories of Nazism. Now, race talk is never easy or comfortable anywhere. Despite how unsettling, frustrating, and unsatisfying discussions of racism remain in North American theological and feminist conversations, they are now practically unavoidable across most disciplines in religious studies, humanities, and social sciences. The European situation is different in terms of how race and racism appear in public and academic discourses. Not that racism doesn't exist in Europe – alas, it does. Nevertheless, it is inspiring to see as Mithu Sanyal recently pointed out from her German perspective that new paths are explored in the European context on how to address it more openly and constructively. Even though a new openness for engaging race in racism is emerging, Sanyal observes that still "we're all walking on eggshells; the discussion about racism is on the agenda but we're whispering 'race' as if it were a dirty word."[8]

Meanwhile, hardly a day goes by without new and very troubling knowledge – such as the scientifically researched "existential risks" – emerging about the climate change and its impact on virtually all spheres of life.[9] But what often slips to the sidelines of the climate change discussions is its impact on migration – which also means dealing with cultural, racial, and religious

---

[7] Ruby Hamad, *White Tears/Brown Scars* (Melbourne University Press: Melbourne 2019). The quote is from her article "White Women Were Colonisers Too: To Move Forward, We Have to Stop Letting Them Off the Hook," *Guardian*, 30 August 2019 (https://www.theguardian.com/world/2019/aug/30/white-women-were-colonisers-too-to-move-forward-we-have-to-stop-letting-them-off-the-hook, 2 September 2019).

[8] Mithu Sanyal, "Suddenly, it's OK to be German and to talk about race," in *Guardian*, 18 September 2019 (https://www.theguardian.com/commentisfree/2019/sep/18/germany-race-conversation-afd-openness?CMP=Share_AndroidApp_Gmail, 19 September 2019).

[9] For a global overview of risk analysis in relation to the climate change see, for example, the work of Cambridge's *Centre for the Study of Existential Risk* (https://www.cser.ac.uk, 1 September 2019).

strangers! This impact will only swell to add more momentum and complexity to what such unlikely bedfellows as the Ecumenical Patriarch Bartholomew and the late sociologist Zygmunt Bauman have already described as "humanity's crisis."[10] Migrants, especially as the current bugbear of choice for ethno-nationalist campaigns across the globe, are like a disconcerting sign of the times not only for political and cultural soul-searching but, even more consequentially, for spiritual assessment and theological analysis of Christianity's existential risks of idolatry.[11] This is one more reason to foreground migration as a *locus theologicus* in Euro-Atlantic theological imagination.

Like Rabbi Sacks, I also see the real presence of strangers as globalization's "supreme challenge" to world's religions. Interacting and co-existing with strangers has never been an easy-going business. Sacks probes deeper with a seemingly disarming simplicity: "Can we find, in the human 'thou', a fragment of the Divine 'Thou'? Can we recognize God's image in one who is not in my image?"[12] And, "can I do so and feel not diminished but enlarged?" precisely as every generation all over again discovers that we "must now make space for those who are different and for another way of interpreting the world"[13] in ways that are fitting for our unique historical location.

I would like to add that we are no longer just asking the perennially frustrating question as Sacks does, namely, "can we see the presence of God in the face of a stranger"[14] but also wondering what does it even mean to "see" (to recognize, to acknowledge, to affirm, to respect) the presence of the Divine in those who are not like me/us? Indeed, how? Through what theological optics can we see difference without prematurely negating or triumphantly colonising

---

[10] Patriarch Bartholomew, "Address by His All-Holiness Ecumenical Patriarch Bartholomew at the Concordia Europe Summit 'Migration Challenging European Identity'," taking place on 7 June 2017 in Athens, Greece. (https://www.patriarchate.org/-/address-by-his-all-holiness-ecumenical-patriarch-bartholomew-at-the-concordia-europe-summit-migration-challenging-european-identity-june-6-2017-athens, 18 August 2019) See also, Brad Evans and Zygmunt Bauman, "The Refugee Crisis is Humanity's Crisis," *The New York Times*, 2 May 2016 (https://www.nytimes.com/2016/05/02/opinion/the-refugee-crisis-is-humanitys-crisis.html, 2 July 2019).

[11] Some of the most respected North American theologians from a wide ecumenical spectrum have recently called attention to the profound theological challenges that currently amplifying forms of nationalism present to many societies around the issues of xenophobia. See "Against the New Nationalism: An Open Letter," *Commonweal*, 146:15, October 2019, 2-4.

[12] Jonathan Sacks, *The Dignity of Difference: How to Avoid the Clash of Civilizations*. Revised edition with a new preface (Continuum: London and New York 2003), 17.

[13] Sacks, *The Dignity of Difference*, 8.

[14] Sacks, *The Dignity of Difference*, 5.

it in this age when dealing with difference "is the greatest religious challenge of all?"[15] In our time, when millions of human beings are on the move and are increasingly portrayed as disgusting, threatening, malicious, and as not deserving any mercy or understanding from the late postmodern nation states in the global North which are still more or less (it seems) inculturated in Christian lifeworlds, how can theological imagination be deployed to profoundly recraft the Western Christian operative theologies of shared human creaturehood? How can theological optics empower the capacity to see personality, resilience, courage, creativity, hope, love, agency, and dignity in those that are being vilified to the point of becoming invisible precisely as fellow human beings?

Postmodern Differences, Borderization, and Noticing the Subaltern Eyes

And this is where postcolonial and decolonial angles can be useful in the quest for new anthropological imagination that also affects the dominant imaginaries of gendered difference. Is it not time, especially in the affluent and relatively peaceful enclaves of the "First World," to retool our operative theological anthropologies that (should) inform the attitudes and actions toward all those human persons whose shared humanity and shared stake in being part of God's creation is overshadowed by lingering colonial conventions as well as constructions of such radical otherness (racial, cultural, religious) that their suffering and death seems to give our societies no pause, no notice, and no grief? Is it not high time for theological feminist discourses to commit more expansively, especially in Europe, to critical engagement with racism and "go planetary" in order to break open some methodological and cultural taboos that still often result in diplomatically avoiding the issues of race? Having lived the first half of my life in Soviet and postsoviet Eastern Europe and now living in the United States, I have yet to find a place where an honest conversation about our human constructions of race, racism, ethnicity and all the myriad of hierarchies and inequities that such construction entail would be comfortable.[16] Most of us want to avoid such conversations at all costs. Feminist discourses

---

[15] Sacks, *The Dignity of Difference*, 46.

[16] The recent Jena Declaration of the Institute for Zoology and Evolutionary Research of Friedrich Schiller University in Jena, Germany, points to the difficulty in some European cultures of finding a constructive way of addressing racism. Indeed, "simply removing the word 'race' from our daily language will not prevent racism and intolerance. A feature of current forms of racism is precisely the tendency in far-right and xenophobic circles to avoid the term 'race.'" (https://www.uni-jena.de/en/190910_JenaerErklaerung_EN.html, 11 September 2019).

and gatherings have not presented many exceptions so far. In other words, as an Eastern European living and working in North America, I keep wondering what kind of theological imaginaries would allow us in the (still, at least, "ambiently"[17] Christian) Global North to see, sense, shape, and enact a shared grasp of humanity of those who are unlike us in quite a few ways? Regardless of how we proceed, in the Global North it would behoove us not to forget that there is a significant difference between "what is concealed and what is by nature invisible…," in the words of decolonial philosopher Boaventura de Sousa Santos, while – and this is of supreme importance – also remembering that "subaltern eyes are different and unequal."[18]

In the quest for a new shared grasp of other human persons and their humanity, it is time to seriously reassess *both* the dualistic, hierarchical, and inherently competitive modern constructs of difference as an allergic nuisance to be kept under tight control as well as postmodernity's intoxication with flamboyantly radical(ised) difference.

On the one hand, playing the postmodern game of difference until exhaustion over the past three decades indeed did unleash a suppressed flood of visceral resentment against the hypocrisies of modern Western totalizing universalism. The darker sides of modernity were exposed as precisely having imposed Eurocentric imaginaries of being and knowing elsewhere through colonial subjugation. Additionally, postmodern discourses of difference also uncovered at least some of its dark colonial and patriarchal undersides.

On the other hand, the same postmodern sensibilities rapidly waltzed into the terrains of decadent fragmentation of lifeworlds. The momentum of fragmentation now appears only to be accelerating. More and more of us find ourselves separated in various silos of identity politics, culture wars, economic disparities, and conflicting worldviews on everything from eating meat and shaving legs to nuclear weapons and physician assisted suicide… Obviously, the decadent fragmentation is reaching its apogee in the brave "new" cyberworld. It offers seemingly unlimited potential for both extreme visibility and unprecedented authenticity despite the sense (or perhaps rather a mirage?) of intimate and instantaneous connections across social networks and flows of

---

[17] I am referring to the notion of "ambient faith" by the anthropologist Matthew Engelke. See his "Angels in Swindon: Public Religion and Ambient Faith in England," in: *American Ethnologist* 39/1 (2012), 155-170.

[18] Boaventura de Sousa Santos, *The End of the Cognitive Empire: The Coming of Age of Epistemologies of the South* (Duke University Press: Durham and London 2018), 172, 174.

information. Amidst the Covid-19 social distancing provisions, cyberworld surely offers a new regime of normality and connections. It also provides whole new parallel galaxies of social and discursive networking in which the cybercitizens can dwell without any awareness of those who might physically be just around the corner and yet maybe on the other, more disinherited, side of the digital divide. Moreover, alongside experiences of cozy intimacy, our fascinating cyberworld also offers possibilities for endless pretense and a very profitable invisibility (and camouflage!) for multi-pronged and cowardly hatred. Nevertheless, it is so often the material and visible bodies of those who are being "othered" that end up bearing the cruel brunt of virtual hate.

All of these vectors of friction and disparity acquire a particular poignancy within the broader horizon of the global postcolony. It this postcolony all differences – big and small, readily apparent or barely visible and audible – are coloured by the fact that we inhabit a world that remains structured in hegemony, dominance, and inequity. It plays out in countless mutations in the inescapable entanglement of not just gender, race, and class but now also increasingly of nationality, citizenship, statelessness, and immigration status. For more and more people on this planet, these are no academic categories nor abstract dimensions of identity politics. These categories of identity can be a matter of life or death. The "old" world of jagged materiality is still here. And it is becoming even more viscerally a world "of bodies and distances" but most alarmingly, as the postcolonial philosopher Achille Mbembe has argued, a world of "borderization" and "separation" that no one else knows more painfully than migrants.[19] Emerging theological visions, indeed poetics, of human creaturehood including the crucially significant dimensions of gender cannot be spiritually or existentially disengaged from these enforced regimes of identity – as invisible as they may be to those who never need a visa to cross a border or can easily obtain one without a life-threatening ordeal to have fun, to connect with loved ones, or to take on yet another new job if they so desire.

Bare Life, Migration, and Theopolitics

This crucible of borderization is where the challenge of global migration for Christian theological anthropology grows even deeper if we actually allow its methodological understructure to be postcolonized through, among other

---

[19] Achille Mbembe, "Deglobalization," Translated by Isabelle Chaize. *Editions Esprit* 2018/12 (2018), 2-3. (https://www.cairn-int.info/article-E_ESPRI_1812_0086--deglobalization.htm, 12 June 2019).

things, theological and moral imaginaries that emerge from the roots migratory experience.[20] With record numbers of people on the move globally, I suggest, theological anthropology will need to develop a desire for a broad methodological hospitality. Such a hospitality would dare not only to acknowledge and honor visions from the eyes that are not only different but also unequal but, furthermore, also allow itself to be reconfigured (never a painless process!) by these such visions. I can see three vectors of attention emerging from within such a methodological hospitality:

First, no theological constructs, be they patriarchal or feminist or whatever else, can go unquestioned while more and more people on this planet are considered redundant and disposable. Judging from what Pope Francis accurately diagnosed as the frightening "globalization of indifference"[21] toward migrants worldwide, it would perhaps not be too surreal to wonder how often migrants are actually – and practically – considered not fully human? In what sense those who are drowning in the Mediterranean – or dying at the U.S./Mexico border – are seen as human vis-à-vis those who are "natives," "host societies," and "citizens" with certain inalienable human rights and certain human dignity? How else can one comprehend the relative silence or even endorsement by so many Christians of the kind of rhetoric and policies that designate whole ethnic groups of asylum seekers and refugees as "swarm" as the former UK Prime Minister David Cameron described it?[22] Or, worse, "rapists" who "bring crime" and "animals" that "infest" our countries as the present U.S. President Donald Trump put it?[23]

---

[20] On the particularities and complexities of postcolonial diasporic imagination in relation to theological methodology I have already written elsewhere. For example, see Kristine Suna-Koro, *In Counterpoint: Diaspora, Postcoloniality, and Sacramental Theology* (Pickwick Publications: Eugene, OR 2017), see particularly 15-89.

[21] Pope Francis, "Homily at Lampedusa, 8 July 2013." (http://w2.vatican.va/content/francesco/en/homilies/2013/documents/papa-francesco_20130708_omelia-lampedusa.html, 20 August 2019).

[22] BBC News, "David Cameron: 'Swarm' of migrants crossing Mediterranean," in: *BBC*, 30 July 2015. (https://www.bbc.com/news/av/uk-politics-33714282/david-cameron-swarm-of-migrants-crossing-mediterranean, 21 June 2019).

[23] Among numerous other reports, for a summary of some of the strongest language President Trump has used publicly and among the members of his administration about migrants up to date with links to previously reported utterances, see Eugene Scott, "Trump's most insulting – and violent – language is often reserved for immigrants," in: *Washington Post*, 2 October 2019. (https://www.washingtonpost.com/politics/2019/10/02/trumps-most-insulting-violent-language-is-often-reserved-immigrants/, 10 October 2019).

As the exceedingly inequitable arc of globalized neo-liberal economy still bends onward, Robert J. C. Young accurately observes that multitudes are "condemned to the surplusage of lives full of holes, waiting for a future that may never come, forced into the desperate decision to migrate illegally across whole continents in order to survive."[24] What many in Western societies ignore or conveniently overlook is the fact that, as Saskia Sassen aptly summarizes, we are already entering that stage in the age of migration when "even more people will be on the move, not because they are in search of a better life but because they are in search of bare life."[25] Among theological voices that have the clearest understanding of what is at stake in these circumstances is Pope Francis.

In his homily on 8 July 2019 to commemorate the 6th anniversary of his visit to the island of Lampedusa, Pope Francis once again raised the thorny issue of migrants and refugees. What was true in 2013 became even more poignant in 2019 if we look at the United Nations latest available record high figures about forcibly displaced persons alone without even addressing the manifold desolations of millions of economic refugees: 70.8 million people were forcibly displaced worldwide. Among them, there were 25.9 million refugees, 3.5 million asylum seekers, and 41.3 million internally displaced persons.[26] The United Nations High Commissioner of Refugees also reports that it has data on 3.9 million stateless persons "but there are thought to be millions more."[27] Shortly after these figures were released on 19 June 2019 on the World Refugee Day, Pope Francis observed that "the existential peripheries of our cities are densely populated with persons who have been thrown away, marginalized, oppressed, discriminated against, abused, exploited, abandoned, poor and suffering."[28] Indeed, "these are not mere social or migrant issues! 'This is not just about migrants', in the twofold sense that migrants are first of all human persons, and that they are the symbol of all those rejected by today's globalized society."[29]

---

[24] Robert J.C. Young, "Postcolonial Remains," in: *New Literary History* 43 (2012), 19-42, here 27.
[25] Saskia Sassen, "The Making of Migrations," in: Agnes M. Brazal and Maria Teresa Davila (eds.), *Living With(out) Borders: Catholic Theological Ethics on the Migrations of Peoples* (Orbis: Maryknoll, NY 2016), 11-22, here 11.
[26] United Nations High Commissioner for Refugees, (UNHCR) "Figures at a Glance," 19 June 2019. (https://www.unhcr.org/en-us/figures-at-a-glance.html, 21 June 2019).
[27] United Nations High Commissioner for Refugees (UNHCR), "Figures at a Glance."
[28] Pope Francis, "Homily on 8 July 2019." (http://w2.vatican.va/content/francesco/en/homilies/2019/documents/papa-francesco_20190708_omelia-migranti.html, 1 August 2019).
[29] Pope Francis, "Homily on 8 July 2019."

Second, such methodological hospitality entails a commitment to an ongoing examination of protracted and lingering colonial constructs of power, being, and knowledge. It entails a robust examination of European theological traditions and initiatives as positively, hopefully, and affirmatively "provincial."[30] That is, such an examination would be eager to cross-pollinate and to engage in transformative conversations with other "provincial" modes of inquiry and fabrics of imagination to foster a creative glocal dialog. Why glocal? Simply because so much of what imperils our lives today goes beyond one "provincial" locality – ecological degradation, human trafficking, drug and weapons trade, environmental pollution, and yes, migration, too. Cultural and methodological cross-pollination will be fruitful only if it avoids mimicking the inertias of patriarchal Western modernity when it comes to conversing with the whole spectrum of indigenous and decolonial movements across many disciplines, including feminist thought. As a response to the moral exigencies of global migration, Euro-American feminist theological imagination can be most consequential if it joined hands with the whole spectrum of movements mentioned above to explore what it means to theologize from one of the many undersides of postcolonial globalization.

Theologizing from the undersides of postcolonial globalization in the Global North, especially through feminist-oriented modalities, should discern its accountability and theological vocation by connecting its analyses and visions of the Divine with the punishing realities of people on the move in general if transformative liberation still remains among the priorities of feminist commitments in theology. In particular, there should be a meaningful and constructive theological engagement with the massive gender-specific challenges that women (and to an extreme extent, queer and transgender women) migrants, refugees, and asylum seekers face as gendered subjects while being on the move or stranded in camps or locked up in detention centers. How might feminist theological inquiry challenge and aspire to transform the awareness of the suffering women in the ice-cold border detention facilities in the United States who are separated from their children and being told to drink water from toilet bowls as so many news reports from the United States revealed in 2018 and 2019? Or, how will that challenge and aspiration relate to the reality of

---

[30] I refer to the postcolonial concept of "provincializing" the mythical colonial notion of Europe as exposed by Dipesh Chakrabarty in his seminal *Provincializing Europe: Postcolonial Thought and Historical Difference*. New edition with a new preface (Princeton University Press: Princeton 2008).

migrant women drowning in the Mediterranean (if they somehow managed to survive trafficking nightmares in Libya and other North African launching points) while European powers try find legal ways to avoid responsibility for rescuing those who are already literally drowning in the water? Or, how will that challenge and aspiration relate to the reality of women and their families stuck in the Idomeni refugee camp (among others) in Greece that the Greek interior minister Panagiotis Kouroublis not too long ago described as a "modern-day Dachau"[31] – to name just a few examples closest to home for European societies?

Feminist philosopher Kelly Oliver has recently cautioned that the plight of women refugees calls for new categories of inquiry going beyond what both Western feminist and decolonial feminist critiques have offered so far. She argues that "even intersectionality cannot begin to address the special plight of women refugees who leave their homes with nothing but what they can carry, and often that means their children, and then only for as long as their strength holds out. And in terms of transnational feminism, women refugees challenge the very notion of national sovereignty assumed by the idea of transnational."[32]

Third, such a methodological hospitality means not avoiding the fact that theological anthropology involves theopolitics. The last thing theologizing from the undersides of postcolonial globalization can afford, I submit, is a gnostic flight from politics. Or, perhaps, should we call it a retreat into the comfort zones of self-preservation and privilege, be they academic, economic, or cultural? Of course, as Johann Baptist Metz pointed out already decades ago "no theology can hold itself to be politically innocent or neutral without self-deception or self-delusion."[33] Catherine Keller puts it even more pithily, "theology always means – whatever else it means – theopolitics."[34] Under the

---

[31] Will Worley and Lizzie Dearden, "Greek refugee camp is 'as bad as a Nazi concentration camp', says minister," *Independent*, 18 March 2016. (https://www.independent.co.uk/news/world/europe/idomeni-refugee-dachau-nazi-concentration-camp-greek-minister-a6938826.html, 20 July 2019).

[32] Kelly Oliver, "The Special Plight of Women Refugees," in: Margaret A. McLaren (ed.), *Decolonizing Feminism: Transnational Feminism and Globalization* (Rowman and Littlefield: Lanham 2017), 177-200, here 192.

[33] Johann Baptist Metz, *Faith in History and Society: Toward a Practical Fundamental Theology*. A New Translation by J. Matthew Ashley with Study Guide (Crossroad, Herder and Herder: New York 2013), 60.

[34] Catherine Keller, *God and Power* (Augsburg Fortress: Minneapolis 2005), 135.

aegis of global migration, the theological intersects the political ever more relentlessly. The "ground zero" of this intersection resides in theological anthropology and in the poetics of creaturehood (of which more is to be said later) at a time when more secularized social imaginaries of human dignity and rights are gradually being drowned out by pragmatic nihilism of political convenience and manipulative mobilizations of postmodern neo-tribalism precisely where they grate against the inequities of global postcolony.

Is Being Human Still – or Again – (Not) Enough?

The emerging postcolonial visions and poetics of creaturehood will need to start with basics. Is being human enough for survival, let alone leading or aspiring to flourishing life? This is a simple and yet a very troublesome question. Observing the attitudes of many Western societies amidst the migration surge, Tony Fry attributes the category of "the abject" to the displaced, the dislocated, and "instrumentally dehumanized" who are, today, "the world's unseen, unheard, the 'they' who are unfeelingly ignored, [the] neoliberal capital's human waste."[35] Today, refugees and migrants are the instrumentally dehumanized *par excellence* of our convoluted globalization. They are made invisible precisely as humans with dignity and integrity while being rendered hypervisible as threats, burdens, and invaders. Some years ago (and that was before Syria, before the Rohingya ethnic cleansing and many other more recent catastrophic events!) Giorgio Agamben already re-actualized Hannah Arendt's ominous questions about refugees as the very epitome of the postmodern precariousness of life as well as the crisis of the very concept of human rights and nation state. It is worth pondering a bit over Agamben's observation that the marginal figure of the refugee deserves to be regarded as the "central figure of our political history."[36]

On the one hand, Agamben observed, there is no space in our world for the naked life of human beings or the "pure human in itself" – and yet, on the other, "growing sections of humankind are no longer representable inside the nation-state."[37] Refugees constitute nothing less than a "radical crisis of the

---

[35] Tony Fry, "Design for/by 'The Global South'," *Design Philosophy Papers* 15/1 (2017), 3-37, here 18.
[36] Giorgio Agamben, "Beyond Human Rights," in: *Social Engineering* 15 (2008), 90-95, here 93. Agamben mostly engages with Hannah Arendt's poignant essay dating back to 1943 "We Refugees."
[37] Agamben, "Beyond Human Rights," 93.

concept" of human rights although it is precisely the refugees who "should have embodied human rights more than any other."[38] Again and again contemporary migration illustrates the fragility of human rights precisely because they seem to depend on citizenship. But citizenship itself is an increasingly contested and manipulated concept in today's globalized and re-tribalizing world (think of, for example, the stateless Rohingya who are denied citizenship in their native Myanmar but now stuck in massive refugee camps in Bangladesh as well as living in the shadows of other host societies elsewhere in the region).

This is the state of affairs within which the feminist theorist Kelly Oliver, like Agamben, also dialogues with Hannah Arendt's thought. Oliver argues that we have reached a point when it is only fair to stop pretending and admit that "being human in not enough" because "human beings are not born with rights. They are not born equal"[39] in the world as we know it. The present wretchedness of so many migrant lives in the present era of building walls resurrects the specters of a socio-political imaginary that is associated with Carl Schmitt's approach from the Nazi era where it became acceptable to recognize that "not every human being with a human face is human."[40]

Let's consider this once more, and with a feeling: being human is not enough.

Is there something that religious traditions and theological imaginaries can offer – indeed are compelled to offer with a renewed urgency – to constructively challenge the callous reality of this resigned yet pragmatically accurate *Realpolitik* of migration?

What I am about to suggest is something that many in the Global North may easily find disconcerting, obsolete, or futile. Namely, during the persistent chipping away at the social imaginary of human rights (especially exemplified in the growing precariat of refugees, asylum seekers, and economic migrants across all continents in justified search for survival and dignified life) theological imagination can critically and constructively draw from the depths of religious traditions to offer a new post-secular spectrum of ethical imaginaries. Such post-secular imaginaries may also need to be robustly ecumenical,

---

[38] Agamben, "Beyond Human Rights," 92.
[39] Oliver engages Arendt's reflections on forced displacement and predicaments on refugees in the context of human rights debates in "The Special Plight of Women Refugees," 194.
[40] Michael J. Perry, *Toward a Theory of Human Rights: Religion, Law, Courts* (Cambridge University Press: Cambridge and New York 2006), 67.

interreligious, and even post-institutional in terms of the gradually dissolving structures of institutionalized religion in Western societies but I don't want to be too hasty in this regard – yet. The mission of such imaginaries is to modulate the momentum of polarization, of practical dehumanization and of the demonization of migrants and refugees as political bargaining chips in ethnonationalist ideologies. During the protracted collision of identity and morality which migration now constantly unleashes throughout the social fabric of the Global North and its theological visions, here nothing less will do than taking Agamben's call to use such crises "for a renewal of categories that can no longer be delayed"[41] seriously.

Of course, quite a few may insist that theological (that is, with Metz and Keller, theopolitical) responses to the multiplying conundrums of human rights must be met with a priori skepticism or indifference in the secular Global North. Many might see them as outdated or untrustworthy. As a postcolonial theologian, I can agree that there are good reasons for deploying a robust hermeneutic of vigilance toward all religious concepts, theological constructs, and spiritual practices. Vigilance, however, ought not to automatically imply a wholesale dismissal of theological imagination as merely nostalgic or as intransigent by default. My purpose here is not to present an argument like Michael Perry's that the morality of human rights can still be effectively grounded in religious discourse.[42] That is a conversation for another time. Here I merely suggest that migration crisis presents a fecund and deeply consequential opportunity, precisely during such messy times as ours, to prioritize re-envisioning theological imaginaries of human life through a poetics of creaturehood which is rooted in the conception of shared yet irreducibly diverse human embodiment and embeddedness within the mysterious planetary web of life which ought to be perceived as nothing less than the creation of God.

Difference, Similitude, and a (Counter)Poetics of Creaturehood

How might a postcolonially inflected vision – indeed, a poetics – of creaturehood within the planetary web of creation unfold? All of us are, at least to some degree and at some point, strangers and others to one another. Yet despite all the differences who doesn't yearn to flourish and have abundant life on our common planet? In Christian perspectives, abundant life is what creation, incarnation, and salvation are all about as presented by the gospel of

---

[41] Agamben, "Beyond Human Rights," 94.
[42] Perry, *Toward a Theory of Human Rights*, 7-13.

John 10:10: "I came that they may have life, and have it abundantly" (New Revised Standard Version). Other English translations render this remarkable verse as "I came to give life that is full and good" (Easy to Read Version). Or "I have come so that they may have life, life in its fullest measure" (Complete Jewish Bible). Or, Christ has come so that they have life "in its fullest" (Contemporary English Version). However one might choose to translate the Greek adverb περισσὸν, the gospel is a fundamental counter-poetics to the hardnosed concession that "being human is not enough."

A theological counter-poetics of resistance and transformation could manifest, I reckon, as something old and yet new: as a theological poetics of creaturehood in which our human *imago dei* can be re-envisioned in a non-hegemonic and non-competitive way. Right off the bat, I must clarify that such a poetics does not endorse the still ongoing fixations on warped anthropocentric self-glorification with its narcissistic logic of domination over the rest of the planetary community of creation. The relational entanglement is not singularly vectored toward the Uncreated at the expense of or in competition with the rest of the planetary community of life. It is simultaneously an entanglement with the rest of the creation precisely because this entanglement originates in, with, and through the Uncreated. Consequently, while this kind of poetics of creaturehood is by no means limited to intra-human differences alone, the scope of the present reflections allows me to merely flag this dimension while prioritizing here some other aspects of poetics of creaturehood in a more direct correlation with strangers, migrants, and refugees.

Moreover, I seek a poetics of creaturehood that unsettles not only the colonial and patriarchal forms of life, thought, relations, and power, but also the deeply ingrained anthropocentrism that has permeated most modern and postmodern Western theologies and critical theories. That includes certain professed feminist orientations. This is why ecofeminist, ecowomanist, postcolonial, and decolonial discourses that foreground ecojustice rightly deserve a methodological priority in our historical moment. These minoritarian imaginaries prioritize the enormity of the climate change and the accompanying extinction of species with its myriad implications (including migration and, consequently, encountering strangers in our backyards!) for all life forms on this planet. Even without providing absolute guarantees, such prioritizing offers the most accountable way to ensure that the lived wounds of racial, ethnic, and cultural violence remain visible and audible in the broader horizon of feminist theological creativity.

As far as our locus of enunciation as human persons attempting to envision a poetics of creaturehood is concerned, a fruitful place to begin is pretty traditional and yet in need of a certain re-orchestration. Christian anthropology traditionally recognizes human persons as marked by a distinct relation to the Divine which is captured in the trope of *imago dei*. Despite exaggerations and distortions of human self-aggrandizement, the relational identity of *imago dei* does not float in a vacuum. Rather, it is contextualized within a deeply relational and interdependent web of evolving creation. On the one hand, *imago dei* is a figure of transparency and intimacy with God. On the other, it is simultaneously a figure of opacity, distance, and difference: whatever else they might be or become, humans are not God! It marks the human self-awareness of being a derivative mystery – an offshoot, so to say, of the Holy Mystery of the Divine. This relation and this awareness grounds the aspiration toward a distinctive sanctity and dignity of all human life in Jewish and Christian traditions.

So retrieving *imago dei* today is about self-critical and responsible contextualizing of human lives within the intricate circle of all sentient creatures as unique participants in a planetary *perichoresis* of the whole creation, visible and invisible, in all its exciting and bewildering beauty. The dignity of human lives matters precisely as we, humans, are participants – unique, distinct, purposeful, self-reflective, mysterious – but resolutely and only as participants[43] and not as unaccountable oligarchs of that more expansive and interdependent *perichoresis* of creation in which everything, visible and invisible, matters in its own distinct way.

That being said, there is another feature of *imago dei* which is particularly relevant in the present context. Some versions of the broad idea of *imago dei* were not unique to the cultural milieu of Hebrew tradition. Power and privilege have oppressively long histories of presenting itself, and only itself, as uniquely endowed by the Divine and reflecting the Divine. Yet the Hebrew scriptures de-throne these decadent versions of allegedly special relationship of the elite few with the Divine while relegating all others to the scrapheap of intelligence, beauty, and ability. Meanwhile the Genesis narratives affirm that all human creatures are inscribed into this distinct relational interface of intimacy, awareness, responsiveness, and accountability in relation to God. *Imago dei* is a unique and yet utterly democratic human entanglement with God.

---

[43] As those working in the area of animal ethics have clearly reminded us all, the second creation story in Genesis 2 should significantly modulate the triumphalist anthropocentric readings of Genesis 1:26-27 since according to the second story, *nephesh* or the breath of life, the very aliveness of being, is not an exclusive property of human persons but rather of a whole host of creatures.

Furthermore, next to the notion of *imago dei* in the creation narrative in Genesis 1:26 stands the equally enigmatic trope of likeness, *similitudo*. Now, similitude does not need to be exclusively vectored toward God as the goal of *theosis*, deification/divinization. Similitude can express a proleptic Janus-faced trait of being invited to yearn and to strive toward the likeness of God while also realizing that all those who yearn and strive in a myriad of unique ways nevertheless participate in the same mimetic movement toward the same ultimate fulfillment. And this is where reading the biblical trope of similitude/likeness as a dually vectored dynamic relational process interfaces with the poetics of creaturehood that is slanted not only God-wardly but also laterally, toward the fellow human creatures. I was drawn to reflect on the Genesis interplay of the image and likeness by the postcolonial philosopher Achille Mbembe's call for a postcolonial "politics of the similar."[44] He observes the need for a "politics of humanity that is fundamentally a politics of the similar, but in the context in which what we all share from the beginning is difference. It is our differences that, paradoxically, we must share."[45] Of course, all such sharing on the planetary scale ought to aspire to be post-hegemonic and actively decolonial for it to actually work. It would entail intentionally steering the course away from the historically entrenched cultural structures of dominance that continue to mutate across all terrains of life. As Mbembe is quick to underscore, such a politics of the similar is relational, reciprocal, and multi-directional: "There is no relation to oneself that does not also implicate the Other. The Other is at once difference and similarity, united."[46]

While our creaturely similitude to God should always be handled with a generous helping of apophatic and eschatological reserve, the poetics of creaturely similitude allows for connections and interactions among human creatures which honor difference yet without reifying it to alienate, exclude, wound, and disinherit other human persons. Whereas the human entanglement with the Uncreated leans into an apophatic dissimilarity even amidst its yearning and striving for similitude, our entanglement with the rest of creation leans into an interface of similitude. All human persons begin with something we share in common: *imago dei* is our original similitude even while we are invited to participate in a transformative movement toward a similitude ever

---

[44] Achille Mbembe, *Critique of Black Reason*. Translated by Laurent Dubois (Duke University Press: Durham and London 2017), 178.
[45] Mbembe, *Critique of Black Reason*, 178.
[46] Mbembe, *Critique of Black Reason*, 178.

greater and ever more Godward. So while its Godward vector is eschatological, its interhuman vector of shared aspiration can legitimately call for not only a more laterally slanted theopoetics of creaturehood but even more consequentially, for a theopolitics of creaturehood. The lateral slant of similitude embodies the transformative postcolonial counter-thrust in the theopoetics of creaturehood to unsettle the cosmologies of demeaning dominance by highlighting the analogous, the similar, the resonant, and the shared dimensions of creaturehood while the pertinent differences are suitably recognized as "united" according to Mbembe's idiom. From this perspective, differences that often seem so profoundly alienating among all those who are supposedly created in the image of God (race, gender, class, ability, sexuality, ethnicity, language, culture, religion and so forth) are nevertheless counterpointed by a theopoetics and theopolitics of similitude which is so often practically invisible in the sinful antagonisms of life. This balancing theopoetics and theopolitics of creaturehood, I hasten to add, absolutely need not degenerate into a sneaky totalitarianism of "the same."

To discern similitude amidst difference is to resist both the decadent amplification of difference into alienation and dehumanisation as well as the temptation to camouflage it by totalitarian coercion into artificial and equally dehumanising uniformity and compliance. To discern similitude, thus, requires a kind of postcolonial/decolonial restart of what the medieval folks called "spiritual senses" to (re)activate the capacity for a reciprocity of vision or spiritual intervisibility. Spiritual intervisibility depends on the capacity to see the diverse refractions and modulations of *imago dei* in the like and the unlike precisely as real, as fascinating, as evolving, as mysterious and as sometimes very frustrating, very discouraging, and even frightening. Nevertheless, through the lens of poetics of creaturely similitude, these differences live and move under the apophatic proviso of not being the ultimate word about the shape and destiny of our as well as all other human lives. In this sense, even the strangest stranger who comes from a far country and who is not in my image is still someone bearing God's image across which no other human creatures can impose any ultimate borders of separation except by engaging in idolatry. Ultimately, what begins with spiritual senses only becomes visible as sensibilities, practices, and politics of hospitality – or not. The poetics of creaturehood as a *theopoetics* of similitude becomes visible, recognizable, and real as an embodied and performed *theopolitics* of similitude for the life of the world in which all can have a lane on the path toward flourishing and abundant life.

Similitude, Borderlands, and Choices

What does theopoetics and theopolitics of similitude have to do with strangers, migrants, and refugees? To answer that question, a short detour into borderlands and border thinking may be helpful. As a diasporic theologian, I find the Chicana feminist thinker Gloria Anzaldua's border-thinking approach particularly interesting as it resonates with Mbembe's "Other" being united, at once, in difference and similarity. Anzaldua's imaginary of thinking of differences and similarities from the in-betweenness of *nepantla* – the geographical, cultural, religious, and political borderzones – is useful as it foregrounds the webs of existence and webs of connections.

What is needed, according to Anzaldua, is the "web-making faculty" of border-thinkers to entertain "less rigid categorizations and thinner boundaries that allow us to picture ... similarities instead of divisions."[47] Such a capacity can enable us to "weave a kinship entre todas las gentes y cosas."[48] We are talking about kinship and not some type of homogenizing sameness. Perhaps this is how we can seek more fruitfully for ways to conceive of *imago dei* with thinner boundaries and with thicker edges of solidarity?

Yet another way to re-imagine the theopoetics and theopolitics of similitude without falling back into the traps of both sameness and radicalised difference is to consider the decolonial imaginary of pluriverse. According to Walter Mignolo, decolonial pluriverse refers to the imaginary of a world in which many worlds can coexist in a convivial way without an absolutist force of domination.[49] Meanwhile Arturo Escobar proposes pluriverse as a political ontology of "really existing" and "partially connected worlds" which can be part of each other and radically different at the same time."[50] Escobar's

---

[47] Gloria E. Anzaldua, *Light in the Dark/Luz en lo oscuro: Rewriting Identity, Spirituality, Reality*. Edited by Analouise Keating (Duke University Press: Durham and London 2015), 83.

[48] Anzaldua, *Light in the Dark/Luz en lo oscuro*, 83. Anzaldua habitually performs linguistic code-switching in her texts. The quote reflects her original writing in which Spanish parts of sentences are not always italicized in texts that are written predominantly in English.

[49] Among several texts in which Mignolo explores a notion from the Zapatista movement, see his recent "Foreword: On Pluriversality and Multipolarity" and "On Pluriversality and Multipolar World Order: Decoloniality after Decolonization; Dewesternization after the Cold War," in: Bernd Reiter (ed.), *Constructing the Pluriverse: The Geopolitics of Knowledge* (Duke University Press: Durham and London 2018), ix-xvi and 90-116 respectively. Also see Walter D. Mignolo and Catherine E. Walsh, *On Decoloniality: Concepts, Analytics, Praxis* (Duke University Press: Durham and London 2018).

[50] Arturo Escobar, *Designs for the Pluriverse: Radical Independence, Autonomy, and the Making of Worlds* (Duke University Press: Durham and London 2018), 216.

pluriverse resonates with Mbembe's move toward "the similar" amid difference as Escobar describes pluriverse to be "fractal, or endowed with self-similarity; anywhere you look at it, and at any scale, you find similar (yet not the same) configurations, meshes, assemblages ... that is, the pluriverse."[51]

If both *imago dei* and *similitudo* can be perceived as pluriversal or fractal, perhaps they can undergird a theo-ontology of similitude that connects even as it differentiates but without intractable racial, sexual, economic, and other hierarchies? Perhaps there might emerge a theo-ontology which could render visible the shared creaturely desire for flourishing and the yearnings for abundant life lived to the fullest measure in, with, under whatever manifestations of creaturely diversity? Perhaps it is worth risking, as Anzaldua poignantly put it, to take on a comportment in which, she says, "I have chosen to struggle against unnatural boundaries."[52] She is convinced that "we revise reality by altering our consensual agreements about what is real, what is just and fair. We can trans-shape reality by changing our perspectives and perceptions. By choosing a different future, we bring it into being.[53]

Perhaps this sort of discernment and action can engender a poetics pushing back against the intentional disruptions of human flourishing of our time – which are, as Shawn Copeland forcefully argues in her recent *Knowing Christ Crucified: The Witness of African American Religious Experience*, matters of social suffering precisely as a theo-social problem.[54]

Imago, Similitude, and the Sacrament of the Stranger

Finally, how might the vision of creaturehood which is rooted in the theopoetics and theopolitics of similitude relate to strangers? The growing indifference and even hostility toward migrants and refugees as the paradigmatic "abject" of our time convey quite clearly that our Euro-Atlantic societies continue to "despoil and degrade, violate and desecrate the very meaning of human being, of being human."[55] Despoiling, violating, and desecrating is not limited, of course, to displaced and uprooted people but also afflicts those multitudes who are trapped in systemic poverty and discrimination in the crevices of metropolitan affluence.

---

[51] Escobar, *Designs for the Pluriverse*, 257, note 15.
[52] Anzaldua, *Light in the Dark/Luz en lo oscuro*, 23.
[53] Anzaldua, *Light in the Dark/Luz en lo oscuro*, 21.
[54] M. Shawn Copeland, *Knowing Christ Crucified: The Witness of African American Religious Experience* (Orbis: Maryknoll, NY 2018), 132.
[55] Copeland, *Knowing Christ Crucified*, 174.

For far too many persons in far too many places, the recognition of *imago dei*, in oneself and in others, remains a strenuous effort. As Copeland asserts based on the aspirations of BlackLivesMatter movement, to strive toward an understanding of "what authentic human being means – to love self, to stand up for ourselves and with and for others, to throw off stifling and negating images, to take joyful possession of our subjectivity, to love, to work, to hope"[56] – demands a hard and courageous labour of transformative healing.

Love: seeing *imago dei* through rekindled spiritual senses and choosing to risk a poetics of creaturehood that plays out in the world as an anthropology and theopolitics of similitude is as relational a matter as is love. As is compassion. As is solidarity. As is hospitality. As is righteous action for and with those who are not in my/our image. Hans Urs von Balthasar once insisted that "love alone is credible."[57] Love divine that is credible can be no otherwise than radically relational and radically incarnate. Which means, as I interpret von Balthasar here, that love that has anything to do with God is radically practical, embodied, and enacted in the world of God's creation by those summoned by God. Love, in this sense, is not something just felt or thought about, or even believed into. As von Balthasar puts it, "love exists only between persons...God who is for us the Wholly-Other, appears only in the place of the other, in the 'sacrament of our brother' [and sister]."[58] Although God is the "Wholly-Other (in relation to the world)," God is also "at the same time the Non-Other (Cusanus: *De Non-aliud*), the one who, in his otherness, transcends even the inner-worldly opposition between this and that being."[59] While keeping in mind the apophatic proviso of transontological dissimilarity between the Divine and the created world, wouldn't the creatures who bear the image of and aspire to the likeness of *this* God also be inscribed in the theo-ontology of non-otherness vis-à-vis all fellow creatures of *this* God at least to some degree? Here is, I suggest, yet another way of articulating the poetics and theopolitics of similitude that leans laterally while remaining faithful to the apophatic reserve to refrain from overplaying the analogical interval between the created and the Uncreated.

---

[56] Copeland, *Knowing Christ Crucified*, 174.
[57] Hans Urs von Balthasar, *Love Alone is Credible*. Translated by D.C. Schindler (Ignatius Press: San Francisco 2004).
[58] Von Balthasar, *Love Alone is Credible*, 150. It seems that, at least theoretically, von Balthasar would include all genders in his notion of revelatory encounter with God.
[59] Von Balthasar, *Love Alone is Credible*, 150.

But interestingly, the sacrament of our brothers and sisters is not where the analogies are consummated when it comes to the embodying the revelations of divine love. Von Balthasar urges an extension of the sacramental analogy even further, even closer to the spirit of Matthew 25:35: "For I was hungry and you gave me food, I was thirsty and you gave me something to drink, I was a stranger and you welcomed me" (New Revised Standard Version). The most sacramental encounter with divine love does not just happen, Balthasar ponders, with those whom we effortlessly see as "brothers/sisters" or "neighbors." So I read von Balthasar's idea, perhaps stretching it otherwise than he would have done while still insisting on such a reading as a legitimate elaboration of his insights, that such a revelatory encounter with God takes place through righteous and compassionate action for and with those who appear to us as "strangers."

In resonance with the enigmatic trope of *imago dei*, the face of a stranger is simultaneously the most transparent and yet the most opaque sacrament of divine love. This is, as I call it in conversation with von Balthasar's reflections, the sacrament of the stranger. It reveals the unfathomably borderless love divine, all human loves and filial and tribal relations excelling, to paraphrase Charles Wesley's verses,[60] to culminate precisely in encounters with those on the farthest edges of our comfort and cultural kinship.

Even though it may not have been the primary goal of his argument in *The God Question and Modern Man* – after all, my reasoning here proceeds as a *constructive* conversation with von Balthasar – his reflections on love intimate a sacramental revelation. Sacramental revelations are nothing other than a making-real, a making-credible (a sort of *Wirklichwerdung*) of love precisely where the borders of ordinary relationships of kin, and of religious and cultural familiarity become, as Anzaldua put it, "thinner." Where that happens, no one else but Christ himself, as von Balthasar argues

> ...is not even a little more present in the Christian than in the stranger who does not know him at all, and who precisely for this reason is all the poorer and more needy, hence all the more the Sacrament of Jesus Christ. This stranger is always the primary 'object' of love, while the love within the Church is rather the sacred sign of the love that passes over into world. Of itself it does not stop short at the frontier of the Church, indeed, being love, it does not know this frontier at all. It is its essence to transcend it...[61]

---

[60] I'm referring to Charles Wesley's hymn "Love Divine, All Loves Excelling" (1747).
[61] Hans Urs von Balthasar, *The God Question and Modern Man*, Translated by Hilda Graef (Seabury Press: New York 1967), 146.

Love divine is *sans frontiers*. Isn't it a crazy idea screaming against all the instincts of individual, societal, and ecclesial self-preservation and self-perpetuation? It is certainly not much crazier than Jesus Christ breaking the taboos of tribes, silos, and pious conventions about what it is that puts human creatures in the right relationship with the God of life and love by identifying himself with the social outcasts including strangers ξένος, (yes, the same term that appears in "xenophobia") in Matthew 25:35.

Today, for European and North American theologians alike, texts like Genesis 1:26-27 and Matthew 25 – among others – need to be read, reflected about, preached about, and researched while keeping an eye on the news from the Mediterranean, the Sonoran Desert, the Rio Grande Valley, and the Greek islands. These borderzones where the boundaries between life and death, humanity and dehumanization are so thin are the indispensable *loci theologici* of our time. Poetics and theopolitics of creaturehood, of *imago dei*, of similitude will become real – or not – as we exercise our decolonised spiritual senses by choosing to see and to hear what it means and feels to be visible, invisible, or camouflaged precisely *in those places* as racialised, gendered, displaced, marginalised, victimised, and often criminalised subjects. As dehumanised subjects.

And yet the disinherited nevertheless persist in their courage to struggle for a flourishing life in these borderzones which are now purposefully rendered more and more inhospitable to life and dignity. They do it against unbelievable odds and stubbornly stand up for themselves in circumstances that most people in our Euro-Atlantic societies have only seen in nightmares, war documentaries, or horror movies. It is their sacramental claim on our theological imagination and practice to see *imago dei* and discern similitude in those who are not in "our" image but who take joyful possession of their subjectivity as much as they can muster to love, to work, and to hope.

Keeping an eye on "the migrant multitude as the planetary outcasts of the globalizing world"[62] is becoming a theological vocation and a practice of discipleship today. It also compels us, Western Europeans and Eastern Europeans alike, to remember the inconvenient postcolonial fact for all our theological endeavors that we live in a historical time when the colonial empire not only "writes back" but sometimes "arrives back" and becomes visible in

---

[62] Hyo-Dong Lee, *Spirit, Qi, and the Multitude* (Fordham University Press: New York 2013), 41.

a whole new way precisely here – here, in Europe, where the colonial matrix of power, knowledge, and being set sail from in the first place.[63]

Shawn Copeland insists that people whom our collective "corrupt consciences and crooked systems" have effectively "crucified" are nevertheless "the only sure sign of God's presence in our world."[64] This is a very strong claim – the *only sure* sign of God's presence! It seems to me that what we have here is a broad invitation to consider what kind of power, what kind of agency, what kind of identity, what kind of theopoetics-*cum*-theopolitics of creaturehood and similitude can and should become visible and real when strangers are seen as surprisingly and actually… human. Imagine this: strangers as sacramental signs of creating, redeeming, and sanctifying God. No doubt, these are risky and opaque sacramental signs for, indeed, "hosting a stranger is always a risk, never a fait accompli."[65] Engaging in a sacramental encounter is always a risk, too. Whatever else these sacramental encounters and entanglements unveil, the business of inviting in and coming together with strangers is about love, actually: ours to some extent, but above all, God's love.

Reverend Dr. **Kristine Suna-Koro** is Associate Professor of Theology at Xavier University, Cincinnati, Ohio, USA. She is a Latvian-American diasporic theologian working at the intersections of postcolonial thought, sacramental and liturgical theology as well as modern historical theology and migration studies. She is the author of *In Counterpoint: Diaspora, Postcoloniality, and Sacramental Theology* (2017) and numerous articles and chapters on postcolonial theology, liturgy, sacramentality, migration, and theological aesthetics. She is a pastor in the Latvian Evangelical Lutheran Church in America and currently serves as the Delegate for Membership of the North American Academy of Liturgy (NAAL) and co-chair of Religions, Borders, and Immigration seminar of the American Academy of Religion (AAR). sunakorok@xavier.edu

---

[63] A fellow immigrant and professor of journalism from New York, USA, Suketu Mehta, provides a fabulous and pithy reminder about what the current migration discussions often obscure (or actively obfuscate) – namely, the destructive legacies of colonialism. So when today's migrants from the former colonies are asked "Why are you here?" they can justly respond, "We are here because you were there" – just as Mehta's grandfather did in a park in London. Suketu Mehta, *This Land is Our Land: An Immigrant's Manifesto* (Farrar, Straus and Giroux: New York 2019), 3.
[64] Copeland, *Knowing Christ Crucified*, 145.
[65] Kearney and Taylor, "Introduction," 1.

Silvia Martínez Cano

Claves teológicas para la construcción de un imaginario a favor del reconocimiento del otro

Resumen

Las migraciones, la crisis ecológica y las consecuencias del sistema económico neoliberal son en la actualidad tres urgencias planetarias. Para dar respuesta a estas urgencias, este texto pretende profundizar en el imaginario cultural que las sociedades aportan sobre la in/visibilización de las personas, en función de su raza y género, y, de esta manera, analizar cómo son nuestros imaginarios teológicos acerca del diferente. En este sentido, una revisión de la noción de *imago Dei* puede trastocar el imaginario patriarcal que afecta a la relación entre Dios y la persona, y las consecuencias que tiene esto en el ecosistema social macroplanetario. El texto se pregunta sobre la posibilidad de situar el cuerpo violentado de las mujeres migrantes como lugar teológico para poder reelaborar la noción de *imago Dei* a la luz de una ontología relacional que permita encontrarse y reconocer al otro-otra como hermana-hermano e hijo-hija de Dios.

Palabras clave: migración; antropología teológica; *imago Dei*; mujeres migrantes.

Abstract

Migration, the ecological crisis, and the consequences of the neoliberal economic system are currently three planetary emergencies. In response to these emergencies, this text seeks to delve into the social imaginary that societies provide on the in/visibility of people, depending on their race and gender, and in this way, analyze how our theological imaginary about the different is. In this sense a review of the notion of *imago Dei* can disrupt the patriarchal imaginary affecting the relationship between God and the individual, and its consequences in the macro-planetary ecosystem. The text wonders about the possibility of placing the abused bodies of migrant women as a theological *locus* to reproduce the notion of *imago Dei* illuminated by a relational ontology that enables them to find themselves and recognize the other as sister-brother and son-daughter of God.

Keywords: migration; theological anthropology; *imago Dei*; migrant women.

Silvia Martínez Cano
Claves teológicas para la construcción de un imaginario a favor del reconocimiento del otro

Zusammenfassung
Migration, die ökologische Krise und die Konsequenzen des neoliberalen Wirtschaftssystems sind gegenwärtig drei globale Notlagen. Als Antwort auf diese Notlagen will dieser Text die kulturelle Imagination vertiefen, die Gesellschaften über die Un-/Sichtbarkeit von Menschen, abhängig von ihrer Rasse und ihrem Geschlecht, bereitstellen, und auf diese Weise analysieren, was unsere theologischen Imaginationen über die Unterschiede sind. In diesem Sinn kann eine Revision des Begriffs der *imago Dei* die patriarchalische Imagination, die die Beziehung zwischen Gott und der Person betrifft, und die Folgen, die das für das makroplanetarische soziale Ökosystem hat, stören. Der Text fragt nach der Möglichkeit, den verletzten Körper der Migrantinnen als theologischen Ort zu positionieren, um den Begriff der *imago Dei* im Licht einer relationalen Ontologie neu zu formulieren, die es erlaubt, einander zu begegnen und die andere/den anderen als Schwester/Bruder und Sohn/Tochter Gottes anzuerkennen.

Schlagwörter: Migration; theologische Anthropologie; *imago Dei*; Migrantinnen.

La noción de *imago Dei* en el contexto de tres urgencias planetarias

Tres son, hoy, las urgencias planetarias a las que dar respuesta: las migraciones, la crisis ecológica y el devorador sistema económico neoliberal. Unas urgencias que obligan a tener en cuenta los múltiples factores que provocan crisis continuadas en los sistemas sociales y económicos que inciden sobre la salud del planeta. No son cualquier cosa, son cuestiones de primera línea que meditar y resolver. Una secuencia de la película *Children of Men* del director Alfonso Cuarón (*Hijos de los hombres*, 2006)[1] puede servirnos para visualizar su profunda relación y su extrema necesidad de resolución. La película describe una distopía en un tiempo futuro no muy lejano (¡2027!), en la que el planeta vive en el caos y solo una zona geográfica muy pequeña, protegida por un gran muro, mantiene los privilegios de las sociedades del bienestar. Pero se enfrenta al problema de que no nacen bebés, y la sociedad está advocada a la extinción. La escena que he elegido para visualizar esta problemática es aquella en la que el protagonista, Theo, acompaña a una mujer africana, Kee, que milagrosamente está embarazada, a través de la frontera, en un ambiente de violencia descontrolada, donde las personas que pretenden pasar la frontera son maltratadas y asesinadas. Todo el entorno está arrasado, quemado, contaminado. No hay color ni alegría. Todo es

---

[1] Entrevista a Alfonso Cuarón por Annie Wagner el 28 de diciembre de 2006, "Politics, Bible Stories, and Hope. An Interview with Alfonso Cuarón", en *The Stranger*. Disponible en https://www.thestranger.com/seattle/Content?oid=128363, 19 marzo 2020.

violencia y oscuridad, gritos, sufrimiento. Theo, muy significativamente, atraviesa la frontera sin zapatos, símbolo de absoluta precariedad en el mundo de los humanos.

A trece años de esta profética película con tintes claramente cristianos hoy, vemos escenas similares: la acumulación de refugiados en Turquía y Grecia, y las condiciones en esos campamentos de refugiados, sin saber qué sucederá los días venideros; la frontera del Mediterráneo y los miles de muertos que pueblan sus fondos marinos; el ascenso de la extrema derecha en distintas partes del mundo y su soberbio desinterés por lo que sucede (una muestra es las declaraciones de Bolsonaro acerca de los incendios del Amazonas o el desprecio del partido político español Vox por las víctimas de la violencia machista especialmente las mujeres extranjeras); la guerra de Siria inconclusa y de la que ya nadie habla; el Estado fallido de Guatemala y la violencia extrema que se extiende por todo Centroamérica; las separaciones de los niños de sus familias en la frontera de México y las condiciones de su detención... Como teóloga y como madre de cuatro hijos, estas imágenes me hacen pensar, sintiendo mucho dolor, que nos aproximamos rápidamente a un contexto similar al de la película.

Quisiera hacer surgir con la lectura de este texto varias preguntas al respecto de estas urgencias planetarias, pero especialmente centradas en la problemática de los migrantes, los desheredados y desarraigados. Pretendo profundizar en el imaginario cultural que las sociedades aportan sobre la in/visibilización de las personas, en función de su raza y género, y de esta manera, analizar cómo son nuestros imaginarios teológicos (y por lo tanto, nuestros lenguajes) acerca del diferente. Considero, *a priori*, si ya estamos en esta situación, que estos imaginarios han de ser reeducados, reevangelizados. La dificultad de esta reeducación está en la complejidad de los factores en los que se aloja el imaginario cultural. Tener en cuenta a la vez la crisis ecológica, los movimientos migratorios causados por diferentes motivos –hambre, guerra, etc. – y la complejidad de la producción de cultura a través del mundo virtual y consumista es francamente difícil, y más cuando estamos en una situación de fragmentación absolutamente extrema de la vida.

La interpretación bíblica de la relación entre ser humano y resto de la creación no solo ha ignorado la evolución, sino que ha posicionado al ser humano fuera de la creación, objetivándola como un objeto de uso y disfrute más dentro del modelo consumista heteropatriarcal de la modernidad. Esto supone que todo aquello que excede los márgenes de la definición de ser humano dentro del presupuesto neoliberal-heteropatriacal, queda, en esta bipolaridad, automáticamente desplazado en el lado de la naturaleza, es decir objetivado y expuesto a su uso y abuso. Así sucede con la naturaleza, pero también con los migrantes en general y, en concreto, con los cuerpos de las mujeres cuando se exponen y se usan en las redes reales y virtuales como objetos de consumo. Es preocupante la situación de las mujeres. Ellas son las que han salido, desde su piel indígena, a defender el Amazonas, son las que cruzan con sus hijos las fronteras esquivando la muerte, son las que se venden en los anuncios de prostitución para pagar deudas o las que son utilizadas como vasijas calientes cuando se ponen sus vientres al servicio de la venta de bebés.

Para abordar las urgencias humanas del hoy, necesito acudir a la comprensión de la creación de forma holística, evitando los binomios ser humano-naturaleza que desequilibran la creación de Dios. Pretendo revisar brevemente algunas claves de la antropología teológica desde el marco de las urgencias planetarias nombradas, para poder trazar una herramienta teológica que se exprese en términos de liberación y sanación. Si atendemos a la dinámica interna de la creación, esto es, a su capacidad de evolucionar a medida que la etapa creativa anterior lo permite, podemos comprender mejor algunas de las características antropológicas del ser humano: voluntad, interdependencia, responsabilidad, solidaridad. El texto de Gn 1 nos habla de estos pasos, desde la metáfora de la tensión dinámica de la separación: sin la luz-tinieblas no habría tiempo, sin la separación de las aguas no habría tierra (lo seco), sin la tierra no habría vida vegetal, sin ella no habría vida animal ni vida humana. Dios no controla este proceso, sino que es la propia creación la que fluye para desarrollarse con sus propias normas. Es autónoma. El texto también nos dice que la libertad humana interferirá en este fluir de la creación[2], por lo que en ella, de forma natural, se trazan interdependencias entre sus criaturas.

Sin embargo, una intervención que vulnere las propias normas autónomas de la creación da lugar a una des-creación (o destrucción). Es decir, los propios mitos de Gn 3 (la violencia y la muerte representada por Caín y Abel) y Gn 7 y 12 (la destrucción de toda la creación representada en el diluvio y en la torre de Babel) nos advierten de las consecuencias de la libertad-responsabilidad desvinculada de la interdependencia-solidaridad.

---

[2] Mercedes Navarro "A imagen y semejanza divinas. Mujer y varón en Gn 1-3 como sistema abierto", en Mercedes Navarro e Irmtraud Fischer (eds.), *La Torah* (LBLM1) (Verbo Divino: Estella 2010), 209-262.

Cuando la hermenéutica bíblica no es capaz de superar las claves de lo que Schüssler Fiorenza llama "kyriarcado"[3], entonces, el mandato de dominar la tierra se comprende como una tensión dinámica en desigualdad, sin tener en cuenta que el ser humano es un microcosmos que participa de la armonía y desarmonía de la creación. El imaginario patriarcal de Dios que le representa como autoritario, jerárquico, impasible afecta a la dinámica y desequilibra la tensión, subordinando la naturaleza al ser humano, la mujer al hombre. Así, la imagen de Dios afecta directamente a la definición de persona desde los términos de poder y perfección. Se es imagen de Dios cuando existe una similitud con la imagen de Dios autoritaria, jerarquizada y racional, por lo tanto, si se es varón, se tiene poder y se ejerce sobre otras personas y sobre la naturaleza[4]. Las jerarquías de poder son poseídas por los varones mayoritariamente de raza blanca. Los hombres y mujeres racializados asumen su condición de subalternos y por lo tanto de dominados, como Dios domina la creación. Esta narrativa kyriarcal de percibir la realidad interioriza esta relación desigual y los subaltenos se convierten en agentes y víctimas a la vez de su propia dominación. De esta manera, la comprensión de *imago Dei* queda también jerarquizada, categorizando quién se asemeja más a Dios y quién no.

Desde algunas voces de la teología ecofeminista[5] se anima a la utilización de la categoría de "extranjera" (*foreigner woman*) como una estratificación de *imago Dei*[6] unida a una segunda categoría, la "autonomía"[7], para comprender la antropología teológica desde una perspectiva más amplia. Las mujeres son reducidas en su semejanza a Dios por causa de su sexo, en primera instancia, pero también por su procedencia (etnia/raza). Esto supone una marginalización doble que se convierte en estructural también en el imaginario teológico. Cuando las mujeres dejan de ser imagen de Dios en su plenitud, pierden capacidad de autonomía, pues quedan sometidas a las relaciones desiguales del imaginario cristiano que las someten. La *relacionalidad* humana, base para

---

[3] Cf. Elisabeth Schüssler Fiorenza, *Cristología crítica feminista: Jesús Hijo de Miriam, Profeta de la Sabiduría* (Trotta: Madrid 2000).
[4] *Cf.* Mary Daly, *Beyond God the Father: Toward a Philosophy of Women's Liberation* (Beacon Press: Boston 1985).
[5] *Cf.* Mary Judith Ress, "Espiritualidad ecofeminista en América Latina", *Investigaciones Feministas* 1 (2010), 111-124.
[6] Janet W. May, "Foreigners", en Rosemary Radford Ruether (ed.) *Women Healing Earth: Third World Women on Ecology, Feminism and Religion* (Orbis Books: Maryknoll 1996), 39-43.
[7] Ivone Gebara, *Longing for Running Water: Ecofeminism and Liberation* (Augsburg Fortress: Minneapolis 1999), 71-73.

comprender la tensión entre lo semejante y lo diferente en la persona, queda dañada, pues el sistema kyriarcal controla la autonomía y el cuerpo de las mujeres reduciendo su capacidad de decisión, y por lo tanto su relacionalidad, en otros términos que no sean los permitidos por el imaginario machista. La autonomía es libertad creadora, propia de la *imago Dei*.

Las mujeres, despojadas de su libertad creadora

Por otro lado, algunas voces de la teología poscolonial apuntan a la dificultad de comprender la *imago Dei* en términos sexuados. Si *imago Dei* es ser imagen de Cristo en plenitud, y si esta imagen se entiende sexualizadamente, el cuerpo de las mujeres, y especialmente de las mujeres no blancas, no puede asemejarse al cuerpo de Cristo, por lo que las mujeres no son tan imagen de Dios como los hombres[8]. La feminidad queda en un segundo plano para alcanzar la plenitud humana y, por tanto, la cristificación de las mujeres es una situación inalcanzable. Por ello, por su lejanía a la plenitud, las hace más vulnerables al pecado y, en una perspectiva patriarcal, sujetos de pecado por su corporalidad.

La convergencia entre las dos perspectivas teológicas nos hace preguntarnos con qué claves responden estas teologías feministas para favorecer un cambio radical que rompa la concepción androcéntrica de la *imago Dei*. Ambas perspectivas convergen en no renunciar a la corporalidad de las mujeres para redefinir el concepto de *imago Dei*, pues rechazan reducir la semejanza a Dios al puro intelecto y racionalidad[9]. Además, apuestan por la "relacionalidad" humana como clave para una antropología teológica inclusiva. Esta relacionalidad se expresa en términos de solicitud hacia la alteridad, es decir, en relaciones de justicia y compasión, como expresión de la imagen divina mostrada en la humanidad[10]. Se entendería la *imago Dei* como una relacionalidad corporal y dinámica, donde no se acepta la legitimación de un ejercicio jerárquico y abusivo de la creación de Dios. A eso, la teología ecofeminista añade otra clave que puede ayudar a redirigir la relacionalidad, esta es, la reconfiguración de la perspectiva kyriocéntrica en una perspectiva biocéntrica. Aquí tomaría

---

[8] Delores S. Williams, "A Womanist Perspective of Sin", en Emilie M. Townes (ed.), *A Troubling in My Soul: Womanist Perspective on Evil and Surffering* (Orbis Books: Maryknoll, 1996), 130-149, aquí 146.

[9] Michelle A. González, *Creada a imagen de Dios: Antropología teológica femenina* (Mensajero: Bilbao 2006), 186.

[10] Mercy Amba Oduyoye, *Introducing Áfrican Women´s Theology* (Sheffield Academic Press: Sheffield 2001), 76. *Cf*. Elizabeth A. Johnson, *La que es: el misterio de Dios en el discurso teológico feminista* (Herder: Barcelona 2002).

de referencia la propuesta de Sally McFague de comprender la creación como "cuerpo de Dios"[11] para comprender la estrecha relación e interdependencia entre ser humano y naturaleza, pues Dios sostiene y alimenta[12] toda la creación con su sobreabundante amor. La *imago Dei* se expresaría al estar en comunión con todos los seres, criaturas de Dios y desplazar al varón blanco del centro y meta de la creación[13]. La *imago Dei* situa a toda la humanidad en distintos niveles de relaciones solidarias con las otras criaturas. Esto sería una mirada biocéntrica. La *imago Dei* capacita al ser humano para relacionarse con Dios a través de su "cuerpo". Por lo tanto, la corporalidad del ser humano, hombre o mujer, y la bondad del mismo (por ser *imago Dei*) forma parte de las relaciones compasivas que permiten la relación con Dios[14]. Una mirada biocéntrica de la creación desplazaría la economía neoliberal y el tecnopatriarcalismo hacia prácticas más ecodependientes, donde la relación con el otro (y forma de vida) determina la toma de decisiones y la acción. La encíclica Laudato Si, apunta al "paradigma tecnocrático" como raíz humana de la crisis ecológica (LS 101-136). La descentralización de lo humano hacia una biodiversidad mayor haría pasar de un modelo de negación de la vida, no solo de las personas, sino también del ecosistema global, a un modelo de vida compartida, ya que "ecosistema natural y el ecosistema humano, son lo mismo y se degradan juntos" (LS 17-61).

Desde un modelo biocéntrico solidario, la insostenibilidad del modelo neoliberal podría ser abordada con categorías de justicia y solidaridad que reconfiguraban un orden planetario desde el protagonismo de los márgenes y no desde el abuso y devastación de los poderosos. Los planteamientos de la teología feminista poscolonial afirman que la descentralización de la mirada biocéntrica afectan directamente a los sistemas económicos y sociales que utilizan la raza, el género, la sexualidad, la capacidad intelectual, la clase y la capacidad económica como discurso interseccional para mantener

---

[11] Cf. Sally McFague, *Modelos de Dios: Teología para una era ecológica y nuclear* (Sal Terrae: Santander 1994).
[12] Gabriele Dietrich, "The world as the body of God", en Rose Mary Radford Ruether (ed.) *Women Healing Earth. Thrid World Women on Ecology, Feminism and Religion* (Orbis Books: Maryknoll 1996), 82-98, aquí 97.
[13] González, *Creada a imagen de Dios,* 190.
[14] González, *Creada a imagen de Dios,* 191, citando a Mary McClintock Fulkerson, "Contesting the Gendered Subject: A Feminist Account of the imago Dei", en Rebecca Chopp y Sheila Greeve Davaney (eds.), *Horizons in Feminist Theology: identity, Tradition and Norms* (Fortress Press: Minneapolis 1997), 99-115, aquí 107.

sistemas tecno-patriarcales, incluso en el ámbito religioso[15]. Nuestras urgencias –migraciones, crisis ecológica y no sostenibilidad del sistema económico neoliberal– consecuencias visibles de este discurso, están profundamente relacionadas, por la complejidad rizomática de la cultura actual. Hablar de una es hablar de las otras. Tomarlas en cuenta nos obliga a tener presentes todas las categorías que utiliza la teología feminista postcolonial para reconstruir una comprensión de la *imago Dei* centrada en la relacionalidad justa y compasiva. La teóloga Namsoon Kang[16] propone cinco instrumentos para reconfigurar este discurso teo-antropológico: 1. deconstruir la construcción occidental de fijeza binaria; 2. descentrar el etnocentrismo, el geocentrismo, el androcentrismo y el heterocentrismo; 3. proponer la hipersensibilidad hacia los marginados; 4. ser radical en la afirmación de los otros, a pesar de todo; 5. rehabilitar a los colonizados/marginados/oprimidos como *imago Dei*. Aunque todos están presentes en este texto, me he ayudado especialmente de los tres últimos para desarrollar el recorrido desde "las mujeres migrantes son lugar teológico" (segundo apartado) hasta la propuesta de que "el reconocimiento del otro como diferente" es una clave profética ineludible de nuestros días.

Las mujeres migrantes como lugar teológico

La urgencia de reconfigurar la comprensión de imago Dei, pasa por una reformulación de los puntos de partida de la antropología teológica desvinculándola del ejercicio jerárquico del poder y de la búsqueda de la perfección. Las corrientes teológicas feministas a las que he aludido anteriormente hacen el esfuerzo de visibilizar otras narrativas que puedan ser, como decía Elisabeth Johnson, "elemento cognoscitivo"[17] de la realidad y del Misterio de Dios. En palabras de Ivone Gebara:

> Lo que afirmamos como las verdades de la Teología son en verdad experiencias diferentes, que algunos hicieron e intentaron expresar según su cultura y sus vivencias. Nosotros/as las repetimos como si fueran nuestras, pero, muchas veces, sin apropiarnos de ellas. Las repetimos como una lección aprendida en la escuela, o

---

[15] Kwok Pui-Lan, *Postcolonial Imagination and Feminist Theology* (Westminster John Knox Press: Louisville 2005), 127-128.

[16] Namsoon Kang, "Teología desde un espacio de intersección del poscoloniamismo", *Concilium* 350 (2013), 79-84.

[17] Elizabeth A. Johnson, *Friends of God and Prophets: A Feminist Theological Reading of the Communion of Saints* (SCM Press: London 1998), 164.

como un argumento de autoridad, y es aquí que comienza la pérdida de sentido de los significados religiosos[18].

Esto quiere decir que las experiencias diferentes que nos apropiamos, o que asimilamos por imposición, debilitan la comprensión de la compleja relación entre el ser humano y Dios. Gebara busca con esta afirmación recordarnos que la pérdida de significados teológicos está directamente relacionada con reducción de la capacidad de aceptar, a la vez, varias narrativas diferentes del ser humano en su encuentro con Dios. Para solucionar esta problemática (aumentar en significados) necesitamos acceder a la memoria y la narrativa que normativamente se invisibiliza. A mi parecer, en la mayor parte de la historia, y prácticamente en todas las culturas, las narraciones invisibilizadas son las de las mujeres. Cuando pensamos en migrantes, nos imaginamos a un varón, cuando la realidad de muchas mujeres migradas está a nuestro alrededor muy frecuentemente. Incluso en el relato del desplazado/extranjero, las mujeres quedan invisibilizadas. Cuenta Pepa Torres, teóloga activista en el barrio de Lavapiés de Madrid, que:

> Su nombre es Jadiya, era de Casablanca. Vivía en España desde hacía doce años. Sus dos hijos han nacido quí y ella era madre y padre a la vez, porque hacía ya mucho tiempo que su marido los había abandonado. Desde hace cinco años trabajaba en una empresa de limpieza y aunque su contrato era de media jornada trabajaba doce horas diarias sin apenas descanso. Una vecina también marroquí cuidaba de sus hijos mientras ella estaba fuera de casa y les daba de comer, pero el día anterior había tenido que ir al colegio del pequeño por un asunto urgente y aunque avisó a la encargada de que iba a llegar un poco más tarde, esta le acababa de decir que se pasara al día siguiente a recoger el finiquito por la oficina de la empresa. No podía más con tanta carga, no dormía bien y le dolía mucho el estómago. Su médico le había dicho que lo suyo no se curaba con medicinas, sino con tranquilidad, pero ¡cómo iba ella a estar tranquila con todo lo que tenía en la cabeza! [...] Vivimos rodeadas de Jadiyas y su ahogo es también el nuestro[19].

La situación de muchas mujeres migrantes reivindica una *imago Dei* desde la invisibilizada: ¿qué pueden aportar las mujeres desde sus narrativas personales a la cuestión antropológica? ¿Qué puede aportar Jadiya, desde su experiencia

---

[18] Ivone Gebara, *Intuiciones ecofeministas: Ensayo para repensar el conocimiento y la religión* (Trotta: Madrid 2000), 71.
[19] Pepa Torres, *Decir haciendo: Crónica de periferias* (San Pablo: Madrid 2018), 165-66.

de sufrimiento a la experiencia religiosa de la comunidad? La identidad de estas mujeres, como decía Metz[20], está definida por su exclusión y su sufrimiento. En ellas se intersectan distintos factores: mujer, pobreza, en tránsito, sin poder, vinculadas a la naturaleza. Ser humana, para ellas es sufrir y resistir[21]. Es a ellas a las que se las despoja de humanidad; quedan excluidas del modelo blanco enriquecido. Se trata de un olvido cultural y social pero también religioso, pues potencia su condición corpórea como carne pecadora. El imaginario religioso nos da muestras de ello. Marca a las mujeres, las reconfigura y las fragmenta, como sujetos vulnerables y frágiles en espacios de marginalidad y pobreza. La imagen de las mujeres en el imaginario religioso no es Agar, la esclava extranjera expulsada a la que Dios le hace justicia, sino el cuerpo sexualizado de María Magdalena que implora perdón a Dios por sus faltas.

Las mujeres quedan invisibilizadas porque la dinámica kyriarcal no permite empatizar con la dolida y desplazada. Se convierten así, en números, cuerpos que no importan, dirá Judith Butler[22], cuerpos que son daños colaterales necesarios, objetos prescindibles. No se empatiza con estos cuerpos, pues son cosas, y, si no se empatiza, no puede haber misericordia[23].

La vulnerabilidad es violentada y quebrada. Sus cuerpos son ignorados, insultados, incluso maltratados o violentados. Sometidos a la disciplina de la culpa. Son culpables de la violencia que se ejerce sobre ellas, y son estigmatizadas si se atreven a salirse de esta disciplina. En las periferias de nuestro entramado planetario las mujeres soportan las injusticias de una forma pasiva, como única forma posible se existir. Se ignora/invisibiliza a los sujetos femeninos de estas periferias, en las periferias de sus lugares de origen y en las periferias de los lugares donde emigran. Se las ignora procurando que no desarrollen la capacidad de cuestionar las circunstancias de sus vidas y sobre la vida de los demás. Se las invisibiliza para que no tomen la palabra, para que no se organicen y tracen vínculos con otros y otras que puedan fraguar alianzas liberadoras.

---

[20] Cf. Johann Baptist Metz, *Dios y tiempo: Nueva teología política* (Trotta: Madrid 2002).
[21] Chung Hyun Kyung, *Introducción a la teología feminista asiática: luchar por ser el sol una vez más* (Verbo Divino: Estella 2004), 39.
[22] Judith Butler, *Cuerpos que importan* (Paidós: Barcelona 2002), 60; Silvia López, *Los cuerpos que importan en Judith Butler* (Dosbigotes: Madrid 2019), 70-71.
[23] Recordemos como en algunas ocasiones Jesús llora y, como consecuencia, se compadece. Cf. Elisa Estévez, *Mediadoras de sanación* (Universidad Pontificia de Comillas y San Pablo: Madrid 2008), 195-205; Cf. Walter Kasper, *La misericordia: Clave del Evangelio y de la vida cristiana* (Sal Terrae: Santander 2015), 65-86.

Su quebranto, su grito silencioso de dolor, es el sacramento de la Iglesia, pues las mujeres encarnan hoy la vulnerabilidad de la vida en su totalidad[24]. Vida vulnerable y dolorida que se expresa en el cuerpo quebrantado de Cristo en torno al que nos reunimos los cristianos y cristianas.

Podemos decir, entonces, que las mujeres son el "lugar teológico"[25] desde donde hoy podemos comprender el sacramento que nos une a los cristianos y cristianas, el cuerpo entregado, la vida dada, para que otros puedan florecer. En las historias de las mujeres migrantes, en su memoria sufriente, podemos encontrar una narrativa de liberación que entronca en la salvación de Dios. Pues la inclusión de la experiencia de la experiencia de Dios de las mujeres es un ejercicio de búsqueda de la Verdad, de desvelamiento del rostro de Dios[26]. La experiencia de las mujeres extranjeras no debe disolverse en la lucha social y considerarse como un sacrificio necesario para que otros puedan salir de la pobreza. Si esto sucede, "se aprisionaría la verdad con la injusticia" (Rom 1,18) o, dicho de otro modo, la injusticia deformaría, enmascararía la realidad para legitimarse. El patriarcado, la dictadura de los mercados y su lógica excluyente niegan la realidad de las mujeres para poder mantener situaciones de privilegio del poder masculino y capitalista[27]. El "sacramento de la extranjera", el sacramento de las mujeres migrantes, nos obliga a luchar contra su situación de marginalidad y opresión.

El lugar teológico no es solo su vida y sus experiencias de sufrimiento, sino la experiencia de violencia en las fronteras de la precariedad laboral y vital. Debilidad, sufrimiento, enfermedad, incomprensión, culpa, miedo, etc. Esto es imagen de Dios: es vida en tránsito, desde la necesidad y las marginaciones que se intersectan. Se trata de un lugar teológico que se yergue como hermenéutica multidireccional, pues habla de género, raza, pobreza, familia, economía, historia, relaciones en un todo global. En esta red de hilos que se entretejen, debemos encontrar aquellos elementos que liberan y aquellos que oprimen. Una visión antropológica renovada de la *imago Dei* pasa inevitablemente por

---

[24] Ivone Gebara, *El rostro oculto del mal: Una teología desde la experiencia de las mujeres* (Trotta: Madrid 2000), 44.
[25] Cf. Jon Sobrino, *El principio-misericordia. Bajar de la cruz a los pueblos crucificados* (Sal Terrae: Santander 1992), 31-45.
[26] Ann O'Hara Graff, "The Struggle to Name Women's Experience", en Ann O'Hara Graff (ed.), *In the Embrace of God. Feminist Approaches to Theological Anthropology* (Wipf and Stock Publishers: Eugene 1995), 71-89, aquí 83.
[27] Torres, *Decir haciendo*, 171.

esos nodos de convergencia, como diría Deleuze[28], pero también recorre aquellos hilos que tensionan y dificultan visualizar todo el entramado en su conjunto. Por eso, el lugar teológico que articula un discurso sobre Dios y sobre el ser humano, no se reduce solo a una hermenéutica, sino que las narrativas femeninas, sus experiencias, sufrimientos y aspiraciones son también parte de ese lugar: "son un *logos* pronunciado desde la vida y la praxis histórico-eclesial de las mujeres"[29].

Transformar la mirada: de la víctima a la empoderada
Para que se dé realmente un cambio antropológico que permita llamar al migrante hermana o hermano, hay cuestiones relativas al trabajo teológico que deben ser necesariamente abordadas. Nos centraremos en tres de ellas que son imprescindibles de reflexionar.

La primera cuestión es la sexualización del lenguaje sobre Dios. El modelo patriarcal de Dios se expresa con un lenguaje masculino, machista y excluyente que constantemente invisibiliza a las mujeres y su experiencia religiosa. Una propuesta de transformación de este lenguaje no trataría de reemplazarlo totalmente por otro femenino, pues pasaríamos de nuevo a una tiranía lingüística (y por tanto discursiva), sino que trataría de señalar los límites y carencias del mismo. Esto es lo que O´Hara[30] reconoce como una "iluminación mutua" de forma que se reconoce la diversidad y se acepta lenguajes diversos a un mismo acontecimiento religioso. Y al mismo tiempo, se provocaría un reconocimiento de que el lenguaje utilizado es un lenguaje parcial que produce tres efectos: aceptar que varios lenguajes pueden convivir juntos, desvelar las distorsiones que hay en la hermenéutica bíblica y en la teología tradicional y elaborar lenguajes más inclusivos a través de la creatividad y la asociación de conceptos y experiencias (*insight*).

La segunda, se entrelaza con la anterior, pues apuesta por abandonar la bipolaridad sexual que sitúa a los géneros como totalidades enfrentadas y articula un discurso desigual. Habría que abordar la crítica al modelo de complementariedad muy interiorizado en la antropología teológica cristiana y que corresponde a una concepción patriarcal de los sexos y da como resultado la "subordinación" de las mujeres; desde ahí incorporar otras comprensiones no

---

[28] *Cf.* Gilles Deleuze y Felix Guatari, *Rizoma* (Pre-textos: Madrid 2015).
[29] Virginia Azcuy, "Hacia una Iglesia más solidaria con las mujeres. Conversando con tres teólogas latinoamericanas", en: *Erasmus* III,1 (2001) 77-95.
[30] O´Hara, "The Struggle to Name", 83

polares como la cooperación o *"partnership"*,[31] la "mutualidad interpersonal"[32] o la "referencialidad mutua".[33]

Por último, es también necesario, a mi modo de ver, evitar la tendencia de la cultura colonialista de buscar identidades esenciales, estáticas y distinguibles. El modelo colonial patriarcal construye sistemas binarios (los unos, los otros) jerárquicamente estructurados[34] y, al establecerse la comunicación, la relación de diferencia se constituye en una relación de poder. En el pensamiento occidental, varones y mujeres, negros y blancos, homosexuales y heterosexuales, europeos y latinos, no solamente son diferentes, sino que son "esencialmente" diferentes, no pueden ser iguales, y, por lo tanto, no merecen derechos iguales. Se constituyen, así, fronteras entre individuos (en el sentido simbólico del término, pero también en el sentido literal: Melilla, México...) y desencadenan una rigidez en las formas de relación que conlleva incomprensión e incapacidad de fraguar vínculos.

Para combatir el rechazo (o a veces colapso) de las identidades esenciales al encontrase con otras identidades, creo que sería útil utilizar al menos una hermenéutica diatópica, es decir, una hermenéutica que aprovecha en sus elaboraciones de pensamiento aquellos saberes de otras culturas para articular "un proceso recíproco de traducción de saberes, valores, creencias, concepciones"[35]. Para ello, pone en contacto las narrativas de cada cultura y abre la comprensión a través de los "lugares" diferentes *(dia-topos)* de partida y de los encuentros entre ellos.

A efectos prácticos, en la teología –y, en concreto, la reflexión de la *imago Dei*– supone asumir el carácter de incompletud de todas las tradiciones teológicas, huyendo de universalismos y ofreciendo espacios de relación entre ellas donde cooperen para dar respuesta a las distintas realidades vitales/culturales.

---

[31] Cf. Letty M. Russell, *The Future of Partnership* (Westminster Press: Philadelphia 1979); Letty M. Russell, *Growth in Partnership* (Westminster Press: Philadelphia 1981).
[32] Cf. María Teresa Porcile, *La mujer espacio de salvación* (Publicaciones Claretianas: Madrid 2004).
[33] Cf. Karl Lehmann, "The place of Women as a Problem in Theological Anthropology", *Communio* (1983), 219-239. Cf. Michelle Schumacher, *Women in Christ: Toward a New Feminism* (Eerdmans: Grands Rapids 2004).
[34] Kang, "Teología desde un espacio de intersección", 79.
[35] Cf. Boaventura de Sousa Santos, *Descolonizar el saber, reinventar el poder* (Trilce: Montevideo 2010).

Para operar en estos términos, esto es, para construir una nueva antropología teológica inclusiva, es necesario ahondar en las "ontologías relacionales", que surgen del diálogo horizontal entre iguales[36]. Partimos de la experiencia de las mujeres migradas para poder comprender cuál es el sacramento de comunión de la Iglesia hoy. Por tanto, cada narrativa, cada mirada subjetiva, refuerza los lazos de comunidad que se intersectan en esas experiencias, no porque sean iguales, sino porque al ser diferentes las palabras se encuentran en los cuerpos, los espacios y los tiempos, las emociones y las intuiciones de los otros/as, dando importancia a aquello que no es mío. Se trata así de un "sentipensamiento"[37] subalterno, que rescatamos y actualizamos de las Escrituras y incorporándolo a las intuiciones de la bondad de la persona, sea su raza o género la que sea.

Poner en práctica esta ontología relacional puede dar como resultado algunos beneficios para el trabajo teológico. Lo primero es la expansión del imaginario en un lenguaje más plural, más rico y diverso en nuevas analogías[38]. Provoca un movimiento del mismo, en continuo diálogo (diatópico) de las subjetividades. Así va adquiriendo matices vivos, más apegados a lo concreto y a las vivencias cotidianas, por lo que tendremos una teología encarnada, preocupada por la vida y sus sufrimientos. Pone en el centro, además, la experiencia de un Dios que libera y empodera a los que son desposeídos de su dignidad en el sistema tecnoneoliberal-heteropatriarcal.

Por otro lado, se educa a la comunidad cristiana, o en realidad, la comunidad cristiana se "autoeduca". A través del lenguaje y del imaginario inclusivo se establecen unas relaciones nuevas donde la diferencia se acoge como un don de la creación, pues Dios, en su infinito amor, creó una pluralidad de especies y ecosistemas para que hubiera vida en abundancia[39].

---

[36] Arturo Escobar, *Sentipensar con la tierra: Nuevas lecturas sobre desarrollo, territorio y diferencia* (UNAULA: Medellín 2014).

[37] *Sentipensamiento* es el ejercicio de vincular la razón y la emoción para interpretar la vida y su sentido. Las emociones experimentadas en la vida y la experiencia sobre ellas, repiensa y narra la vida teniéndolas en cuenta. Arturo Escobar recoge este término del sociólogo Orlando Fals Borda y lo desarrolla afirmando que es un ejercicio cognitivo que supera al pensamiento abstracto (razón cartesiana), pues visibiliza otras fuentes de conocimiento, por ejemplo, aquellas basadas en experiencias somáticas, emocionales e intuitivas, o experiencias espirituales, místicas u oníricas. Escobar defiende que este tipo de experiencias ofrecen, a veces, formas más directas de acceder y comprender a la realidad ya que transcienden la mediación de la reflexión abstracta. Cf. Escobar, *Sentipensar*, 2010.

[38] O'Hara, "The Struggle to Name", 85.

[39] Recordemos que las semillas no nacen normalmente solas, sino que en muchas ocasiones flora y fauna produce miles de semillas o embriones de los que solo algunos fructifican. Esta sobreabundancia es la sobreabundancia de Dios, Cf. David Jou, *Dios, cosmos, caos* (Sígueme, Sala-

La comunidad, entonces crece en un clima de sobreabundancia, donde se cumple la máxima de Gál 3,28, que proclama que la diferencia es un bien querido por Dios.

El reconocimiento del otro como diferente. Fronteras que abrir, jardines que construir

Nancy E. Bedford afirma en su libro *Teología a tres voces* que la antropología teológica debe responder "de manera vivificante a las asimetrías de género que desembocan en el feminicidio. En este asunto, la escatología futurista de San Agustín necesita ceder a una escatología realizada y presente: una igualdad de género que pueda comenzar a experimentarse hoy, en la esperanza de una nueva creación en todo su esplendor"[40].

Necesitamos repensar el encuentro con el otro como una fiesta de la creación. Repensar significa intervenir en dos cuestiones y provocar una transformación en ellas. La primera tiene que ver con el auto-descentramiento. La modernidad nos ha conducido a un autocentramiento mayor que en épocas anteriores. El ser humano, situado en el centro del universo proyecta una visión sobre la realidad profundamente subjetiva, que reduce los acontecimientos a la percepción personal que se tiene de ellos. Esto supone un acortamiento de la mirada, mermando la capacidad de comprensión de la realidad. El auto-descentramiento busca una perspectiva subjetiva más amplia donde la persona pueda identificar en su experiencia religiosa otros factores, y no solamente los que le afectan personalmente. Así puede establecer relaciones de interdependencia con el medio que habita en lo concreto y con toda la creación en general.

Por otro lado, al tener una visión centrada en las propias experiencias y necesidades, absolutizamos lo que nos sucede, descompensando las relaciones de equidad con los otros, considerando que lo que nos sucede es lo más importante y por lo tanto, tiene prioridad sobre lo demás. Es lo que llama Marina Garcés el tiempo de la "credulidad", o la necesidad imperiosa de dar siempre nuestra opinión, pues es lo único valioso que tenemos y sabemos[41]. Como consecuencia, nos atrofiamos, porque nos incapacitamos para realizar una

---

manca 2015), 159-188; Cf. Elizabeth A. Johnson, *Pregúntale a las bestias* (Sal Terrae: Santander 2015), 45-99.

[40] Virginia Azcuy y Nancy Bedford y Mercedes Bachman, *Teología feminista a tres voces* (Ediciones Universidad Alberto Hurtado: Buenos Aires 2017), 323-24.

[41] Marina Garcés, *Nueva ilustración radical* (Anagrama: Barcelona 2017), 9.

observación activa (una crítica) de la realidad, es decir, percibir los detalles que nos describen la realidad del otro. Es cada vez más frecuente que pasemos por la cotidianeidad sin observarla, sin analizar las circunstancias y los factores que la conforman y propician unas u otras situaciones y consecuencias. Perdemos la conciencia de la realidad, de su paso por nosotros.

La propuesta para auto-educar la experiencia religiosa personal sería hacer el proceso contrario, auto-descentrarnos para salir al encuentro con el otro, pues en la diferencia se da el fenómeno maravilloso del reconocimiento personal, al tiempo que se reconoce al otro con el que me encuentro.

La segunda cuestión tiene que ver con el des-androcentramiento desde una perspectiva colonial, es decir, un des-androcentramiento del modelo de hombre blanco y europeo, que monopoliza las miradas antropológicas sobre la *imago Dei*. El desarrollo de unas prácticas políticas y económicas más individuales, propician un refuerzo de centramiento en la realidad masculina[42]. Cuando lo público y lo privado se ha desdibujado con la pluralidad y la globalidad, lo masculino se impone sobre lo femenino con violencia, y las categorías culturales globales se piensan y se ejecutan en masculino, sin tener en cuenta la voz de las mujeres y las problemáticas que les afectan. Nos encontramos, por tanto, con unas prácticas androcéntricas que dificultan el empoderamiento femenino y la conquista de la equidad. La participación en este mundo, pensada desde las categorías machistas, depende del grado de asimilación que las mujeres hagan de estas prácticas. Con la aceptación del modelo, las mujeres abandonan las formas de pensamiento propias y las respuestas que dan –desde su diversidad– a sus problemas y a los de los demás.

La tarea de auto-educación de la experiencia religiosa, en este caso, sería aceptar la crítica antropológica feminista postcolonial[43] como una herramienta para recordarnos la diversidad de la realidad humana, al tiempo que aprendemos a pensar la alteridad como diversidad, pensar la interculturalidad como identidad, y pensar la convivencia como herramienta de cohesión y crecimiento. El otro se ve, entonces, como una oportunidad de ampliar nuestra concepción del mundo a partir de su diferencia, con todas sus peculiaridades. También se recibe como una oportunidad de profundizar en el misterio de la experiencia de Dios del que participamos como imagen de Dios y cauce la misericordia de la divinidad en la creación.

---

[42] Gebara, *Intuiciones Ecofeministas*, 96.
[43] Cf. O'Hara, *In the Embrace of God*, 161-189.

Es un proceso de aproximación a la otra o el otro, en el que tienden a surgir elementos propicios para la práctica de la paz, la tolerancia, la igualdad y la justicia. Partimos pues de un modelo de sociedades interculturales que suponen "interacción, intercambio, apertura y solidaridad efectiva: reconocimiento de los valores, de los modos de vida, de las representaciones simbólicas, bien dentro de los códigos de una misma cultura o bien entre culturas distintas"[44]. Somos hombres y mujeres creados a imagen de Dios, portadores de plenitud y afectados a la vez de limitaciones humanas. Esta ambigüedad es el lugar teológico que nos pone en salida hacia el otro/la otra entendiendo su diferencia como propia de la imagen de Dios.

Por último, mucho más profunda es la conversión personal a la empatía, que tiene que ver con las raíces de misericordia que hay alojadas en nosotras y nosotros por nuestra condición de *imago Dei*. La capacidad empática del ser humano está anclada en la capacidad de gemir y clamar de Dios al lado de la creación que sufre y clama[45]. La empatía compasiva bien ejercida supera el concepto de tolerancia para ahondar en la noción de solidaridad. La idea de que la narrativa de las mujeres es lugar teológico (presente en la obra de Johnson[46]) va acompañada de otro concepto fundamental, el de la solidaridad o sororidad. Memoria y narrativa aseguran el carácter práctico de la fe[47], que: (a) reinterpreta las fuentes antropológicas; (b) reconoce, interpreta y explica la biografía de las mujeres como lugar teológico y (c) adquiere una estructura solidaria[48] encaminada al empoderamiento. Es la solidaridad-sororidad, derivada de lo anterior lo que permite una comunión-inclusiva.

La empatía unida a la sororidad produce prácticas discursivas deliberativas y persuasivas y tiene un imaginario rico. Educa las distintas formas humanas

---

[44] Mary Nash, "Diversidad, multiculturalismos e identidades: perspectivas de género", en M. Nash y D. Marre (eds.), Multiculturalismos y género: un estudio interdisciplinar (Bellaterra: Barcelona 2001), 21-47.

[45] William A. Dyrness y Oscar García-Johnson, *Theology without borders* (Baker Academic: Grand Rapids 2015), 81-83.

[46] Cf. Elizabeth A. Johnson, *La que es: el misterio de Dios en el discurso teológico feminista* (Herder: Barcelona 2002); Elizabeth A. Johnson, *Pregúntale a las bestias* (Sal Terrae: Santander 2015); Johnson, Friends of God and Prophets. Una teología sororal-solidaria que Johnson ha desarrollado a partir del pensamiento de J.B. Metz: "narrative memory in solidarity".

[47] Johnson, Friends of God and Prophets, 164.

[48] La "memoria narrativa" alcanza su verdadera estatura "dramática" – en el sentido de Balthasar – , cuando se traduce en un plan de practicar la solidaridad, entendiendo a ésta como «un tipo de comunión en la cual se llega a una conexión profunda con los otros de modo tal que los sufrimientos y alegrías devienen parte de lo que concierne a cada uno y una huella hacia la acción transformativa." Johnson, Friends of God and Prophets, 175.

de sentir, de ser, de comunicar, de comprender, de relacionarse, de expresar la propia cosmovisión, deja que la subalterna sea capaz de convivir en contextos plurales y cambiantes sin sentirse sola.

Conclusiones

Parafraseando a Bedford, nos toca realizar una antropología teológica en clave escatológica. La experiencia de Dios nos conduce hoy a dotar a los cuerpos de esperanza. Dios se revela como cuerpo encarnado, Mayra Rivera lo llamará Spirit-flesh[49]. Los cuerpos humanos, de mujeres y hombres, los cuerpos de los seres vivos, todos ellos, que conforman el cuerpo ecológico que es el universo, necesitan del amor de Dios para la plenitud de la vida. Cuerpos materiales, sexualizados, finitos, estigmatizados, vulnerables. Todos, imagen de Dios, son cauce de expresión del mayor misterio de nuestra carne (*flesh*), Jesús de Nazareth[50]. Esta expresión del misterio de la encarnación – "el mayor misterio de nuestra carne (*flesh*)" – amplia la forma metodológica con la que apreciamos lo real y lo finito de nuestros cuerpos[51], en los cuales descubrimos la sabiduría con la que Dios sostiene nuestras vidas y la Vida de la creación. En este sentido, nuestra vida (nuestros "cuerpos de carne") es un río de esperanza que empapa el sustrato de la Vida, y que está destinado a construir un jardín renovado. Y los jardines solo pueden mantenerse abonándose con el desarrollo de cuatro actitudes: la resistencia, la resiliencia, el decir-nos y la creatividad:

- Una antropología teológica en resistencia, que se compromete en dotar a las personas y a la naturaleza de estrategias de supervivencia, de cooperación y de reciprocidad para poder enfrentar la conflictividad y poder transformar la realidad desde la resistencia frente al mal que nos aborda. Dios, Espíritu-encarnado (*spirit-flesh*) da forma con su presencia en nosotras a

---

[49] Mayra Rivera, "Thinking bodies", en Ada María Isasi-Díaz y Eduardo Mendieta (eds.), *Decolonizing Epistemologies: Latina/o Theology and Philosophy* (Fordham University Press: New York 2012), 221-225. El término *flesh* en inglés tiene difícil traducción al español, pues hace referencia a la carne de la piel, al "pellejo" en un vocabulario castellano más vulgar. Se aleja del concepto de carne de la teología tradicional, para darle una sentido más cercano a la idea de que a través del cuerpo estamos conectados a la realidad (a través de los sentidos) y también trascendemos a ella al hacernos conscientes de su vulnerabilidad y a la vez de nuestra capacidad de albergar la infinitud de Dios en una carne finita.

[50] Gebara, *Longing for Running Water*, 184

[51] Rivera, "Thinking bodies", 221.

una nueva realidad histórica[52] y perturba y rompe las normas kyriarcales en favor de los cuerpos femeninos que sufren.
- Una antropología teológica resiliente, que desarrolla aprendizajes basados en la confianza en Dios y el diálogo con lo diferente. Asume los conflictos y los enfrenta buscando soluciones creativas, desde la hospitalidad y la justicia[53], que reconstruyan a las mujeres y las empodere como ciudadanas que construyen solidaridad desde una experiencia religiosa compasiva.
- Una antropología teológica del decir-nos, que desarrolla estrategias para nombrarnos y visibilizarnos[54]. Que solo encuentra su propia definición en las palabras y miradas que dirige al diferente donde se reconoce la imagen de Dios. Desde el reconocimiento del otro como rostro del Espíritu-encarnado, se trabaja para que estas miradas sean devueltas en igualdad, recordando que la relacionalidad y la comunidad que esta produce, son fuente de co-creación (capacidad de dar vida).
- Una antropología teológica creativa, que apuesta por la exploración de oportunidades y por la asunción de riesgos para obtener una justicia mayor. Esta antropología profética/escatológica aprende de los errores como oportunidad de reflejar más plenamente a Dios en el cuerpo de las mujeres, no a pesar de sus cuerpos[55], sino a través de sus cuerpos. Una antropología que está siempre alerta a las distorsiones que el sistema patriarcal destructor produce en la comprensión de la plenitud humana, buscando caminos disruptivos para plenificar el don de Dios recibido.

Tengo la esperanza de que en 2027 no confundamos realidad con ficción. Que las escenas de la película de Anfonso Cuarón no sean precursoras de una realidad similar. Tengo la esperanza de que el cuerpo migrado de las mujeres se encarnará en el sacramento de salvación de la Iglesia. El "sacramento de la extranjera" pondrá a prueba nuestra fe y nos salvará.

Silvia Martínez Cano (1975), Doctora en Educación Artística por la Universidad Complutense de Madrid, Licenciada en teología Fundamental por la Facultad de Teología de la Universidad Pontificia de Comillas, Master en Artes Visuales y

---

[52] Rivera, "Thinking bodies", 223.
[53] Cf. Namsoon Kang, *Cosmopolitan Theology: Reconstituting Planetary Hospitality, Neighbor-Love, and Solidarity in an Uneven World* (Chalice Press: Saint Louis 2013), 21-31, 126-179.
[54] Kang, "Teología desde un espacio de intersección", 83.
[55] González, *Creada a imagen de Dios,* 236. Cf. Johnson, *La que es,* 287-290.

Educación, Licenciada en Bellas Artes y Restauración. Actualmente está realizando un doctorado en Trinidad y estética teológica.

Es profesora de Teología Fundamental en el Instituto Superior de Pastoral (Universidad Pontificia de Salamanca) y profesora de Artes en la Universidad Pontificia de Comillas.

De formación interdisciplinar: Trinidad, estética teológica, arte religioso, arte e iconografía, arte y religiones, arte y educación religiosa, Teología Feminista, arte y espiritualidad, Eclesiología, Teología Pastoral... Además, domina la investigación desde perspectiva de género, siendo su tesis doctoral un trabajo interdisciplinar entre teología, arte, didáctica de la educación y género.

Pertenece a la Asociación de Teólogas Españolas (ATE) a la European of Women in Theologican Research (ESWTR) y a la Asociación de Mujeres en las Artes Visuales (MAV). smartinez@comillas.edu

Bess Brooks

She Who Is ... Invisible? A Glimpse of the Mothering God in the Church of England's Eucharistic Prayers

Abstract
This article contends that, when we think of regimes of (in)visibility, we should begin with God and, specifically, how we describe God in public worship. The essay highlights the invisibility of female aspects of God in the current Church of England (CofE) Eucharistic Prayers. There is a single reference to God as mother in Prayer G and the author argues that the inclusion of this reference is characterised by defeminisation: that is, the masculine aspect of something dominates to the extent that the female aspect cannot manifest. The author suggests that defeminisation occurs at three levels: in the historic dominance of the Father metaphor as a way of describing God, in the lack of value placed on feminist scholarship in the CofE General Synod debates about Prayer G, and in the inadequacy of the mother reference itself. The mother God, as depicted in Prayer G, does not feed her children, unlike the father God in Prayers B, E, and F. The author suggests that future revisions of CofE Eucharistic Prayers should increase the visibility of female aspects of God. The article is set within the overall context of Gail Ramshaw's hermeneutical approach to liturgy, YES-NO-YES, and her concept of liturgy as primary speech.

Keywords: Defeminisation; mother God; eucharistic prayer; feminist; liturgy; Church of England.

Resumen
Este artículo sostiene que, cuando pensamos en regímenes de (in)visibilidad, deberíamos comenzar por Dios y, específicamente, por cómo describimos a Dios en el culto público. El ensayo resalta la invisibilidad de aspectos femeninos de Dios en las oraciones de eucaristía de la actual Iglesia de Inglaterra (CofE). Hay una sola referencia a Dios como madre en la Oración G (Prayer G) y la autora discute que la inclusión de esta referencia es caracterizada por la desfeminización: es decir, el aspecto masculino domina hasta tal punto que el aspecto femenino no puede manifestarse. La autora sugiere que la desfeminización ocurre en tres niveles: en el dominio histórico de la metáfora del Padre como forma de describir a Dios, en la falta de valor dado a debates del Sínodo General de la CofE sobre la Oración G en la investigación feminista y en la inadecuación de la referencia a la madre en sí. La madre Dios, tal y como se la

describe en la Oración G, no alimenta a sus hijos, contrariamente al padre Dios en las Oraciones B, E y F. La autora sugiere que futuras revisiones de las Oraciones de Eucaristía de la CofE deberían incrementar la visibilidad de aspectos femeninos de Dios. El artículo se ubica en el contexto general de la aproximación hermenéutica de Gail Ramshaw a la liturgia, SÍ-NO-SÍ y su concepto de liturgia como diálogo primario.

Palabras clave: Defeminización; madre Dios; oración eucarística; feminista; liturgia; Iglesia Anglicana.

Zusammenfassung
Dieser Artikel macht geltend, dass wir, wenn wir an herrschende Systeme von (Un-) Sichtbarkeit denken, mit Gott beginnen sollten und besonders daran, wie wir Gott in öffentlichen Gottesdienst beschreiben. The Beitrag hebt die Unsichtbarkeit der weiblichen Aspekte Gottes in den gegenwärtigen Eucharistischen Gebeten der Church of England (CofE) hervor. Es gibt einen einzigen Bezug auf Gott als Mutter im Gebet G und die Autorin argumentiert, dass die Einbeziehung dieses Bezugs von De-Feminisierung gekennzeichnet ist, d. h. der männliche Aspekt von etwas dominiert so sehr, dass der weibliche Aspekt nicht sichtbar werden kann. Die Autorin weist darauf hin, dass De-Feminisierung auf drei Ebenen stattfindet: in der historischen Dominanz der Vatermetapher als eine Weise Gott zu beschreiben, in der fehlenden Wertschätzung der feministischen Forschung in den Debatten der CofE-Generalsynode über Gebet G und in der Unangemessenheit des Bezugs auf die Mutter selbst. Die Mutter Gott, so wie sie im Gebet G dargestellt wird, nährt nicht ihre Kinder, anders als der Vater Gott in den Gebeten B, E und F. Die Autorin schlägt vor, dass zukünftige Revisionen von Eucharistischen Gebeten der CofE die Sichtbarkeit der weiblichen Aspekte Gottes verstärken sollten. Der Artikel ist im größeren Kontext von Gail Ramshaws hermeneutischem Zugang zur Liturgie, JA-NEIN-JA, und in ihrem Konzept von Liturgie als ursprünglicher Sprache verortet.

Schlagwörter: Entweiblichung; Mutter Gott; eucharistisches Gebet; feministisch; Liturgie; Kirche von England.

Introduction
"Liturgical language is [...] the essential and primary [Christian] speech," according to the liturgical scholar Gail Ramshaw.[1] "[It is] the basic language

---

[1] Gail Ramshaw, *Liturgical Language: Keeping It Metaphoric, Making It Inclusive* (Liturgical Press: Collegeville and Minnesota 1996), American Essays in Liturgy, 5.

from which all other speech flows in exposition and reflection and to which, when Sunday comes around again, all Christian talk returns."[2]

What happens if key facets of God, so far as we can understand and describe them, are not visible in the liturgical language with which the people of God engage on Sunday morning? How does this relate to the theme of the ESWTR conference in Leuven, September 2019, "Gender, Race, Religion: De/constructing Regimes of In/visibility"? I suggest that the issue of invisibility "starts at the top." It is present in the reduced visibility of any female aspect of God in the current Church of England (CofE) liturgy – that is to say, in the eight Eucharistic Prayers published as Order One of Common Worship (CW) in 2000, and labelled A to H. Specifically, there is only one explicit reference to God as a mother (as opposed to a father) in all the eight Prayers – and that is in Prayer G. Yet CW was published after several decades of feminist scholarship in this area. What factor(s) might have contributed to this state of affairs?

I attempt to answer this question by looking at three separate, but related, issues. Firstly, I briefly look at some of the feminist scholarship on metaphors and models for God in the two to three decades before the publication of *CW*. I particularly consider the dominance of the father metaphor, to the exclusion of the mother one. Secondly, I look at the process by which Prayer G became part of the Eucharistic Prayers of the CofE. Unfortunately, the papers of the Liturgical Commission of the CofE are subject to a 30-year rule of confidentiality and cannot be accessed at this time. I have, however, studied relevant public documents debated by General Synod,[3] and the transcripts of those debates published in the Synod's *Report of Proceedings* (*RoP*) in 1998 and 1999.[4] Thirdly, I make a close analysis of the mother phrase in Prayer G and

---

[2] Ramshaw, *Liturgical Language*, 5.
[3] Particularly, The Liturgical Commission, *Report by the Liturgical Commission to General Synod: Eucharistic Prayers, GS 1299* (General Synod of the Church of England: London June 1998); The Liturgical Commission, *Report by the Liturgical Revision Committee: Eucharistic Prayers for the Celebration of Holy Communion Also Called the Eucharist and the Lord's Supper, as revised in Committee May 1999, GS 1299A* (The Liturgical Commission: London May 1999); The Liturgical Commission, *Report by the Revision Committee* GS 1299Y (General Synod of CofE: London 1999); The Liturgical Commission, *Draft Eucharistic Prayers: Second Report of the Revision Committee* GS 1299X (General Synod of CofE: London 1999); The Liturgical Commission, *The Order for the Celebration of Holy Communion also called The Eucharist and The Lord's Supper together with Eucharistic Prayers: As presented for Final Approval February 2000, GS 1211C/GS 1299C* (General Synod of the Church of England: London 2000).
[4] General Synod of the CofE, *Report of Proceedings (RoP): General Synod July Group of Sessions 1998* (London 1998), vol. 29/2; General Synod of the CofE, *RoP: General Synod July*

compare it to similar phrases in other Eucharistic Prayers. In all of this I make use of Ramshaw's hermeneutical method when considering liturgy, that of YES-NO-YES, which I will detail below.

Of course, all liturgy is inadequate in some sense – we can never describe all that God is or all that the Divine means to us. I would like to suggest, however, that the whole process of arriving at the single comparison of God to a mother in Prayer G is characterised, at least in part, by a kind of drive towards female invisibility. This invisibility is multi-layered:

a) Firstly, there is the dominance of the father metaphor for God over all other metaphors in our Christian heritage, including the mother metaphor.
b) Secondly, I would argue that 30 years of feminist scholarship into the naming of God was apparently sidelined, at least by some of the relevant parties, when the General Synod of the CofE was considering the inclusion of Prayer G in the Eucharistic Prayers.
c) Thirdly, the single reference to God being like a mother in Prayer G is itself inadequate, as I shall demonstrate below.

In order to describe the phenomenon of female invisibility in Prayer G, I use the term "defeminisation." I understand this concept as originating in the biological sciences, referring to "an aspect of the process of sexual differentiation by which a potential female-specific structure or behaviour is changed by one of the processes of male development"[5] but now in wider use in a variety of fields such as feminist economics and gender studies. While it sometimes refers to the "'removal' of female characteristics," I am using it here to describe an aspect, or process, of male development causing the *"prevention* of an aspect of female development from manifesting."[6]

Ramshaw's hermeneutical approach to liturgy: YES-NO-YES

Gail Ramshaw, the renowned American liturgical scholar, argues that the hermeneutical method needed when we encounter liturgy is "YES-NO-YES."[7]

Group of Sessions 1999, (London 1999), vol. 30/1; General Synod of the CofE, *RoP: General Synod November Group of Sessions 1999*, (London 1999), vol. 30/2.

[5] "Defeminisation: Definition and Meaning," *Collins Dictionary* (https://www.collingsdictionary.com). Cited as a reference in the Wikipedia article on defeminisation footnoted below.

[6] "Defeminization," *Wikipedia: The Free Encyclopedia* (11 April 2018), https://en.wikipedia.org/wiki/Defeminization, 10 May 2019. Italics in original.

[7] Gail Ramshaw, *Reviving Sacred Speech: The Meaning of Liturgical Language: Second Thoughts on Christ in Sacred Speech* (OSL Publications: Akron 2000), 32.

Our initial YES is a deep-seated response to the holy status of the words we speak and the relevance of them in our lives; the subsequent NO reflects our work as liturgy-students, critically examining the symbols and phrases that we use; our final YES, a statement which Ramshaw describes as "hard and easy,"[8] is our (re)acknowledgement of the sacred standing of what we are saying and that we speak the communally-accepted words as a people of faith to an invisible God.[9]

The context of this article – the initial YES

In the case of this article, the initial YES takes place in the context of the Eucharistic Liturgy of the CofE and its development over nearly 500 years, the CofE being part of the world-wide Anglican Communion. Revisions of the CofE's liturgy are not exactly commonplace; in fact, there have been more in the last 90 years than from 1662 onwards.[10] Although the CofE arguably existed for centuries before the Reformation, and the 1662 *Book of Common Prayer* (*BCP*) was not the first version of the Prayer Book, the *BCP* is often taken as a kind of liturgical touchstone, given that it was the only authorised liturgy for 350 years.[11] The obligatory use of the *BCP*, published under Charles II following the restoration of the monarchy in 1660, was an attempt at establishing uniformity throughout the Church in the wake of the upheaval of the preceding years. Setting aside the unsuccessful attempt to persuade Parliament to authorise a revised Prayer Book in 1928, the *BCP* remained largely unassailable until the middle of the 20th century when pressure to modernise the liturgy resulted in various "alternative services," that is to say "alternative to the *BCP*," in the 1960s and -70s. This movement culminated in the landmark publication of the *Alternative Service Book* (*ASB*) in 1980.[12] However, the perceived need for change did not stop there; further reflection on the importance of the shape of the liturgy and the desire to give CofE parishes a breadth of liturgical freedom in their own particular context led to the publication of

---

[8] Ramshaw, *Reviving Sacred Speech*, 35.
[9] See Ramshaw, *Reviving Sacred Speech*, 32.
[10] See Paul Bradshaw (ed.), *Companion to Common Worship* (SPCK: London 2001), 1, 8-37.
[11] The *BCP* itself was largely based on Archbishop Thomas Cranmer's 1552 Prayer Book with subsequent revisions of the latter in 1559 and 1604. See Bradshaw (ed.), *Companion to Common Worship*, vol. 1, 10-13, for more detail.
[12] See Bradshaw (ed.), *Companion to Common Worship*, vol. 1, 12-20.

CW in 2000 CE. *CW* included the eight Eucharistic Prayers of Order One, labelled A–H,[13] (the Prayers).[14]

The Prayers, therefore, were the product of many years of thought and development. Indeed, one commentary on the process of publishing *CW* (written for a general audience) comments that the Prayers of Order One "[were not] dropped fully made out of heaven. Rather [they were] the fruit of over 30 years of working, celebrating and reflecting with new forms."[15]

My personal NO

With the easy perspective of hindsight, however, it is possible to see that while this 30 years of reflection and experimentation was taking place in respect of the CofE Eucharistic Liturgy, a concurrent, and sometimes connected, work was carried out in the field of feminist theology in the area of metaphor and the naming of God. I suggest that the result of this scholarship is not particularly obvious in the Prayers that emerged in *CW*, 2000. It is here that my personal "NO" is situated.

At the heart of my "disagreement" lie two interconnected issues. First of all, there is the duty to use the language we have (in this case, British English) to express the nature and character of God to the best of our limited human ability, even though we are simultaneously attempting the impossible. As Augustine says, "Have I said anything, solemnly uttered anything that is worthy of God? On the contrary, all I feel I have done is to wish to say something; but if I have said anything, it is not what I wished to say. How do I know this? I know because God is inexpressible."[16] In my opinion, this aforementioned duty includes the need to try and capture the beyond-genderedness of God in a non-reductionist manner. This is not achieved by simply describing God as non-male, but by exposing female aspects of the Divine.

---

[13] The Archbishops Council 2000, *Common Worship: Services and Prayers for the Church of England* (Church House Publishing: London 2000), 184-205.

[14] From this point on, the word Prayer with an uppercase P refers to one of this particular set of Prayers unless otherwise stated.

[15] Colin Buchanan, Jeremy Fletcher, James Jones et al., "Holy Communion," in: Mark Earey and Gilly Myers (eds.), *Common Worship Today: An Illustrated Guide to Common Worship* (Harper Collins Religious: London 2001), 156.

[16] John E. Rotelle (ed.), *Augustine: Teaching Christianity*, translated by Edmund Hill (New City Press: New York 1996), 11: *The Works of Saint Augustine: A Translation for the 21st Century*, 107-108, quoted in Gail Ramshaw, *Treasures Old and New: Images in the Lectionary* (Fortress Press: Minneapolis 2002), 297.

Secondly, and intimately connected to the first point, lies the issue of women's perception of their own "status." If God is male, according to our liturgy, what does that say about my own position as a woman made in the image of God and my status vis-à-vis the men in my congregation? I would argue that these issues are of current relevance in the CofE even though women can be licensed as Readers, ordained as Priests, and consecrated as Bishops.

Elizabeth Johnson, writing in 1992, ably puts these issues into context using the "lens of women's flourishing."[17] In her view, "right speech about God"[18] cannot take place as something distinct from caring for all created things, particularly "for human beings in the rightness of their personal, interpersonal, social and ecological relations."[19] Taking Irenaeus' maxim *Gloria Dei vivens homo* (The glory of God is the living human being), she makes the point that God is decreased in some way whenever people including women, are "violated, diminished, or have their life drained away."[20] This kind of interdependence between God and human beings works in both directions. Johnson quotes Segundo as saying, "[o]ur falsified and inauthentic ways of dealing with our fellow men [sic] are allied to our falsification of the idea of God. Our unjust society and our perverted idea of God are in close and terrible alliance."[21] Johnson brings the position of women in society and the Church to the fore, when she argues:

> Inherited Christian speech about God has developed within a framework that does not prize the unique and equal humanity of women, and bears the marks of this partiality and [male] dominance. This language is now under fire both for its complicity in human oppression and its capacity to rob divine reality of goodness and profound mystery.[22]

Johnson views attempts to find new ways to talk about God as very important for the Church. Such an exercise serves both to combat the oppressiveness of sexism, among other evils, and to increase our perception of the glory of God.[23] However, within the CofE, there is a strongly regulated liturgy: the

---

[17] Elizabeth A. Johnson, *She Who Is: The Mystery of God in Feminist Theological Discourse* (Crossroad: New York 2002), 10th Anniversary Edition with new Preface, 17.
[18] Johnson, *She Who Is*, 14.
[19] Johnson, *She Who Is*, 14.
[20] Johnson, *She Who Is*, 14.
[21] Juan Luis Segundo, *Our Idea of God*, translated by John Drury (Orbis: Maryknoll, NY 1974), 8, quoted in Johnson, *She Who Is*, 14.
[22] Johnson, *She Who Is*, 15.
[23] See Johnson, *She Who Is*, 15.

Eucharistic Prayers of Order One were published twenty years ago in 2000 and the limitations of this "inherited speech about God" remain, namely the almost complete lack of female imagery for God of any kind. So, my personal NO lies more precisely here – in the way we describe and name God in our Eucharistic Prayers, as one aspect of the liturgical experience.

Defeminisation in the Creation of the Mother Metaphor in Prayer G
Example 1. The Dominance of the Father Metaphor

Liturgy is not purely an exercise in linguistic theory. Nevertheless, at the crux of this matter, the describing and naming of God, lies the nature of metaphor. More particularly, perhaps, there is the issue of the metaphor-gap, the distance between the nature of metaphor and our understanding of it. A brief look at metaphor and its role in liturgical language is therefore relevant here. I have chosen the few authors represented in this short overview because they were feminist theologians influential in this field in the twenty to thirty years before the publication of *CW* in 2000.[24] I hope by this means to indicate that the Eucharistic Prayers A–H were drafted in an era where discourse concerning the describing and naming of God was very much alive in certain sections of the academy.

Human beings cannot fully comprehend or describe God and so we need to search for ways to express the inexpressible. We take refuge in talking about things we know, for example, rock, water, light, and try to use these to help define something which is beyond our human capacity to capture in words. That is to say, we speak metaphorically in order to try and grasp reality. Metaphor is the "principal means" by which we are able to speak about an inexpressible God.[25]

Often the effectiveness of a metaphor lies in the understanding of an underlying model. Sallie McFague says that "[t]he simplest way to define a model is as a dominant metaphor, a metaphor with staying power."[26] "God the Father" is one such "metaphor which has become a model" with its "comprehensive, ordering structure and its impressive interpretive potential."[27]

---

[24] A complete overview of the work undertaken in this area between 1970 and 2000 is outside the scope of this essay.
[25] Janet Martin Soskice, *Metaphor and Religious Language* (Clarendon Press: Oxford 1985), x.
[26] Sallie McFague, *Metaphorical Theology: Models of God in Religious Language* (Philadelphia: Fortress Press, 1982, ⁴1988), 23.
[27] McFague, *Metaphorical Theology*, 23.

McFague is concerned about the dominance of this "paternal model" in credal language.[28] For her, this "undercuts both the *content* and the *form* of metaphorical theology. It undercuts the *content* of the relationship with God as one based not on merit but on grace because paternal imagery alone is not capable of modelling this pattern."[29] It then "undercuts the *form* of metaphorical theology" not because of the model itself but because of its dominance and "its status as *the* interpretative grid for Christian faith, which elevates it to an absolute, literalistic, and virtually idolatrous position."[30]

The question becomes: should any one model be allowed to become so dominant as has the paternal one?[31] Given that any single metaphor is inadequate, how can we encourage a fuller and more perceptive encounter with God? McFague highlights Phyllis Trible's work on Genesis 1: 26-30, and the gender of God.

> God is neither male nor female, nor a combination of the two. And yet, detecting divine transcendence in human reality requires human clues. Unique among them, according to our poem, is sexuality. God creates, in the image of God, male and female. To describe male and female, then, is to perceive the image of God; to perceive the image of God is to glimpse the transcendence of God.[32]

McFague understands Trible's work as demonstrating the legitimacy of *both* female and maternal images of God as *part* of the way in which we attempt to describe the inexpressible.[33]

That is not to say that the use of the mother metaphor is free from complexity as far as feminist liturgical theologians in this period are concerned. Firstly, there is debate about the difference between naming God as mother and stating that God is like a mother.[34] Secondly, there is concern about how the term 'mother' might be interpreted. Marjorie Proctor-Smith notes the problem of absolutising motherhood in a way that can be exclusive of women's actual experience. She also recognises the complexities inherent in understanding the

---

[28] McFague, *Metaphorical Theology*, 114.
[29] McFague, *Metaphorical Theology*, 114. Italics in original.
[30] McFague, *Metaphorical Theology*, 115. Italics in original.
[31] See McFague, *Metaphorical Theology*, 128.
[32] Phyllis Trible, *God and the Rhetoric of Sexuality* (Fortress Press: Philadelphia 1978), 121, *non vidi*, quoted in Sallie McFague, *Metaphorical Theology*, 169.
[33] See McFague, *Metaphorical Theology*, 169.
[34] For example, Gail Ramshaw contended with this issue in the early part of her career. See Gail Ramshaw, "Lutheran Liturgical Prayer and God as Mother," *Worship* 52/6 (1978), 517-542.

term 'mother' within a patriarchal framework.[35] Thirdly, just as the father metaphor dominates female metaphors in liturgy, so the liturgical context itself might be a further source of female invisibility.[36]

The work described here is only a small subsection of the scholarly texts available. The point is that it took place during the twenty to thirty years in which the development of the CofE Prayers is said to have occurred. McFague's work in particular highlights the dominance of the father metaphor, or model,[37] to the almost-exclusion of any other, including that of the mother. This domination is despite the legitimacy of both paternal and maternal metaphors and/or models.

I would argue that this is the first example, or layer, of defeminisation in the Prayers that I mentioned in my introduction. Let us return to part of the definition of defeminisation outlined above: "[a]lthough the term might seem to imply 'removal' of female characteristics, in nearly all biological contexts it refers to *prevention* of an aspect of female development from manifesting."[38] It is not the father metaphor itself which poses a problem, but rather its dominance to the extent that the mother metaphor becomes sidelined or overlooked. The female is indeed prevented from "manifesting."

As Janet Soskice says, the difficulty is that: "Metaphors become not only part of our language but also part of the way in which we interpret our world, and the implications of one metaphor are very different from those of another."[39] That is to say, if the father metaphor dominates all other metaphors then that metaphor begins to define how we actually perceive God. Any parental model for God has been defeminised; only the male portion flourishes.

Defeminisation in the Process of Including the Mother Metaphor in Prayer G Example 2. The Sidelining of Feminist Scholarship in the General Synod debates concerning Prayer G

I have argued that the development of the CofE Eucharistic Prayers A–H occurred during a period of significant feminist scholarship concerning metaphor and the describing and naming of God. I now consider the sidelining of this scholarship, at least by some of the relevant parties, when the General Synod debated the

---

[35] See Marjorie Procter-Smith, *In Her Own Rite: Constructing Feminist Liturgical Tradition* (CreateSpace Independent Publishing Platform ²2013), Chapter 4, especially 97-100.

[36] See Janet H. Wootton, *Introducing a Practical Feminist Theology of Worship* (Sheffield Academic Press: Sheffield 2000), Introductions in Feminist Theology 5, 17-33.

[37] See McFague, *Metaphorical Theology*, 147-152.

[38] "Defeminization," *Wikipedia*, accessed 10 May 2019. Italics in original.

[39] Soskice, *Metaphor and Religious Language*, 62.

inclusion of Prayer G in the Prayers and some of its wording in the period from July 1998 to November 1999. I suggest that this is the second example, or layer, of defeminisation in the process of including the mother metaphor in Prayer G.

To reiterate, Prayer G contains the sole reference in the Prayers to God as mother or female in anyway:

> "As a mother tenderly gathers her children, you embraced a people as your own."[40]

God is compared to a mother, though not addressed or named as such.[41] Given the breadth and depth of relevant feminist scholarship during the preceding 30 years, the "female" is surprisingly absent in this collection of Prayers in general, indeed almost invisible.[42] I will now briefly outline the process by which Prayer G, and the mother phrase within it, was included in the Eucharistic Prayers, Order One of *CW*.

The Role of the Liturgical Commission and the General Synod

In order to understand what follows, it is helpful to have a general understanding of the CofE's Liturgical Commission and its relationship to the General Synod. The Liturgical Commission comprises a group of ordained and lay liturgical scholars, and others, who work together principally to "prepare [...] forms of service and promote [...] the development and understanding of liturgy and its use in the Church."[43] The membership of the Liturgical Commission from 1996-2000 consisted of 22 members (including two co-opted members and four consultants) of whom five were women.[44]

---

[40] The Archbishops Council 2000, *Common Worship: Services and Prayers for the Church of England*, 201.

[41] See, for comparison, the second of the four Thanksgiving Prayers for Ordinary Seasons of the Methodist Church in England, which reads "God our Father and our Mother." Trustees for Methodist Church Purposes, *The Methodist Worship Book* (Peterborough: Methodist Publishing House, 1999), 204. The date of publication of this volume is a year before that of the CofE's *Common Worship*.

[42] There are three references to Jesus being born of Mary in the Prayers: Prayer A "giving him to be born of a woman;" Prayer B "born of the blessed Virgin;" Prayer G "born of Mary." See The Archbishops Council 2000, *Common Worship: Services and Prayers for the Church of England*, 184, 188, 201.

[43] *The Liturgical Commission,* s.a., https://www.churchofengland.org/prayer-and-worship/worship-texts-and-resources/liturgical-commission, 19 May 2019.

[44] The five female members of the committee were Dr. Carole Cull, Revd. Susan Hope, Mrs. Anna de Lange, Revd. Canon Jane Sinclair, Revd. Anna Tilby. As received in an attachment to an email sent to me on 5 June 2018 from Ms. Sue Moore, Administrative Secretary to the Liturgical Commission, quoting from The Church of England Year Book 1999 (London:

One of the main tasks of the Commission is to prepare the drafts of potential CofE services and submit them to the General Synod and the House of Bishops of the CofE for debate, reference to diocesan synods, request for revision, and final acceptance.[45]

The General Synod comprises three houses: (1) the House of Bishops (diocesan bishops and their elected suffragan bishops, (2) the House of Clergy (elected clergy representatives from each diocese of the CofE, and some universities), and (3) the House of Laity (elected lay representatives from each diocese).[46] Revisions of the liturgy must be accepted by the General Synod to pass into legal usage in the CofE.[47] New services require the approval of a two-thirds majority of each house within the Synod.[48]

A brief history of the inclusion of Prayer G in the Prayers of Order One, Common Worship

The 1662 *Book of Common Prayer* (*BCP*) was the liturgical point of reference within the CofE until the mid-20th century, when pressure to modernise the liturgy resulted in various "alternative services" to the *BCP* in the 1960s and -70s. This movement culminated in the highly significant publication of the *Alternative Service Book* (*ASB*) in 1980, which was authorised for 20 years.[49] The four Eucharistic Prayers of Rite A in the *ASB* contained no reference to God as mother.[50]

Church House Publishing 1999), *non vidi*. Not all these members would have been involved in drafting all the Eucharistic Prayers (Information contained in same email). We do not know what the contribution of these five women was to the process as there is a 30-year rule of confidentiality governing the work of the Liturgical Commission.

[45] The General Synod, "is the national assembly of The Church of England. It came into being in 1970 under the Synodical Government Measure 1969, replacing an earlier body known as the Church Assembly. The General Synod considers and approves legislation affecting the whole of The Church of England, formulates new forms of worship, debates matters of national and international importance, and approves the annual budget for the work of the Church at national level." *The General Synod*. https://www.churchofengland.org/about/leadership-and-governance/about-general-synod, 19 May 2019.

[46] See *The General Synod*.

[47] In this situation, the General Synod is acting on behalf of Parliament. This is in line with the Prayer Book (Alternative and Other Services) Measure 1965, delegating powers from Parliament to the then Church Assembly and later the General Synod for the approval of new services. See Bradshaw, *Companion to Common Worship*, vol. 1, 16-17.

[48] See Earey and Myers (eds.), *Common Worship Today*, 101.

[49] See Bradshaw (ed.), *Companion to Common Worship*, vol. 1, 20.

[50] *The Alternative Service Book 1980 Together with the Liturgical Psalter* (CUP: Cambridge 1980), 130-141. The Third Eucharistic Prayer contains a reference to Mary, 136.

Work began in earnest on the *ASB*'s successor in the early 1990s[51] and it is important to note that this included a move towards more explicitly inclusive language for the congregation (as opposed to frequent references to 'fellow men', for example).[52]

The phrase,

> As a mother tenderly gathers her children
> you embraced a people as your own [...][53]

appeared in Eucharistic Prayer 2 of six Eucharistic Prayers prepared by the Liturgical Commission in 1996. However, this proposal was rejected by the General Synod. Colin Buchanan, member of the Revision Committee on Eucharistic Prayers 1995, and Trevor Lloyd, chairman of the Steering Committee on Eucharistic Prayers 1995, commented as follows on the outcome of this process:

> On 13 and 14 February 1996, for the first time in over sixteen years, the General Synod of The Church of England voted on a motion to give Final Approval to six new eucharistic prayers. To our deep regret, the House of Laity of the Synod failed to give the prayers the two-thirds majority needed for authorisation and they were accordingly defeated.[54]

Buchanan and Lloyd noted that the reasons for the defeat were unknown.

> On 13-14 February 1996 the Synod debated 'Final Approval.' The voting, requiring a two-thirds majority in each House, was: Bishops 25-10: Clergy 164-44: Laity 135-81. And that was that. For the first time liturgical texts had been rejected in Synod without anyone knowing what was determinative in that defeat.[55]

So, the Liturgical Commission was obliged to produce amended Prayers for consideration. The Report of the Liturgical Commission to General Synod dated June 1998 mentions six potential Eucharistic Prayers for inclusion within

---

[51] See Bradshaw (ed.), *Companion to Common Worship*, vol. 1, 32.

[52] A full treatment of this issue is outside the scope of this essay but see Bradshaw (ed.), *Companion to Common Worship*, vol. 1, 26-27 and The Liturgical Commission, *Making Women Visible: The Use of Inclusive Language With The ASB, A Report by the Liturgical Commission of the General Synod of the Church of England* (Church House Publishing: London 1988), GS 859, for more information.

[53] Colin Buchanan and Trevor Lloyd, *Six Eucharistic Prayers as Proposed in 1996* (Grove Booklets: Cambridge 1996), Worship Series 136, 12.

[54] Buchanan and Lloyd, *Six Eucharistic Prayers as Proposed in 1996*, 3.

[55] Buchanan and Lloyd, *Six Eucharistic Prayers*, 9.

Order One of *CW* (now Prayers A-F)[56]. However, the Prayer which was to become Prayer G, including the sentence 'as a mother tenderly [...],' was not among them. Buchanan and Reid summarised the situation:

> This prayer came into the set of eight Eucharistic Prayers at a very late stage. It has its origins in a text composed by the Roman Catholic International Committee for English in Liturgy (ICEL) in 1984, and a text very like it was among the six proposed to General Synod in February 1996 and then defeated there – which is why it was not among the new texts proposed by the Commission in 1998.[57]

This summary does not completely clarify the reasons why a Prayer G-like text was not included, but it is interesting that there was no reintroduction of a Prayer containing a 'mother' phrase at this point. This speaks to defeminisation in a subtle way: The Prayers which used the father metaphor dominated and a text containing the mother metaphor did not manifest at this point.[58]

Considerable thought was then given at the July 1998 meeting of the General Synod as to what should be included in each of the approved Eucharistic Prayers:

> Yet what should go into such a prayer? The jury is still out on many of the details but the consensus seems to be an opening dialogue that signals the prayer's uniqueness, a thanksgiving for creation and redemption which might focus on a particular aspect or mystery, the *Sanctus* hymn borrowed by Christians at an early stage from the synagogue to sing of the union of earth and heaven (namely the particular historical occasion of the Eucharist within the eternal work of Christ), the thanksgiving continued with the institution narrative which provides the pivot, the psychological heart of the prayer, and the thanksgiving concluded, linking this narrative to the work of Christ and praying for the presence of the Spirit on the Eucharist for the renewal of the people of God and for the whole creation.
>
> This is the broad consensus at this moment in history.[59]

---

[56] The Liturgical Commission, *Report by The Liturgical Commission to General Synod: Eucharistic Prayers*, GS 1299.

[57] Colin Buchanan and Charles Reid, *The Eucharistic Prayers of Order One, Reprint of First Edition with Corrections* (Grove Books Limited: Cambridge 2001), Worship Series 158, 24.

[58] As a side issue, the Report in June 1998 still questioned whether a choice of Prayers was actually needed at all. See The Liturgical Commission, *Report by The Liturgical Commission to General Synod: Eucharistic Prayers*, GS 1299, 1-2. It is slightly surprising that this question was raised at this point, given the *ASB*, published in 1980, already had four Eucharistic Prayers within Rite A. This question speaks, albeit peripherally, to the idea of defeminisation: given that there was no reference to God as mother in the six Prayers included in the June 1998 report, it is very unlikely that a solitary Eucharistic Prayer would contain such a phrase.

[59] The Bishop of Portsmouth, the Rt. Revd. Kenneth Stevenson, consultant to the Liturgical Commission from 1996–2000, *RoP: July Group of sessions 1998*, vol. 29/2, 641.

However, the report of this July 1998 Synod debate contained no suggestion of including some of the maternal metaphors for God found in Scripture within the Eucharistic Prayers. This is despite the fact that there had been a reference to God as mother in Eucharistic Prayer 2 of the six Prayers that were rejected back in 1996 by the House of Laity of the Synod, as detailed above.

The Sidelining of Feminist Scholarship Within the General Synod Debates of July 1999 and November 1999
By the time of the General Synod of July 1999, the Liturgical Revision Committee had produced revised versions of the 6 Prayers A to F[60] and submitted a draft Eucharistic Prayer for consideration, annexed in a further report.[61] This draft text was similar to Eucharistic Prayer 2, part of the six Prayers that were defeated by General Synod in 1996.[62] In line with the wishes of Synod, the draft Prayer was not offered as an independent entity, that is, as a future Prayer G, but as "material [...] [which] might be incorporated in the extended Prefaces and for use with the Eucharistic Prayer F."[63]

During the July 1999 General Synod debate, the Bishop of Oxford, Richard Harries, indeed moved that the first part of this annexed Prayer be returned to the revision committee with a view to it becoming an alternative preface to Prayer F.[64] That is, it would still not be a distinct Eucharistic Prayer. He commented:

> I am not going to go through all the merits of the first part of that prayer;
> I would just like to draw members' attention to lines 35-43 on page 48:
> 'How wonderful the work of your hands, O Lord!
> As a mother tenderly gathers her children
> you embraced a people as your own.
> When they turned away and rebelled

---

[60] The Liturgical Commission, *Report by The Liturgical Revision Committee: Eucharistic Prayers for The Celebration of Holy Communion Also Called The Eucharist and The Lord's Supper, as revised in Committee May 1999*, GS 1299A (The Liturgical Commission: London May 1999).

[61] The Liturgical Commission, *Report by the Revision Committee* GS 1299Y, (General Synod of CofE: London 1999), 48-50. Referenced in *RoP: July Group of Sessions 1999*, vol. 30/1, 91.

[62] See Buchanan and Reid, *The Eucharistic Prayers of Order One*, 24, and Buchanan and Lloyd, *Six Eucharistic Prayers as Proposed in 1996*, 12.

[63] Comments by the Bishop of St Albans, the Rt. Revd. Christopher Herbert, *RoP: General Synod July Group of Sessions 1999*, vol. 30/1, 93.

[64] Comments by the Bishop of Oxford, the Rt. Revd. Richard Harries, *RoP: General Synod July Group of Sessions 1999*, vol. 30/1, 406-407.

your love remained steadfast.
[...]
It would be a terrible pity if those lines were lost. They are biblical – in those first few phrases we have a direct echo of the words of Our Lord: 'O Jerusalem, Jerusalem, stoning the prophets and those who have sent you, how often would I have gathered you to me as a hen gathers her children under her wing.'[65]

However, when it came to the General Synod meeting of November 1999, what had been suggested as an alternative preface to Prayer F was now under serious consideration as a Eucharistic Prayer in its own right, namely Prayer G.[66] At that point, the suggested Prayer had several detractors, although their criticisms generally concerned the procedure by which Prayer G had been accepted for discussion and various points of Eucharistic and Christological theology, rather than the mother phrase.[67] Nevertheless, had those detractors held sway, the final group of Eucharistic Prayers would have contained no reference to God as mother.

The supporters of Prayer G commented favourably on the mothering phrase. The Bishop of Oxford, Richard Harries, strongly defended the acceptance of the Prayer because he believed "it has particular literary strengths and theological insights:"[68]

> After the *Sanctus*, 'How wonderful the work of your hands, O Lord! As a mother tenderly gathers her children you embraced a people as your own.' As the Bishop of Portsmouth has already pointed out, this is not to address God as mother; it is using fully biblical imagery from the Book of the Prophet Isaiah and from the Gospels, where Jesus for example lamented over Jerusalem and said, 'How I longed to gather you to me as a hen gathers her chicks under her arms.' Is it not vital today to have some imagery of motherhood, some feminine imagery? Personally, I would like to have far more; I would like to have something of this in every eucharistic prayer. Given the importance of this for so many people today, surely we need it in at least one eucharistic prayer?[69]

---

[65] Comments by the Bishop of Oxford, *RoP: July Group of Sessions 1999*, vol. 30/1, 406.
[66] The Liturgical Commission, The Liturgical Commission, *Draft Eucharistic Prayers: Second Report of the Revision Committee* GS 1299X (General Synod of CofE: London 1999); 11-12 and Annex 2. Referenced in *Second Report by the Revision Committee* GS 1299X. Referenced in *RoP: November Group of Sessions 1999,* vol. 30/2, 261, 291.
[67] For example, Doctor Peter Capon, delegate for Manchester; Mrs Rosalind Campbell, delegate for Chester; Revd Simon Killwick, delegate for Manchester; the Bishop of Peterborough, the Rt. Revd. Ian Cundy, General Synod of the CofE, *RoP: General Synod November Group of Sessions 1999* (General Synod of the CofE: London 1999), vol. 30/2, 294-295, 297-298 and 311 respectively.
[68] Comments by the Bishop of Oxford, *RoP: November Group of Sessions 1999*, vol. 30/2, 309.
[69] Comments by the Bishop of Oxford, *RoP: November Group of Sessions 1999*, vol. 30/2, 310.

And the Bishop of Salisbury, David Stancliffe, added his support:

> I know that the Bishop of Oxford has championed this prayer for theological reasons for some time. [...] I think that there is nothing in this prayer that we should not welcome and much that we should, and I hope that the Synod will vote for it.[70]

However, one general supporter of the Prayer was the Bishop of Portsmouth, Kenneth Stevenson, who commented negatively on the work of feminist scholars in relation to the mother phrase:

> Some concern has been expressed about the mother image in this prayer, but I would direct members of the Synod to Isaiah 49.15, "Can a mother forget her nursing child?;" and "A hen gathering her children" – Matthew 23.37, Luke 13.34. This ancillary allusion to motherhood in the Godhead is not a creation of strident late twentieth-century feminism. It is deep in the tradition and is to be found in Julian of Norwich. In saying that, I would like to allay some fears and open up that memory – which we are doing all the time when we write prayers, because we are standing where we are, and gathering the information and knowledge that we have.[71]

There are various issues of note here:

(1) It is surprising that there has been "concern [...] expressed" at all. This was the only maternal reference concerning God in all the eight prayers under discussion at this point in the process.
(2) It is interesting that the concern over references to "motherhood in the Godhead" were about an "ancillary allusion" to such motherhood, indicating a lack of recognition that the mother phrase expresses an important characteristic of God. To quote Trible again:

> God creates, in the image of God, male and female. To describe male and female, then, is to perceive the image of God; to perceive the image of God is to glimpse the transcendence of God.[72]

---

[70] Comments by the Bishop of Salisbury, the Rt. Revd. David Stancliffe, chairman of the Liturgical Commission from 1996–2000, *RoP: November Group of Sessions 1999*, vol. 30/2, 312.
[71] Comments by the Bishop of Portsmouth, *RoP: November Group of Sessions 1999*, vol. 30/2, 296.
[72] Phyllis Trible, *God and the Rhetoric of Sexuality* (Fortress Press: Philadelphia 1978), 121, *non vidi*, quoted in McFague, *Metaphorical Theology*, 169.

(3) The use of the adjective "strident" to describe "late twentieth-century feminism" in general. This seems a particularly negative way of talking about the collective work of many different scholars. It sidelines the importance of the academic work done in the area of metaphor and describing God in liturgy.

Nevertheless, the Bishop expressed the very biblical nature of the mothering phrase and supported the inclusion of Prayer G in the Prayers in general.

Finally, Prayer G was accepted into the final collection of "draft eucharistic prayers contained in [the document] GS 1299B,"[73] although there are no records in the relevant *RoP* as to the voting pattern in this case. Prayer G was then included in the document GS 1211C/ GS 1299C, which included all eight Prayers A–H for final approval by the General Synod in February 2000.[74] *CW* itself was launched on the first Sunday in Advent 2000.

There was now one Prayer with one reference to God being like a mother (as opposed to a father) in the Eucharistic Prayers of Order One. However, the contribution of feminist scholarship in the area of metaphor and the description and naming of God was either not mentioned or was described somewhat negatively in this particular process. This is the second example, or layer, of defeminisation in Prayer G, as I see it. The category of scholar has been defeminised here; the female has been prevented from manifesting.

Defeminisation in the creation of the mother metaphor in Prayer G
Example 3. The mother who does not feed her children

What kind of mother is God like in Prayer G?

The phrase which we are considering suggests that the mother "gathers" her offspring in a tender manner. The word "gather" or "gathers" appears in some of the other Eucharistic Prayers too, specifically Prayers B, E and F. This section will look at the close context of the "gathering phrase" in each case and what that might say about the God who "gathers". Is there a difference between a father who "gathers" or a mother who "gathers"? The relevant material reads as follows:

> Prayer B – "[...] **gather** into one in your kingdom all who share this one bread and one cup [...]"

---

[73] See *RoP: November Group of Sessions 1999*, vol. 30/2, 312.
[74] *The Order for the Celebration of Holy Communion Also Called The Eucharist and The Lord's Supper Together with Eucharistic Prayers* GS 1211C/GS 1299C (General Synod of the Church of England: London February 2000), 37.

Prayer E – "Look with favour on your people, **gather** us in your loving arms and bring us with [N and] all the saints to feast at your table in heaven […]"
Prayer F – "**Gather** your people from the ends of the earth to feast with [N and] all the saints at the table in your kingdom,"
Prayer G – "As a mother tenderly **gathers** her children, you embraced a people as your own."[75]

Significantly, B, E and F all mention feeding or feasting in some way as part of the "gathering phrase" itself; Prayer G, the mother prayer, does not. However, one task that a human mother is (usually) capable of doing is feeding a child herself, although that is not to say that all human mothers do so.

Of course, any metaphor for the Divine is necessarily limited, the mother metaphor or anything else. No single metaphor can say everything about God, nor should we fall into literalism. However, I think this is a strange and telling omission; the one activity the God as mother could do naturally from within herself (in the case of breastfeeding), and which is totally sustaining of life, is not identified and celebrated in the Eucharistic Prayers. Only the father God plays this role in any way.[76]

This seems to be a prime example of the dominance of the father metaphor or, you could say, the paternal model (following McFague). The mother God is defeminised: the father takes over the role that she could play at least in part, in addition to everything else he is doing. This is despite the fact that, according to one Synod debate, one of the supporting biblical verses for this phrase is Isaiah 49:15,[77] a verse in which God is compared to a nursing mother. Here in the "gathering phrases" of the Eucharistic Prayers, the father "feeds" his people to the exclusion of the mother, even though she has children (a close personal relationship) while he appears to have subjects or citizens in the phrases I have indicated. She only "gather[s] her children," as opposed to all the tasks which are performed by the father God, and she cannot even look after those children fully.

---

[75] See The Archbishops Council 2000, *Common Worship: Services and Prayers for the Church of England*, 190, 197, 201. Emphasis is mine.

[76] In saying this, I do not want to get distracted by the fact that some women cannot breastfeed or choose not to do so. I do not think this is a comment on their ability to be a good mother, nor does it define motherhood in general. And, of course, fathers can feed their children in other ways. That is not what I am talking about here.

[77] Comments by the Bishop of Portsmouth, *RoP: November Group of Sessions 1999*, vol. 30/2, 296.

One of the un-nuanced and disparaging criticisms levelled at some kinds of feminist scholarship is that everything is simply all about female bodily function. Whatever the truths or otherwise of such criticism, that is not a reason for overlooking the female body as a site for theology.[78] In this case, I think that it is perfectly reasonable to question why the one image of God as a mother in the current CofE Eucharistic Prayers does not include the idea of feeding her children, while there are several references to God the father doing so.

The omission of feeding or feasting from the mothering phrase in Prayer G is highly relevant, given the biblical references to God as a nursing mother mentioned in the relevant Synod debates. Why does only the father God feed his people in these Eucharistic Prayers? The mother God appears to be the protector of her children but, bizarrely, does not feed them. She is, I would argue, defeminised. An important part of her being is prevented from manifesting.

Conclusion

In reflecting on this work, I have highlighted a recurrent theme, which I have called "defeminisation." To remind ourselves of the definition from the world of biological sciences:

> In developmental biology and zoology, **defeminisation** is an aspect of the process of sexual differentiation by which a potential female-specific structure, function, or behavior is changed by one of the processes of male development. Although the term might seem to imply "removal" of female characteristics, in nearly all biological contexts it refers to *prevention* of an aspect of female development from manifesting.[79]

I am obviously not suggesting taking a biological definition and applying it directly to the area of liturgical prayer. That would be an absurd simplification. However, I think that the last part of the definition, "the prevention of an aspect of female development from manifesting," is relevant here. It is a thread which appears to run right through the process surrounding the mothering metaphor in Prayer G.

---

[78] See for example Linda Hogan, *From Women's Experience to Feminist Theology* (Sheffield Academic Press: Sheffield 1997) for a positive stance on this.

[79] "Defeminization", *Wikipedia: The Free Encyclopedia*, 11 April 2018, (https://en.wikipedia.org/wiki/Defeminization, 10 May 2019).

First of all, it appears in the dominance of the father metaphor within our Christian heritage and so, of course, in our liturgy. The father metaphor is prevalent to the point of excluding other metaphors, including the maternal one. The paternal model pervades all; the female is prevented from manifesting.

Secondly, there is the sidelining of 30 years of feminist scholarship into the naming and describing of God when Prayer G was being considered for use as part of *CW*. One of the interesting things to notice about the 1998 and 1999 debates which took place concerning the acceptance of Prayer G is the lack of reference to such feminist scholarship. I mention this period of time, of course, because of the quote cited above: "[The Eucharistic Prayers of Order One were not] dropped fully made out of heaven. Rather [they were] the fruit of over 30 years of working, celebrating and reflecting with new forms."[80] The feminist scholars mentioned in this essay are only a few of the many feminist theologians at work during this same 30-year period and I have only cited certain of their works. I could have mentioned many others, both systematic and liturgical theologians, who studied the father metaphor, and/or the patriarchal model, in different ways in the period 1970 to 2000.[81] Yet in his comments on the mother image in Prayer G in 1999, the Bishop of Portsmouth (albeit only one commentator) negates the work of feminist scholars – the capacity of scholarship is taken away from them. You could say the category of scholar is defeminised. They have only contributed stridency, not detailed academic work which has received international recognition: "This ancillary allusion to motherhood in the Godhead is not a creation of strident late twentieth-century feminism."[82] Neither the Bishop of Oxford nor the Bishop of Salisbury, although supporters of the mother phrase in Prayer G, mention (in the November 1999 debate) the contribution of feminist scholars to the process.

I wonder about a possible chicken-and-egg situation concerning defeminisation in liturgy and life. If you put so little value on female academic scholarship

---

[80] Earey and Myers (eds.), *Common Worship Today*, 156.
[81] A tiny sample includes Mary Daly, *Beyond God the Father: Toward a Philosophy of Women's Liberation* (Beacon Press: Boston and Toronto 1993); Daphne Hampson, *Theology and Feminism* (Blackwell: London 1990); Elisabeth Schüssler Fiorenza, *In Memory of Her*, (Crossroad: New York 1994, Tenth Anniversary Edition); Jane Shaw, "Women, Rationality and Theology," in: Daphne Hampson (ed), *Swallowing a Fishbone: Feminist Theologians Debate Christianity*, (SPCK: London 1996), 50-65; Sarah Coakley, "Kenosis and Subversion: On the Repression of 'Vulnerability' in Christian Feminist Writing," in: Hampson (ed.), *Swallowing a Fishbone*, 82-111.
[82] Comments by the Bishop of Portsmouth, *RoP: November Group of Sessions 1999*, vol. 30/2, 296.

and its conclusions, does this influence how keen you are, or not, to increase the number of female metaphors for God in liturgy? Or vice-versa?

Thirdly, the single reference to God being like a mother in Prayer G is itself deeply inadequate; it is here that my suggestion of defeminisation as a characteristic of the whole process is most apparent. Above all else, it is there in the person of God herself as depicted in the phrase in Prayer G. As indicated in my analysis of the "gathering phrases" in Prayers A–H above, the God as mother who "gathers" her children in Prayer G does not feed them, whether you imagine this as breastfeeding or any other kind of nourishment. This is very different to the father God in "gathering phrases" in the other Eucharistic Prayers.

If Ramshaw is right and liturgy really is "the essential and primary speech, the basic language from which all other speech flows in exposition and reflection,"[83] then it seems to me that what we codify in our liturgies really matters. This is because it expresses what we really think about the Divine, in so far as we can humanly express it at all. And, if that is the centre, or the starting point of all that we say in life, then, in a very real sense, everything ripples out from that. If there is defeminisation in liturgy (the "primary speech" in which we participate), then what is the relationship between defeminisation in liturgy and defeminisation in the sense that it occurs, or might occur, in other walks of life. If there is a relationship does it, in part, account in any way for the invisibility with which we wrestled at the ESWTR conference, Leuven, September 2019?

What happens when we rewrite our liturgy? If we are prepared to change or develop the metaphors we use to try and express God and to write such changes into our Eucharistic Prayers, does this effect change in life in general, in society, in our work practices, in our churches? Would re-writing what we say on Sunday morning mitigate the invisibility with which we contend?

Whatever the response to these wide-ranging questions, I think that I have demonstrated a specific case for suggesting that the process of creating the mothering phrase in Prayer G is characterised by defeminisation, or you could say by a drive towards female invisibility: there is the over-dominance of the father metaphor to the detriment of other metaphors including female ones, the lack of regard given to female scholarship of the 1970-1990s in the debates about Prayer G in the General Synod in 1988 and 1999, and the defeminisation

---

[83] Ramshaw, *Liturgical Language: Keeping It Metaphoric, Keeping It Inclusive*, 5.

of God herself in the single mothering reference which does occur. I am aware that some may think that such a concentration on the need for appropriate references to a mothering God is something of an old-fashioned argument; a striving after a dualistic view of the Divine which feels slightly out-of-date. I would argue against this position. Yes, I am discussing a historical situation which perhaps took place in a specific climate of thought about the naming of God, which might have changed direction in some ways now (although I am not totally convinced that this is the case). However, the liturgy itself is current and is repeated Sunday by Sunday now by the people of God. It is the primary speech which we utter today and so is of the utmost relevance.

Towards a final YES

To conclude with Ramshaw, we have to find a way from YES through NO and back to YES again where liturgy is concerned. We have to stand up in Church on Sundays and say something to which we can give our assent. I am bringing the issue of defeminisation to the fore in the hope that those within the relevant C of E bodies will be moved to reconsider the lack of female metaphors for God in Prayers A–H, or their successors, and that such things might one day form a more significant part of the "primary speech" of the CofE.

Bess Brooks is a mature student in the Research Masters Programme in the Faculty of Theology and Religious Studies, KU Leuven, supervised by Professor Dr. Joris Geldhof. Her current research interests are female representations of God in liturgy, the work of Gail Ramshaw and the historical debates of the Church of England's General Synod concerning liturgical reform. She will soon be licensed as a Reader in the Church of England (Diocese of Europe). bess@family-brooks.org

Jadranka Rebeka Anić – Ana Thea Filipović

Gehört die Ausbeutung zum System? Missbrauch von Ordensfrauen in der Katholischen Kirche

Zusammenfassung
Im Rahmen einer erhöhten gesellschaftlichen Sensibilität für sexualisierte Gewalt sind Delikte von Geistlichen an Minderjährigen, aber auch Missbrauch von Ordensfrauen ans Licht gekommen. Der Beitrag widmet sich der Frage der Arbeitsausbeutung und des sexuellen Missbrauchs von Ordensfrauen. Aufgrund der zugänglichen Berichte, Publikationen, Filme und Medieninformationen wird das Phänomen geschildert und es wird auf einige kontextuell spezifische Unterschiede hingewiesen. Darauf werden innerkirchliche Ursachen dieser Erscheinung befragt, theologische Orientierungspunkte zur Lösung angedeutet und die verabschiedeten kirchenrechtlichen Maßnahmen vorgetragen.

Schlüsselworte: Katholische Kirche, Ordensfrauen, Missbrauch, Macht, sexualisierte Gewalt, Kirchenstruktur.

Summary
In the context of an increased social sensitivity to sexualised violence, offences committed by clergy against minors, but also the abuse of religious women, have come to light. This article deals with the question of labour exploitation and sexual abuse of religious women. Based on accessible reports, publications, films and media information, the phenomenon is described and some contextually specific differences are pointed out. The causes of this phenomenon within the Church are questioned, theological points of reference for a solution are suggested, and the measures adopted under canon law are presented.

Keywords: Catholic Church; religious women; abuse; power; sexualised violence; structure of the Church.

Resumen
En el contexto de una creciente sensibilidad social que sexualiza la violencia, los delitos cometidos por clérigos contra menores, así como también el abuso de religiosas, han salido a la luz. Este artículo aborda la cuestión de la explotación social y el abuso sexual de religiosas. Basado en informes accesibles, publicaciones, películas e información de los medios de comunicación, se describe el fenómeno y se señalan algunas

diferencias específicas culturales. Las causas de este fenómeno dentro de la Iglesia son cuestionadas, se sugieren puntos de referencia teológicos como solución y se presentan las medidas adoptadas por el derecho canónico.

Palabras claves: Iglesia Católica; mujeres religiosas; abuso; poder; violencia sexualizada; estructura de la Iglesia.

Einführung

In der letzten Zeit werden in der Öffentlichkeit immer mehr Fälle des sexuellen Missbrauchs und der Arbeitsausbeutung von Ordensschwestern durch Medien bekannt, da die Betroffenen in verschiedenen Teilen der Welt angefangen haben, gegen diese Praxen zu protestieren und darüber zu sprechen. Einige Ordensfrauen, Opfer sexualisierter Gewalt, haben Bücher veröffentlicht, in denen sie von ihren Erfahrungen schreiben.[1] Es wurden auch Dokumentarfilme gedreht.[2] Eine erste Dissertation zum Thema ist geschrieben und verteidigt worden.[3] In diesem Zusammenhang ist ebenso eine historische Forschung von Hubert Wolf zu erwähnen, die unter dem Titel *Die Nonnen von Sant'Ambrogio - Eine wahre Geschichte*[4] veröffentlicht wurde. Nachdem die

---

[1] Vgl. zum Beispiel: Doris Wagner, *Nicht mehr ich. Die wahre Geschichte einer jungen Ordensfrau* (Droemer Knaur: München 2016); Marie-Laure Janssens, *Le silence de la Vierge. Abus spirituels, dérives sectaires: une ancienne religieuse témoigne* (Bayard: Montrouge 2017).

[2] Vgl. Eric Quintin und Marie-Pierre Raimbault, *Gottes missbrauchte Dienerinnen* (Dream Way Productions/Arte France, 2019: https://devtube.dev-wiki.de/videos/watch/7fa4ea08-efe8-4742-8fa7-23f9c5f90b28, 8. November 2019); Florian von Stetten, *Im Namen Gottes – Frauen gegen Missbrauch in der Kirche* (Phoenix 2019: https://www.youtube.com/watch?v=UUa16dp3Q_g, 8. November 2019); Astrid Harms-Limmer und Stephan Keicher, *Eine ehemalige Ordensfrau klagt an* (Bayerischer Rundfunk, 2019: https://www.youtube.com/watch?v=PfF_ArkQzFY, 8. November 2019).

[3] Die erste Doktorarbeit, die das Thema des sexuellen Missbrauchs von Ordensfrauen durch Priester erforscht, hat Sr. Mary Makamatine Lembo aus Togo geschrieben. Diese auf Französisch geschriebene Arbeit unter dem Titel *Relations pastorales saines et matures: maturité affective et sexuelle pour une collaboration entre prêtes et consacrées, témoignage pour le Règne de Dieu* hat sie am 26. September 2019 an der Päpstlichen Universität Gregoriana in Rom mit Summa cum laude öffentlich verteidigt. Sr. Lembo erforschte, am Fall von neun Opfern in fünf afrikanischen Ländern südlich der Sahara, relationale Dynamiken, im Rahmen derer der sexuelle Missbrauch von Ordensfrauen passiert, und die durch Machtungleichgewicht und wirtschaftliche Abhängigkeit gekennzeichnet sind. Die Mentorin der Dissertation war Prof.in Karlijn Demasure. Vgl. Gregorio Borgia, „Pontifical university takes up sex abuse of nuns by priests" (https://thepublicsradio.org/article/pontifical-university-takes-up-sex-abuse-of-nuns-by-priests, 10. November 2019).

[4] Hubert Wolf, *Die Nonnen von Sant'Ambrogio. Eine wahre Geschichte* (C. H. Beck: München 2013).

#MeToo-Bewegung in 2006 begann und 2017 eine Expansion erlebte,[5] wurde inzwischen auch eine #NunsToo-Bewegung initiiert.[6]

Die Internationale Vereinigung der Generaloberinnen der Ordenskongregationen, die weltweit mehr als 500.000 Ordensfrauen vertritt, hat im November 2018 eine „Kultur des Schweigens und der Geheimhaltung" verurteilt, die im Zusammenhang mit dem Missbrauch in Kirche und Gesellschaft herrscht.[7] Dennoch ist in vielen Ländern, einschließlich Kroatien, die sexualisierte Gewalt gegen Ordensschwestern immer noch ein Tabuthema.[8] In diesem Beitrag wird das Phänomen des Missbrauchs von Ordensfrauen geschildert, einige kontextuell spezifische Unterschiede werden ans Licht gebracht, die innerkirchlichen Ursachen werden befragt, theologische Orientierungspunkte zur Lösung angedeutet und die verabschiedeten kirchenrechtlichen Maßnahmen vorgetragen.

Der Begriff „sexueller Missbrauch" wird im öffentlichen Diskurs, d.h. in den Medien, in Vorträgen, und von den Betroffenen selbst verwendet. Häufig wird er aber auch durch die Bezeichnung „sexualisierte Gewalt" ersetzt, um deutlich zu machen, dass im Vordergrund die Gewalt, und nicht die Sexualität steht.[9] Unter dem Begriff „sexuelle Gewalt" versteht man nämlich Handlungen, mit deren Hilfe *sexuelle Interessen* gegen den Willen Dritter durchgesetzt werden. Das Motiv des Handelns ist dabei in erster Linie ein sexuelles. Der Terminus „sexualisierte Gewalt" meint hingegen, dass mittels sexueller oder sexualitätsbezogener Handlungen primär *nichtsexuelle Interessen* durchgesetzt werden. Es geht um eine besondere Ausdrucksform von Macht, die mit

---

[5] Vgl. Tamara Janušić, „Svi #metoo skandali: Analitičari tvrde da će pokret utjecati i na dodjelu Oscara" (https://www.vecernji.hr/showbiz/svi-metoo-skandali-analiticari-tvrde-da-ce-ovaj-pokret-utjecati-i-na-nadolazecu-dodjelu-oscara-1301484, 5. September 2019).

[6] Vgl. Sylvia Poggioli, „After Years Of Abuse By Priests #NunsToo Are Speaking Out" (https://www.npr.org/2019/03/18/703067602/after-years-of-abuse-by-priests-nunstoo-are-speaking-out?t=1567622952228, 4. September 2019).

[7] Vgl. Catholic News Service, „Prominent nun says Polish priests must stop abusing women religious" (https://www.globalsistersreport.org/news/equality/prominent-nun-says-polish-priests-must-stop-abusing-women-religious-55873, 22. August 2019).

[8] Die Bewegung #MeToo hat in Kroatien in der Gesellschaft insgesamt kaum Folgen gehabt. Vgl. Eda Vujević, „Posljedice #MeToo pokreta: žene se još teže zapošljavaju, pogotovo ako su – atraktivne" (https://www.slobodnadalmacija.hr/novosti/hrvatska/clanak/id/635024/posljedice-metoo-pokreta-zene-se-jos-teze-zaposljavaju-pogotovo-ako-su--atraktivne, 27. November 2019).

[9] Vgl. Ruth Habeland, „Definition sexuelle Gewalt und sexueller Missbrauch" (https://www.bjr.de/fileadmin/redaktion/allgemein/Praevention/Praetect_Materialien/Fachbeitraege/Gesamt_Inhalte_Habeland_01.pdf 10. Januar 2020).

hierarchisierten Geschlechterbeziehungen verbunden ist.[10] In diesem Beitrag werden daher die Begriffe „sexueller Missbrauch" und „sexualisierte Gewalt" synonym verwendet, da die Problematik in einem breiteren Rahmen von Geschlechterhierarchien und Machtmissbrauch in der Katholischen Kirche betrachtet und befragt wird.

Arbeitsausbeutung
In der offiziellen Zeitung des Heiligen Stuhls, *L'Osservatore Romano,* vom 1. März 2018 berichtete die Journalistin Marie-Lucile Kubacki über die Geschichten und Erfahrungen der Ausbeutung von Ordensfrauen, von denen viele aus den ärmeren Ländern des Südens kommen. Diesem Bericht zufolge würden die genannten Ordensschwestern ohne Arbeitsvertrag, Regelung der Arbeitszeiten und den gerechten Lohn im Haushalt oder in der pastoralen Mitarbeit eingesetzt. Sie werden in privaten Haushalten des Klerus sowie in kirchlichen Institutionen den Priestern und Bischöfen und auch den Seminaristen als kostengünstige und zuverlässige Arbeitkräfte, über deren Zeit nach Belieben verfügt werden kann, zur Verfügung gestellt.[11]

Ähnliche Verhältnisse waren während der sozialistischen Zeit auch in Osteuropa verbreitet. Da viele Ordenskongregationen während der kommunistischen Herrschaft ihre Institutionen und bisherige öffentliche Tätigkeiten verlassen mussten, waren die Gemeinschaften in sozialer Not, und auf ein Honorareinkommen durch die Pfarrer, Bischöfe oder kirchliche Institutionen zur Ausbildung des Klerus angewiesen.[12] Diese Abhängigkeit verband sich mit den autoritären Verhältnissen innerhalb der Ordensgemeinschaften von Frauen selbst, und kreierte in vielen Fällen eine (Un)Kultur von Ungleichheit, mangelnder Transparenz (in Blick auf Entscheidungen, auf Finanzen und anderes), Misstrauen und Unzufriedenheit. In Ordensgemeinschaften gelten traditionell die

---

[10] Vgl. Renate-Berenike Schmidt, „Sexualisierte und sexuelle Gewalt – Herausforderungen in schulischen Kontexten," in: Karin Böllert und Martin Wazlawik (Hg.), *Sexualisierte Gewalt* (Springer VS: Wiesbaden 2014), 59-74; Marlene Stein-Hilbers, *Sexuell werden* (Verlag für Sozialwissenschaften: Wiesbaden 2000), Geschlecht und Gesellschaft, 16, 148-161, hier: 148-149.

[11] Vgl. Marie-Lucile Kubacki, „Il lavoro (quasi) gratuito delle suore, L'Osservatore Romano" (http://www.osservatoreromano.va/it/news/il-lavoro-quasi-gratuito-delle-suore, 21. November 2019).

[12] Vgl. Josip Baloban, „Pokoncilska situacija žene u Hrvata," in: *Bogoslovska smotra* 60 (3-4/1990), 257-272; Jadranka Rebeka Anić, „Franziskanerinnen in der ‚Männerkirche'. Zustand und Erneuerung, in: Michaela Sohn-Kronthaler, Willibald Hopfgartner und Paul Zahner (Hg.), *Zwischen Gebet, Reform und sozialem Dienst. Franziskanische Frauen in den Umbrüchen ihrer Zeit* (Tyrolia-Verlag: Innsbruck und Wien 2015), 279-302, hier: 290.

Ordensschwestern als Mitglieder eines Kollektivs, das im Dienste höherer Zwecke steht, weshalb ihre eigenen Bedürfnisse bedeutungslos und zu verdrängen sind. Darum werden die Einzelnen der Macht der Oberinnen ausgesetzt.[13]

Die inzwischen bekannt gewordene ehemalige Ordensfrau Doris Reisinger (geb. Wagner), die einer in relativ neuer Zeit gegründeten Ordensgemeinschaft mit stark ausgeprägter autoritärer Struktur angehörte, weist auf ein Klima der Angst in der Kirche hin. Diese Angst sei auch daran zu erkennen, dass die Ordensfrauen, die im erwähnten Artikel von *L'Osservatore Romano* sprachen, anonym bleiben wollten. Reisinger schließt aber: „Es ist allerdings ein bemerkenswerter und hoffnungsvoller Schritt, dass sie sich überhaupt zu Wort gemeldet haben."[14]

Sexueller Missbrauch
Neben den Berichten zur Arbeitsausbeutung gibt es aber auch Erhebungen, die vom sexuellen Missbrauch der Ordensfrauen in der Katholischen Kirche sprechen. Erste Erhebungen zu dieser Frage in der Katholischen Kirche haben ihren Anfang Mitte der neunziger Jahre des 20. Jahrhunderts genommen.[15] Eine erste ausführliche Berichterstattung zum sexuellen Missbrauch von Ordensschwestern in Afrika hat 1994 die irische Ordensfrau Maura O'Donohue geschrieben und am 18. Februar

---

[13] Vgl. Kubacki, „Il lavoro."
[14] Doris Reisinger, „#NunsToo. Sexueller Missbrauch an Ordensfrauen – Fakten und Fragen," in: *Stimmen der Zeit* 143 (6/2018), 347-384, hier 382-383. In der Kirche in Kroatien kann man auch ein Klima von Angst beobachten. Dafür spricht die These von einem „Schweigen der Frauen", das sich von den Zeiten vor dem II. vatikanischen Konzil bis heute nicht geändert hat, trotz einer erhöhten Anzahl der Frauen, die sich inzwischen in allen, auch in leitenden Funktionen in kirchlichen Institutionen befinden. Vgl. Jadranka Rebeka Anić, „Žene i službe u Katoličkoj crkvi: mogućnosti, stanje, perspektive," in: *Bogoslovska smotra* 89 (4/2019), im Erscheinen.
[15] Der Jesuit Klaus Mertes, der in 2010 als damaliger Leiter der Berliner Jesuiten-Schule Canisius-Kolleg die Fälle des sexuellen Missbrauchs erstmals in Deutschland bekannt gab, schreibt später auch von den Missbrauchsfällen in buddhistischen Klöstern und anderen religiösen Milieus. Er erwähnt das Beispiel eines Zen-Klosters, wo der Autor des Tibetischen Buches vom Leben und Sterben, Sogyal Rimpoche, entlarvt wurde: „ein menschenunwürdiges System von psychischen und materiellen Abhängigkeiten um den geistlichen Despoten kam ans Tageslicht." Mertes führt weiter an: „Mir selbst begegnete das Phänomen des geistlichen Missbrauchs zum ersten Mal Ende der 1970er Jahre, als der Bruder eines Schulfreundes von der Mun-Sekte akquiriert wurde. Alle üblichen Methoden von anfänglichem Love-Bombing bis hin zu umfassender Gehirnwäsche mit psychisch-physischer Versklavung wurden dort für mich sichtbar, Phänomene, von denen ich mir lange Zeit wünschte, dass sie in ‚meiner', der katholischen Kirche nicht vorkommen mögen. Aber sie kommen vor. Und das ist erschreckend." Klaus Mertes, „Vorwort," in: Doris Wagner, *Spiritueller Missbrauch in der katholischen Kirche* (Herder: Freiburg, Basel und Wien 2019), 5-12, hier: 7.

1995 an den damaligen Präfekten der Ordenskongregation Kardinal Eduardo Martínez Somalo und das Personal aus seinem Büro gegeben. In ihrem Bericht nannte sie 23 Länder, und zwar die folgenden: Botswana, Burundi, Brasilien, Ghana, Indien, Irland, Italien, Kenia, Kolumbien, Lesotho, Malawi, Nigeria, Papua Neu Guinea, Philippinen, Südafrika, Sierra Leone, Tanzania, Tonga, Uganda, Vereinigte Staaten, Zambia, Zaire, Zimbabwe.[16] Über den Missbrauch von Ordensschwestern in Afrika, aber auch in Rom, hat gleichfalls Sr. Marie McDonald am 20. November 1998 auf einem Treffen in Rom berichtet, an dem höhere Ordensoberen und -oberinnen sowie Vertreter der „Kongregation für die Institute geweihten Lebens und für die Gesellschaften apostolischen Lebens" teilgenommen haben.[17] Im Jahre 1995 befragten die Forscher der Universität von St. Louis in einem Pilotprojekt 578 Ordensfrauen aus drei verschiedenen Instituten in den USA.[18] Aufgrund der Ergebnisse dieses Pilotprojektes wurde eine nationale Erhebung durchführt, die 1.164 Ordensfrauen umfasste, die den apostolischen Frauenkongregationen angehörten. Die Leitung dieser Gemeinschaften wurde in die Vereinigung der Ordensoberinnen in den USA, *Leadership Conference of Women Religious (LCWR)*, versammelt.[19] Die Ergebnisse dieser Untersuchungen sind aber geheim geblieben. Da die *LCWR* besorgt war, dass die Daten sensationslüstern ausgenutzt werden könnten, musste sich die Forschergruppe der Universität von St. Louis damals verpflichten, keine Pressemitteilung über die Studie zu geben. Über die Studie wurde jedoch in zwei amerikanischen Fachzeitschriften im Jahr 1998 berichtet.[20] Offizielle Reaktionen auf die Studie blieben in den Ordensinstituten aus.[21]

---

[16] Vgl. John L. Allen JR. und Pamela Schaeffer, „Reports of abuse. AIDS exacerbates sexual exploitation of nuns, reports allege" (https://natcath.org/NCR_Online/archives2/2001a/031601/031601a.htm, 2. August 2019).

[17] Vgl. Marie McDonald, „The Problem of the Sexual Abuse of Arican Religious in Africa and in Rome. Strictly Confidential Text" (https://natcath.org/NCR_Online/documents/McDonaldAFRICAreport.htm, 11. November 2019).

[18] Vgl. Paul Duckro, John Chibnall und Ann Wolf, *Histories of Sexual Abuse. Exploitation, and Harassment in Catholic Women Religious: A Pilot Study of Three Communities* (Saint Louis University: Saint Louis 1995), unveröffentliches Manuskript.

[19] Vgl. John T. Chibnall, M. Ann Wolf und Paul N. Duckro, „A National Survey of the Sexual Trauma Experiences of Catholic Nuns," in: *Review of Religious Research* 40 (2/1998), 142-167, hier: 146-147. 149.

[20] Es geht um: Chibnall, Wolf und Duckro, „A National Survey"; Paul N. Duckro – John T. Chibnall und M. Ann Wolf, „Women Religious and Sexual Trauma," in: *Review for Religious* 57 (3/1998), 304-313.

[21] Vgl. Bill Smith, „Nuns as sexual victims get little notice" (https://www.snapnetwork.org/female_victims/nuns_as_victims.htm, 24. November 2019).

Die oben genannten Berichte der Schwestern Maura O'Donohue und Marie McDonald kamen 2001 an die Öffentlichkeit und wurden unter anderem von den Zeitungen *National Catholic Reporter* und *New York Times* aufgegriffen. Erst darauf gab der damalige vatikanische Pressesprecher Joaquín Navarro-Valls zu, dass der Heilige Stuhl mit diesen Fällen des sexuellen Missbrauchs von Ordensfrauen vertaut war. Allerdings versuchte er das Problem durch die Erläuterung zu minimalisieren, dass das Problem auf einen kleinen geographischen Raum beschränkt sei. Er fügte hinzu, dass man daran arbeiten würde, die Ausbildung auf diesem Gebiet zu verbessern und einzelne Fälle zu einer Lösung zu bringen.[22]

Letzte Berichte von Fällen des sexuellen Missbrauchs an Ordensschwestern, meistens durch Priester und sogar Bischöfe, kommen aus dem Fernen Osten: aus Indien, Osttimor, den Philippinen und Südkorea.[23] In die Öffentlichkeit kommen aber auch immer mehr Fälle aus Europa, wie der Fall des Gründers einer kontemplativen Frauengemeinschaft, der Johannesgemeinschaft, in der der Missbrauch an Schwestern der Gemeinschaft Anfang der achtziger Jahre des 20. Jahrhunderts durch 20 Jahre hindurch begangen wurde, bis zum 2009 aber unbekannt blieb.[24] Bekannt geworden ist auch der Fall von Gérard Croissant, dem Bruder Ephraim. Er war der Gründer der Gemeinschaft der Seligpreisungen und hat über Jahre hinweg junge Ordensfrauen in sogenannten „mystischen Vereinigungen" zum Geschlechtsverkehr gezwungen.[25]

Dem Verein AVREF *(Aide aux Victimes de mouvements Religieux en Europe et Familles)* aus Paris, der sich um die Opfer des geistlichen Missbrauchs in katholischen Gemeinschaften kümmert, sind viele Opferberichte

---

[22] Vgl. Reisinger, „#NunsToo," 377-378.
[23] Vgl. Michael Sainsbury, „Allegations of abuse in two Asian nations make some worry more to follow" (https://www.globalsistersreport.org/news/trends/allegations-abuse-two-asian-nations-make-some-worry-more-follow-55866, 22. August 2019); Tim Sullivan, „Nuns in India tell AP of enduring abuse in Catholic church" (https://apnews.com/93806f1783f34ea4b8e-9c32ed59cdc06, 24 August 2019).
[24] Vgl. Elisabeth Auvillain, „French Catholics raise voices, demand measures to prevent further clergy sex abuse" (https://www.globalsistersreport.org/news/trends/french-catholics-raise-voices-demand-measures-prevent-further-clergy-sex-abuse-56083?utm_source=GSR%20digest:%204-16-19&utm_campaign=cc&utm_medium=email, 16. April 2019).
[25] Vgl. Emmanuel Lalande und Sophie Bonnet, „Les Béatitudes: dans l'enfer d'une communauté religieuse" (https://www.lesinrocks.com/2011/11/29/actualite/actualite/les-beatitudes-dans-lenfer-dune-communaute-religieuse, 21. November 2019).

bekannt, denen zu entnehmen ist, dass es sich nicht um Einzelfälle handelt. Das Muster ist, wie Doris Reisinger bemerkt, immer dasselbe:

> Oft sehr junge Ordensfrauen werden von Priestern missbraucht, die ihre Rolle als Gründer, Beichtväter oder geistliche Begleiter ausnutzen, um die Frauen zu – bisweilen spirituell überhöhten und vermeintlich einvernehmlichen, bisweilen aber auch gewaltsam erzwungenen – sexuellen Handlungen zu nötigen. [...] Die meisten Opfer sind von ihren Erlebnissen so verletzt, verwirrt und nicht selten traumatisiert, dass sie schlicht nicht in der Lage sind, an die Öffentlichkeit zu gehen, wenn sie es überhaupt fertig bringen, sich jemandem anzuvertrauen. Auch das geschieht oft nur zaghaft und erst viele Jahre nach den Missbrauchserfahrungen.[26]

Die Ursulinenschwester Jolanta Olech, Generalsekretärin der polnischen „Konferenz der höheren Ordensoberinnen" mit dem Sitz in Warschau, behauptete aufgrund der Informationen, die sie erhielt, dass der sexuelle Missbrauch von Ordensfrauen seitens der Priester in Polen ein langanhaltendes Problem sei. Auch wenn die Daten über den Missbrauch von Ordensschwestern in Polen nicht systematisch erforscht worden sind, seien ihr „sehr schmerzhafte" Fälle bekannt, die während der zwölf Jahre geschehen sind, in denen sie das Amt der Vorsitzenden und der Sekretärin der genannen Vereinigung der Ordensoberinnen inne hatte. Auch wenn die Schwestern sich bei den männlichen Ordensoberen beschwert haben, war nicht bekannt, ob etwas in dieser Hinsicht unternommen wurde. In die Öffentlichkeit sind die Fälle nicht gelangt. Sie erzählte von dem Fall einer jungen Ordensfrau, die schwanger geworden ist, und ihre Gemeinschaft selbstverständlich verlassen musste, während der Priester, Vater des Kindes, weiter in seinem Amt geblieben ist, ohne größere Konsequenzen daraus zu haben müssen.[27]

Kontextuell spezifische Unterschiede

Die bisherigen Untersuchungen zum sexuellen Missbrauch von Ordensschwestern haben gezeigt, dass die Methoden der Täter von Region zu Region spezifische Merkmale aufweisen.

In Europa und Nordamerika sind die Ordensschwestern häufig von den Priestern zunächst geistlich und psychologisch abhängig geworden. Ihre Beziehungen zu den Priestern als geistlichen Begleitern und Beichtvätern haben deren Wahrnehmungen beeinträchtigt, und sie der Manipulation und dem Missbrauch ausgesetzt.

---

[26] Reisinger, „#NunsToo," 381.
[27] Vgl. Catholic News Service, „Prominent nun says."

In ärmeren Ländern spielte die finanzielle Abhängigkeit und die bildungsbezogene Unterordnung eine zusätzliche Rolle, sodass es zu einem wahren Menschenhandel kommen konnte. Der Priester gilt in vielen Kulturen als der Gesandte Gottes. Aufgrund der patriarchalen Wertekonstellation hat er Vorteile, ohne etwas dafür zu leisten müssen. Die Ordensfrau müsse gehorsam und als Frau ohne weiteres unterwürfig sein. Die Not der Familien, aus denen die Ordensschwester stammen oder der Wunsch der Schwestern ihre Begabungen durch eine Schulung oder ein Studium zu verwirklichen waren nicht selten Gründe dafür, dass sie zu Gegenleistungen im Bereich der Sexualität genutzt und gezwungen wurden.[28]

Der Missbrauch von Schwestern in Afrika hat noch weitere regionalspezifische Züge. Die Befürchtung der Priester, sich bei den Prostituierten oder anderen sexuell aktiven Frauen mit AIDS anzustecken, ließ sie die Ordensfrauen als „sichere" Sexualpartnerinnen betrachten. Da die Ordensoberinnen von den Priestern die Empfehlungsschreiben für Gelder bei den Wohfahrtsorganisationen benötigen, fühlen sie sich oft verpflichtet, den Priestern die gewünschten Schwestern in ihre Pfarrgemeinden zu schicken, die sie nachher zum sexuellen Verkehr ausnutzen. Das Sakrament der Versöhnung und die geistliche Begleitung werden missbraucht, um sexuelle oder sexualitätsbezogene Leistungen zu erhalten. Es gab auch Fälle, in denen die Schwestern schwanger und von den Priestern zur Abtreibung genötigt wurden. Die Strafen für die Priester sind banal, wie die Versetzung in eine andere Pfarrei, geistliche Exerzitien zu machen oder sogar zum Weiterstudium gesandt zu werden, was auch als Belohnung betrachtet werden kann. Die betroffenen Ordensfrauen müssen dagegen den Orden verlassen, was sie nicht selten in extreme existenzielle Notlagen bringt. Für ihre Familien ist das eine Schande, von ihren Gemeinschaften werden sie verstoßen. Manche sahen sich dann als alleinstehende Mütter gezwungen, als Zweit- oder Drittfrauen in eine Ehe einzuwilligen oder sogar sich zu prostituieren, um ihr eigenes Überleben und das ihres Kindes zu sichern. Im Hintergrund des sexuellen Missbrauchs steht immer eine Abwertung der Frau in der Gesellschaft und in der Kirche. Priester werden als Autoritätsfiguren angesehen, haben höhere theologische Ausbildung, sind materiell besser versorgt und erwecken wegen ihres Status das Vertrauen von Schwestern, das sie ausnutzen.[29]

---

[28] Vgl. Matthias Drobinski, „Missbraucht im Namen des Herrn" (https://www.sueddeutsche.de/medien/arte-doku-missbrauch-nonnen-sexuelle-gewalt-katholische-kirche-1.4354003, 24. August 2019).

[29] Vgl. McDonald, „The Problem of the Sexual Abuse"; Chris Hedges, „Documents Allege Abuse of Nuns by Priests" (https://www.nytimes.com/2001/03/21/world/documents-allege-abuse-of-nuns-by-priests.html, 11. November 2019).

Laut der Untersuchung der Gruppe von der Universität St. Louis in den Vereinigten Staaten aus dem Jahr 1996 haben mindestens 34.000 von 85.000 der katholischen Ordensschwestern der apostolischen Kongregationen zur Zeit der Forschungsdurchführung unter der einen oder anderen Form sexueller Traumata gelitten, zuweilen mit bedeutenden psychischen oder spirituellen Folgen.[30] Am häufigsten handelte es sich um sexuelle Ausbeutung im Sinne einer Verletzung der Berufsethik. Das geschieht, wenn eine Person in einer Verantwortungsposition die Abhängigkeit und Verwundbarkeit einer ihr professionell zugeteilten oder anvertrauten Person ausnutzt. Da eine sinnvolle Zustimmung zu sexuellen Handlungen nur in einer Atmosphäre der Gegenseitigkeit und Gleichheit erfolgen kann, handelt es sich oft um Ausbeutung auch dort, wo die/der Unterlegene sich der Freiwilligkeit der Beziehung nicht sicher ist.[31] Viele Opfer realisieren erst spät, dass sie ausgenutzt und missbraucht wurden. Das passiert, laut Doris Reisinger, etwa wenn die vermeintlich liebende Person ihr freundliches Gesicht ablegt, ein „Nein" des Opfers nicht akzeptiert oder über dessen Nöte und Ängste gleichgültig oder gewaltsam hinweggeht. Das Machtungleichgewicht wird dadurch wieder im vollen Umfang spürbar.[32]

Die Studie zeigte, dass es in kirchlichen Institutionen auch Täterinnen gab. Um die 13% der Befragten gaben an, sexuelle Ausbeutung oder Belästigung durch eine Mitschwester erlebt zu haben. In den meisten Fällen waren die Täter aber männlich und Kleriker, meistens die Beichtväter oder geistliche Begleiter der Opfer.[33] Als Folge der Missbrauchserfahrungen entwickeln die Opfer unter anderem Schuld- und Schamgefühle, haben eine gestörte Gottesbeziehung, leiden unter Depressionen, sogar bis zu Suizidgedanken hin.[34]

An die Wurzeln gehen

Wie ist es möglich, dass Ordensfrauen in einer so erschreckend hohen Zahl Opfer von sexuellem Missbrauch werden konnten? Die Frage der sexualisierten Gewalt in geistlichen Gemeinschaften ist im Kontext des geistlichen Missbrauchs, der psychologischen Manipualtion und des Missbrauchs von Macht zu verstehen.

---

[30] Vgl. Chibnall, Wolf und Duckro, „A National Survey," 158. Siehe auch: Duckro, Chibnall und Wolf, „Women Religious," 158; Bill Smith, „Nuns as sexual victims."
[31] Vgl. Chibnall, Wolf und Duckro, „A National Survey," 144.
[32] Vgl. Reisinger, „#NunsToo," 379.
[33] Vgl. Duckro, Chibnall und Wolf, „Women Religious," 310.
[34] Vgl. Reisinger, „#NunsToo," 379.

Sr. Véronique Margron hebt hervor, dass die Berichte, in denen der Missbrauch gegen Ordensfrauen aufgedeckt wurde, auf interne Ursachen in der Kirche schließen lassen. Es geht um die Macht der Priester, die Sakralisierung von deren Rolle und Person, um die Idee eines für die Person erniedrigenden Gehorsams, der von den Ordensfrauen gefordert wird, um den Hintergrund eines patriarchalen Denkens und des Machismo-Phänomens.[35] Im Herzen dieses Phänomens und dieser tiefen Krise der Glaubwürdigkeit der Kirche steht die Frage nach der Macht und nach dem Umgang mit der Macht in der Kirche. Letztendlich geht es um die Frage einer jahrhundertelangen Aufteilung der Kirche auf den Klerus und die Laien, wobei die ersteren die Macht haben, zu definieren, was die letzteren zu glauben und zu tun haben. Das hat strukturelle Basis für eine Doppelmoral geschafft.[36] Der Ausschluss der Frauen von dem kirchlichen Amt hat weitere Konsequenzen für den Umgang des Klerus mit den Frauen, wie auch auf eine ganze Kultur der Unterwerfung. Diese Kultur und diese Art des Umgangs mit Macht ist aber auch auf die Ausübung von Autorität in den Ordensgemeinschaften von Frauen übertragen worden.

Die Stilisierung der Macht in der Kirche zu einer sakralisierten Macht[37] und das Phänomen des Klerikalismus als Konzentration der Macht und deren Missbrauch, den Papst Franziskus als „eine echte Perversion in der Kirche"[38] verurteilt, muss radikal und unwiderruflich in Frage gestellt und überwunden werden, denn er schafft systematisch immer neue Opfer. Dafür ist eine kopernikanische Wende notwendig, die sich auf das Kirchenverständnis bezieht und tiefgreifende Reformen in der Katholischen Kirche verlangt.[39]

---

[35] Vgl. Elisabeth Auvillain, „Q & A with Sr. Véronique Margron, leader of religious addressing abuse in church" (https://www.globalsistersreport.org/blog/qas-social-justice/q-sr-v%C3%A9 ronique-margron-leader-religious-addressing-abuse-church-56033, 10. November 2019).
[36] Vgl. Hans-Joachim Sander, „Wenn moralischer Anspruch schamlos wird. Von der Unverschämtheit im sexuellen Missbrauch und in der kirchlichen Schuldkultur," in: *Stimmen der Zeit* 144 (2/2019), 83-92.
[37] Vgl. Gregor Maria Hoff, „Sakralisierung der Macht. Theologische Reflexionen zum katholischen Missbrauch-Komplex," 1-5. (https://dbk.de/fileadmin/redaktion/diverse_downloads/ presse_2019/2019-038c-FVV-Lingen-Studientag-Vortrag-Prof.-Hoff.pdf, 18. November 2019)
[38] Vgl. Antonio Spadaro, „Il dialogo del Papa con i gesuiti di Mozambico e Madagascar" (https:// www.vaticannews.va/it/papa/news/2019-09/colloquio-papa-con-gesuiti-africa-civilta-cattolica. html, 22. November 2019).
[39] Vgl. Geschäftsleitung der Synode der Römisch-katholischen Körperschaft des Kantons Zürich, „Wir brauchen tiefgreifende Reformen. Erklärung zu den Missbräuchen in der Katholischen Kirche" (http://blog.aufbruch.ch/wir-brauchen-tiefgreifende-reformen?utm_campaign=2017_ ersterNewsletter&utm_source=hs_email&utm_medium=email&utm_content=71833204&_

Auch wenn die Wende von einer hierarchisch-pyramidalen Ekklesiologie zu einer Communio-Ekklesiologie, die auf dem Zweiten Vatikanischen Konzil wieder aktualisiert wurde, deklarativ schon stattgefunden hat, scheint sie in Wirklichkeit erst mit dem Pontifikat von Papst Franziskus (seit März 2013) ernsthaft umgesetzt zu werden. Sie drückt sich in der Auffassung des kirchlichen Amtes, vor allem der Autorität der Bischöfe in der Kirche, in der jesuanischen Logik des Dienstes und nicht der Macht aus (LG 22-23). Sie basiert auf dem allgemeinen Priestertum aller Gläubigen, nach dem alle getauften Mitglieder der Kirche die gleiche Würde haben (LG 10). Sie beginnt sich in Form von Synodalität auszudrücken, auf der Papst Franziskus fest beharrt, und in deren Zentrum wieder die Frage der Subjektwerdung, der Partizipation, der Verteilung von Macht und der geistlichen Unterscheidung steht.[40] Sie muss weiter die Frage nach der Stellung der Kirche zu den Frauen einbeziehen. Es ist an der Zeit, dass die klerikale und patriarchale Struktur in der Kirche aufgebrochen wird, damit es zu einem gleichberechtigten Miteinander aller Gläubigen, einschließlich der Geschlechter, kommen kann. Die Kirche im Sinne Jesu Christi muss sich in Richtung auf eine echte und gleichwertige Partnerschaft zwischen Laien und Kleriker, zwischen Frau und Mann entwickeln.

Doris Wagner meint, dass es eine ziemlich einfache Antwort darauf gibt, warum geistlicher Missbrauch in der Kirche möglich ist, trotz der gängigen Meinung, dass wir heute in der Katholischen Kirche eine grundsätzlich aufgeklärte und menschenfreundliche Theologie haben. In der Kirche hat es immer beides gegeben, „eine freiheitliche und eine autoritäre Tradition."[41] Die freiheitliche Tradition ermöglicht die spirituelle Selbstbestimmung, die vor dem geistlichen Missbrauch schützt, der auch zu anderen Formen von Missbrauch führt. Die autoritäre Tradition fördert die spirituelle Fremdbestimmung, und somit verschiedene Formen des geischtlichen Missbrauchs: Vernachlässigung, Manipulation und Gewalt. Diese beiden Traditionen sind schon im Neuen Testament anzutreffen, sie finden sich in den Schriften der Kirchenväter, in lehramtlichen Texten, im Kirchenrecht und in aktuellen theologischen Debatten über das Verhältnis von Wahrheit und Freiheit. Es bleibt zu hoffen,

---

hsenc=p2ANqtz-_HtYPcAjwcjc4Db8MEjk2CzSwD4cCxZ7uw0ZwMYeLmK0G8SqVX1-PAjUkxgSRTBe80v3jy3Zm_ktHXoYuHka4_ue2Whw&_hsmi=71833204, 17. April 2019).

[40] Vgl. Ana Thea Filipović, „Neu lernen Kirche zu sein. Synodalität im Kontext der Jugendsynode," in: *Bogoslovska smotra* 89 (5/2019), im Erscheinen.

[41] Doris Wagner, *Spiritueller Missbrauch in der katholischen Kirche* (Herder: Freiburg, Basel und Wien 2019), 148.

dass die Kirche es schafft, sich auf die Seite ihrer eigenen freiheitlichen Tradition zu stellen.[42]

Notwendig ist der spirituelle Vorgang der Unterscheidung der Geister, die Fähigkeit, Versuchungen zum Machtmissbrauch zu durchschauen und sie zurückzuweisen. Der klassische theologische Weg der *via negativa* besagt, dass es keine Erkenntnis Gottes im eigenen Leben ohne ein ständiges Ringen um diese Abgrenzung gibt, „gerade deswegen, weil alle Rede von Gott immer wieder instrumentalisiert werden kann."[43]

Das Ringen um die Freiheit der Kinder Gottes
Der in der jetzigen kirchlichen Struktur tief sitzende Gebrauch von Macht hat sich auf das Verständnis des Gehorsams in der Kirche und in den Ordensgemeinschaften so ausgewirkt, dass Gehorsam als Unterwerfung verstanden wird, die als höchste Tugend stilisiert wurde, die aber für Manipulation jeder Art anfällig ist.[44] Das richtig verstandene Gelübde des Gehorsams geht aus einem Prozess des gemeinsamen Suchens im Prozess eines echten Dialogs und der geistlichen Unterscheidung hervor, handelt aber niemals gegen das Gewissen einer Person. Es geht um einen freien Gehorsam, und nicht um servile Unterwerfung.

Mehrere Fälle des Missbrauchs sind in den neueren geistlichen Gemeinschaften vorgekommen, die im 20. Jahrhundert gegründet worden sind. Diese Gruppen, oft aus der Mitgliedschaft mit Ordensgelübden und mit Laienversprechen bestehend, sind zu einer Art Parallelkirche geworden. Der Gehorsam zur kirchlichen Autorität ist in ihnen sehr ausgeprägt, weil er ein Nachweis der Loyalität zur Kirche ist, wodurch diese Gemeinschaften hohe Wertschätzung durch die kirchliche Hierarchie erhalten. Zugleich wird eine emotional beladene Spiritualität gepflegt. Die Figuren der Gründer haben eine große Bedeutung und werden nicht in Frage gestellt.[45] Unter diesen gibt es in der Katholischen Kirche „sektenähnliche, in sich geschlossene Gemeinschaften, die ein elitäres Selbstbild, eine ideologische Selbstüberhöhung, ein dualistisches Welt- und Menschenbild, eine apokalyptische Weltanschauung und eine radikale Leidensmystik pflegen, die den einzelnen Mitgliedern die vollkommene Selbstaufgabe abverlangt."[46] In allen spirituell totalitären Gemeinschaften

---

[42] Vgl. Wagner, *Spiritueller Missbrauch*, 148-162.
[43] Mertes, „Vorwort," 10.
[44] Vgl. Auvillain, „French Catholics raise voices."
[45] Vgl. Auvillain, „French Catholics raise voices."
[46] Wagner, *Spiritueller Missbrauch*, 77.

werden religiöse oder quasireligiöse Bilder, Worte und Rituale benutzt, die von den geistlichen Führern und Führerinnen entwickelt wurden, mit denen Andersdenkende abgewertet und jede eventuell kritische Stimme aus der eigenen Gefolgschaft im Keim erstickt wird. Wo die Freiheit einzelner Menschen untergraben wird, entsteht ein weiter Raum für spirituelle Manipulation, die im Einzelfall geradezu menschenverachtende Merkmale annehmen kann.[47] Auf diesem Hintergrund finden der Missbrauch von Macht und der spirituelle Missbrauch einen fruchtbaren Boden.

Jungen Leuten geben solche Gemeinschaften oft ein verlockendes Sicherheitsgefühl, Nähe zu einer charismatischen Führungspersönlichkeit, Zugehörigkeit zu einer Elite und ähnliches. Die dunklen Seiten sind aber die Verschließung und Isolierung von der Außenwelt, der Bruch mit der Familie, die Kontrolle der Kontakte nach außen, die Erstickung des selbständigen, kritischen Denkens, die Falle eines radikalen Welt-Kirche-Dualismus, Instrumentalisierung der Beichte und der Spiritualität, die zur Manipulation und Gewalt führen kann.[48] Da diese Institute autonom sind, gibt es keine wirkliche externe Kontrolle ihnen gegenüber.[49]

Was in diesen radikalen Bewegungen vor sich geht, ist zum Teil auch in den klassischen Ordensgemeinschaften anzutreffen, vor allem bezüglich der Ausübung von Autorität, des Verständnisses von Gehorsam, der (In)Transparenz der Vorgehensweisen, der Entscheidungen und der Finanzen, der (Miss)Achtung der Menschenrechte usw. Der Weg zur Manipulation und zum Missbrauch ist unter solchen Umständen weit offen. Die Täter des spirituellen und dann in mehreren Fällen auch des sexuellen Missbrauchs wählen sich Opfer aus, die sich in einer verletzlichen und anfälligen Phase befinden. Sie bauen eine Vertrauensbeziehung auf. Oft leben die Schwestern, und auch die Brüder, unter solchen Bedingungen, dass sie die ganze Zeit erschöpft sind: durch Überarbeitung, wenig oder gar keine Freizeit und Erholung, mangelnde Behandlung im Krankheitsfall. All dies kann das Urteilsvermögen, das Selbstvertrauen und das Selbstwertgefühl einer Person schwächen. Eine spezifische Dynamik der geistlichen Begleitung zwischen zölibatär lebenden Menschen spielt dabei auch eine Rolle.[50]

---

[47] Vgl. Wagner, *Spiritueller Missbrauch*, 116-117.
[48] Vgl. Mertes, „Vorwort," 11.
[49] Vgl. Auvillain, „Q & A with Sr. Véronique Margron."
[50] Vgl. Auvillain, „Q & A with Sr. Véronique Margron."

Einige Untersuchungen zeigen, dass eine gewisse Anzahl von Opfern schon Opfer sexuellen Missbrauchs waren, bevor sie der Gemeinschaft beigetreten sind. Durch den Beitritt wollten sie der Frage der Sexualität ausweichen. Dann sind sie aber erneut zu Opfern geworden.[51]

Der Missbrauch und die Ausbeutung führt

> deswegen immer auch zu Rückfragen an die Hintergründe, die den Missbrauch begünstigen, ermöglichen oder Systeme anfällig und attraktiv machen für Täter und Täterinnen. In der Aufarbeitung von Machtmissbrauch und sexualisierter Gewalt in Institutionen ist der Blick auf die unauflösliche Verbindung von verantwortlichen Personen mit systemischen Zusammenhängen Standard – gerade auch im Hinblick auf Prävention.[52]

Unmittelbare Maßnahmen

Die Opfer des sexuellen Missbrauchs leiden und brauchen Hilfe, und zwar nicht nur in Form von Therapien. Sie brauchen ebenso die offizielle Anerkennung des erlittenen Unrechts. Die mitschuldig gewordenen Institutionen sollen dafür die Verantwortung übernehmen und die Täter zur Rechenschaft ziehen. Das Verbergen und Vertuschen der Geschehenisse um des institutionellen Ansehens willen sowie das Befürworten von „internen Lösungen" stärkt noch einmal die Täter und erniedrigt die Opfer.[53]

Das langjährige Verschweigen der Missbrauchstaten in der Kirche zeigt, dass der Schutz der Reputation der Institution Kirche viel wichtiger war als der Schutz der betroffenen Personen. Papst Franziskus hat die Kirchenrechtsnormen im Kampf gegen den sexuellen Missbrauch durch Geistliche drastisch verschärft. Er erließ für die gesamte Katholische Kirche eine Meldepflicht für Fälle sexuellen Missbrauchs. Sein Schreiben in Form eines *Motu proprio* mit dem Titel *Vos estis lux mundi*[54] („Ihr seid das Licht der Welt") vom 7 Mai 2019 sieht neue Verfahrensweisen für die Strafanzeige vor und führt eine weltweite Anzeigepflicht ein. Erstmals regelt es die Untersuchung gegen Bischöfe,

---

[51] Vgl. Katharina Kluitmann, „Das Ohr der Kirche. Orden und Missbrauch – ein Zwischenstand," in: *Herder Korrespondenz* 73 (8/2019), 35-37, hier: 36; Chibnall, Wolf und Duckro, „A National Survey," 158.

[52] Mertes, „Vorwort", 6.

[53] Vgl. Reisinger, „#NunsToo," 383.

[54] Franziskus, „*Vos estis lux mundi*". *Apostolisches Schreiben in Form eines „Motu proprio"* (https://w2.vatican.va/content/francesco/de/motu_proprio/documents/papa-francesco-motu-proprio-20190507_vos-estis-lux-mundi.html, 23. November 2019).

die Ermittlungen vertuscht oder verschleppt haben.[55] Zudem müssen alle Diözesen bis spätestens Juni 2020 ein leicht zugängliches Meldesystem für Anzeigen einrichten.[56] Zu den wichtigsten Neuerungen gehört ein Verfahren, mögliche Unterlassungen von Verantwortlichen aufzuspüren. Im Fall der entsprechenden Voruntersuchungen gegen Bischöfe erhalten die Metropolitan-Erzbischöfe eine besondere Rolle. Diese können sich weiterer Fachleute, vor allem auch Nicht-Kleriker, bedienen. Um Verfahren zu beschleunigen, muss der Vatikan binnen 30 Tagen über den Stand der Voruntersuchungen informiert werden.[57] Alle Kleriker und Angehörige von Ordensgemeinschaften werden auch rechtlich verpflichtet, Informationen über möglichen Missbrauch oder eventuelle Unterlassungen beim Kirchenoberen zu melden. Dies scheint zukünftig nicht nur im Fall minderjähriger und schutzbefohlener Opfer zu gelten, sondern auch wenn abhängige volljährige Seminaristen oder Ordensnoviz_innen und Ordensfrauen betroffen sind sowie im Fall von Kinderpornografie.[58]

In den letzten Jahren und Monaten hat sich eine Atmosphäre zu entwickeln begonnen, die darauf bedacht ist, den Opfern die Angst vor dem Sprechen zu nehmen und ihnen Gehör zu schenken. Es ist die Aufgabe aller, besonders jener, die Verantwortung in der Kirche und in Ordensgmeinschaften tragen, den Opfern von offizieller Seite zu sagen: „Ihr habt das Recht zu reden!"[59] Den Opfern soll psychologische, rechtliche und andere Art von Hilfe angeboten werden. Die Täter sind mit den Misstaten zu konfrontieren und zur Rechenschaft zu ziehen. Nur wirksame Maßnahmen können zur Vermeidung künftiger Fälle beitragen. Zur Schaffung eines neuen Klimas und neuer Strukturen in der Kirche, die den Missbrauch, dessen Verschweigung und Verheimlichung verhindern können, sollen auch die Theolog_innen ihren Beitrag leisten.

Schlussfolgerung

In einem Klima der erhöhten Sensibilität bezüglich der sexualisierten Gewalt in der Gesellschaft von heute sind in den letzten Jahren zahlreiche Fälle von sexuellen Verbrechen an Minderjährigen durch Geistliche, aber auch Fälle der

---

[55] Vgl. Franziskus, „*Vos estis lux mundi*", Art. 8 und 9.
[56] Vgl. Franziskus, „*Vos estis lux mundi*", Art. 2, § 1.
[57] Vgl. Vgl. Franziskus, „*Vos estis lux mundi*", Art. 10-14.
[58] Vgl. KNA, „Kirchenrecht drastisch verschärft. Papst erlässt Meldepflicht für Missbrauchsfälle in der Kirche" (https://www.domradio.de/themen/papst-franziskus/2019-05-09/kirchenrecht-drastisch-verschaerft-papst-erlaesst-meldepflicht-fuer-missbrauchsfaelle-der-kirche?utm_source=%22push%22&_gb_c=03C8243CAFD14A8699C2C6AC693723F4, 27. Mai 2019).
[59] Reisinger, „#NunsToo," 384.

Ausbeutung und der sexualisierten Gewalt an Ordensfrauen durch Priester aufgedeckt worden. Der Einblick in die Berichte, Publikationen, Interviews, Filme und Medieninformationen zeigt, dass die Ordensfrauen sowohl Arbeitsausbeutung als auch sexuellen Missbrauch von Seiten des Klerus erleben. Das passiert auf allen Kontinenten, wobei das Phänomen in einzelnen Kontexten spezifische Merkmale aufweist. Diese Merkmale sind mit der Lage der Frauen in der Gesellschaft, mit dem sozialen Status der Familien und der Ordensgemeinschaften, mit der Art des Umgangs zwischen den Priestern und Ordensschwestern in einer Kultur sowie mit der Ausübung von Autorität in der Kirche und den Ordensgemeinschaften verbunden.

Das Bild des Problems weist auf strukturelle Ursachen in der Kirche hin. Konkret geht es um die traditionelle, in der Praxis aber noch weit verbreitete Aufteilung der Kirche auf Klerus und Laien, wo eigentlich nur der Klerus über die Macht verfügt. Es geht spezifisch auch um die Lage der Frauen in der Kirche, die wesentlich durch ihren Ausschluss vom Amt gekennzeichnet ist. Die Macht des Klerus wurde zu einer sakralisierten Macht stilisiert. Die gesamte Geschichte der Kirche lässt ein Spannungsverhältnis zwischen einer autoritären und einer freiheitlichen Tradition in ihr erkennen. Die Aktualisierung und eine konsequente Durchführung des Programms der Communio-Ekklesiologie des Zweiten Vatikanischen Konzils durch Papst Franziskus macht Mut, dass die Bildung einer neuen Wertung und Stellung der Frauen (und Ordensfrauen) in der Kirche und einer neuen Art des Verstehens und der Ausübung von Macht in Kirche und Ordensgemeinschaften möglich ist.

Jadranka Rebeka Anić promovierte zur Dr.in theol. an der Katholisch-Theologischen Fakultät der Universität Wien. Aktuell ist sie als wissenschaftliche Forschungsberaterin am Institut für Sozialwissenschaften Ivo Pilar, Reginalzentrum Split in Kroatien tätig. Ihr Hauptforschungsgebiet ist Feministische Theologie und Genderstudies. Im Jahr 2017 erhielt sie den Herbert-Haag-Preis für Freiheit in der Kirche. Sie ist Mitglied der Kongregation der Franziskanischen Schulschwestern der Christ-König-Provinz, Split. Liste der Veröffentlichungen siehe unter: https://www.bib.irb.hr/pretraga?operators=and|Ani%C4%87,%20Jadranka%20Rebeka%20(277285)|text|author rebeka.anic@pilar.hr

Ana Thea Filipović ist (seit Januar 2019) ordentliche Professorin am Lehrstuhl für Religionspädagogik und Katechetik an der Katholisch-Theologischen Fakultät der Universität Zagreb in Kroatien. Sie forscht zu den Themen religiöser Bildung und Erziehung, der kirchlichen Praxis sowie zu Kirche und Christentum in der Gesellschaft

von heute. Im Sommersemster 2017/18 war sie Gastprofessorin für Theologische Gender Studies (Fachbereich Pastoraltheologie) an der Theologischen Fakultät der Universität Luzern. Aktuell ist sie Vorsitzende der Kroatischen Sektion der ESWTR. Sie ist Mitglied der Kongregation der Schwestern von unserer lieben Frau in Zagreb. Liste der Veröffentlichungen siehe unter: https://www.bib.irb.hr/pretraga?operators=and|Filipovi%C4%87,%20Ana%20(209322)|text|author
thea.filipovic1@gmail.com

Sylvia Hübel

Herstory of Epistemic Injustice: Wo/men's Silencing in the Catholic Church

Abstract
This article addresses some aspects relating to the intersections of gender, knowledge and authority in the Catholic Church. We will argue that Catholic women have been suffering for centuries gender-based injustices, ranging from inequitable access to theological educational and scholarly work to exclusion from doctrinal development and authoritative knowledge sharing.

This sort of harm has been coined by the British philosopher Miranda Fricker as *epistemic injustice* (Fricker, 2007). She implies by this a distinctive type of injustice when someone is wronged specifically in her capacity of knower, informant, or participant in a community's sharing of knowledge. Drawing on feminist epistemology and this conceptual framework, we will focus on the injustice of systematically dismissing the voices and knowledges of women. First, we shall provide a brief introduction to Fricker's work, demonstrating why it lends itself so well to women's situation in the Church. We will illustrate its potential to help us understand the inner working of the Catholic Church as an epistemic community, where official doctrine has been produced, shaped and authoritatively shared by male agents, mostly members of the clergy. The lenses of epistemic injustice could further contribute to the critical understanding of the role of knowledge practices in perpetuating gendered, oppressive practices. Through historical and contemporary examples, we will take under scrutiny some of the sources and mechanisms of *hermeneutical and testimonial injustice* embedded in the doctrine and practices of the Church. We will also explore their ideological function in legitimating and inculcating structures of domination and clerical hegemony.

Last, we will depict some manifestations of epistemic resistance through the examples of outstanding feminists *avant la lettre* and contemporary dissenters who countered this sort of injustices. We will refer to the significant role played during the last fifty years by feminist theological scholarship and the currently emerging lay movements seeking to resist and disrupt "kyriarchy" (Schüssler-Fiorenza, 1993).

Keywords: epistemic injustice; gender; knowledge; clerical status; feminist theology; kyriarchy.

Sylvia Hübel
Herstory of Epistemic Injustice: Wo/men's Silencing in the Catholic Church

Resumen
Este artículo aborda algunos aspectos relacionados con las intersecciones de género, conocimiento y autoridad en la Iglesia Católica. Se argumentará que las mujeres católicas hayan estado sufrimiento injusticia en base a su género, alcanzando desde un acceso no equitativo a trabajo teológico-educacional y académico hasta la exclusión del desarrollo doctrinal y del reparto de conocimiento autoritativo.

Este tipo de daño ha sido denominado por Miranda Fricker como "injustica epistémica" (Fricker, 2007). Con ello, se refiere a un tipo de injusticia en la que una persona es perjudicada en su capacidad de sujeto conocedor, informante o participante del reparto de conocimiento de una comunidad. Trazando una epistemología feminista y este marco conceptual, me centraré en la injusticia que supone desoír sistemáticamente las voces y los saberes de las mujeres. Primero, proporcionaré una breve introducción a la obra de Fricker, demostrando por qué se adecúa a la situación de las mujeres en la Iglesia. Ilustraré su potencial para ayudarnos a comprender el funcionamiento interno de la Iglesia Católica como comunidad epistémica, donde la doctrina oficial se ha producido, moldeado y compartido de forma autoritativa entre agentes masculinos, mayormente clérigos. Las lentes de la injusticia epistémica podrían además contribuir a un entendimiento crítico del rol de las prácticas de conocimiento a la hora de perpetuar prácticas opresivas y basadas en el género. A través de ejemplos históricos y contemporáneos, someteré a escrutinio algunas de las fuentes y mecanismos de injusticia hermenéutica y testimonial incrustados en la doctrina y prácticas de la Iglesia. También exploraré su funcionamiento ideológico al legitimar e inculcar estructuras de dominación y hegemonía clerical.

Por último, describiré algunas manifestaciones de resistencia epistémica a través de ejemplos de algunas destacadas feministas *avant la lettre* y disidentes contemporáneos que contraargumentaron este tipo de injusticias. Me referiré al significante papel jugado por la teología feminista y los emergentes movimientos laicos que buscan resistir y alterar el "kyriarcado" (Schlüssler-Fiorenza, 1993) durante los últimos cincuenta años.

Palabras clave: injusticia epistémica; género; conocimiento; estatus clerical; teología feminista; kyriarcado.

Zusammenfassung
Dieser Artikel spricht einige Aspekte in Bezug auf die Intersektionen von Gender, Wissen und Autorität in der katholischen Kirche an. Die Autorin argumentiert, dass katholische Frauen seit Jahrhunderten auf dem Geschlecht basierende Ungerechtigkeiten erleiden, vom ungleichen Zugang zu theologischer Bildung und wissenschaftlicher Arbeit bis zum Ausschluss von der Lehrentwicklung und dem Teilen des autoritativen Wissens.

Diese Art der Benachteiligung wurde von der britischen Philosophin Miranda Fricker als *epistemische Ungerechtigkeit* bezeichnet (Fricker, 2017). Sie bezieht darin einen besonderen Typ von Ungerechtigkeit ein, wenn jemand spezifisch wegen ihrer

Fähigkeit als Wissende, Informantin oder Teilhaberin am Teilen des Wissens in einer Gemeinschaft Unrecht erleidet. Auf der Basis feministischer Epistemologie und dieses konzeptuellen Rahmens fokussiert der Beitrag auf die Ungerechtigkeit einer systematischen Ablehnung der Stimmen und des Wissens von Frauen. Zuerst wird eine kurze Einführung in Frickers Werk gegeben, die aufzeigt, warum es sich so gut eignet, die Situation von Frauen in der Kirche zu beschreiben. Wir werden sein Potential beleuchten, uns zu einem Verständnis des inneren Funktionierens der katholischen Kirche als epistemische Gemeinschaft zu verhelfen, wo die offizielle Lehre durch männliche Akteure, meist Mitglieder des Klerus, produziert, gestaltet und autoritativ geteilt wurde. Die Linse der epistemischen Ungerechtigkeit kann außerdem zu einem kritischen Verständnis der Rolle von Wissenspraktiken bei der Aufrechterhaltung gegenderter unterdrückender Praktiken beitragen. Mit Hilfe von historischen und gegenwärtigen Beispielen sollen einige Quellen und Mechanismen von Ungerechtigkeit in Hermeneutik und Zeugenschaft untersucht werden, die in der Lehre und den Praktiken der Kirche eingebettet sind. Wir werden auch deren ideologische Funktion bei der Legitimierung und Einschärfung von Strukturen der Dominanz und klerikalen Hegemonie ergründen. Zuletzt sollen einige Manifestationen epistemischen Widerstands durch Beispiele einiger herausragender Feminist*innen *avant la lettre* und gegenwärtiger Dissident*innen beschrieben werden, die sich dieser Form der Ungerechtigkeit entgegenstellten. Dabei wird auf die bedeutende Rolle, die die feministische theologische Wissenschaft in den letzten fünfzig Jahren und die gegenwärtig aufkommenden Laienbewegungen dabei spielten, dem „Kyriarchat" (Schüssler Fiorenza, 1993) Widerstand zu leisten und es zu unterbrechen, Bezug genommen.

Schlagwörter: epistemische Ungerechtigkeit; gender; Wissen; Klerikerstand; feministische Theologie; Kyriarchat.

Introduction

Feminist scholarly endeavours often start with a self-reflective part about the writing or research process, so with this, I will share the sparkles that brought me to this topic and the approach chosen in this article. Besides my rather disheartening lived experiences as a feminist theologian, there have been some specific events unfolding during the last couple of years reminding me that the censorship and silencing of women's voices have been to date compelling in the Catholic Church. I took note of these cases from the media, first in the spring of 2018 when *Voices of Faith*, an international Catholic women's group was hindered in the organisation of an event advocating a more significant role for women in the Church. Since 2014 this meeting has been held at the Vatican yearly around *International Women's Day*. However, in 2018, the head of the *Dicastery for Laity, Family, and Life*, refused to approve some of the speakers. The personal profile and activities of the targeted contributors were showing in the direction of the issues that the Church treats as taboos, non-topics and where usually some form of silencing is imposed: feminist scholarship and activism; pro-choice stance; lesbian and gay advocacy. Finally, the organizers countered this act of censorship by relocating the event to the Jesuit Curia, a few blocks away.

Around the same time, the beginning of March 2018, women's monthly supplement of *L'Osservatore Romano*, titled *Women Church World* – came out with testimonies of women religious denouncing their widespread exploitation as housekeepers for the clergy. They reported that religious sisters were treated like servants, ordered to do domestic work, and even the highly educated ones were given chores with no relationship to their intellectual formation and vocation. This magazine continued to deliver ground-breaking work during the following year. For instance, they played a crucial role in breaking the taboo around the sexual abuse of religious sisters. Nevertheless, after a series of publications revealing the culture of power abuse ruling in the Church, the staff of the magazine has been put under so much pressure that they decided to resign with the whole editorial group. In an open letter addressed to Pope Francis, founder and editor Lucetta Scaraffia quoted among the main reasons a campaign of progressive discrediting and delegitimisation directed towards them: "We throw in the towel because we feel surrounded by a climate of mistrust and progressive delegitimization, by a gaze in which we do not feel the esteem and credit necessary to continue our collaboration. (...) Now it seems to us that a vital initiative is reduced to silence and that we return to the antiquated and arid custom of choosing from above, under direct male control, women deemed reliable. In this way, a positive work and a beginning of a frank and sincere relationship, an occasion of parresia, is discarded in order to return to clerical self-referentiality."[1]

These and other similar cases brought me to reflect on the hostility proved to date towards women's agency and voice in the Catholic community. It gave me the impulse to analyse how this stubborn bastion of patriarchy with its system of gender apartheid still censors and silences the testimonies of women who take the courage to utter inconvenient truths. Nothing new under the shallow glass ceiling of the Vatican – one could say. Women have been acting as agents of change in the Church ever since its beginnings. Besides, feminist theologians have been tackling the issue of gender inequality within the

---

[1] Lucetta Scaraffia, *Open letter to Pope Francis* (https://www.futurechurchnews.org/article/scarrafias-open-letter-to-pope-francis, 13 November 2019).

ecclesial community already for a few decennia. However, the censorship of women's testimonies, suppression of their voices, and limitation of their roles run to date as a scarlet thread through the history of the Church. Leading and decision-making, being listened to are still privileges not readily available to most women. Even if they represent the vast majority of practising Catholics attending mass daily or volunteering in myriad church activities, they are still barred from most forms of authority.

Epistemic Injustice
Women have been unable to contribute to the processes through which knowledge and meanings had been produced and exchanged in the Church for almost two thousand years. Their voices and testimonies have been questioned, censored or discarded ever since the dawn of Resurrection. Moreover, testimony occupies a central place in the tradition of the Catholic Church, so credibility is a fundamental issue. If only we look at the resurrection narrative itself, which represents the cornerstone of Christian faith, women's lived experience of this event has been officially told, transmitted in writing and interpreted for a long time only by men. Furthermore, women have been unable to participate in the areas which created the official discourse of the Church and its hermeneutical understanding, simply because they were excluded from theologising.

By force of their ordination and the powers invested in them, the members of the clergy have always played the role of institutional gatekeepers of knowledge production and sharing, claiming unique access to truth and its interpretation. Besides, historically, the exercise of clerical powers extended much beyond the institution of the Church, reaching the cultural, social, and political realms equally. Church leaders and the clergy, in general, were by their office in a position to define morality, and thus to influence or regulate practically all essential aspects of women's life – from their role in the society and the family till their intellectual endeavours.

This sort of harm and injustice has been coined by the British philosopher Miranda Fricker as *epistemic injustice*. She defines this situation as a distinctive type of injustice when someone is wronged specifically in her capacity of knower, informant, or participant in the community's production or sharing of knowledge.[2] The scenarios quoted in the introduction are, in fact, textbook examples of how epistemic injustice operates. Hence, in the following, we will

---

[2] Miranda Fricker, *Epistemic Injustice: Power and the Ethics of Knowing* (Oxford University Press: Oxford 2007).

connect Fricker's theory with the sources and manifestations of epistemic injustice, as well as the practices that kept it going for so long in the institution of the Church. I will demonstrate why this theory can provide an invaluable contribution to the discussions on the intersections of clerical power, knowledge/or claim to knowledge, and gender.

In her theory, Fricker brings together innovatively the issues of power, knowledge, and participation in knowledge production and sharing. Her attention goes primarily to the ethical and political dimensions of processes of knowledge exchange. This is one of the most influential theories to have emerged in philosophy in recent years. The impact of her work has been enormous, and her conceptual frame has been used in many contexts: from human rights issues in general or specific forms of discrimination (based on gender, racial or other elements), in the healthcare context or for the analysis of concerns regarding climate change. Fricker distinguishes two forms of epistemic injustice: *hermeneutical* and *testimonial*.

The first one, *hermeneutical injustice* belongs to the domains of understanding and interpretation, and it refers to situations when due to unequal power relations, some people are denied the access to epistemic goods (such as education, knowledge, or interpretive discourses). Further, due to the lacunae thus created in their conceptual resources, they would also be unable to formulate their experiences and interpret their world. Fricker defines this as: "the injustice of having some significant area of one's social experience obscured from collective understanding owing to structural identity prejudice in the collective hermeneutic resource."[3] This marginalization has also a direct consequence the lack of active participation in the pool of social meanings.

In our case, although women represent the majority group in the active life of the Catholic community, the ones without whom the pews would be empty, and most activities would be stagnating, until the end of the 20th century, they had minimal access to knowledge shaping and sharing tasks. Male clergy have formulated the doctrine of the Church, and this failed to capture the experiences of lay people in general and women in particular. Women have been prevented from participation in creating and shaping hermeneutical understanding in the Church, simply because they were excluded from theologising or interpreting the Bible. Hence, they also lacked the conceptual means and opportunities to articulate their lived experience.

---

[3] Fricker, *Epistemic Injustice*, 155.

Moreover, the official religious discourse has been used to justify women's invisibilization and silencing. The Church as a shaper of morals and social influencer has played for long centuries a significant role in initiating, orchestrating, and conducting the persecution of women who expressed a claim to knowledge. Throughout history, women were judged as not corresponding to gender norms if only they expressed their wish for access to knowledge, reading and studying, sharing ideas, or speaking up in a public context. These gender norms have been regulating and restricting the production and dissemination of knowledge. Anyone deviating from these norms was considered dangerous; hence, persecuted, tortured, sanctioned, or robbed of their lives.

The second form, *testimonial injustice* occurs when due to structural inequalities, a hearer fails to treat the speaker as a source of knowledge, systemically questioning, censoring, or finally discarding her testimonies. Fricker argues that this form of injustice is primarily a matter of credibility deficit, due to the lower status of the epistemic agent or the prevailing negative stereotypes around her person. For instance, those who do not possess a certain social standing are ignored or dismissed, so they cannot participate in the production or exchange of knowledge.

Testimonial injustice can occur in a one-on-one transactional exchange when a member of the clergy does not personally give credit to the knowledge of a woman due to the prejudices deeply embedded in his education or culture.[4] However, instead, we would rather zoom out to the systemic manifestations of testimonial injustice on a structural level. Due to longstanding patriarchal ideas, practices and implicit biases, women members of the church in general and women theologians, in particular, have been positioned as less than competent knowers. They have been hermeneutically marginalized and their testimonies systemically dismissed. We refer here not only to the silencing of women's voices in the discipline of Theology, but all acts of restricting their access to knowledge, interpretation of their own experiences, and the sharing of knowledge across the centuries. We use testimony in a broad sense, as being able to speak and to be heard, to narrate and interpret, to participate, to dissent and to be believed. Even though these are crucial prerogatives of membership in any community, the lay faithful have been to date prevented from participating in fair epistemological exchanges in the institution of the Church.

---

[4] Fricker distinguished between transactional and structural varieties of testimonial injustice, and she focused mainly on the one-on-one individual exchanges.

The Sources of Epistemic Injustice in the Catholic Church

As we said, women's voices have been almost entirely shut out of theological reflection until the second half of the 20th century. Official Church teaching in its current form is the product of exclusively male members. The long history of the development and interpretation of Church doctrine and practice is also a man-made history. Male members of the Church have decided what orthodoxy was and they formed people's common understanding of what orthopraxis should be. They used their authority to limit, dismiss or silence all forms of alterity in attitudes and knowledges. The same way, Canon Law, the church's legislation applying to Christian life has been formulated without any input of women. Moreover, a whole set of canons has been sustaining to date the inequality of the sexes.[5] And last, but not least, the liturgical language of the Church still renders women invisible. The institution of the Church has thus created, shaped and sustained a system in which women have been denied the status of epistemic agents.

The main strategies of women's silencing were: the non-sharing or unjust sharing of epistemic goods; the unjust distribution of epistemic authority; unequal hermeneutical participation (denying women access to decision-making in councils, synods or acts of public teaching and speech such as sermons). In the following, we will review a few of the historical sources and contemporary manifestations of these specific forms of injustice.

Persisting Negative stereotypes and Suppressive Female Roles

Some of the most significant sources of epistemic injustice in the Church have been the long persisting negative stereotypes and prejudices against women. Our theological tradition has, implicitly or explicitly, provided a negative characterization of 'women' and the 'feminine' millennia-long. Already during the first centuries of Christianity, the church fathers created and sustained such stereotypes about women and their weak, sinful nature. Women were regarded as inferior and weak in both intellect and character. While they perceived men as primarily spiritual beings, women were characterized as carnal beings defined by their sexuality and lust. Hence, the church fathers outdid each other in describing them in the vilest and profoundly dehumanizing ways.

---

[5] For instance, women do not even enjoy the full rights and duties of lay people as the role of reader and acolyte are still explicitly reserved to lay men (c. 230). Further, women are excluded the positions of judges in the diocesan courts (c. 1421 §2), all these roles being reserved for priests (c. 1421 §1) or deacons (c. 266 §1).

The patriarchal interpretation of the fall narrative was primarily at the root of these ideas. Tertullian, Chrysostom, Augustine, Jerome – they all blamed women for the fall and the eviction from paradise. They identified women with Eve, who through her disobedience, introduced sin into the world, causing the death of all human race. Therefore, they warned men against these lustful temptresses who continuously reproduced Eve's initial temptation of Adam.

For instance, Tertullian in his *Apparel of Women* referred to women as the originators of sin: "And do you not know that you are (each) an Eve? [...] You are the devil's gateway: you are the unsealer of that (forbidden) tree: you are the first deserter of the divine law: you are she who persuaded him whom the devil was not valiant enough to attack. You destroyed so easily God's image, man. On account of your desert – that is, death – even the Son of God had to die."[6] So an even more important consequence of the patristic exegesis of the fall was that our theological tradition and more specifically our soteriology had been built around the dichotomy of female sinfulness versus male salvific action. Based on this core myth of the Judeo-Christian tradition, women had to atone for their collective guilt and redeem themselves by the gender roles assigned to them. The church fathers concluded that it was according to the natural order for men to rule over women and for women to be subservient to their husbands.

Further, they based their teaching on women's inferior position in the church and the family on The Epistles of Paul.[7] A passage often misused in this regard was the pronouncement from the First Letter of Paul to Timothy (1:2,11-14) stating that women were not allowed to teach nor communicate their faith in public, due to their inherent sinfulness and moral corruption: "A woman must receive instruction silently and under complete control. I do not permit a woman to teach or to have authority over a man. She must be quiet. For Adam was formed first, then Eve. Further, Adam was not deceived, but the woman was deceived and transgressed."[8] John Chrysostom, in his Homily IX on this same passage, contended that because Eve sinned, all women were punished with subjection: "The woman taught once, and ruined all. On this account therefore he saith, let her not teach. But what is it to other women, that she suffered this?

---

[6] Tertullian, *Chapter I. Introduction: Modesty in Apparel Becoming to Women, in Memory of the Introduction of Sin into the World Through a Woman* (http://www.tertullian.org/anf/anf04/anf04-06.htm, 28 April 2020).

[7] The passages often cited and used as a justification for gender inequality were: 1Corinthians 11:7-9, 1Corinthians 14:33-35 and Ephesians 5:22-23.

[8] *The New American Bible, Revised Edition* (Saint Benedict Press: Charlotte, NC 2010).

It certainly concerns them; for the sex is weak and fickle, and he is speaking of the sex collectively. For he says not Eve, but 'the woman', which is the common name of the whole sex, not her proper name. Was then the whole sex included in the transgression for her fault? As he said of Adam, After the similitude of Adam's transgression, who is the figure of Him that was to come" (Rom. 5:14); so here the female sex transgressed, and not the male. Shall not women then be saved? Yes, by means of children (…) God has granted you another opportunity of salvation, by the bringing up of children, so that you are saved, not only by yourselves, but by others."[9]

The patristic influence on later thinking was so profound that the idea of women's inferiority has been reiterated and reinforced by Saint Thomas Aquinas a thousand years later. Even much later, up to the late 19th century, encyclicals proclaimed the inferiority of women, insisting on the headship of men over women in marriage and condemning as heretics those who taught the equality of the sexes. Trivialized preservations of the Fall narrative persisting to date everywhere around the globe are still caricaturing and undermining women's trustworthiness.

What is the harm perpetrated in these cases? First of all, due to the patristic misinterpretations of the Fall narrative centered around the question of knowledge and access to knowledge, women suffered a significant credibility deficit. They were deemed epistemically untrustworthy, and their experiences, testimonies, knowledge have been invalidated, discounted, or silenced. Hence, also, women's lived experiences of religious life, their understanding of God and faith have been dismissed by the dominant group. Secondly, not being taken seriously as a knowing subject meant not being respected in a fundamental human capacity. The harm and damage incurred were at once moral and epistemological. In this regard, Fricker emphasized that while at instances testimonial injustice could have minor consequences, the harm was growing in gravity when it was persistent and systematic.

An indirect and more implicit way of epistemic silencing and invisibilization was prescribing women passivity, sacrifice, and selflessness as typically feminine virtues. Some of the ways of keeping women in a silent, powerless position are deeply hidden in the hagiography and spiritual tradition of the Church. Men

---

[9] Saint Chrysostom, "Homily IX. 1 Timothy ii. 11-15", in: Philip Schaff (ed.), *Homilies on Galatians, Ephesians, Philippians, Colossians, Thessalonians, Timothy, Titus, and Philemon* (T&T Clark: Edinburgh and Eerdmans: Grand Rapids, MI 1988), Nicene and Post-Nicene Fathers series 1, 13. (https://www.ccel.org/ccel/schaff/npnf113.v.iii.x.html, 29 April 2020).

formulated, shaped and set the criteria for sanctity and wrote the hagiographies. All through the centuries of our history, the vast majority of female saints canonized by the Church and set as role models for women were examples of endurance, humbleness, and obedience, who kept silent even in the face of male power abuse and suppression. Even the official teaching of the Church on women and their role in the world and the family has been dictating a passive, servile role. The feminine model invoked with consistency to reinforce and sacralize this subordination and passivity of women was Mary, the Mother of Jesus.

Hermeneutic Marginalization and Epistemic Labour Invalidation

In most places, women have been admitted to theological training only in the second part of the 20th century. For instance, the Gregorian University opened its doors to women's training in 1965, the first PhD defended by a woman was in 1973. The timing was approximately the same in other Western European countries, such as Germany and Belgium. In the United States, the admission happened a bit earlier, as specific courses opened to women in the fifties. By the eighties, some women theologians were already enjoying a particular position and voice in academia.

In the recent decennia, women theologians have not been so much prevented from the process of knowledge production, as from the authoritative forms of sharing it. Despite the massive corpus of work delivered since the seventies, for women theologians in general and feminist ones in particular, it has been disproportionately harder to complete epistemic tasks. Deeply embedded gender biases have been undermining the credibility of their theological work. Primarily the contributions not conforming to mainstream theological methods and preoccupations, have been disregarded, devalued, and systematically dismissed as not real scholarship. As Foucault's theorizing of the power/knowledge nexus puts it, their knowledges "have been disqualified as non-conceptual knowledges, as insufficiently elaborated knowledges: naïve ... hierarchically inferior knowledges ... that are below the required level of erudition and scientificity."[10] The works dealing with women's disadvantaged position in the Church or any topic questioning the foundations of clerical hegemony have been harshly invalidated by mainstream theology. Assuming feminist labels in one's publications could imply destroying one's epistemic credibility and all opportunity to pursue an academic career.

---

[10] Michel Foucault, *Society Must Be Defended: Lectures at the Collège de France, 1975-1976*, translated by David Macey (Picador Press: New York 2003), 7.

Even after half a century of feminist contributions to the theological landscape, most male theologians, academics or members of the clergy do not show the openness and willingness to familiarize themselves with women's work. One of the theorists of epistemic resistance, José Medina qualifies this attitude as a form of *willful hermeneutical ignorance*.[11] He zooms into the characters of privileged subjects and refers to this attitude as a culpable state arising out of a cluster of epistemic vices: epistemic arrogance, laziness, and closed-mindedness. He calls them epistemically spoiled: "the powerful can be spoiled not only by enjoying in a disproportionate way the privilege of knowing (or, rather, being assumed to know) but also by having the privilege of not knowing or of not needing to know. Sometimes there are entire domains that people in a position of privilege do not have to familiarize themselves with."[12]

Even if the injustice being thus inflicted is not deliberate but emerging from "residual" bias and prejudices inherited from a long tradition of patriarchal views, dismissing the voice and input of more than half of the community is a sign of moral failure. Besides, the effects of the credibility deficit suffered by women can run very deep: if someone experiences persistent testimonial injustice, she may lose confidence in her intellectual abilities to such an extent that she would be hindered in her education or intellectual development. And if we understand theology as more than an intellectual endeavour, and rather as personal "faith seeking understanding", then women might also experience a profound moral dissonance and a real crisis of faith because their community which confesses egalitarian values, is systematically discriminating them.

Scrutiny, Canonical Warnings, and Censorship

Critically inquisitive and dissenting voices have never really been appreciated in the Catholic Church, nor tolerated as expressions of a sincere quest for meaning. The Church has a long and disheartening history of silencing, ostracising, and removing those who raised issues which could shake the structural foundation of power concentrated in the clergy. So, a more outspoken way of silencing has undoubtedly been the exercise of doctrinal authority.

---

[11] José Medina, *The Epistemology of Resistance: Gender and Racial Oppression* (Oxford University Press: Oxford 2012). Medina's account of epistemic injustice departs from Fricker's in some points that can be especially insightful for our analysis. He develops for instance the idea of responsibility of the privileged ones who commit epistemic injustice.

[12] Medina, *The Epistemology of Resistance*, 32.

When analysing the meaning and practice of ecclesial authority, we could resort to the theories around regimes of power/knowledge which intersect Fricker's concerns.[13] Since the 4th century, the institution of the Church had been enmeshed with monarchical forms of power in which church leaders played the role of guardians of knowledge. Throughout the history of Christianity, various levels and forums were set up to monitor and admonish theological work, from local or regional doctrinal committees to centralized ones such as the Congregation for the Doctrine of the Faith. These forums were charged with prescribing disciplinary actions whenever they deemed to discover doctrinal irregularities. Church leaders have thus basically determined who can speak and what counted as correct and true. In order to maintain a unitary discourse, the dissenters have been marginalised or silenced.[14]

Even in our days, many of women's theoretical and practical preoccupations, such as the concerns for inclusivity and social justice have been scrutinised, censored and silenced by doctrinal forums at both national and Vatican levels. Feminist theologians, religious sisters have been pioneering in areas which mainstream male theologians consider as doctrinal minefields. Women have attended to contemporary human experience and the empirical reality, raising difficult questions about official teachings which seemed at variance with believers' deepest intuitions and experiences. They tackled such issues, lending their voice to the voiceless, the marginalised and ostracised of our societies. As a reaction, they were confronted with investigations and various severe sanctions, from the suspension of their activities and tasks to ex-communication. Such an example would be the investigation of the *Leadership Conference of Women Religious* in the United States, which started in 2012 under the authorisation of Pope Benedict. This scrutiny concluded that the sisters had challenged the church teaching on homosexuality, the ordination of women, and the healthcare reform. Similar action was often taken against the theological work of individuals. For instance, the Congregation for the Doctrine of the Faith scrutinised professor Margaret Farley's work *Just Love: A Framework for Christian Sexual Ethics* (2006) and contended that her theological method was

---

[13] Amy Allen, "Foucault and Epistemic Injustice", in: Ian James Kid et al. (eds.), *The Routledge Handbook of Epistemic Injustice* (Routledge: London 2017), 187-194; Foucault, *Discipline and Punish: The Birth of the Prison*, translated by Alan Sheridan (Vintage Books: New York 1978).

[14] Steven G. Ogden, *The Church, Authority, and Foucault: Imagining the Church as an Open Space of Freedom* (Routledge: London 2017).

not consistent with authentic Catholic theology, due to its understanding of the role of the Church's Magisterium, its method and attendance to contemporary experience. Many more women theologians who addressed thorny issues in the fields of sexual or medical ethics received warnings, sanctions, or have been excommunicated.[15]

Moreover, as we have illustrated it in the part dealing with the negative stereotypes, Christian theology built on a long tradition of debates and arguments regarding women's moral, intellectual and natural shortcomings. These negative views on women and their sinful nature fueled many forms of harsh doctrinal persecution at different moments in history.

For instance, during the late Middle-Ages women who devoted themselves to different fields of human knowledge, going beyond the limits of the gender roles ascribed to them were regarded as suspicious. As all formal access to knowledge and education was under male-control, women who operated outside the realm of men's authority were perceived as a threat. Hence, one of the strategies to consolidate patriarchal power was to directly suppress and prosecute women who mastered knowledges beyond the control of Church authorities (such as medicine, biology).[16] This resulted in massive violence against female healers, midwives who were all labelled as witches at some point in history. Feminist historical critique uncovered horrendous stories of persecution of women at the hands of the Church through the collaboration of inquisitors (especially in the 14th–17th centuries).

Witch hunts had at their base the previously mentioned prejudices on women's weakness of character inherited from the church fathers and the theology of their times. Medieval theology still saw women as descendants of Eve, temptresses and possible associates of the devil. Besides, the medieval Church had significant power in influencing social ideologies. *Malleus Maleficarum* (1487), is just one of the works which illustrate how misogyny and negative

---

[15] For instance, Sister Margaret McBride, a hospital executive and member of St. Joseph's Hospital Ethics Committee in Phoenix, Arizona was relieved of her position and excommunicated for approving the termination of the life-threatening, 11-week pregnancy of a 27-year-old mother of four. Or, Sister Jeannine Gramick spent three decades building a pioneering ministry to the gay and lesbian community, despite relentless and unsuccessful efforts made by then Cardinal Ratzinger to silence her and ban her work.

[16] For instance, the women who acted as healers in their communities were in the possession of popular wisdom transmitted orally from one generation to the other. The healing practices and the medicinal applications of many herbs and plants could have costed Hildegard von Bingen her life just 200–300 years later.

stereotypes could impact the societal views on women. This work written by the Dominican monks Kramer and Sprenger became the manual of witch hunts. It listed a whole set of typically feminine weaknesses which made women susceptible to sin and an easy prey to the devil. To build credibility for his book, Kramer relied on quotes from the church fathers and Aquinas about why women were more likely to be led astray. At his request, pope Innocent VIII issued the bull known as *Summis desiderantes* (1484) in which he acknowledged the practice of witchcraft and condemned it as the worst of all heresies. The pope also authorized Kramer and Sprenger to prosecute witchcraft in Germany.

Clerical Status: Epistemic Privilege and Credibility Excess

Even though all the elements mentioned before contributed to epistemic injustice in the Church, the primary source from which all of them originate is the two-tiered lay-clergy structure itself. This asymmetry has created two epistemic classes, one of knowers and the other of sub-knowers, which have been sustained to date. According to the official doctrine of the Church, the community is made up of a teaching part *(docens)* and a taught part *(discens)*: "In the dominant episteme, the laity made up the *ecclesia discens*, or that element of the church taught by the hierarchy, and the hierarchy existed as *ecclesia docens*, or the teaching church."[17] The pre-Vatican II neo-scholastic understanding of the Church viewed truth and revelation as coming from God through the hierarchy to the faithful in a top-down fashion. This pyramidal, hierocratic ecclesial model implied that reception of doctrine was perceived as a unidirectional movement from teacher *(magisterium)* to receiver *(fideles)*.

Even though Christianity started out as an equality-based community, it gradually transformed into a hierarchical structure, and the tasks initially shared among the members have been later concentrated on the person of the priest. While the clergy received all the authority of knowledge production and sharing, lay people have been placed in a passive, receptive position, and this prescribed a leader/follower dynamic.

Along the centuries, as a result of this epistemic privilege and credibility excess enjoyed by the members of the clergy, a whole set of attitudes and practices had been constructed around priesthood. In order to contextualize the power dynamics operating to date inside the Catholic community, we need to look into the

---

[17] Mark Kowalewski, *All Things to All People. The Catholic Church Confronts the AIDS Crisis* (SUNY Press: Albany, NY 1994), 132.

development of clerical status itself. A mere glimpse into the history of the Church reveals that during its first millennium, priesthood comprised a more restricted territorial and ministerial jurisdiction. Up to the 12th-13th century, ordination meant being entrusted with leadership and liturgical role for a specific community; it encompassed at the same time election as its starting point and consecration as its term. The term *ordinatio* signified the fact of being designated and consecrated to take up a particular place, or better a specific function, *ordo*, in the community and at its service.[18] This definition has gradually shifted, and by the 12th century, ordination came to signify the investment with an irrevocable power to be exercised in any community in the universal church.

Further, a very potent source of epistemic privilege is the triple office priests are granted in ordination, namely the office of *teaching* (*munus docendi*), *governing* (*munus regendi*), and *sanctifying* (*munus sanctificandi*). Through ordination and the so-called concomitant ontological change they undergo, priests are formed to act as alter Christus – other Christs. They "are configured to Christ in such a way that they are able to act in the person of Christ the head."[19] First of all, the *teaching munus* implies that they possess a transcendental warrant to claim knowledge over what is truthful and right in issues of faith and morals. When they speak in the name of Christ and the Church, when they preach and teach, they do this with an authority that no member of the laity can ever enjoy (*Presbyterorum ordinis*, n. 5). Secondly, the priest, as a sharer in Christ's kingship, can also exercise a *governing function* (*Presbyterorum Ordinis*, n. 6–7). The conferred pastoral power covers the legislative, judicial, and punitive aspects in the life of the community. And last, through *the sacerdotal power* invested on them in ordination, they become mediators of God's grace or forgiveness in the sacraments. As such, if Catholic priests are seen as mediators between God and humans, linking the human and divine realms, their role is utterly indispensable.

The epistemic authority has further been reinforced by liturgical acts and language. The transcendental dimensions of priestly status have been deeply embedded in the catholic public imagination through the discourses, which

---

[18] See: Yves Congar, "My Path-findings in the Theology of Laity and Ministries", in: *The Jurist* 32 (1971), 180.

[19] See: *Dogmatic Constitution on the Church. Lumen Gentium* n. 28 (1964). (http://www.vatican.va/archive/hist_councils/ii_vatican_council/documents/vat-ii_const_19641121_lumen-gentium_en.html 11 November 2019); *Decree on the Ministry and Life of Priests/Presbyterorum ordinis* n. 2 and n. 13 (1965). (http://www.vatican.va/archive/hist_councils/ii_vatican_council/documents/vat-ii_decree_19651207_presbyterorum-ordinis_en.html 11 November 2019).

could reach the faithful (the language of the liturgy, spiritual writings and catechesis). The theologically uneducated lay people were exposed to the essential points of the theology of priesthood every time they participated in a liturgical service. The over-emphasis of the divine selection, indelible mark, the role of mediation between God and humans, and the ontological difference acquired in the order became thus the bedrock of clerical identity and their status in the communities. The elevated, metaphorical language of piety and obedience used in the liturgy obscured the asymmetrical power relations. French sociologist Pierre Bourdieu argued that euphemisms and the very abstract vocabulary played a crucial role in the Catholic Church's reproduction of inequality between the hierarchy and the laity. Church officials used this language "to inoculate themselves from the acknowledgement of the real truth of church practices and to convince the laity (and others) that there is nothing arbitrary about hierarchical power and the clerical privilege it embeds."[20]

Last, but not least, the idea of the priest as someone set apart due to his divine calling has also been closely associated with him as a person endowed with particular virtues. However, this moral authority and credibility are not (necessarily) based on personal virtues, but on the power invested in ordination and the constructs emerging from this. As the sacrament of order would endow the members of the clergy with a sanctifying grace enabling them to lead a holy life, the role of personal morals became minimised or lost out of sight. Moreover, the sacramental powers operated 'mechanistically,' meaning that the personal merit of the priest would not affect the quality of the sacraments conferred by him.

The divide between the class of clerics possessing all the governing power and the laity restricted to a followers' obedient role, resulted as we know in a plethora of abusive practices and unethical behaviour patterns. The overemphasis of ontological difference often contributed to a somehow aloof attitude, the sense of superiority and entitlement prevailing among some ordained men. Besides, the demographic reality of priest shortage has given rise to lowered selection criteria and minimalist expectations concerning the moral, spiritual, and intellectual character of the candidates for the priesthood.

---

[20] Michele Dillon, "The Catholic Church's Euphemization of Power", in: *National Catholic Reporter* 15 (February/2019) (https://www.ncronline.org/news/accountability/catholic-churchs-euphemization-power 15 August 2019); see also: Pierre Bourdieu, *Practical Reason: On the Theory of Action* (Stanford University Press: Redwood City, CA 1998).

All public revelations of cases of sexual abuse started as a competition between the word of a clergy member to be trusted by virtue of his divine selection and his assumed moral superiority and the word of the victims (be it children or adults, women or men). These abominable conditions could be sustained for such a long time due to a well-established culture of obedience on which the pastoral relations were built. If the priest was the man of God who continued Christ's ministry on earth, he was also perceived as the one who could cut people off from the kingdom of God. Hence, understanding clericalism is crucial for grasping the various manifestations of abuse of power, as well as the epistemic harms suffered by all those who advocated for the discriminated or silenced groups in the Church.

The economy of credibility is a quite complicated issue and a site of numerous intersecting aspects. For instance, today, the members of clergy enjoy quite varying degrees of authority and credibility in different regions of the world. In the Western world, their societal influence and authority have significantly declined already in the second part of the 20th century. In more traditional societies from Eastern Europe to Latin America or African countries, the clergy has been enjoying until recently a quite authoritative role. This positioning has partly contributed to the delayed outburst of the abuse crisis in these areas. If we look at the example of the recent outburst of the abuse crisis in Poland, we will understand that the more traditional Catholic a country is, the harder it is to break through the layers of taboo and cover-up. Even though the cases coming to the light today are at least as old as the ones revealed in other parts of the world much earlier, in traditional settings, they surface with greater difficulty. On many sites around the world, this drama has not even managed to unfold.

Epistemic Smothering and the Culture of Cover-up

Feminist philosopher Kristie Dotson identified a subcategory of testimonial injustice, called *testimonial smothering* when the speaker self-silences for fear that her testimony will be misinterpreted or rejected, when one "perceives one's immediate audience as unwilling or unable to gain the appropriate uptake of proffered testimony."[21] For instance, although the first extensive reports on the abuse of nuns in the church go back to the 1990s, the scale at which the reports come up today confirms the fact that most of the victims kept silent for fear of the consequences. Personal narratives reveal that raped

---

[21] Kristie Dotson, "Tracking Epistemic Violence, Tracking Practices of Silencing", in: *Hypatia* 26 (2011), 244.

nuns did not dare to complain to their superiors, because they knew they would not be given credit or even worse, they would be blamed for seducing a member of the clergy. Cases from India, Africa, and Europe confirmed that those who finally spoke up revealing the abuse they suffered, have been intimidated, ostracized, dismissed from their communities even when pregnant.

Epistemic smothering is the reason why in most cases no complaints or no criminal charges have been filed. The reactions of disbelief and the unwillingness of Church officials to acknowledge or handle the cases of abuse were nothing else than expressions of profound testimonial injustice. Survivors have been searching for listeners among those whose role would have been by virtue of their ministry to support the vulnerable. Instead, they have been blamed even with outright accusations of seduction. Moreover, when a member of the clergy or the entire group invested with significant moral authority denied the lived experience of survivors, they were re-experiencing epistemic injustice. Personal stories of survivors confirmed that the repeated experience of testimonial injustice – being questioned, dismissed, blamed often resulted in new traumas. This was especially damaging to their spiritual lives, causing a crisis of faith and alienation from their communities.

Cover-up has been very much a part of the Catholic institutional culture and the commonly used policy in cases of clerical misconduct.[22] The culture of secrecy, internal protocols, the closed circuits of communication such as those revealed in *Crimen Sollicitationis* (1962) enabled these strategies.[23] The explosion of the abuse crisis revealed that the institution of the church protected the clergy at all costs, hiding their crimes as long as it was feasible. The mere acknowledgement of the problems would have meant exposing the system to critique and weakening their absolute power. Under the guise of protecting the good name of the Church, they were defending the authority and sovereign power of clergy; they deemed these as more important than the protection of the most vulnerable or the commitment to the values of the Gospel. On the other hand, everything has been done to silence the victims and their families: dissuading them at all costs from filing official complaints, imposing legal clauses in settlements.

---

[22] Véronique Magron, moral theologian and president of the Conference of Religious Sisters and Brothers in France, uses the term *omerta* to describe this code of silence and secrecy. This term is typically used in the context of criminal organisations as the mafia.

[23] The Supreme Sacred Congregation of the Holy Office, *Instruction on the Manner of Proceeding in Causes involving the Crime of Solicitation*, (Vatican Polyglot Press: Vatican 1962). (http://www.vatican.va/resources/resources_crimen-sollicitationis-1962_en.html, 6 September 2019)

Epistemic Resistance: From Feminists *avant la lettre* to Contemporary Dissenters

Women Resisting Epistemic Injustice

Even if women theologians' formal participation in epistemic labour goes back only half a century, women had been involved in denouncing and resisting epistemic oppression much before this time. Throughout the history of Christianity, there have emerged courageous, intelligent and erudite figures who raised their voice against the injustice of women's epistemic silencing. We had some outstanding examples of feminists *avant la lettre* who resisted and tackled epistemic injustice in all its manifestations, such as Hildegard von Bingen, Catherine of Siena, Theresa of Avila, Mary Ward or Sor Juana Inés de la Cruz.

Numerous women saints challenged and transgressed the established norms of female roles. In their attempts to reform corrupted institutions and practices, they have opposed the Church authorities. As a reaction, they suffered severe persecutions; their educational and spiritual projects got suppressed. Some of them enjoyed though a certain level of authority and had the opportunity to speak up and teach. Often it was due to their visions and mystical experiences they were able to gain support and credibility. For instance, Catherine of Siena and Hildegard of Bingen used very smartly the arguments of their mystical revelations with the purpose of corrective reformative interventions.

Hildegard (1098–1179), whose genius spanned many fields (including science, music, visual arts, healing, and mysticism) contested the negative stereotypes affecting women and their unfair treatment in the Church. By assuming the role of a channel for divine messages, she gained official support and dispensation for preaching to the masses. She went on preaching tours across Germany and delivered not very flattering sermons about the moral corruption of the clergy. She entered into conversations, debates and advised abbots, bishops, emperors, and Popes. Her controversial ideas resulted in her being reprimanded by the clergy, but she could go unpunished as the pope acknowledged and respected her as a visionary.

Another such example is that of Teresa of Avila (1515–1582) who spent most of her religious life under the scrutiny of the Inquisition. When she set out to reform the Carmelite order, she met harsh opposition and myriad trials at the hand of the Inquisition and the priests appointed to spiritually guide her. In her autobiography, she remarked that these persecutions were enough to drive her insane. At a time when women were forbidden to practice contemplative prayer without the strict guidance of male spiritual directors, Teresa exhorted her sisters to believe in their own ability to access God and continue on their contemplative path.[24]

The 17th-century Mexican scholar, Sor Juana Inés de la Cruz was an autodidact, writer, poet, and philosopher. She contested the prohibition of women's education and the misogynistic biblical misinterpretations which led men to bar women from studying. Sor Juana criticised the Church's oppressive treatment of women, and she claimed intellectual equality. In her *Respuesta* (1691) she brilliantly used both the Scripture and patristic texts to support women's right to intellectual endeavours. She discredited Paul's statement ordering women to be silent and its misogynous interpretation. Further, she drew on the tradition of wise women (*mujeres sabias*) of the Bible and Church history, demonstrating that in the past, women had been allowed intellectual freedoms with great benefit to the community. Her spirit of independent inquiry, thirst for knowledge and advocacy for women's right to intellectual endeavours got her in conflict with the church establishment. Finally, she was banned from her library, silenced, forbidden to share her ideas and knowledge through writings.

Feminist Scholarship and the Reconstruction of Herstory
Even though intellectual efforts to counter epistemic injustice have popped up at various moments in our history, until the second half of the 20th century, women have not really enjoyed access to formal theological education. The fact that they were deprived of access to theological knowledge implied as well that they absented from the development of hermeneutical and epistemic tools (language, concepts, symbols, theology, liturgy). Hence, they could not participate in the areas that created the hermeneutical understanding in the Church. It was after Vatican II that Catholic women started to pursue theological education in increasing numbers.

Feminist scholarship came first of all, as an expression of resistance to the patriarchal regime of truth. During the initial stage of feminist theological endeavours, starting with the 1970s, women tackled what we defined in the previous as *hermeneutic injustice*. The primary aim was to deconstruct the hegemony of the male-made discourse of theology. Deconstruction involved a process of questioning and critical reading of centuries-old misinterpretations of religious texts. Feminist scholars set out to identify patriarchal knowledge practices and address the various forms of exclusion and infringement on the

---

[24] Teresa of Avila, *Interior Castle: Classics of Western Spirituality*, translated by Kieran Kavanaugh and Otilio Rodriguez (Paulist Press: New York 1979), 83 and 101.

epistemic agency of women. In order to achieve this, they revisited the mainstream concepts and methods of theologising. They revealed the ideological role of religious discourse in legitimating and inculcating oppressive structures, gender inequality and women's exclusion from knowledge creation and sharing. Awareness-raising of the mechanisms of epistemic marginalization was a critical step towards in the transformation of malestream epistemological frameworks.

Further, they revisited the biblical and historical sources. They created tools to uncover and reconstruct *herstory* (women's version of history*)* from under the deposits of two thousand years of ideological debris. They approached the sources through the lenses of *a hermeneutics of suspicion*. The term coined in the 1970s by Paul Ricoeur has become synonymous with a deconstructive practice of inquiry and interpretation. According to this theoretical approach, there can be no objective or absolute knowledge of the meaning of texts (including literary, philosophical or even biblical texts).[25]

This reading strategy was critically subversive of all forms of power and domination, and its aim was to reveal not only the structures of domination inscribed in texts but also in their interpretations. For instance, a pioneer in this field, biblical scholar Elisabeth Schüssler Fiorenza argued that a feminist reading of the biblical texts should be rooted in suspicion and it should ask whose interests and point of view do these interpretations support in the earthly realm. The ultimate goal was a feminist theological reconstruction. With this in mind she examined male-centred texts in the light of their social-historical contexts and origins. She used the methods of historical criticism to reinterpret the beginnings of the Christian religion. Remembrance, she argued, could operate as a form of *counter-memory*, empowering women to resist experiences of repression. *In Memory of Her* reconstructed early Christian beginnings in terms of a democratic model of *discipleship of equals*.[26]

---

[25] For an introduction and definition of the term see: Hans-Georg Gadamer, "The Hermeneutics of Suspicion", in: Gary Shapiro and Alan Sica (eds.), *Hermeneutics: Questions and Prospects* (University of Massachusetts Press: Amherst 1984), 63; G. D. Robinson, "Paul Ricoeur and the Hermeneutics of Suspicion: A Brief Overview and Critique", *Premise* 8 (1995), 12. (http://individual.utoronto.ca/bmclean/hermeneutics/ricoeur_suppl/Ricoeur_Herm_of_Suspicion.htm 12 November 2019); David Stewart, "The Hermeneutics of Suspicion", *Journal of Literature and Theology* 3 (1989), 296-307.

[26] Elisabeth Schüssler Fiorenza, *In Memory of Her: A Feminist Theological Reconstruction of Christian Origins* (Crossroad Publishing: New York 1983).

Christian feminists looked in particular at the communities of the early church where women were still playing leadership roles – founding and leading church communities (Lydia, Prisca, Euodia and Syntyche), prophesying (Philip's daughters, Corinthian women), teaching (Prisca) or playing the role of apostles (Mary of Magdala).

The language, the doctrine of the Church as well as its imagery and liturgy, created an overwhelming sense of God as male. For this reason, feminist theology set out to create an inclusive language and took a firm methodological commitment to women's lived experience. They designated women's experience as a central methodological concept and the starting point for theological reflection: "the lens through which one does theology", "a filter through which theological sources must pass in order to be included in the doctrine."[27]

Feminism, with its liberatory epistemology, emerged not only to diagnose and contest inherited epistemic hierarchies but also to eliminate structural injustices. After almost two thousand years of unequal hermeneutical participation, marginalisation, exclusion, all-male decision-making and authority, feminist theologians came to denounce and eliminate kyriarchal power relations inside our religious communities. *Kyriarchy* is another term coined by Schüssler Fiorenza in her ground-breaking work *But She Said: Feminist Practices of Biblical Interpretation* (1992). It is a neologism derived from the Greek κύριος (kurios – lord, master) and ἄρχειν (archein – to rule, to dominate) by which she described all intersecting systems of domination based on the rule of a lord/master. By this definition, she extended the focus from sexist relations of discrimination in a patriarchal system to all other forms of oppression.

Feminist theology is a liberation theology sensitive to the intersections of power with gender, race, social and economic vulnerabilities. Hence, feminist scholars have been committed not only to the elimination of women's subordination but promoted inclusivity towards all other oppressed or vulnerable groups – all *wo/men*. Schüssler Fiorenza introduced this spelling to express that feminist concern was directed to all marginalised, women and men equally, independently of race, class, or religion. "Hence the spelling wo/men seeks to communicate that whenever I speak of wo/men I mean not only to include all women, but also to speak of oppressed and marginalized

---

[27] Elizabeth A. Johnson, *She Who Is: The Mystery of God in Feminist Theological Discourse* (Crossroad Publishing: New York 1992), 15.

men. Wo/men must be therefore understood as an inclusive expression, rather than as an exclusive universalized gender term."[28]

Feminist scholarship accomplished very much in these few decennia of struggle against epistemic injustice. Today, thanks to the zealous work of the last 50 years, women are not any longer *only* the objects of man's theologising but also the subjects of theology. Even though they managed to create a more inclusive hermeneutical climate, they have not reached yet the impact they should have on mainstream theological discourse and church practices. The reason is that women are still not in the position to participate in decision-making; they still lack epistemic authority. Accordingly, the feminist efforts have been more recently redirected towards reaching more recognition as knowledge producers.

Lay Reform Movements Leading from Kyriarchy to a Discipleship of Equals
The Church, in its role of a meaning-making community, has created and sustained too long its unfair differentials in epistemic authority. This injustice is insurmountable in the form in which Church governance, doctrine and regulation of morals happen today. José Medina refers to the imperative of epistemic interaction manifested in various forms of activism and political resistance. He underscores the importance of genuine dialogue between groups requiring an attitude of respect, recognition, and enabling "mutual resistance and beneficial friction."[29]

Partly thanks to the monumental work delivered by feminist scholars and advocates, we are testimonies of an encouraging momentum. We are witnessing the emergence of an unprecedented movement of resistance advocating structural change and demanding a renewed moral epistemic conduct from the part of the beholders of power and authority. A significant number of lay initiatives (*Voices of Faith, Future Church, Wijngaards Institute for Catholic Research, The Women's Ordination Conference*) engage today in epistemic resistance, cracking open the spaces of single understandings, making room for women/lay people's voices, experiences, their understanding of faith, God and being in the world as Christians today. They are seeking a more collaborative relationship with the ordained leadership and a more democratic church structure. They are trying to address the moral dissonance experienced between

---

[28] Elisabeth Schüssler Fiorenza, *Jesus: Myriam's Child, Sophia's Prophet: Critical Issues in Feminist Christology* (The Continuum International Publishing Group: London 1994), 191.

[29] Medina, *The Epistemology of Resistance*, 198.

the teachings of the Gospel and clerical abuse of power. They are urging the Church leaders to engage in authentic dialogue, practising the virtue of epistemic justice to restore the credibility of the Church.

Conclusion

Even though women can participate today in the production of knowledge as theologians, teachers, exegetes, ethicists, pastoral associates, they are still unable to participate in sound epistemic practices. Even though in some places they are represented on church bodies and diocesan advisory groups, these are unfortunately still sporadic examples. Even though they share their knowledge and experience on family life and faith in thousands of works, they still follow the synods of the Church from the back rows.[30] This disenfranchisement will persist as long as they cannot enjoy full participation as equals in decision-making bodies, governance and ministries. Epistemic justice and equality will be accomplished, only when our male counterparts lend a listening ear to the imperative of equality inside religious communities.

In order to transform the Catholic Church from a *kyriarchy* into a *discipleship of equals* we need epistemically virtuous men like the Jesuits who opened their Curia in Rome to welcome the censored speakers of the Voices of Faith event; or like some priests who assumed their suspension from ministry just because they advocated equality for women. Until then, we should engage and persist in our epistemic disobedience, challenging the privileged group to unlearn their ignorance and become aware of their oppressive norms and practices. The momentum is asking for more epistemic friction.

Sylvia Hübel is a feminist theologian and bioethicist committed to advocating and promoting women's equal participation in church and society. She earned a Sacrae Theologiae Licentiatus degree in Systematic Theology at the Université Catholique de Louvain with a thesis on *The Deconstruction of Male Discourse in the Theological Work of Elisabeth Schüssler Fiorenza*. Afterwards, she continued her endeavours at the University of Leuven with a PhD thesis on *Women's Lived Experiences of Reproductive Technologies* in a feminist bioethical approach. She furthered her professional skills with postgraduate courses in Family and Sexuality Studies, Bioethics and Psychology. She has held various positions as a researcher,

---

[30] Of the approximately 360 attendees at the Synod on the Family in 2015, only 30 were women who could follow in silence everything from the back pews. They couldn't vote. This was a carefully selected group of married women and women religious, who did not necessarily reflect Catholic women from all walks of life.

adult trainer, teacher, and parliamentary adviser. Besides, she has volunteered in a variety of contexts: parishes and schools, social and healthcare institutions, student residences. Her research interests include theological ethics; medical ethics and humanities (phenomenology of illness, lived experiences of illness and medical care); women's reproductive health and rights; healthcare policy. sylviahubel@gmail.com

Monica Ruset Oanca

Julian of Norwich: The Visible Writings of an Invisible Recluse

Abstract

Julian of Norwich's *Revelations of Divine Love*, written in the 14th century Norwich, described her mystical visions without telling much about her personal life. The article attempts to discuss the contrast between her lack of physical visibility, and the abundance of complex visions which outline quite clearly her theological views. This mystic was an anchorite observing the rules specific to her station, and a few details about her can be learnt from Margery Kempe's autobiography, as a meeting between the two is mentioned. Margery's visit and her trust in Julian's opinion shows how respected the latter was.

Julian's work is not only a recording of religious images, but rather it presents a profound theological insight, which insists on an optimistic understanding of the world and an unshaken confidence in its bright future. Although the official point of view of the Church differs greatly from her perception, and despite the controversial images she depicts sometimes, her text has always been accepted by the Church and has become a point of reference for all Christians interested in a mystical approach to theology. By starting from Julian of Norwich's apparent invisibility, locked inside her cell, the author aims to reveal new aspects of her theology and to probe into the relevance of her work and life for the 21st century society.

Keywords: medieval; mystical theology; optimistic perception.

Resumen

La obra de Juliana de Norwich *Revelaciones del Amor Divino*, escrita en el siglo XIV en Norwich, describe sus visiones místicas sin contar demasiado sobre su vida personal. Este artículo intenta discutir el contraste entre su falta de visibilidad física y sus abundantes y complejas visiones, que subrayan de forma notable su visión teológica. Esta mística fue una ermitaña que observó las normas específicas de su condición. Unos pocos detalles sobre ella se pueden encontrar en la autobiografía de Margery Kempe, puesto que se menciona un encuentro entre ambas.

La obra de Juliana no es solo un registro de imágenes religiosas, sino que también presenta un profundo conocimiento teológico, que hace hincapié en una comprensión optimista del mundo y una confianza inquebrantable en su brillante futuro. Aunque el punto de vista oficial de la Iglesia difiere sobremanera de su percepción, y a pesar de las imágenes controvertidas que a veces describe, su texto siempre ha sido aceptado por la Iglesia y se ha convertido en un punto de referencia para aquellas personas cristianas interesadas en una aproximación mística a la teología. Comenzando por la aparente invisibilidad de Juliana de Norwich, encerrada en su celda, la autora tiene como objetivo revelar nuevos aspectos de su teología e indagar en la relevancia de su vida y obra para la sociedad del siglo XXI.

Palabras clave: Edad Media; teología mística; percepción optimista.

Zusammenfassung

Die *Offenbarungen der göttlichen Liebe* von Juliana von Norwich, geschrieben in Norwich im 14. Jahrhundert, beschreibt ihre mystischen Visionen, ohne viel über ihr persönliches Leben zu sagen. Der Artikel diskutiert den Gegensatz zwischen ihrer fehlenden physischen Sichtbarkeit und dem Überfluss komplexer Visionen, die deutlich ihre theologischen Ansichten umreißen. Diese Mystikerin war eine Einsiedlerin, die die spezifischen Regeln ihres Standortes befolgte. Einige Details über sie können aus Margery Kempes Autobiographie entnommen werden, in der ein Treffen der beiden erwähnt ist. Margerys Besuch und ihr Vertrauen auf Julianas Meinung zeigt, wie sehr letztere respektiert war.

Julianas Werk ist nicht nur eine Aufzeichnung religiöser Bilder, sondern präsentiert vielmehr eine tiefgehende theologische Einsicht, die auf einem optimistischen Verständnis der Welt und einem unerschütterlichen Vertrauen in ihre leuchtende Zukunft besteht. Obwohl der offizielle Standpunkt der Kirche stark von ihrer Wahrnehmung abweicht und trotz kontroversieller Bilder, die sie manchmal zeichnet, wurde ihr Text immer von der Kirche anerkannt und wurde ein Bezugspunkt für alle Christ*innen, die an einem mystischen Zugang zur Theologie interessiert sind. Ausgehend von Julianas offensichtlicher Unsichtbarkeit, eingeschlossen in ihre Zelle, will die Autorin neue Aspekte ihrer Theologie aufdecken und die Relevanz ihres Werkes und Lebens für die Gesellschaft des 20. Jahrhunderts untersuchen.

Schlagwörter: Mittelalter; mystische Theologie; optimistische Wahrnehmung.

> *[...] al shal be wel, and al shal be wel,
> and al manner of thyng shal be wele.*
> Chapter XXVII (the 13th revelation)

Julian of Norwich's work was appreciated in medieval times in the monastic environment. It was often copied by nuns, and a few manuscripts can still be analysed nowadays.[1] However, hardly any facts regarding her personal life are known, and the only fact known with certainty is that she was a recluse in 14th-century Norwich and as such she observed the rules specific to this station, which made her at the same time invisible to and respected by her contemporaries.

The present article will insist on the sharp discrepancy between the lack of information regarding Julian's physical existence (as she is known only by association with the place where she lived and the people she met) and the wealth of information regarding her inner perception of God, which can be clearly inferred from her work. A specific feature of her theology is her insistence on God's kindness and forgiveness, and her conviction which can be summed up in the words "all will be well," despite the existence of sin and pain.

Julian of Norwich's invisibility, as vocation

Medieval records are notorious for omitting women's achievements and thoughts, so it becomes necessary to make an effort in order to bring to light women's contribution to history, and this essay is part of the body of research clearly outlined by Kathleen Biddick and Joan Wallach Scott in their work: *The Shock of Medievalism,* who explain that much recent work in medieval women's history has focused on women mystics in a "vowed effort to rewrite a traditional historiography whose contempt and fear of these women's bodily practices had rendered them 'invisible' [...] the desire to make historical women visible is both the effect of modern visualizing technologies and the possibility for their resignification."[2]

---

[1] There still are eight medieval manuscripts (of which the oldest are: The Amherst Manuscript, early 15th century, The Westminster Manuscript, around 1500, The Paris Manuscript, around 1580 in the region near Antwerp). The first edition of The Revelations of Love was supervised by Serenus Cressy, O.S.B. and was published in 1670 (Julian's Showing of Love in A Nutshell: Her Manuscripts and Their Contexts http://www.umilta.net/tablet.html, 20 November 2019).

[2] Kathleen Biddick and Joan Wallach Scott, *The Shock of Medievalism* (Duke University Press: Durham and London 1998), 135-136.

Up until late 20th century research, our understanding of female mystical devotion was based on medieval male interpretations, as the writing of historical records and the authenticating of cult and miracles were controlled by (clergy)men.[3] Naturally, such a perspective was biased, and thus a more holistic and profound approach is required in order to better comprehend the dynamics of popular devotion to female saints and the benefits 20th century audiences can draw from reading their works.

Details regarding Julian's quiet life, living as an anchoress near Saint Julian Church in Norwich, are almost unknown, and the little information that we have about her existence comes from wills[4] which mentioned her as the beneficiary. Actually, not even her name is known, since the name Julian was the name of the patron saint of the church next to which she resided. Although her solid theological education is indisputable, there is no clear evidence where she acquired it, nor is her social status known but "there is a strong possibility she was a nun at the Benedictine convent at Carrow, a mile from the church of St. Julian's, Conesford, in Norwich where she was later enclosed as an anchoress," according to the introduction of the 2006 edition of her work.[5] It is certain that she lived in Norwich[6] at least between 1393 (when she was mentioned in a will) and 1413 (when she was visited by Margery Kempe), but nothing of the turmoil specific to a prosperous harbour, nor any hint at the Hundred Years' War can be found in her work, which deals strictly with the recording of her mystical experiences and their interpretation for the spiritual benefit of those who read them.

A few details about her can be learnt from Margery Kempe's autobiography (as a meeting between the two is mentioned), and also from *Ancrene Riwle*, the book regulating the life of the recluses· which she probably used in order

---

[3] Margaret Schaus, *Women and Gender in Medieval Europe: An Encyclopedia* (Routledge: New York 2006), 351.

[4] Very often the wills are the most reliable sources with regards to the place were recluses lived, because they were legal documents, and as such they recorded the actual situation, and in addition they were preserved in archives.

[5] Nicholas Watson and Jacqueline Jenkins (eds.), *The Writings of Julian of Norwich* (The Pennsylvania State University Press: Pennsylvania 2006), 4.

[6] It is of importance to point out that she was just one of many other recluses who lived in Norwich anchorage and Blomefield's *History of Norfolk* (vol. iv. p. 81) enumerates other women who lived as recluses there: in 1472 Dame Agnes; in 1481, Dame Elizabeth Scott; in 1510, Lady Elizabeth; in 1524, Dame Agnes Edrygge – as it is mentioned in the introduction to *Revelations of Divine Love*, Recorded by Julian, Anchoress at Norwich, (Methuen & Company: London 1901), xvii.

to organise the practical aspects of her life. Just like other anchoresses, Julian lived all her life in a cell, which had three windows: one for the Holy Communion (which opened inside the church), one for food (the window of the house, used for the maid to communicate with her), and another one that opened into a parlour, where she could talk to people asking for her advice. These means of communication with the outside world were carefully supervised, because seclusion was essential for strengthening her connection with God. Thus *The Ancrene Riwle describes:* "Hold no conversation with any man out of a church window, but respect it for the sake of the holy sacrament which you see therein, and sometimes take your woman to the window of the house; the other men and women to the window of the parlour, to speak when necessary; nor ought you but at these two windows."[7]

It is probably through the parlour window that Margery Kempe talked to Julian, when the former came to ask for the anchorite's advice and support. Unfortunately, they talked exclusively about Margery, or at least this is what she recorded, so there is no information about Julian as a person, her habits or her preferences. Julian's words for Margery were a confirmation of the latter's choice of life and an urge to persevere.[8]

A brief comparison between these two women, who both wrote on mystical issues, may help better understand the religious context in Norfolk area. There is a sharp contrast between the ways in which Julian and Margery chose to express their devotion to God, and this divergence is obvious from the first vision they each received. Despite the fact that they both first saw Jesus Christ while they were gravely ill, so much so that they both believed they would die of their respective illnesses, their visions differed: Julian of Norwich saw Jesus during His Passion, wearing the crown of thorns, whereas Margery Kempe saw Him in the likeness of a pleasant visitor "most beauteous and most amiable."[9]

---

[7] "Ancrene Riwle," paragraph 48–Chapter 2, Of the Senses, part 2: Of Speech, "The Ancrene Riwle" http://readeralexey.narod.ru/Library/AncreneRiwle2.html, 20 November 2019.

[8] "Any creature that has these tokens [the abundant tears whenever she prayed to God], may steadfastly believe that the Holy Ghost dwells in his [Margery's] soul. And much more, when God visits a creature with tears of contrition, devotion or compassion, he may and ought to believe that the Holy Ghost is in his [Margery's] soul. [...] Patience is necessary for you, for in that shall you keep your soul", Margery Kempe, *The Book of Margery Kempe* (Penguin Books: London 2004), 78.

[9] Kempe, *The Book of Margery Kempe*, 42

As a matter of fact, Julian and Margery were situated at opposite ends of the spectrum of 14th century feminine devotion (which encompassed different aspects: nuns, beguines[10] or devout women leading an ordinary existence): the anchorite was invisible, living a quiet existence which involved a certain degree of anonymity, whereas Margery needed to cry out her devotion and her loud tears as well as her outspokenness turned her into a conspicuous, controversial figure[11] everywhere she went. Moreover, people's distrust of her vocation was not surprising, as she was not part of an acknowledged form of consecrated life, a fact which made her vulnerable to accusations of heresy and dissent.

Despite Julian's traditional stance with respect to lifestyle, her work is unique and different from the norm, as it emphasises a distinct mystical path towards God. Julian can hear Jesus's voice loud and clear, and she quotes God's words, an experience which brings about the feeling of comfort, as she feels the constant and strong connection with God. Actually, the word which characterises Julian's *Revelation* is "joy," which is perhaps the first step to feel "bliss." The visions she receives are a constant and inexhaustible source of joy and bliss, which she constantly feels whenever she writes, talks or thinks about God. Therefore, her *Revelations of Divine Love* is not only a recording of mystical visions, but rather presents a profound theological insight, which insists on an optimistic understanding of the world and an unshaken confidence in its bright future.

The image of the Passion of Christ is the first revelation which was granted to her, after her prayer and it is not unexpected since it was the focus of people's devotion in the 14th century. For instance, one of the most famous

---

[10] Although there is no clear evidence of beguinages in England, considering the trade between Norwich and the Low Countries it is probable that the notion was known to Julian' contemporaries. Furthermore, there is an accepted theory that Briton's Arms in Elm Hill (dating from the late 14th century), which is a three-storied timber frame building in Norwich, was used as a residence by several unmarried, or widowed devoted Christian women, making it a kind of beguinage. "Norfolk Record Office" https://norfolkrecordofficeblog.org/2019/11/19/an-elizabethan-beguinage-in-hempstead-cum-eccles-norfolk/, 16 April 2020.

[11] Despite Margery Kempe's preoccupation with listening to and obeying God's will, as well as with respecting the doctrine of the Church, she was often considered an outcast in the 14th-century patriarchal society, which desired and admired silent obedient women. However, she was not unique in such behaviour, as there were other holy women (even saints), who had an abnormal, and even scandalous behaviour: Christina (*Mirabilis*) the Astonishing or Marie of Oignies (both living in the early 13th century), both mentioned in her book; the former was incarcerated twice for her shocking actions, while the latter was described as crying unceasingly for several days during Holy Week.

treasures of Norwich Cathedral was the Despenser Retable (late 14th century), which depicts the Passion of Christ, His crucifixion and Resurrection in five conventional scenes. Unlike these simple and rather static depictions, Julian's words are powerful and emotional, as she insists on details like "the red blood trickle down from under the Garland hot and freshly and right plenteously, as it were in the time of His Passion." While watching closely details from the crucifixion scene, she also experiences a profound feeling of joy: "Trinity fulfilled my heart most of joy."[12] So in this first instance, as well as in all the others, the vivid image of the suffering face of Christ (regardless of how sorrowful it is) awakens in her a feeling of joy, because her mind does not stop at the level of contemplation, but rather it moves beyond, as she understands the spiritual implication of this sufferance, namely it is exactly this sacrifice that opens the way towards salvation.

Unlike other mystical writers, who seem confident in what they experience and what they know (for instance Richard Rolle or the author of the *Cloud of Unknowing*), Julian confesses to a feeling of surprise that she (a simple, ordinary human being) is granted such powerful, and yet intimately warm visions: "full greatly was astonished for wonder and marvel [...] that He that is so reverend and dreadful will be so homely with a sinful creature living in wretched flesh."[13] These two feelings, of joy and of humble astonishment, characterise her work and define the uniqueness of her style setting her apart from other mystical writers.

The Invisible Body of the Female Mystic

Although today there is no trace left of the anchorites' presence, in the 12th century (and up until the 14th century) there were hundreds of them spread all over Europe. This institution was well-known and supported financially not only by affluent people, but also by the city, given that there are documents which attest to the fact that a small amount of the municipality's expenses, one

---

[12] "sodenly the Trinite fullfilled the herte most of joy," Julian of Norwich, chapter IV, the 1st vision. I have used the original medieval text: *The Shewings of Julian of Norwich*, TEAMS Middle English Texts, https://d.lib.rochester.edu/teams/publication/crampton-shewings-of-julian-norwich, 21 November 2019; and the modern version: *Revelations of Divine Love Recorded by Julian, Anchoress at Norwich*, edited by Grace Warrack (Methuen & Company: London 1901).

[13] "full gretly was astonyed for wonder and mervel [...], that He that is so reverend and dredfull will be so homley with a synfull creature liveing in wretched flesh." Julian of Norwich, chapter IV, the 1st vision.

or two percent, were used for the maintenance of the recluses.[14] It shows that this practice was accepted and esteemed by the community. In time though, isolation started to acquire negative connotations, especially since the judicial system used inclosing as penance for female offenders.[15]

Our present effort to make the anchorites' (and Julian's) body visible is partly in contradiction with their desire, as, obviously, one of the purposes of being enclosed was to remain outside the ordinary, daily existence and to focus on their inner spiritual life. It has been pointed out that "Life in an anchorhold offered women protection from intrusive relatives or lustful men and the guarantee that they could not be brushed aside as hypocrites or frauds. They lived in full view of the people, which in itself ruled out deception. It was convincing proof of divine inspiration."[16] Thus, being an anchoress offered at the same time security and a recognised social status, which in time granted her authority in theological matters. Although this choice implied a wish not to be disturbed by her contemporaries, that did not actually mean that the recluse was invisible to them, but rather that she had a profound desire to be extremely visible to God.

However, according to Carolyn Walker Bynum, the emphasis on the salvation of the soul did not imply a neglect of the body, since it was not perceived as something negative, or an impediment to receiving divine revelations. Rather, any reference to the body was an attempt to elevate it, and thus to use it in order to obtain a spiritual benefit "control, discipline, even torture of the flesh is, in medieval devotion, not so much the rejection of physicality as the elevation of it."[17] In Julian's case her physical illness and weakness were the starting point for her revelations. Her prayer is to use bodily suffering in order to be united spiritually with God: "that my body might be fulfilled with mind and feeling of His blessed Passion. For I would that His pains were my pains,

---

[14] Paulette L'Hermite-Leclercq, "Le reclus dans la ville au Bas Moyen Âge," *Journal des Savants* t. 3, no 3-4, 1988, 219-262, hier 254.

[15] L'Hermite-Leclercq believes that one reason for the fall in the number of recluses could be the fact that life imprisonment in a small place resembling a reclusory became a type of punishment which replaced death penalty. Once enforced reclusion (incarceration) became common, voluntary reclusion did not seem so attractive, any more, L'Hermite-Leclercq, "Le reclus dans la ville au Bas Moyen Âge," 256-257.

[16] Anneke B. Mulder-Bakker, *Lives of the Anchoresses: The Rise of the Urban Recluse in Medieval Europe*, (University of Pennsylvania Press: Philadelphia 2005), 46.

[17] Caroline Walker Bynum, *Fragmentation and Redemption*, (Zone Books: New York 1994), 182.

with compassion and afterward longing to God. [...] therefore I desired to suffer with Him."[18]

Moreover, her choice of living in an isolated hermit's cell might tempt the modern audience to consider it as her renunciation of the beautiful aspects of life, and thus a way of suppressing the body and its needs. Nevertheless, this would be a grave misunderstanding of her motivation, for living in the anchorage made it possible for her to shape her life according to her will: "she wanted for her daily living to be measured by the standard of Christ[19] [...] Every thought and action and decision"[20] were motivated by her will to strengthen her connection with Christ. Hence, physical enclosure is only a means of helping her remain completely absorbed by and available to God.

For a bishop blessed the reclusory when the recluse first entered it, she (or he) was under the supervision of the Church. For Julian, this was confirmed by her writings which have been accepted by the Church. However, Julian's authority was not due to her rigorous rendering of the ideas that circulated in the ecclesiastical circles, but to her reputable and chaste station. She did not feel the constraint to rehash ideas which were usually found in sermons, but rather, her work is sometimes unexpectedly original, and one of her most quoted controversial images is her presentation of Christ as Mother: "And furthermore I saw that the Second Person, which is our Mother as anent the Substance, that same dearworthy Person is become our Mother as anent the Sense-soul [...] For in our Mother Christ we profit and increase, and in Mercy He reformeth us and restoreth, and, by the virtue of His Passion and His Death and Uprising, oneth us to our Substance."[21] I will not insist on this image, but I have to point out the feminization of Christ, which stems from the recognition of the fact that traditionally the giver of life, as well as the giver of food, is the mother, in other words, the woman.

This gendered assessment of human behaviour, which regarded obedience and silence as feminine features, may have placed religious men in a rather awkward position, as, in order to follow their vocation, they had to form their

---

[18] "that my body might be fulfilled with minde and felyng of His blissid passion, for I would that His peynes were my peynes, with compassion, and, afterward, longeing to God. [...] therefore I desired to suffer with Him." Julian of Norwich, chapter 3.
[19] Grace Jantzen, *Julian of Norwich: Mystic and Theologian* (Paulist Press: New Jersey 2000), 90.
[20] Jantzen, *Julian of Norwich*, 157.
[21] "And ferthermore I saw that the Second Person, which is our Moder substantial, that same derworthy person is become our Moder sensual [...] For in our Moder Criste we profitten and encresin, and in mercy He reformith us and restorith; and, be the vertue of His passion and His deth and uprisyng, onyth us to our substance" – Julian of Norwich, chapter 58.

habits using characteristics exalted in women as a point of reference. It has been mentioned that medieval times witnessed a feminization of the clerics' behaviour and appearance once they renounced their worldly life: "religious men became extraneous to contemporary gender construction."[22] It comes as no surprise that when Richard Rolle adopted the status of a hermit, he used one of his sister's dresses to make a habit, since the clerical clothes resembled the feminine attire. This situation seems to raise another issue, that of genderless appearance or in terms of visibility and invisibility the apparent effacement of gender differences in devoted Christians.

An issue which was often debated in medieval sermons and literature and which tended to make the body at the same time invisible and genderless was chastity. This choice appears as a denial of carnal desires, asserting, thus, the power of the soul over the body and it was expected of all religious people. However, Julian did not mention it at all, so, clearly, although she took this vow, she did not consider it an essential topic as most male theologians[23] did. Julian emphasised just the need to create a close relationship with God, and to rely completely on God's love. This absolute spiritual commitment was essential, whereas bodily restrictions were just means to achieve it.

Therefore, the body was just a tool for Julian, to be used in order to elevate the soul. For instance, the pain felt within the body was turned from a weakness into a means of experiencing the unity with God, as He Himself felt pain. The visibility of the body was neither an impediment nor an advantage, as it was just a connection with the world around her, a link which was not really important for Julian. She loved her fellow Christians and advised them if they so desired, but she did not really need their presence for her spiritual advancement, and, thus, did not choose to be visible to them

Julian's serenity versus 14th century anxiety

A Christian's purpose in life was (and still is) salvation and Julian often mentioned how Christ's incarnation was the source of "our endless salvation,"[24] since one can be saved through prayer and devotion only because of Christ's sacrifice. Thus in Julian's *Revelations* His Passion was part of "all the deeds

---

[22] Dawn Hadley (ed.), *Masculinity in Medieval Europe*, (Routledge: Abingdon 2014), 168.

[23] For instance, in "The Fire of Love", Richard Rolle dedicates an entire chapter (no. 24) to "the stink of lechery and the peril of touching." Richard Rolle, *The Fire of Love* (Methuen & Company: London 1920), 102-106.

[24] Julian of Norwich, Chapter VI.

that Jesus hath done about our salvation"[25] and thus, it did not bring about sadness, despite the excruciating pain that Christ's Passion involved and which was minutely described. On the contrary, remembering it engendered a feeling of gratitude and love, as well as hopes for an endless life in His presence. Kari Elisabeth Børresen, also emphasises this aspect in her study on Julian of Norwich, "Julian's focus on Christ's passion is typically late medieval, but she does not share the fascination with Christ's suffering as such. In contrast to the period's anguished search for a merciful God, Julian's basic trust in universal salvation."[26] Her strong optimism is rooted in her visions and she presents it fearlessly, unconcerned that it might differ from the official policy of the Church.

The message conveyed by the Church, and which can be witnessed in most of the 14th-century sermons and chronicles, produced the impression of "immense sadness"[27] and depicted a gruesome life after death, with horrors and punishment, being thus in stark contradiction to Julian's optimistic message, which insisted on salvation. Huizinga further points out that: "Since the thirteenth century the popular preaching of the mendicant orders had made the eternal admonition to remember death swell into a sombre chorus ringing throughout the world." [28] And even more than the sermons, the walls of churches and cathedrals presented for the illiterate a rather gloomy picture of their life, as demons interfered almost freely on Earth and every single sin was punishable by pain, either immediately or on the Judgement Day. One such example of people being overwhelmed by demons is the medieval limestone frieze of Lincoln Cathedral (late 12th century) which depicts the Torments of the Damned in Hell – for instance on the West Front of the cathedral, one can see an adulterous couple being punished by wyverns (*id est serpent-dragons*) by having their hair pulled. These freezes were, in a way, religious caricatures of salvation and damnation, aimed at an illiterate, vulnerable public, in an attempt to scare them so that they became obedient and submissive to the will of the Church.

This fear-provoking ideology contrasts profoundly with Julian's words, which emphasise the omnipotence of God's love, as well as the conviction that Jesus' sacrifice can cleanse man's sins, while his duty is only to believe and

---

[25] "al the dedes that Jesus hath done aboute our salvation," Julian of Norwich, Chapter XXII.
[26] Kari Elisabeth Børresen and Adriana Valerio (eds.), *The High Middle Ages* (SBL Press: Atlanta 2015), 169.
[27] Johan Huizinga, *The Waning of the Middle Ages* (Penguin Books: London 1922), 31.
[28] Huizinga, *The Waning of the Middle Ages*, 140.

rely on Jesus Christ. This complete confidence in God's love has been regarded as the core of her theology:

> "because the starting point for Julian's understanding of creation is the love of God, and because this permeates her reflection, her emphasis is on the nobility of the soul and the delight God takes in it, rather than upon the sin [...] For Julian the primary fact is that we are loved by God and are the honourable place of his dwelling.[29]

However, Julian was not blind to human suffering, but she interpreted it as God's manner of bringing people closer to Him. Misfortune and suffering became instruments that were used to cure people of their spiritual illnesses, like selfishness or pride. Accordingly, a rather violent image is projected, of Christ "breaking" Christians – (allowing for the sufferance to happen) in order to rid them of their "vicious pride" (in other words to purify them) and then "gathering" – reconstructing them – making them "clean and holy," in order to unite them with Him:

> "And this He does for to hinder the harm that they should take from the pomp and the vain-glory of this wretched life, and make their way ready to come to Heaven, and up-raise them in His bliss everlasting. For He saith: 'I shall wholly break you of your vain affections and your vicious pride; and after that I shall together gather you, and make you mild and meek, clean and holy, by oneing to me."[30]

It is through this process that people should understand their pains, in other words their misfortunes and tribulations, and bear them without despair. Sin was regarded as a grave impediment for acceding to the Kingdom of God and salvation, and people regarded daily the horrors that were the consequences of their sins. While "Julian is fully aware that her fundamental belief in divine love affronts traditional concepts of sin, damnation and God's jealous justice,"[31] she gives logical and mystical arguments to support her vision and encourage people to follow her optimism. So just like Christ's Passion brought

---

[29] Jantzen, *Julian of Norwich*, 130.

[30] "And this He doith for to lettyn the harme that thei shuld take of the pompe and the veyn glory of this wrechid lif, and mak ther way redy to come to Hevyn, and heynen them in His bliss without end lestyng. For He seith, I shall al tobreke you for your veyn affections and your vicious pryde, and after that I shal togeder gader you, and make you mylde and meke, clene and holy, by onyng to me." Julian of Norwich, chapter XXVIII.

[31] Børresen and Valerio (eds.), *The High Middle Ages*, 170.

about the salvation of the world, 14th-century people's misfortunes become a source of salvation. Regardless of the present hardships, or of the sins committed, we receive the reassurance in Christ's words: 'It is truth (sothe) that sin is the cause of all this pain; but all shall be well, and all shall be well, and all manner [of] thing shall be well.'[32] Therefore, there is no despondency or lamentation anywhere in her lines, but rather the constant mentioning of the joy she feels when receiving the divine revelations and the bliss she expects in Heaven together with the other human beings. Perhaps the most conclusive vision is the image of the world being the size of hazel-nut "He shewed me a little thing, the quantity of a hazel-nut, in the palm of my hand; [...] In this Little Thing I saw three properties. The first is that God made it, the second is that God loveth it, the third, that God keepeth it."[33] This delicate image is also very representative of her theology. The world is little, insignificant, and so is each and every one of us, and yet God shows great care and concern for the smallest creature. Visibility in her city was thus irrelevant for Julian, since she wished for divine visibility and believed wholeheartedly that God can see us all and will protect us all, out of His great love.

The purpose of focusing on women's visibility in the Middle Ages is to better ascertain their theology and especially the orthodoxy of their writings, as well as their role (and influence) in contemporary society.[34] Such studies might help us understand the dramatic shift in the perception of the Church with regards to these women[35], as in many cases their personality may be better appreciated by and sometimes even more relevant to 21st-century believers than her contemporaries.

---

[32] "It is sothe that synne is cause of all this peyne, but al shal be wele, and al shall be wele, and all manner thing shal be wele." Julian of Norwich, chapter. XXVII, but this promise which is repeated in subsequent chapters XXXI, XXXII, XXXIV, LXVIII.

[33] "He shewed a littil thing the quantitye of an hesil nutt in the palme of my hand, In this littil thing I saw three properties: the first is that God made it, the second is that God loveth it, the third, that God kepith it." Julian of Norwich, chapter 5.

[34] Julian of Norwich's invisible and secluded life as an anchorite inspired Christians in their resistance against 2020 pandemic, as, when the coronavirus restrictions began, the Bishop of Norwich, the Right Reverend Graham Usher, said, he found himself "going back to the writings of Mother Julian of Norwich." In the midst of all of that, she was self-isolating in her cell with the noise of the street going on roundabout her. (Nic Rigby, *"Coronavirus: Mystic's 'relevance' to self-isolating world,"* BBC News, East, 30 March 2020. (https://www.bbc.com/news/uk-england-norfolk-52020227, 26 April 2020)

[35] Joan of Arc was burned at stake as a heretic in the 15th century, but canonised as a Catholic saint in the 20th (1920).

Conclusions

For Julian of Norwich her lack of visibility was not a source of annoyance or resignation, as it was not relevant for her spiritual path. Her interactions with her contemporaries were restricted to short conversations through a small window, as was the norm for an anchorite. Despite her invisible presence, she was admired and thus financially supported by the Christian community in Norwich.

The most important feature of her theology was an unwavering faith in God's love and in His wish to save all Christians and raise their souls into Heaven. Her optimistic ideology was not part of the official message of the Church, which preached damnation, and neither was it correlated with the visual depictions that were popular at the time. Therefore, her words remained relatively marginal in medieval times, and influenced just a few congregations of nuns who copied her manuscript. However, her ideas are considerably more appealing to 21st-century believers, who are tuned to her all-encompassing love and have a more tolerant and self-possessed approach to life than medieval fearful worshippers used to have.

In addition, her theology of love and undeterred optimism can also help us transcend suffering, as it is considered just a temporary situation unfalteringly followed by relief which is regarded as a miracle. Thus, pain only highlights the miracle that brings about relief. Such a perspective on reality is an example of recovering female mystics' theology, and can become a response to contemporary secularism, as well as an important step in the wide-reaching revival of women's spirituality.

Monica Ruset Oanca, PhD, is a lecturer at the University of Bucharest and she teaches English at the Faculty of Orthodox Theology. She has specialised in theological terminology and she has written extensively on medieval civilization, focusing on medieval English mystic writers (especially on Julian of Norwich and Margery Kempe) and on Arthurian literature (especially *La Queste del Saint Graal*). She has published three books, one of them being her PhD dissertation, which discusses the structure and the functions of medieval castles as well as their religious and social importance. She is interested in emphasising the salvific character of medieval literature and her work on *Visions of Salvation in Late Medieval English Literature* is a first step in this endeavour. monica.oanca@lls.unibuc.ro

Aleksandra F. Michalska

Reverend Stoyna: The Blind Seeing With (de)Constructing Power

Abstract
In this article I analyze the phenomenon of the cult of prepodobna Stoyna – a Bulgarian prophetess, who is far less known than the renowned baba Vanga, but originated from the same region. At the age of 7, she became blind after an illness and since then had the gift of preaching and healing. At the beginning of the 20th century, she appeared in the church of Saint George in the village Zlatolist in Bulgaria, where she lived for 50 years and led the life of an anchorite until her death in 1933. Apparently, baba Vanga herself claimed that her predecessor baba Stoyna had three times more power than herself. Baba Stoyna lived on the balcony part of the church and there, in a room that has been preserved and is still visited to this day, accepted pilgrims. According to the stories, she was endowed with not only the gift of clairvoyance and healing, but also levitation and other powers. The Orthodox Church warns against the idolatry and heresy associated with this cult, yet their warning has no effect on the thousands of people who visit this place and treat prepodobna Stoyna as a saint. How has this blind woman with another form of sight continued to influence society? How does her power construct and deconstruct regimes of the in/visibility of Orthodox religion?

Keywords: prophetess; clairvoyant; Orthodox religion; cult of Stoyna; living saint.

Resumen
En este artículo, analizo el fenómeno de la secta de la prepodobna ('venerable') Stoyna, una profetisa búlgara considerablemente menos conocida que el renombrado baba ('abuela') Vanga pero originaria de la misma región. A la edad de siete, quedó ciega por una enfermedad y desde entonces recibió el don de la prédica y la curación. A principios del siglo XX, apareció en la iglesia de San Jorge, en el pueblo de Zlatolist en Bulgaria, donde vivió cincuenta años y llevó una vida monástica hasta su muerte en 1933. Aparentemente, la propia baba Vanga afirmó que su predecesora baba Stoyna había tenido tres veces más poder que ella. Baba Stoyna vivió en la parte del balcón de la iglesia y allí, en una habitación preservada hasta hoy y aún visitada, aceptaba a peregrinos. De acuerdo con las historias, tenía el don no solo de la clarividencia y la curación, sino además de la levitación y otros poderes. La Iglesia Ortodoxa alerta

contra la idolatría y la herejía asociada con esta secta, pero su advertencia no tiene efecto en las miles de personas que visitan este lugar y tratan a prepodobna Stoyna como a una santa. ¿Cómo ha continuado influenciando a la sociedad esta persona ciega con otro tipo de visión? ¿Cómo construye y deconstruye su poder regímenes de (in) visibilidad en la religión ortodoxa?

Palabras clave: profetisa; clarividente; religión ortodoxa; secta de Stoyna; santa viviente.

Zusammenfassung

In diesem Artikel analysiere ich das Phänomen des Kultes von Prebodobna Stoyna, einer bulgarischen Prophetin, die weit weniger bekannt ist als die berühmte Baba Vanga, aber aus derselben Region stammt. Im Alter von sieben Jahren wurde sie nach einer Erkrankung blind und hatte seitdem die Gabe des Predigens und des Heilens. Am Beginn des 20. Jahrhunderts erschien sie in der Kirche des Heiligen Georg in dem Dorf Zlatolist in Bulgarien, wo sie 50 Jahre lang lebte und bis zu ihrem Tod 1933 das Leben einer Einsiedlerin führte. Offensichtlich behauptete Baba Vanga selbst, dass ihre Vorgängerin Baba Stoyna dreimal mehr Macht hatte als sie selbst. Baba Stoyna lebte auf dem Balkonteil der Kirche und empfing dort Pilger, in einem Raum, der noch erhalten ist und bis heute besucht wird. Nach den Erzählungen war sie nicht nur mit der Gabe der Hellsichtigkeit und des Heilens begabt, sondern auch mit Levitation und anderen Kräften. Die Orthodoxe Kirche warnt vor Idolatrie und Häresie, die mit diesem Kult verbunden sind, aber ihre Warnungen haben keine Wirkung auf die Tausenden Menschen, die diesen Ort besuchen und Prebodobna Stoyna als Heilige behandeln. Wie konnte diese blinde Frau mit einer anderen Art von Sehen die Gesellschaft so dauerhaft beeinflussen? Wie konstruiert und dekonstruiert ihre Macht Regime der Un-/ Sichtbarkeit der orthodoxen Religion?

Schlagwörter: Prophetin; Hellseherin; orthodoxe Religion; Verehrung von Stoyna; lebende Heilige.

Introduction

The phenomenon of clairvoyants and mystics in the territory of orthodox Bulgaria is without a doubt a cultural wonder of this part of Europe. It is especially strong in rural backgrounds and characteristic for so called "local religion,"[1] but

---

[1] Galina Valtchinova, *Балкански ясновидки и пророчици от XX век [Balkan Clairvoyants and Prophetesses in the 20th Century]*, (Университеско издателство "Св. Климент Охридски": София 2006/The University of Sofia Press: Sofia 2006), 18. Translation here and throughout the article: Aleksandra F. Michalska.

representatives of all classes of society take an active part in the cult of "unofficial saints." They create a so called "alternative religious culture,"[2] treating a particular prophetess as a "religious expert" in the mediation between man and the divine sphere. Still, a prophetess does not have an official position in the Church, which in theory has the monopoly on this mediation. In practice, however, it turns out that religious life is created not only in the Church and through the Church (as a space and institution), but also through various non-professional religious activists, who remain outside the institution. In this way, we are dealing with the merging spheres of sacrum and profanum in "local religion" and the blurring of clearly dividing borders.

My research is devoted to the merging of (the) sacred and profane spheres at many different levels of interpretation in the Church of St George, located in the village of Zlatolist in Bulgaria, where the cult of prophetess Stoyna[3] is still alive. This Church, with the living quarters of Baba Stoyna on the balcony of the church has become something of a shrine, and expresses in microscale the mentality, beliefs, superstitions, and concerns of society. These are represented in the space of the church, as well as in her iconography. However, the ceremonies and rituals connected with prepodobna Stoyna, illustrate the changes of religiousness.

Stoyna, as a blind person with the gift of "inner sight," became a "spiritual guide," a "local religious expert," appearing to deconstruct age-old established canons and to construct new canons that are not in line with the official doctrine of the Church. It seems that her behaviour and her lifestyle as an anchorite, living in the isolated space of the St. George church, did not cause any opposition from the Orthodox Church.[4] However, her activity as a prophetess and healer manifest her "deconstructive power," and this has officially been criticized by the Church for centuries. She appears to us as a mystic, who

---

[2] Valtchinova, *Балкански ясновидки и пророчици от XX век [Balkan Clairvoyants and Prophetesses in the 20th Century]*, 13. I use the term instead of denotation "folklore religion," after Galina Valtchinova.

[3] Prophetess Stoyna's life is written by her relative Zoya Petrichka, *Житие на Преподобна Стойна от град Серес [The Vita of the Reverend Stoyna from the City of Serres]* (s.l. 1998). Nowadays, there are mainly two researchers dealing with the phenomenon of reverend Stoyna: Valentina Izmirlieva and Petko Ivanov. They are basing their scientific work on interviews with witnesses or written sources.

[4] There was no precedent in Bulgaria for people to live inside a church. This is how she became an exception not only in her own community, but in the tradition as a whole, somehow deconstructing canons.

responded to the needs of the people of her times, during her life. And since the cult of her person gives rise to contemporary rituals, it encourages cultural and anthropological reflection all the more.

The phenomenon of cult of prepodobna (baba Stoyna)

Prepodobna[5] (baba)[6] Stoyna was a blind, Bulgarian prophetess gifted with a "spiritual precognition" (pic. 1),[7] and is treated by a part of the orthodox faithful as "an unofficial saint." Stoyna Dimitrova appeared in the orthodox church of St. George, in the village of Zlatolist, at the beginning of 20th century, in 1913. She claimed that St. George (the patron of the church) himself had led her to this place.

Born on 9th of September 1883, in the village of Haznatar (Seres district, currently located in the territory of Greece), she died at the age of 50, leading a monastic life. When she was 7 years old, she lost her sight after an illness (probably after severe chickenpox) and at that time she gained the gifts of fortune telling and healing. Apparently, baba Vanga herself, a later world-famous Bulgarian prophetess, claimed that her predecessor had powers three times stronger than her own. In 1903, Stoyna left her birthplace, and came together with her family to the town of Petrich as refugees. Stoyna, however, chose to live in the village Zlatolist (earlier Dolna Sushitza) and occupied a balcony area of the church of St George. There she spent the rest of her life, until her death in 1933.[8] In this church, in a room that is preserved and visited to this day, she received pilgrims (pic. 2).

The church of St. George in the village of Zlatolist (pic. 6), built in 1857, is located not far from Melnik, the smallest Bulgarian town in the Sandanski district, south-west Bulgaria a border district bordering Bulgaria, Greece and

---

[5] „Prepodobna" in literal translation from Bulgarian language means "reverend," "venerable," but it describes a saint of a lower rung, who in their earthly life gave themselves to a monastic, ascetic life.

[6] "Baba" in literal translation from Bulgarian language means "grandmother," and commonly the term is used when addressing elderly females.

[7] Valentina Izmirlieva and Petko Ivanov, "Сушишката светица Стойна. I. Житие" [The saint of Sushitsa, Stoyna. I. Vita], in: *Български фолклор* 3 [Bulgarian folklore 3], (БАН: София 1990/BAN: Sofia 1990), 75-94, here 75. Translation here and throughout the article: Aleksandra F. Michalska.

[8] Zoya Petrichka, *Житие на Преподобна Стойна от град Серес* [The Vita of the Reverend Stoyna from the City of Serres], (s.l. 1998), 2. Translation here and throughout the article: Aleksandra F. Michalska.

Aleksandra F. Michalska
Reverend Stoyna: The Blind Seeing With (de)Constructing Power

North Macedonia. The village is currently inhabited by around 10 people. During religious festivals and holidays, however, thousands of pilgrims come there to visit the church of St. George, in which the prophetess lived and met the faithful for several dozens of years. It has become a special place, mainly thanks to the cult of the unofficial saint.

Officially, the Orthodox Church warns against the idolatry and heresy connected with the cult of prepodobna (baba) Stoyna, but at the same time, the Church fails to dissuade the thousands of people from visiting this place and treating her as a saint. Documents say that she was initially treated as a clairvoyant and wise woman, despite the fact that a local orthodox priest had called her "prepodobna" or "reverend."[9] It was only 50 years after her death, in the 1980s, that noticeable signs of a cult of a saint appear in the context of her person: "two icons located in the church showing her as a saint, and in front of which specific rituals are performed, the grave in the church's courtyard as a destination for pilgrimages, two redactions of her written life, read by clergyman on the days dedicated to her memory."[10]

It seems that from that moment onwards, the cult becomes ever more alive, and the name of prepodobna (baba) Stoyna enters pop culture circulation. For example, she becomes the main character of a fictional literature book series with her name in the title; a mineral water brand is named after her given name *Prepodobna Stoyna Natural Mineral Water*; a great number of videos and recordings from visits at the place of her cult can be found on the internet; there are internet discussion boards as well as social profiles dedicated to miracles performed by the prophetess. Small travel icons with the image of prepodobna (baba) Stoyna are sold in a little church shop (pic. 7) and it is possible to fill bottles of miraculous water from the spring at the church courtyard (pic. 8).

Baba Stoyna's Vita

The life of Stoyna was transcribed by her relative[11] – Zoya Velikova from Petrich, the granddaughter of a sister of Stoyna. She contributed significantly to the promotion of the cult of baba Stoyna by organising pious meetings of women

---

[9] See also Petrichka, *The Vita of the Reverend Stoyna*.

[10] Izmirlieva and Ivanov, "Сушишката светица Стойна. I. Житие" [The saint of Sushitsa, Stoyna. I. Vita], 75.

[11] At the beginning of the 1980s, Zoya Velikova (called also Petrichka), after having numerous dreams about her great aunt, decided to be "chosen" to write Reverend Stoyna's life. The Vita was published in 1998.

7    8

connected with the church, reading religious texts out loud (mainly biblical apocrypha) and visiting churches and monasteries throughout the country. Commonly those meetings were called "circle of baba Zoya."[12] Baba Zoya explains that, because baba Stoyna regularly appeared in her dreams, she understood her relative to be a saint and "a sister of St. George." This stimulated her to write down baba Stoyna's life.[13] This dream appearance echoes a similar incident in Stoyna's life. For when Stoyna as a teenager still lived in her family village currently located in the territory of Greece, St George appeared in her dreams. He ordered her to dig in the backyard. Stoyna found an icon and incense there and, as a result, an orthodox church is built in this place. Since then, St. George is the one who "guides" her actions. It is he who "shepherds" her situation after the forced immigration to the territory of Bulgaria and to choose a church of which he is the patron, in the village of Zlatolist (former Dolna Sushitza). In folklore culture, especially in hagiographic writing, "a vision during a dream" is a factor in "regulating relations with the nether world." And is one of the

---

[12] Izmirlieva and Ivanov, "Сушишката светица Стойна. I. Житие" [The saint of Sushitsa, Stoyna. I. Vita], 75-76.
[13] Izmirlieva and Ivanov, "Сушишката светица Стойна. I. Житие" [The saint of Sushitsa, Stoyna. I. Vita], 76.

obligatory testimonial elements for sainthood.[14] Therefore Zoya Velikova met every condition necessary to popularize knowledge about her saint-relative. She gathered testimonies from people who remembered miracles performed by Stoyna. One of the voices said: "In the village of Dolna Sushitza (former name of Zlatolist), many people were coming to prepodobna Stoyna to receive advice and consolation and each person was left astonished, contented and grateful to her whom St. George helped with God's power. When it happened that Turks passed by, they moved a step away and said: 'Here is God's power.'"[15] She also was given credit for saving the village from Turks in 1916, as well as for saving the church from robbery. The hagiography describes as well the testimonial of Stoyna's levitation, who "being scared by an adder asked God to lift her. With the help of his saints and an angel, he lifted her 2 meters high."[16] Other miracles described in the book include Stoyna's influence from beyond the grave, the appearance of the prepodobna and supernatural phenomena at her grave during a caller's visit. There are many cases recorded of healing and clairvoyance. For example, "healing a child from bad eyes" by casting a spell, healing a dying boy with leeches, curing the hand of an elderly woman and so on. Moreover, Stoyna can also use her powers to punish those doing evil, those sinners who want to show themselves in favourable light. She also takes the role of a moralist explaining specific happenings in other people's lives.

Although physically she cannot see, she sees spiritually and has a mysterious knowledge about faith, life, people and God's orders. She is visited by the most notable figures of social life, amongst others an Italian consul who gifts her with clothes "for every day and for special occasion."[17]

It is worth mentioning the difference in receiving the faithful by prepodobna Stoyna and her successor baba Vanga here. Ida Ciesielska explains in the article "Compleks Vanga in Rupite as a religious sanctuary,"[18] that baba

---

[14] Izmirlieva and Ivanov, "Сушишката светица Стойна. I. Житие" [The saint of Sushitsa, Stoyna. I. Vita], 76.

[15] Izmirlieva and Ivanov, "Сушишката светица Стойна. I. Житие" [The saint of Sushitsa, Stoyna. I. Vita], 82.

[16] Izmirlieva and Ivanov, "Сушишката светица Стойна. I. Житие" [The saint of Sushitsa, Stoyna. I. Vita], 86-87.

[17] Izmirlieva and Ivanov, "Сушишката светица Стойна. I. Житие" [The saint of Sushitsa, Stoyna. I. Vita], 89.

[18] Ida Ciesielska, "Kopleks Wanga w Rupite jako sanktuarium religijne," in: *Slavia Meridionalis (Polish Academy of Sciences 21 October 2016)*, 16: 1-23, (http://cejsh.icm.edu.pl/cejsh/element/bwmeta1.element.ojs-doi-10_11649_sm_2016_028, 25 May 2019).

Vanga engaged in political affairs, gave in to commercial activities and received pilgrims at a set charge. A visit to the Rupite complex does not leave any doubt that at some point the place became a place attracting pilgrimage (and not only) tourists in a calculated way, and lost (if it ever had) an atmosphere of spirituality, a feeling of harmonious peace and a refuge for believers. Prepodobna Stoyna, however, never accepted set amounts for her "services," but everyone had the right to show appreciation in their own way. Although it is mentioned that money was left, the gifts were most commonly in the form of chickens, eggs, rye and so on. The story goes that she gave these gifts away to the poor and offered children apples or raisins, whereas the money she left to the church. She herself "ate almost nothing, only fruits, lemon, tea,"[19] says one of the witnesses of her life. In witnesses' comments we hear also: "Тя не беше като другите гледачки" ("She wasn't like other seeresses").[20] The stories also show that she led a truly simple life and did not go anywhere, only to the church courtyard. On Saturdays, when more people appeared in the area, she would lock herself in the room with her two cats and they would say that "(she) is in prayers." The residents of the village referred to this as "she was gossiping with saints" ("със светците си праела моабет").[21] They also recall her as a "good woman, wholly dressed in black." However, it was noted that she was short-tempered when people who visited her to confess seemed to her "not worthy," not deserving to be received.[22] It also befell her to "almost die," that is, she forewarned the priest that for a few days she would look dead and would not move from the bed, but said not to bury her. And then she "was coming back to life" and claimed she had been walking in the nether

---

[19] Valentina Izmirlieva and Petko Ivanov, "Сушишката светица Стойна. II. Фолклорни материали" [The saint of Sushitsa, Stoyna. II. Folklore texts], in: *Български фолклор* 1 [*Bulgarian folklore* 1], (БАН: София 1991/BAN: Sofia 1991), 61-78, here 62. Translation here and throughout the article: Aleksandra F. Michalska.

[20] Valentina Izmirlieva and Petko Ivanov, "Сушишката светица Стойна. III. Проблемът за светостта" [The saint of Sushitsa, Stoyna. III. The question of sanctity], in: *Български фолклор* 2 [*Bulgarian folklore* 2], (БАН: София 1991/ BAN: Sofia 1991), 3-12, here 6. Translation here and throughout the article: Aleksandra F. Michalska.

[21] Izmirlieva and Ivanov, "Сушишката светица Стойна. II. Фолклорни материали" [The saint of Sushitsa, Stoyna. II. Fo

[22] Izmirlieva and Ivanov, "Сушишката светица Стойна. II. Фолклорни материали" [The saint of Sushitsa, Stoyna. II. Folklore texts], 68-69.

world.[23] This phenomenon of the so called "temporary death" is described by ethnologists and anthropologists as an experience of liminality that is a stage of a threshold passage, at the borderline between life and death.[24] When it was actually time for her to die, she informed the priest prior to her death and commanded that she was not to be given injections, knowing that she would die of pneumonia. According to the stories, three orthodox priests came to her funeral (as she had wished), as well as lots of people from neighbouring towns. Interestingly, though, the stories also tell that "from Melnik all residents came apart from the men ("because they did not believe in her"), only men from the village of Zlatolist took part."[25]

The cult of prepodobna Stoyna

During Stoyna's life her image was painted in an icon, which later was copied faithfully or less faithfully. She is presented in a black outfit, which she always wore, with a bouquet of flowers in her hands and with a cross. Pilgrims kneel in front of her and pray to her as to a saint. Today, the faithful, while visiting the room of Stoyna in the church, leave pictures of themselves and their loved ones, so that the power of prepodobna Stoyna can work from afar (pic. 3). In the porch, there is also a notebook with prayers and petitions to prepodobna Stoyna (pic. 4). It is moreover possible to stay overnight on the balcony, where blankets and pillows are arranged in piles for the use of visitors (pic. 5). There are also documented descriptions of miracles, which are experienced by the faithful staying for a night on the church's balcony next to Stoyna's room.[26] Another custom is leaving wheat, bread, and sharing wine on her grave. Women give these offerings "for the salvation of Stoyna's soul."[27]

---

[23] Izmirlieva and Ivanov, "Сушишката светица Стойна. II. Фолклорни материали" [The saint of Sushitsa, Stoyna. II. Folklore texts], 70.
[24] Victor Turner writes about it in his work *The Ritual Process: Structure and Anti-Structure* (Transaction Publishers: New Brunswick/London 1996).
[25] Izmirlieva and Ivanov, "Сушишката светица Стойна. II. Фолклорни материали" [The saint of Sushitsa, Stoyna. II. Folklore texts], 71.
[26] The practice of "incubation" is quite widespread in Bulgarian sanctuaries, famous for miracles, Magdalena Lubańska describes this phenomenon in "Praktyki lecznicze w prawosławnych monasterach w Bułgarii," (Wydawnictwo Uniwersytetu Warszawskiego: Warszawa 2019), here 142-162.
[27] Izmirlieva and Ivanov, "Сушишката светица Стойна. II. Фолклорни материали" [The saint of Sushitsa, Stoyna. II. Folklore texts], 75.

Witnesses of Stoyna's life say without hesitation that: "she is a saint," which is a postscript at the end of a first version of a manuscript of Stoyna's life.[28] In folklore, a "saint" is also always a miracle-worker. "Those saints, who do not perform miracles, do not have authority in a village, regardless of their appreciation by the official Church."[29] Whereas those, who are described as "living saints," those who can have real influence on peoples' lives and can be taken as part of the community, are especially important. [30] "People's saints with God's gifts are at the same time "from here" and "from the nether world," and "heaven's saints are in direct contact with "living saints," appearing in their dreams and talking with them."[31]

This interpretation of the saints can be clarified by turning to literature on the *Mystique*. This is a Greek word taking its origin from the verb μύω (myo) – meaning "to close," interestingly used mainly in relation to "closing eyes." This is interpreted further in a book "The Ill and Healthy Mystique" published by the Orthodox Church in 2014 in Bulgaria, as

> seeing the nether world with closed eyes, experiencing the mystery of religion or spiritual interaction within this intangible world, regardless of external circumstances, in which we are found. (...) Since the invisible world consists of both God's light-paradise and dark-hellish kingdom of demons, also mystique, as per dignity of its subject and quality of character of mystical experience, can be divine and demonic. Interaction with God, angels and apotheosized saints, who after their short earthly life go to heaven is a healthy mystique and always is beneficial to a religious soul. Interaction with demons on the other hand, under any form, is diabolic, demonic and sick mystique. Its results for the soul are extremely fatal.[32]

According to mythologic thinking, blindness, or a lack of ability to physically see, gives the wisdom of "inner sight." Stoyna is widely accepted as a wise

---

[28] Izmirlieva and Ivanov, "Сушишката светица Стойна. I. Житие" [The saint of Sushitsa, Stoyna. I. Life], 78.

[29] Izmirlieva and Ivanov, "Сушишката светица Стойна. III. Проблемът за светостта" [The saint of Sushitsa, Stoyna. III. The question of sanctity], 3.

[30] Izmirlieva and Ivanov, "Сушишката светица Стойна. III. Проблемът за светостта" [The saint of Sushitsa, Stoyna. III. The question of sanctity], 5.

[31] Izmirlieva and Ivanov, "Сушишката светица Стойна. III. Проблемът за светостта" [The saint of Sushitsa, Stoyna. III. The question of sanctity], 8.

[32] Arhimandrit Serafim, *Болна и здрава мистика [The Ill and Healthy Mystique]*, (Православно издателство "Св.Апостол и Евангелист Лука": София 2014/ Orthodox Press „St. Apostle and Evangelist Luke": Sofia 2014), 7-8. Translation here and throughout the article: Aleksandra F. Michalska.

and fair person who has the strength to protect that fairness in life, and somehow keeps order and balance in the community that way.[33]

> All seeresses and clairvoyants act under the influence and regard direct guidelines from saints in the nether world, with whom they work towards a common good. As a result of this, "living saints" and long dead canonized saints have common "clients" and similar positions as patrons in the communities (...), despite their different status from the Church's point of view,

write Bulgarian researchers Ivanov and Izmirlieva.[34] The effectiveness of saints is shown on the one hand through their successful actions, and on the other through their continuous activity in community life, demonstrated by epiphanies (heavenly living saints) and visions (earthly living saints).[35] In relation to prepodobna Stoyna this is an example of her relationship with St George. People say: "Он жив светец, она жив светец!" ("Him living saint, her living saint!"), in which, if necessary "they can count on each other." "Living saints" if necessary, can leave their icons in return for worship. Therefore, the definition of "living saint" is quite flexible and depends on the question whether the saint is active "here and now" and whether they help the community. What is more, a community has the right to sanction "useless" saints, because they breached the "agreement between patron and client." In this event, icons of canonical saints can be punished, for example, by breaking them. In the case of saint seeresses and clairvoyants they can be publicly denuded and symbolically chased away from a village and called pseudo-saints, charlatans, or even witches.[36] Summarising, within the nomenclature of people's religiousness in ordinary religion, a "living saint" is an "active saint"

---

[33] Izmirlieva and Ivanov, "Сушишката светица Стойна. III. Проблемът за светостта" [The saint of Sushitsa, Stoyna. III. The question of sanctity], 9.

[34] Petko Ivanov and Valentina Izmirlieva, "Жив светец в българската фолклорна космология (Опит за (ре)конструкция)" [Living saint of Bulgarian folklore cosmology (Question about (re)construction)], in: *Български фолклор* 3 [*Bulgarian folklore* 3], (БАН: София 2000/ BAN: Sofia 2000), 43-52, here 45. Translation here and throughout the article: Aleksandra F. Michalska.

[35] Ivanov and Izmirlieva, "Жив светец в българската фолклорна космология (Опит за (ре)конструкция)" [Living saint of Bulgarian folklore cosmology (Question about (re)construction)], 45.

[36] Ivanov and Izmirlieva, "Жив светец в българската фолклорна космология (Опит за (ре)конструкция)" [Living saint of Bulgarian folklore cosmology (Question about (re)construction)], 46.

as opposed to a "passive saint," thereby replacing the terminonology used in the church: canonical or uncanonical saint. Stoyna's case leaves no doubt that she is perceived by society as a "living, active saint," although uncanonical for the Church.

Regimes of visibility/ regimes of invisibility

Regarding what is "visible" and what is "invisible" and the relation of those spheres on social life; what are, in Stoyna's case the "regimes of visibility" or the "regimes of invisibility"? In the first place, these have to do with physical conditions relating to her restrictions coming from blindness and a lack of "sight" of what is visible to others. But what then is invisible for many, she sees by her gift of "inner sight." That is why "regimes of invisibility" supposedly do not exist for her, because she is unrestrained in her mystical experiences of "invisible." In the context of Stoyna, I would risk putting an equal sign between those "regimes." And secondly, the way a certain social group in a certain socio-political context "reads" supernatural abilities, revealed by "religious experts," determines if a particular practice will be recognised as a "miracle" (miricalum), or as a "magical aggression" (maleficium).[37] Thus, a particular social group has somehow also power over a person called "fortune-teller," "prophetess" or "folklore saint." In that way this group can "construct" or "deconstruct" "regimes of Her in/visibility."

Edith Stein in her phenomenological vision of the world, writes that the "more someone is focused on the self-inside, lives in his/her inner self, the stronger (she/he) radiates and attracts others"[38] Stoyna, in some ways deprived of natural sight, had restricted possibilities to "distract her attention on other worlds" than the „inner" one. Simultaneously "led in a dream by St George" and pronounced by herself and others to be his "sister," she felt the responsibility to serve others and to show them the correct way. She attracted crowds, even many years after her death. Rudolf Otto also writes about the "gift of sight,"[39] as a sign of "sainthood" and an event treated as a "sign," which cannot be naturally explained. Mentioned earlier, Edith Stein describing a

---

[37] Valtchinova, Балкански ясновидки и пророчици от XX век [Balkan Clairvoyants and Prophetesses in the 20th Century], 25.

[38] Jan Andrzej Kłoczowski, Drogi człowieka mistycznego (Wydawnictwo literackie: Kraków 2001), 72.

[39] Rudolf Otto, Świętość. Elementy irracjonalne w pojęciu bóstwa i ich stosunek do elementów racjonalnych, (Wydawnictwo KR: Warszawa 1999), 166-167.

foundation of "symbolical theology" explains, that "world, indicating something, what exceeds it, is a basic source of recognition, from which natural theology takes its argumentation." God speaks to us through pictures, signs and things. Only those who have an adequate "sense" can read the until now unknown meanings.[40] A great number of followers of prepodobna Stoyna believed that she had this sense, and it is probably because of this that her cult is so widespread. In the context of socio-anthropological studies (as opposed to a purely theological approach), the Bulgarian ethnologist Valtchinova describes the phenomenon of the cult of Balkan prophetesses as "invisible religion," using the term introduced by Luckmann.[41] In this way, she appeals to the secularisation of religion, to a focus on the individual and its individual religious experiences (Valtchinova after Luckmann 1967). Because of its non-institutional spectrum, she also calls it "practical" (Valtchinova after Leach 1968) or "experienced" (Valtchinova after Vauchez 1987, Christian 1989).[42] Characterising this cult as a so called "secular religiousness" releases it from the imposed "official" model of interpretation of senses.[43] That is why instead of religion, Valtchinova rather prefers to talk about "religiousness," which includes processes, actions, institutions, as well as the mentality of a specific community. She defines the term: "it is a system of concepts and explanations of the world surrounding us, natural and social, which assumes participation or influence of supernatural powers in certain moments of life, either with positive (divine sphere) or with a negative sign (demonic sphere)."[44] Therefore, "invisible religion" gives us much more knowledge about the society than what is official and theoretically "visible." All attempts mentioned in the above to give an accurate definition of religion or religiousness lead to creating a formula, that would not fall in the habit of oppositional thinking thereby creating a radical division, such as: "religion" vs. "superstition" (magic), or

---

[40] S. J. Immakulata Adamska OCD, *Światło rozumu i wiary. Duchowa droga Edyty Stein św. teresy Benedykty od Krzyża* (o. Marian Stankiewicz OCD, prowincjał: Warszawa 2002), 138-139.
[41] Valtchinova, Балкански ясновидки и пророчици от XX век [*Balkan Clairvoyants and Prophetesses in the 20th Century]*, 19.
[42] Valtchinova, Балкански ясновидки и пророчици от XX век [*Balkan Clairvoyants and Prophetesses in the 20th Century]*, 19.
[43] Ks. Janusz Mariański, "Niewidzialna religia" w badaniach socjologiczncyh, in: *Studia Płockie* 37 (2009), 191-209, here 191. (http://mazowsze.hist.pl/21/Studia_Plockie/492/2009/16496/, 21 November 2019).
[44] Valtchinova, Балкански ясновидки и пророчици от XX век [*Balkan Clairvoyants and Prophetesses in the 20th Century]*, 20.

"high/official religion" vs. "low/folklore religion."[45] Many modern anthropologists of culture preconceive that those two spheres create one integral world view and that they should not be differentiated, and that scientists should reach deeper in their research, to the roots of Christianity. The cult of prepodobna Stoyna functioning as a part of Bulgarian Orthodox Church, and at the same time outside of official Church doctrine, can be a perfect example of that.

Aleksandra F. Michalska is a graduate of Slavonic studies, post-graduate in cultural studies, art history at Adam Mickiewicz University in Poznan (Poland) and individual specialization in painting and iconography at the Academy of Fine Arts in Sofia (Bulgaria). In the years 2003–2007, she worked as a Polish language teacher at the University Paisi Hilendarski in Plovdiv (Bulgaria). In the years 2007–2009, she worked at the Polish Embassy and the Polish Cultural Institute in Sofia, promoting Polish culture abroad. Since 2011, she has been conducting semester classes of iconography at the University of Arts in Poznan and in parallel from 2017, classes in the same field at the Senior Academy in Collegium da Vinci. From 2012, curator of works and exhibitions of Sylwia Taciak – an artist with Down's Syndrome. From 2018, PhD student at the Department of Semiotics of Culture at the Department of Anthropology and Cultural Studies at Adam Mickiewicz University. michalska.aleksandra@amu.edu.pl

---

[45] Valtchinova, Балкански ясновидки и пророчици от XX век [*Balkan Clairvoyants and Prophetesses in the 20th Century*], 20-21.

Zilya Khabibullina

The Image of a Muslim Woman in the Russian Mass Media: Trying to Overcome Stereotypes in Islamic Media Space[*]

Abstract
The article presents an analysis of media-discourse regarding the position and status of a Muslim woman in Russian society. Consideration is given to the existing stereotypes in the official media, their influence on the formation mode of social visibility of Islam and Muslims in the country, and their use as a resource for constructing political concepts. Another pole of creating visibility is Islamic media (the information resources created by Muslims in the Internet space), with their attempts made to overcome these stereotypes about Muslim women. Almost all Islamic media have material devoted to exposing the existing stereotypes about these women. The research demonstrates how visibility modes can be constructed and deconstructed using the example of the image of Muslim women in a secular and multi-religious society via the modern media resources.

Keywords: Islam; Muslim woman; gender; Mass Media; stereotypes; Islamic media.

Resumen
Este artículo presenta un análisis del discurso mediático acerca de la posición y estatus de una mujer musulmana en la sociedad rusa. Se tienen en cuenta los estereotipos existentes en el espacio público, su influencia en la formación de régimen de visibilidad social del islam y las personas musulmanas en el país y su uso como recurso para construir conceptos políticos. El polo opuesto para crear visibilidad son los medios de comunicación islámicos (medios creados por personas musulmanas), en los que se llevan a cabo intentos de sobrepasar estos estereotipos sobre la mujer musulman. Prácticamente todos los medios islámicos destinan material a exponer estos estereotipos. La investigación demuestra cómo la visibilidad se construye y deconstruye tomando como ejemplo a las mujeres musulmanas en una sociedad secular y multirreligiosa a través de los medios de comunicación modernos.

---

[*] The research was supported by the Russian Science Foundation (RNF), project no. 18-78-10077, entitled "Virtual Ethnicity and Cyber-Ethnography: Innovation and Tradition."

Zilya Khabibullina
The Image of a Muslim Woman in the Russian Mass Media: Trying to Overcome Stereotypes in Islamic Media Space

Palabras clave: islam; mujer musulmana; género; medios de comunicación; estereotipos; medios de comunicación islámicos.

Zusammenfassung
Der Artikel präsentiert eine Analyse des Mediendiskurses im Hinblick auf die Position und den Status der muslimischen Frau in der russischen Gesellschaft. Berücksichtigt werden die vorhandenen Stereotype in offiziellen Informationen, ihr Einfluss auf die Art der Bildung sozialer Sichtbarkeit von Islam und Muslim*innen im Land und ihre Verwendung als Ressource zur Konstruktion politischer Konzepte. Ein anderer Pol der Erschaffung von Sichtbarkeit sind islamische Medien (die Informationsquellen, die von Muslim*innen im Internet geschaffen werden) mit ihren Versuchen, die Stereotypen über muslimische Frauen zu überwinden. Fast alle muslimischen Medien haben Material, das dazu dient die vorhandenen Stereotypen über diese Frauen aufzuzeigen. Der Beitrag zeigt, wie Formen der Sichtbarkeit konstruiert und dekonstruiert werden können, und zwar am Beispiel des Bildes muslimischer Frauen in einer säkularen und multi-religiösen Gesellschaft mittels moderner Medien.

Schlagworte: Islam; muslimische Frau; Gender; Massenmedien; Stereotypen; islamische Medien.

Introduction

Modern media resources are considered to include mass media and modern means of communication, such as the Internet and social networks. They can change social institutions, discourses and social practices, expand the range of interactions, open up new opportunities for believers to express themselves. Most of the information for traditional types of media, such as television, radio and press, comes from the Internet. All of them influence, either directly or indirectly, the formation of the image of the Islamic society. Also today's manifestation and self-presentation of religions are increasingly finding their place on the Internet through forums, social networks and sites. The growing role of virtual life rapidly actualises this sphere of communication and culture giving more opportunities as compared to the ordinary reality to express opinions (sometimes anonymous) on various debatable aspects, including the issues concerning believers.

This paper considers stereotypes broadcast by Russia's official mass media in regard to Muslim women and attempts to overcome them in the Islamic media content. The great majority of the Russian society entertains stereotypes about a Muslim woman and experiences misunderstandings, irony or fear, frequently maintained by mass media. To overcome these negative thinking patterns, the Muslim community uses Internet resources, by which it creates Islamic visibility modes. Actions are taken mainly by cultural associations and private persons who seek to disseminate knowledge on Islam and thus change the image of the Muslim faith in the Russian society and mass media.

The first part of the paper deals with the range of problems associated with stereotyped ideas about the "disempowered" position of Muslim women, the "radical and extremist inclination". It also reveals the sources for the formation of these ideas in Russia. According to the research conducted by Russian scientists, a negative image of Muslim women is frequently formed by the official press and TV. Much was written about these aspects by Aida Soboleva, Natalia Kuzina, Sofia Ragozina, and Shukran Suleymanova who studied the image of Islam using top Russian newspapers (Nezavisimaya Gazeta, Kommersant, Moskovsky Komsomolets, Komsomolskaya Pravda, Rossiyskaya Gazeta, Novaya Gazeta, Izvestiya), federal TV channels (Rain, First Federal TV Channel, Russia 1) and information agencies (Interfax, Lenta.ru). The authors' choice of exactly these print media and TV channels was dictated mainly by their popularity in Russia. The article by Aida Soboleva, a practicing journalist with long time work experience on the national TV describes the evolution of a Muslim woman's image in the Russian information space and points out two persistent stereotypes according to which (1) a Muslim woman is passive and downtrodden and (2) a Muslim woman tends to follow extremism.

The second part of the article corresponds with our research on the Muslim woman's visibility mode, this topic being highlighted in the Islamic Internet resources as opposed to the existing stereotypes. At present the Internet is one of the main Russian Muslims' information platforms. This is explained by the fact that Muslims institutions have no authoritative print media intended for a broad audience. Muslims are poorly involved in creating information and have lower level efficiency in communicating with the journalist community. Our focus is on presenting alternative viewpoints concerning the women's status in Islam disseminated via the websites of Muslim associations and large Islamic information agencies and also those for spiritual knowledge.[1]

---

[1] We have studied publications concerning Muslim women on the sites of two large Russian Islamic organisations – Russian Council of Muftis (www.dumrf.ru) and Central Spiritual Administration of the Muslims of Russia (www.cdum.ru); popular information agency Islam-Today (www.islam-today.ru), sites for spiritual knowledge – Islam and Family (www.islam-isemya.com) and Muslim Fashion (www.muslimfashion.ru).

This research is based on the methods of content analysis of source texts and media-discourse as well as cyber-anthropology, which along with traditional tools of public information through the Internet investigates "new mass media," including social networks and blogs, where different Islamic content is now regularly disseminated.

Islamic content is available in VKontakte, Facebook, Instagram, Odnoklassniki, Twitter and YouTube. In the Russian-language media space, there are more than a hundred different sites on Islamic subjects, regardless of the *mazhab* and target orientation that contain a section devoted to the issues of family and women. Some sites are specially created for female audience members. All of them present the advantages of a Muslim lifestyle; examine the problems that women face who choose to live according to the Shariah rules in the secular state exhibiting publicly their religiosity through dress-code and other symbols.

This investigation is part of the Russian research project on "Virtual Ethnicity and Cyber-Ethnography: Innovation and Tradition" aimed at studying manifestations of ethnicity and religiosity within the network space. This project made it possible to investigate some aspects of Muslim life on the Internet, including those related to the formation of the contemporary Muslim women's image in the mass media space. The bulk of data were collected throughout the course of anthropological research within the Muslim segment of the Internet while performing content analysis of textual material, photos and video images.

Islamic visibility on the Internet

The most rapid development of information technologies has transformed the sphere of communication. Thus, the virtual world has become an integral part of modern life and a reflection of social reality. Being on the threshold of the new millennium, ethnographers and anthropologists have found a new field of research, that is the online (cyber-)space with just the same participation of a person, presentation and self-expression of his/her ethnic and religious identity as in the traditional area. The abundance of online resources poses a great many scientific problems concerning the representation of modern-day cultures in virtual space. Many issues are dealt with theoretically in terms of an interdisciplinary approach.[2] Anthropologists focus their attention on ethnic and

---

[2] Tom Boellstorff, Bonnie Nardi, Celia Pearce and T.L. Taylor, *Ethnography and Virtual Worlds: A Handbook of Method* (Princeton University Press: Princeton, NJ 2012); Christine Hine, *Virtual Ethnography (*Sage: London 2000); Annette N. Markham, *Life Online:*

denominational processes that occur in the online mode and correlate or supplement the obtained results with offline observations.

For the most part, scientists consider the interaction between Islam and the Internet in two aspects. These are "the attitude of Islam towards the Internet" and "the presence of Islam on the Internet." Qualitative research is being performed to describe Islamic online resources.[3] However, research on the Islamic faith using the Internet itself is carried out less frequently.[4] There are many points of contention on Islam debated in the cyberspace. A wide range of topics are in the public eye with the availability of information and possibility to give one's own interpretation of traditional texts. An example of this is the hijab discussion among Muslims because the Quran provides little information about it.[5]

Islam enjoys active development on the Internet. There are a lot of electronic resources created by Muslims to disseminate news, rules of the Muslim lifestyle and information about religious notions and rites. Activities are carried out by web-based parishes, jamaats, "Skype" muftis and sheikhs. Some religious practices, among them sermons, prayers, rites, fasting during Ramadan, took place online. Virtual debates on religious topics have become more informative than in real life; pilgrimage sites and Islamic landmarks of historic and cultural value have been digitized. Virtual disputes concerning religious issues are becoming even more informative and relevant than in real life.

Researching Real Experiences in Virtual Pace (Altamira Press: Walnut Creek, CA 1998); Sarah Pink, Heather A. Horst and John Postill, *Digital Ethnography: Principles and Practice* (Sage Publications Limited: Los Angeles 2016); Liav Sade-Beck, "Internet Ethnography: Online and Offline," in: *International Journal of Qualitative Methods* 2 (3/2004) (https://journals.library.ualberta.ca/tc/index.php/IJQM/ article/view/4472/3597, 26 March 2019) et al.

[3] Rasha A. Abdulla, *The Internet in the Arab World: Egypt and Beyond* (Peter Lang Publishing: New York 2007); Dale F. Eickelman and Jon W. Anderson, *New Media in the Muslim World: The Emerging Public Sphere* (Indiana University Press: Bloomington and Indianapolis 1999); Kristin Zahra Sands, "Muslims, Identity and Multimodal Communication on the Internet," in: *Contemporary Islam* 4 (1/2010), 139-155; Daniel Martin Varisco, "Muslims and the media in the blogosphere," in: *Contemporary Islam* 4 (1/2010), 157-177.

[4] Gary R. Bunt, *Islam in the Digital Age: E-Jihad, Online Fatwas and Cyber Islamic Environments* (Pluto Press: London 2003); Gary R. Bunt, *iMuslims: Rewiring the House of Islam* (University of North Carolina Press: Chapel Hill 2009); Alexis Kort, "Dar al-Cyber Islam: Women, Domestic Violence and the Islamic Reformation on the World Wide Web," in: *Muslim Minority Affairs* 25 (3/2005), 363-383.

[5] Heather Marie Akou, "Interpreting Islam Through the Internet: Making Sense of Hijab," in: *Contemporary Islam* 4 (3/2010), 331-346.

Cyberactivity of Muslims is not only its supplement, but it also expands the area of interactions and offers new possibilities for self-expression.[6]

The communicative and discourse functions in the virtual space are implemented by social networks that connect like-minded people. In virtual groups every participant has his/her own goals, views and opinions, which can either agree with those of other participants or be the subject matter of bitter disputes.

Sociologists made attempts to reveal the essential interrelation between the concepts of "Ummah"[7] and "crowdsourcing."[8] Some of them think that crowdsourcing, as a technology for building social relations, resembles traditional features of the Ummah (Muslim community), and that it therefore has positive prospects for being used both in the format of local projects and on the scale of collective identity.[9] According to this concept, a virtual platform, like a religious community, unites initiative members of society to implement Islam-oriented projects.

A similar principle forms the basis of the international multi-language Muslim social network *Suhba* (Arabic "community") and the social network of basic Muslim values SalamWorld developed by the Muslims of Russia.[10] The main idea of the developers is to record positive things in the world of Islam. The *Suhba* service is intended to be the analog of Facebook, or the so-called "Halal Facebook," functioning on the filtration principle in the case of phenomena negatively perceived by the Muslim community, such as Nazism, violence, terrorism, drugs, gambling, same-sex marriages, etc. The network is intended to unite people with "traditional moral values on the basis of multi-ethnic healthy lifestyle and moral security." Currently, the *Suhba* service is operating in the demonstration version. The developers think that main users of this network will be residents of the states with Muslim population, including China, India, Russia and former Soviet republics.

---

[6] Andrey Golovnev, Svetlana Belorussova and Tatyana Kisser, "Веб-этнография и киберэтничность [Web-ethnography and cyber-ethnicity]," in: *Уральский исторический вестник* 58 (1/2018), 102.

[7] Ummah (Arabic "community," "nation") is a Muslim community in Islam.

[8] Crowdsourcing is the practice of solving socially relevant problems by combined forces of many volunteers using information technologies.

[9] Elena Smolina, "Умма"и "краудсорсинг": связь понятий в рамках интернет-пространства ["Umma" and "crowdsourcing": A Connection Between the Notions Within the Internet Space]," in: *Исламоведение* 4 (2015), 74.

[10] Lauren Bon, "Salamworld: социальная сеть для базовых мусульманских ценностей [Salamworld: A social network for Muslim fundamental values]," in: *Ain.ua*, 3 October 2012 (https://ain.ua/2012/10/03/salamworld-socialnaya-set-dlya-bazovyx-musulmanskix-cennostej, 30 October 2019).

Intense activities of religious organisations in media space and the growing role of electronic mass media in everyday life allow believers to "cover distances and be aware of the life of Muslim communities in different countries; mobile media and mobile communication technologies help open and create spaces where you can be together with others or feel mutual presence."[11]

On the Russian-language Internet there is now formed an almost entirely separate segment. This is the so-called the Islamic Network, which can be self-contained and satisfy all the needs of a Muslim believer. This segment contains nearly all analogs of the Internet resources: from dating sites and clothing stores to search systems where Muslims can find any information about Islam. The Islamic cyberspace has resources aimed against islamophobia and negative attitude towards Islam and intended for the non-Islamic audience. There are also websites focused on Muslims and their problems.[12] Almost all of them include materials contributing to the elimination of the existing prejudices about Muslim women.

Muslim women turn to the Internet in order to assert themselves. They create their own websites; a great many women's blogs have evolved in recent years. Muslim women think it to be one of the most promising ways to struggle against stereotypes. "We are the best source of information about ourselves," they say.[13] Instagram blogs have become a place of creativity where Muslim women can express their thoughts, opinions and attitudes towards religion, family life, motherhood, child upbringing and many other things. The number of women bloggers continues to grow, and this can be partially explained by the fact that the culture of writing and keeping a diary is peculiar to women rather than men. Today's blogs represent a diary as a cultural example in form and content.[14] Blogging topics raised by Muslim women, in common with the female blogosphere on the Russian Internet as a whole, are

---

[11] Zilya Khabibullina, "Селфи в Мекке: харам или досточтимый хадж? [Taking Selfies in Mecca: Haram or Still the Venerable Hajj]," in *Сибирские исторические исследования* 2 (2019), 88-89.

[12] See Daniel Martin Varisco, "Muslims and the Media in the Blogosphere," in: *Contemporary Islam* 4 (1/2010), 157-177.

[13] Nico Colombant, "Активисты раскрывают позитивный образ исламских женщин [Activists Unveil Positive Image of Islamic Women]," in: *Golos-ameriki.ru*, 8 March 2010 (https://www.golos-ameriki.ru/a/muslim-woman-misconcepions-2010-03-08-86878007/183394.html, 15 June 2019).

[14] Anna Gnedash, "Женские сообщества в Online-пространстве: 'Режимы видимости' в публичной политике РФ [Women's Communities in the Online Space: 'Regimes of Visibility' in Public Policy of the Russian Federation]," in: *Человек. Сообщество. Управление* 1 (2012), 98.

oriented towards private issues. Contrastingly, it is socio-political topics that prevail in Islamic blogs written by men. Men's blogs are of great interest for network users; they are the most popular and widely read. Of women's topics in men's blogs, the moral teachings and behaviour of modern Muslim women, their appearance in accordance with Shariah rules, and relations with men are the most popular.

Islam in Russia – "traditional" and "non-traditional"

Russian society often has a misunderstanding about Islam and its followers despite the fact that Islam is the second largest religion in the Russian Federation after Christianity. Similar to Europe, Islam in Russia is often associated in people's minds with violence and fanaticism, whereas Muslims themselves associate their religion with justice and democracy. The confrontation of these two standpoints reinforces "the defense mechanisms" on both parts.[15] Figures that show the number of Muslims in Russia are conditional, since Russian censuses do not reflect the religious denomination. Muslims comprise about ten percent of the population in the country (from fourteen and a half to twenty million people). The majority of Russian Muslims are native Turkic peoples of the Volga-Ural region and ethnic groups of North Caucasus. Islam began to spread over the country in the early 1640s, and nowadays it is the traditional religion among more than thirty indigenous ethnic groups in Russia as well as a considerable number of permanent or temporary migrants. In seven constituent entities of the Russian Federation Muslim people are in the majority: 98% in Ingushetia, 96% in Chechnya, 94% in Dagestan, 70% in Kabardino-Balkaria, 54.6% in Karachay-Cherkessia, 54.5% in Bashkortostan and 54% in Tatarstan.[16] Recent studies report on the progressive increase in the number of Muslims in Russia, both due to their natural growth and migrants primarily from Central Asian countries and Azerbaijan and also due to the growing number of new converts. For example, between 2009 and 2012 Russia saw a decrease in the number of Orthodox Christians (by 6%) and an increase in the

---

[15] Isabelle Rigoni, "Media and Muslims in Europe," in: Jorgen S. Nielsen (ed.), *Yearbook of Muslims in Europe* 1 (Brill: Leiden and Boston 2009), 475.

[16] See Информационные материалы об окончательных итогах Всероссийской переписи населения 2010 года [Information Material on the Final Results of the Russian Census of 2010]. (https://www.gks.ru/free_doc/new_site/perepis2010/perepis_itogi1612.htm, 25 September 2019).

number of the followers of Islam (by 3%).[17] There is fear of islamisation in Russian society heightened by users of the Russian-language segment of the Internet who hold on to the idea of islamisation and tend to publish on the Internet most actively.

Russian Islam is now closely identified by citizens of the country with the Muslim world, especially in terms of Northern Caucasus. Muslims themselves show a growing perception of the Russian Ummah as part of the Islamic world. An inevitable process of Russian Muslims' integration into the global Islamic community is accompanied by growing religiosity and influence of large Islamic centres, such as Saudi Arabia, Turkey and Egypt. Among Muslim peoples of Russia there is a growing need for unity, cohesion and solidarity inherent in the concept of the Muslim Ummah accompanied by the tendency to obey the rules of Islam, including Islamic dress-code, careful fulfillment of rituals, demonstration of religious symbols often poorly understood in secular society.

In the 1990s, Russia saw the subdivision of Islam into "traditional" and "non-traditional" for the purpose to distinguish radical interpretations of Islam and identify the peculiar features of Islam in Russia defined as the religion of "peace and tolerance." In the context of the state's religious policy, "traditional Islam" at the present-day stage is intended to consolidate Russian Muslims within one country and serve as a powerful resource for the formation of civil unity. The term used by representatives of government authorities, religious organizations, ethnic associations, scientific communities and mass media is the commonly accepted notion in the Russian Islamic space. However, there is no unambiguous definition of this notion, and different social groups interpret this word combination in many ways to substantiate their own standpoints on one or another issue of the Russian Ummah. Quite recently, in the course of his meeting with Muftis of the Spiritual Administration of Muslims, the President of the Russian Federation Vladimir Putin stated the need to create Muslim cultural and women's centres. "New socialisation of Islam should be viewed as the development of traditional Muslim lifestyle, way of thinking and opinions in accordance with contemporary social reality, as opposed to the ideology of radical leaders pushing people into the Medieval

---

[17] В России за 3 года доля православных сократилась, мусульман – возросла [In Russia the percentage of Orthodox Christians has decreased and that of Muslims have increased over 3 years], in: *Regnum.ru*, 17 December 2012 (https://regnum.ru/news/1605531.html#ixzz2mnq3ThZy, 10 August 2019).

Ages. New forms of activities are of importance here, including approaches to Muslim cultural centres, Islamic scientific and educational organisations, youth and women's clubs," the Head of the State said at the meeting.[18] In his turn, Mufti Ravil Gaynuddin noted, "Along with the President of our country, we are confident that intense social activities of Russian Muslim women make an inestimable contribution to the future of our country. Through the combined efforts we shall be able to solve hot issues, including the hijab problem, create the matchmaking institution, establish centres for family building, crisis centres for women and centres of confidence; we shall also be able to form a positive image of Muslim women in the country. Around the Internet, Muslim women attract much attention and interest throughout the world becoming trendsetters of fashion and lifestyle."[19]

Research on the Russian mass media shows that there is certainly no unambiguous understanding of what is radical Islam versus traditional Islam in the press. "In mass media, radical Islam is associated with the insecurity in the North Caucasian regions, and also in any other insecure regions of the world. Traditional Islam is mainly described as moderate and loyal to authorities. In this regard, all bad things are considered to come from radical Islam, while all good things from traditional Islam."[20]

In the information space, the visibility mode of Islam follows the lines of "traditional" and "non-traditional" and stereotypes are built on these ideas.

Stereotypes of Muslim women in society and broadcast media

In modern-day societies, mass media (press, radio, television) play a tremendous role in creating the image of the social world. The mass communication system is the most important channel to acquire information about society and one of the main tools of learning new things. The role of mass media in the process of social cognition lies also in the fact that they often propose a

---

[18] Ravil Gaynuddin, Greetings at the conference "Роль женщины в современном обществе [The Role of a Woman in Modern Society]" took place on 9–10 November 2019 in Saratov, in: *Muslim.ru*, 1 December 2019 (https://islam-today.ru/zhenshhina_v_islame/blogery-musulmanki-zavoevyvaut-internet/, 28 October 2019).

[19] Ibid.

[20] Maria Zaprometova, "Есть ли в России исламофобия, и почему русские обращаются в ислам: доклады в МВШСЭН [Is there Islamophobia in Russia, and Why do Russians Convert to Islam: Reports at the Moscow School of Social and Economic Sciences (MSSES)]," in: *Mbknews.today*, 16 October 2019 (https://mbknews.today/sences/est-li-v-rossii-islamofobiy/, 25 November 2019).

ready-made image of one or another social phenomenon. The image of Islam in the Russian information space has frequently been the subject matter of scientific inquiry for Russian specialists.[21] According to these studies, the image of a Muslim is formed in Russian society under the influence of actions undertaken by religious extremists, conflicts with participation of Muslims, and radical statements of Muslim politicians and spiritual leaders.

In the Internet mass media (both in TV channels and publishing houses), there is a stable thematic set concerning the semantic binding between "Muslim – Islam" and terrorism.[22] It is the first federal TV channel and the "News" channel that associate growing terrorism and criminality with Islam in their information agenda. As regards the cultural life and also the issues of inculturation of Muslims in the Russian Federation, the priority in covering the events is accorded to TV Rain, news aggregators Google News, Yandex News and Rossiyaskaya Gazeta.[23]

In official Russian mass media, the most detailed materials on the existing stereotypes about Muslim women's lifestyle were written by Aida Soboleva. Being a journalist and a documentary filmmaker who has been working in the official broadcasting system for many years, she says that the image of a Muslim woman was formed in the Russian information space in accordance with political changes.[24]

---

[21] See, for example, Shukran Suleymanova, "Образ мусульман в ФедеральныхСМИ: мифы о "чужаках"и "врагах России" как угроза единству нации [The Image of Muslims in the Federal Mass Media: The Myth of 'Outsiders' and 'Enemies of Russia' as a Threat to the Unity of the Nation]," in: *Ислам в современном мире* 11 (1/2015), 135-142; Sofia Ragozina, "Анализ лексической сочетаемости лексемы 'ислам'" в российских печатных СМИ (2010-2013) [The co-occurrence range of the word Islam in the Russian Print Media (2010–2013)]," in: *Исламоведение* 8 (1/2017), 112-130.

[22] Natalia Kuzina, "Семантика и контекст лексем 'ислам' и 'мусульманин' в современном российском официальном информационном пространстве и в актуальном общественном сознании (анализ федеральных СМИ, новостных агрегаторов, запросов пользователей сети интернет) [The Semantics and Context of the Lexemes 'Islam' and 'Muslim' in Russia's Official Media Space and in the People's Minds Today (an analysis of the federal media, news aggregators, and Internet users' searches)]," in: Zilya Khabibullina (ed.), *Российский ислам в трансформационных процессах современности: новые вызовы и тенденции развития в XXI веке* (Dialog: Ufa 2017), 165.

[23] Khabibullina, *Российский*, 166.

[24] Aida Soboleva, "К вопросу об образе женщины-мусульманки в российском информационном пространстве [On the Image of Muslim Women in the Russian Media]," in: Irina Frolova and Liliya Gazizova (eds.), *Статус женщины-мусульманки в поликонфессиональном обществе: история и современность* (WorldPress: 2016), 105-111.

After the collapse of the USSR, Russian mass media have got rid of ideological and antireligious principles, but contrarily, they have been commercialised resulting in the dependence on ratings, advertisers, sponsors, and investors. At the state level, broadcasting of Islamic festivals is still financially supported on federal TV channels. Also, educational programs on Islam were broadcast for some time and then got gradually cancelled in the crisis periods. For example, the program called "Now" was cancelled in 1995. The weekly program "The Muslims" on the first Russian TV channel managed to last from 2002 until 2015. In 2004, All-Russia State Television and Radio Broadcasting Company cancelled its radio program "The Voice of Islam" broadcast each Friday since 1991. Programs on the life of Muslims still continue to be broadcast on local TV channels and radio stations. Virtually, every religious organisation has its own publishing arm.

Since the late 1990s, the entire structure of the Russian information space has been radically changed with the development of the Internet. Press has become multimedia and reached a wide audience. In the early 1990s, during the most active renewal of religious life in the post-Soviet space, federal and local mass media considered Islamic topics from the positive standpoint. Muslim women wearing traditional clothes, preparing halal (healthy) food and studying spiritual literature were perceived as the guarantors for renewal and preservation of the best national traditions.

However, with the beginning of the Chechen campaign in the mid-1990s, Islam began to be strongly associated with the image of a female homicide bomber. Over the period from 2000 to 2013 they performed twenty-one terrorist acts in Russia. Formal hijab styling, patriarchal values and gender inequality are still associated with Muslim women by the majority of people. The image of an oppressed Muslim woman remains prevalent. As users of social media platforms write, "They stay at home. There is polygamy in Islam. They give birth to many children and give up a career for the sake of their family. This culture turns a woman into a hostage of her own family. She becomes a slave to her children or has to compete with the other wife. She never goes outside the house and cannot communicate with anyone, because she is afraid of her husband."[25]

---

[25] Мифы о мусульманских женщинах [Myths about Muslim Women], in: *Ислам и семья. Исламский информационный духовно-просветительский портал*, 5 July 2017 (http://www.islamisemya.com/mify-o-musulmanskikh-zhenshchinakh.html#prettyPhoto, 25 August 2019).

We should agree with Aida Soboleva that "in Russian society there are currently two persistent negative stereotypes concerning a woman who follows Islam:

– A Muslim woman is passive and downtrodden;
– A Muslim woman tends to follow extremism."[26]

Islamic themes are actively manipulated by mass media in the political context using standard definitions such as "Vakhabites," "Islamic Fundamentalists," "Mojaheds," "Shakhids," and so on. Political problems acquire a religious subtext growing sometimes to a level of generalisations.

This critique of Muslim women begins with their appearance: Why do they cover the entire body and sometimes even veil the face? People judge these women by appearance and have no interest in their inner world and moral values.

The peculiar features of Muslim clothes are used as a resource to create and dispute the social visibility of Muslims. Mass media promote the image of an anonymous Muslim woman. By means of photos where Muslim women are dressed in black niqabs, they become "homogenised" and are often represented as silent inanimate victims who need to be protected and are unable to accept Western values. However, many Muslim women do not wear headscarves and only few of them in Russia hide their faces completely.

Muslim women's visibility mode in the Russian Islamic Internet content in the fight against stereotypes

Almost all Islamic sites contain material aimed at dispelling myths on passivity, lack of education and aggressiveness of Muslim women. Muslim women are convinced that there is little information in mass media about successful women in Islam and their true status remains concealed. "A Muslim woman" seems now to be a synonym for "a helpless victim," authors say on the site "Islam Today."[27]

---

[26] Aida Soboleva, "К вопросу об образе женщины-мусульманки в российском информационном пространстве [On the Image of Muslim Women in Russian Mass Media]," in: Irina Frolova and Liliya Gazizova (eds.), *Статус женщины-мусульманки в поликонфессиональном обществе: история и современность* (WorldPress: 2016), 108.

[27] Медиа-стереотипы, разрушающие жизнь мусульманки [Media Stereotypes Destroying the Life of a Muslim Woman], in: *Islam Today Kazan*, 23 February 2014 (https://islam-today.ru/zhenshhina_v_islame/media-stereotipy-razrusausie-zizn-musulmanki/, 28 November 2019).

Zilya Khabibullina
The Image of a Muslim Woman in the Russian Mass Media: Trying to Overcome Stereotypes in Islamic Media Space

As regards the religious symbols, in the Internet space Muslim women urge their co-religionists to reject black cloaks in order not to attract people's attention and make a terrifying impression. "Traditional Muslim dark abayas, that is, black clothes covering a woman's figure from head to foot and hiding face completely are inappropriate in Russian society," they think and recommend choosing bright colours and ornate prints.[28] There is now a whole fashion trend of the so-called "hijabists." They show fashionable hijabs and share ideas in their blogs and on Instagram. One can find them by the hashtags #hijabista, #hijabfashionand #hijabstreetstyle.

However, despite appeals on the part of Muslims to fairly reflect the reality, Islamic mass media are mainly focused on missionary work and dissemination of information about the benefit of belief for women. They almost say nothing about scientific, creative and sporting achievements of those Muslim women who lead a lifestyle inconsistent with religious laws and yet identify themselves with Islam by origin. Islamic mass media give little information about women's participation in public and political life of the country and their interaction with the followers of other religions, but much is written about beauty, fashion, clothing, halal cosmetics and rules of behaviour according to the Sunnah.

There is a tendency among Muslim women to keep blogs on the Internet where they have a chance to display their lifestyle and share their thoughts and impressions. In Russia the most popular female Instagram bloggers are:

- Aydan Mamedova (forty thousand followers), the Azerbaijan by origin, is a journalist, a blogger and an anchorperson of the program "Islamic Mosaic" on the TV channel Russia twenty-four.
- Aygul Gabaydulina (twelve thousand female followers) writes a "strict blog for strict Muslim women." The author writes in a very detailed, accessible form about her vision of life in the Muslim countries.
- Aleksandra Golovkova (more than four hundred sixty-three thousand followers) known as "The Most Stylish Muslim Woman of Russia," "Beauty in Hijab," "Modest Beauty." The conversion to Islam by a Russian girl provoked keen interest among the users of social networks. The image created by Aleksandra has become a fashion icon for a great number of young Muslim

---

[28] Как выглядит и кто такая современная мусульманка [What does a modern Muslim woman look like and who is she], in: *Muslim Fashion* – все о мусульманской моде (https://muslimfashion.ru/news/muslim_news/modern_muslim_women,_how_they_look_like, 10 September 2019).

women. Her dress-code, the way of wearing a headscarf, photos, selfies and many other things have gained unprecedented popularity and led to imitation.
- Safiya Umm Ibrahim (forty thousand Muslim followers), the Georgian, is a physician by profession. She writes a medical blog and recommends using *Hijama* known as cupping therapy to treat and prevent diseases.

Such official Islamic organisations as the Russian Council of Muftis and the Central Spiritual Administration of the Muslims of Russia are also engaged in creating a positive image of the Muslim woman. The image of a contemporary female Muslim is presented by Nailya Ziganshina, Head of the Union of Russian Muslim Women, on the website "The Muslims of Russia" in the following words, "We see the image of a Muslim woman in such a way. The beauty of her soul should necessarily be reflected in her appearance. She is well-educated, affable, favourably disposed towards the people around, not indifferent to social problems, eager to earn the grace of Allah, our Almighty, and certainly she is active in solving social problems. All these merits should be incarnated in a genuinely believing woman."[29]

Each year in Ufa the Spiritual Administration holds the All-Russian Women's Forum at which they discuss "the problems of morality, family, parenting, issues concerning Muslim women's self-actualisation in society and their influence on the destinies of both society and country."[30] The event is accompanied by a trade exhibition of halal goods and services and closes with a contest among married women "Super Daughter-in-Law", where each participant presents a written permission from her husband and a recommendation from her mother-in law.[31] The event is a kind of closed entertainment, and unfortunately, it does not aim at solving the problems of Muslim women in society with its stereotypes of mistrust.

A similar situation is observed in the Islamic Internet resources. Muslim women do not try to engage in dialogue with society, often assert their exclusion and claim special rights. In order to find reliable information about the

---

[29] Доклад Наили Зиганшиной "Образ современной мусульманки в России" [Report by Nailya Ziganshina "The Image of a Modern Muslim Woman in Russia"], in: *Мусульмане России. Официальный сайт Духовного управления мусульман Российской Федерации*, 5 May 2012 (http://dumrf.ru/dumer/speeches/3375, 25 August 2019).

[30] В Уфе состоялся V Всероссийский форум женственности [The 5th All-Russian Forum of Femininity was held in Ufa], in: *Центральное духовное управление мусульман России*, 3 December 2017 (http://www.cdum.ru/news/44/8942/, 15 November 2019).

[31] Ibid.

status of a Muslim woman, Islamic sites recommend that the "non-Muslim" part of society read the Quran and hadiths. For example, they advocate the possibility to wear hijab without feeling confused and biased on the part of other people or to be absent during the working hours for *namaz* and Friday sermon. Russian Islamic mass media emphasise women's high status according to the Islamic religious canons and admit the non-performance of religious precepts to a proper degree and, as a result, women's discrimination in family and society. Last year I was lucky to conduct field research in Saudi Arabia during the Hajj. I spent almost a month with Muslim women and had the chance to observe their lifestyle. In fact, the visibility mode among Muslim women includes emphasised piety; they compete with each other in the thoroughness of observing religious rules, ostentatious wearing of headscarves and prescribed clothes, modesty and obedience to the opposite gender.

It should be noted that the Internet is highly efficient in improving the image of one or another religion. The greater part of information for traditional mass media, such as television, radio and press, is found online, that is, the global networks exert either direct or indirect effect on the formation of images and visibility modes. The Internet is filled up with real people, and information put on the website reflects social reality. In order to change the attitude towards religious people and cope with various phobias, Muslims create databases and attract attention to the resources about Islam and its followers informing of their traditions. In our days, the sphere of using the Internet by Muslims is considerably expanded, and the formation of the image of Islam will still continue in the future by means of the Internet.

Conclusions

The problem of the Muslim woman's image is the cross-link for the categories of religion, gender and policy. The negative image of a Muslim woman existing in the Russian mass media attests to the formation of islamophobia. This facilitates the use of the Internet by Muslims as a platform for them to announce protests against information discrimination. On the other hand, there is a feeling of the growing danger of Islam inspired among non-Muslims under the influence of mass media. Eventually, mutual distrust emerges and develops on both parts. The visibility mode of a Muslim woman displayed by Islamic mass media includes beauty, womanhood and piety and fails to break the negative image of a Muslim woman existing in society through the opposition of housekeeping and family values with such harmful stereotypes as backwardness and aggression. The Muslim woman's status is aggravated by her visible closedness to Islamic community, demonstration of outward religiosity, development of patriarchal gender in a society, where Orthodoxy predominates and there are different faiths, but not the aspiration to exhibit her level of education.

The study of Islamic mass media in the gender aspect suggests that there is a specific situation in Russia associated with Islamic feminism among Muslim women spread throughout the Eastern countries, Europe and the United States finds no response on the part of the Russian Muslims. There is no well-organised Islamic feminist association in Russia.[32] The movement of Russian Muslim women does not imply the struggle for gender equality, but is the struggle against the existing stereotypes about Islam in society. Islamic mass media reflect the struggle against stereotypes about the lifestyle of a Muslim woman that develops in two directions. These are overcoming of negative ideas about Islam as a whole and struggle with public opinion for the right to obey religious prescripts. In Europe many Islamic mass media disseminate feminist views, but in Russia we do not observe such a phenomenon.

Zilya Khabibullina, PhD (History), Senior Researcher of the Department of Religiology, R.G. Kuzeev Institute for Ethnological Studies – a Subdivision of the Ufa Federal Research Centre of the Russian Academy of Sciences; Senior Researcher of Peter the Great Museum of Anthropology and Ethnography (Kunstkamera) of the Russian Academy of Sciences; Associate Professor of the Bashkir State Pedagogical University named after M. Akmullah. She is the author of *The Muslim Religious Leaders in the Republic of Bashkortostan at the Turn of the 20th Century* (2015) and numerous articles on the history and development of Islam in secular and multi-denominational society. She edited a volume *Islam in Russia in Current Transformation Processes: New Challenges and Development Trends in the 21st Century* (2017), anthology *Hajj Muslim Peoples of Russia: History and Modernity* (2018). zilyahabibi@mail.ru

---

[32] Alsu Gusmanova, Феминизм в исламе: Как женщины-мусульманки отстаивают свои права [Feminism in Islam: How Muslim Women Defend Their Rights], in: *Enter*, 24 October 2017 (https://entermedia.io/people/feminizm-v-islame-kak-zhenshhiny-musulmanki-otstaivayut-svoi-prava/, 10 September 2019).

Karin Hügel

Queere Auslegungen der Liebesgebote aus Levitikus[1]

Zusammenfassung
Die Liebesgebote aus Levitikus – das Nächstenliebegebot in Lev 19,18 und das Fremdenliebegebot in Lev 19,34 – werden im Anschluss an drei traditionelle Interpretationsvarianten des Nächstenliebegebots aus dem Heiligkeitsgesetz queer ausgelegt.

Erstens kann das Nächstenliebegebot (Lev 19,18) folgendermaßen übersetzt werden: „Du sollst deinen Nächsten lieben, wie *du* dich selbst *liebst* (bzw. *lieben sollst*)". Der oder die Nächste soll in dem Maß geliebt werden, wie jemand sich selbst liebt. Ein solches Verständnis dieses Gebots setzt Selbstliebe voraus. Das Nächstenliebegebot könnte aber auch als Gebot zur Selbstliebe betrachtet werden. Einzelnen queeren Menschen etwa mangelnde Selbstliebe vorzuwerfen, könnte von den Betroffenen als Zynismus aufgefasst werden, wenn ein selbstbestimmtes sexuelles Leben für sie nicht möglich ist. Selbstliebe sollte diesen Leuten durch die Schaffung eines Umfelds leichter gemacht werden, welches ihre Lebens- und Liebesweisen fördert. Ein liebevoller Umgang diverser queerer Leute mit sich selbst wiederum wirkt sich auf ihren Umgang mit anderen Mitmenschen positiv aus.

Zweitens kann das Nächstenliebegebot (Lev 19,18) Folgendes bedeuten: „Du sollst deinen Nächsten lieben, denn er ist *ein Mensch* wie du". In der jüdischen Aufklärung schuf der jüdische Dichter, Sprachwissenschaftler und Exeget Naftali Herz Wessely eine neue jüdische Auslegungstradition des Nächstenliebegebots aus Levitikus, indem er die Gleichheit aller Menschen durch Rekurs auf die Schöpfung theologisch begründete. Aus heutiger feministischer und queerer Sicht gilt es jedoch, eine inklusive Neuinterpretation des biblischen Nächsten- und Fremdenliebegebots einzufordern, sodass die Liebesgebote aus Levitikus als Aufruf zum respektvollem Handeln auch und besonders gegenüber Frauen und diversen Minderheiten wie queeren Personen verstanden werden können.

---

[1] Dieser Artikel ist ein Teil meiner in Entstehung begriffenen Dissertation mit dem Titel „Queere Lesarten der Hebräischen Bibel". Er wurde gekürzt auf der 18. Internationalen Konferenz der Europäischen Gesellschaft für theologische Forschung von Frauen „Geschlecht, Rasse, Religion, De/Konstruieren von Regimen der Un/Sichtbarkeit" an der Katholischen Universität Löwen 2019 und auf der 7. Jahrestagung der Österreichischen Gesellschaft für Geschlechterforschung „Geschlecht und Geschlechterverhältnisse in Transformation: Räume – Relationen – Repräsentationen" an der Universität Innsbruck 2019 vorgetragen.

Drittens und letztens kann das Nächstenliebegebot (Lev 19,18) im Sinne der negativen Goldenen Regel auf folgende Weise verstanden werden: „Du sollst deinen Nächsten lieben, *sodass, was dir verhasst ist, du ihm nicht tun sollst*". Bereits zur Zeit der Abfassung der aramäischen Übersetzung des Targum Pseudo-Jonathan galten die Liebesgebote aus Levitikus als auslegungsbedürftig, sodass die negative Goldene Regel in TPsJ zu Lev 19,18 und zu Lev 19,34 eingeflochten wurde. Nicht nur bedeutsamen Rabbinen wie Hillel oder Akiba, sondern auch Jesus von Nazareth wurde die Goldene Regel zugeschrieben. Auch die Goldene Regel sollte heute – im Unterschied zur Antike – inklusiv verstanden werden und unter Einbezug nicht nur von Männern, sondern auch von Frauen und queeren Personen im Sinne einer Ethik des guten Miteinanders aller Menschen dieser Welt angewendet werden.

Schlagwörter: Queere Lesarten; Nächstenliebegebot (Levitikus 19,18); Fremdenliebegebot (Levitikus 19,34); Selbstliebe; Gleichheit aller Menschen; Goldene Regel.

Abstract
The commandments of love in Leviticus – the one to love the neighbour in Lev 19:18 and the one to love the stranger in Lev 19:34 – are queerly interpreted in connection with three traditional ways of interpretation of the commandment to love the neighbour in the Holiness Code.

Firstly, the commandment of loving one's neighbour (Lev 19:18) can be translated in the following way: "You shall love your neighbour as *you love* (or: *shall love*) yourself". The neighbour shall be loved to the same extent as someone loves him- or herself. Such an understanding of this commandment presupposes self-love. However, the commandment of loving one's neighbour could also be regarded as an imperative to love oneself. Accusing individual queer people for example of lacking self-love could be considered as cynicism by the persons concerned if a self-determined sexual life is not possible for them. Loving oneself should be made easier for those people by creating an environment which sustains their ways of life and love. A loving attitude of various queer people towards themselves, in turn, has a positive impact on their interaction with other fellow human beings.

Secondly, the commandment of loving one's neighbour (Lev 19:18) can mean the following: "You shall love your neighbour for he is *a human being* like you". In the Jewish Enlightenment the Jewish poet, philologist and exegete Naphtali Herz Wessely created a new Jewish tradition of interpreting this commandment in Leviticus by theologically underpinning the equality of all human beings by recourse to the creation. However, from a present-day feminist and queer perspective, it is necessary to demand an inclusive reinterpretation of the biblical commandments to love neighbours and strangers so that the commandments of love in Leviticus can be understood as a call for respectful conduct especially towards women and diverse minorities like queer people.

Thirdly and finally, the commandment of loving one's neighbour (Lev 19:18) can be interpreted in the meaning of the negative Golden Rule as follows: "You shall love your neighbour *so that, what is hateful to you, you shall not do to him*". Already at the time of the composition of the Aramaic translation of Targum Pseudo-Jonathan the commandments of love in Leviticus have been considered as in need of explanation so that the negative Golden Rule has been woven into TPsJ on Lev 19:18 and on Lev 19:34. The Golden Rule was attributed not only to important rabbis like Hillel or Akiba but also to Jesus of Nazareth. Also the Golden Rule should be understood today – in contrast to antiquity – in an inclusive way and should be applied, including not only men but also women and queer people, in terms of ethics for a good coexistence of all human beings in this world.

Keywords: queer readings; Lev 19:18; Lev 19:34; self-love; equality of all human beings; Golden Rule.

Resumen
Los mandamientos de amar del Levítico (aquel de amar al prójimo en Lev 19,18 y aquel de amar al extranjero en Lev 19,34) son interpretados de manera queer en conexión con tres interpretaciones tradicionales del mandamiento de amar al prójimo en el Código de Santidad.

En primer lugar, el mandamiento de amar al prójimo (Lev 19,18) puede traducirse de la siguiente manera: "Deberás amar a tu prójimo tal y como *te amas* (o: *deberás amarte*) a ti". El prójimo deberá ser amado en la misma medida que alguien se ama a sí mismo o misma. Tal comprensión del mandamiento presupone el amor propio. Sin embargo, el mandamiento de amar al prójimo también podría verse como un imperativo para amarse a sí. Acusar a personas queer, por ejemplo, de carecer de amor propio podría considerarse cínico cuando una vida sexual autodeterminada no les es posible. El amor propio debería hacerse más sencillo para aquellas personas creando un ambiente que sustente sus vidas y amor. A cambio, la actitud amorosa de las personas queer hacia sí mismas tiene un impacto positivo en su interacción con sus semejantes.

En segundo lugar, el mandamiento de amar al prójimo puede significar lo siguiente: "Deberás amar al prójimo puesto que es *un ser humano* como tú". En la Ilustración judía, el poeta, filólogo y exegeta Naftalí Herz Wessely interpretó este mandamiento al defender teológicamente la igualdad de todos los humanos recurriendo a la creación. Sin embargo, desde una perspectiva moderna feminista y queer, es necesario demandar una reinterpretación inclusiva de los mandamientos bíblicos de amar al prójimo y al extranjero de tal modo que estos mandamientos del Levítico puedan entenderse como una llamada a la conducta respetuosa, especialmente hacia mujeres y diversas minorías como las personas queer.

En tercer lugar y por último, el mandamiento de amar al prójimo puede interpretarse en el sentido de la regla de oro en negativo: "Deberás amar al prójimo, *de modo que no deberás hacerle lo que te resulta odioso.*" Ya en la época de composición de la traducción aramea del Targum Pseudo-Jonathan, se consideró que los mandamientos de amar del Levítico necesitaban una explicación, de tal manera que la regla de oro en negativo se ha entretejido en TPsJ de Lev 19,18 y 19,34. La regla de oro se atribuye no solo a importantes rabinos como Hillel o Akiva, sino también a Jesús de Nazaret. La regla de oro debería ser entendida hoy en día, al contrario que en la Antigüedad, de manera inclusiva y debería aplicarse, incluyendo no solo a hombres sino también a mujeres y personas queer, en términos éticos para una buena coexistencia entre los seres humanos de este mundo.

Palabras clave: lectura qeer; Lev 19,18; Lev 19,34; autoamor; igualdad de los seres humanos; regla de oro.

Nachdem ich im *Jahrbuch der Europäischen Gesellschaft für theologische Forschung von Frauen* schon zwei Beiträge zu queeren Lesarten der Hebräischen Bibel geliefert habe, nämlich zum Buch Ruth zusammen mit den Schöpfungsberichten[2] und zum Hohelied,[3] präsentiere ich diesmal queere Lesarten zu den Liebesgeboten aus Levitikus.

Sogenannte Homosexualität, ein in mehrerer Hinsicht problematischer Begriff, welcher nicht anachronistisch auf biblische und halachische (das heißt jüdisch rechtliche) Texte der Antike angewendet werden sollte,[4] ist nicht mehr länger nur reines Objekt wie in herkömmlichen wissenschaftlichen Abhandlungen zu den Gesetzen bezüglich Sex zwischen Männern in Lev 18,22 und Lev 20,13. Durch die Entstehung queerer Lesarten der Bibel und weiterer jüdischer und christlicher Schriften im Anschluss an sie fand eine Umkehrung diskursiver Machtverhältnisse statt: Unterschiedliche queere Personen, nämlich Lesben, Schwule, bisexuelle Leute, Transgenderpersonen, intersexuelle und andere Personen, die ihre sexuelle Orientierung oder ihre Identifizierung

---

[2] Vgl. Karin Hügel, „*Queere* Lesarten der Hebräischen Bibel: Das Buch Ruth und die Schöpfungsberichte," in: Lisa Isherwood et al. (eds.), *Wrestling with God/En lucha con Dios/Ringen mit Gott* (Peeters: Leuven 2010) Jahrbuch der Europäischen Gesellschaft für theologische Forschung von Frauen 18, 173-192.
[3] Vgl. Karin Hügel, „Queere Lesarten des Hohelieds," in: Uta Blohm et al. (eds.), *In-between Spaces: Creative Possibilities for Theologies of Gender/Entre espacios: propuestas creativas para las teologías de género/Zwischenräume: Kreative Möglichkeiten für Gender-Theologien* (Peeters: Leuven 2013), Jahrbuch der Europäischen Gesellschaft für theologische Forschung von Frauen 21, 169-185.
[4] Vgl. Exkurs: „Hinweis auf die Zeit- und Ortsgebundenheit unterschiedlicher Verständnisse von Sexualität" in: Hügel, „*Queere* Lesarten. Ruth und Schöpfungsberichte," 185-188.

mit dem soziokulturellen Geschlecht hinterfragen,[5] haben begonnen, alte religiöse Quellen wie die Bibel etc. selbst aus ihren jeweiligen Sichtweisen wissenschaftlich zu untersuchen.[6] Im Zuge queerer bibelwissenschaftlicher und judaistischer Forschung hat sich das Feld der zu analysierenden religiösen Schriften geweitet. Je nach eigener Fragestellung können viel mehr biblische Texte und deren spätere Auslegungen (also auch die Liebesgebote aus Levitikus und jüdische und christliche Interpretationen im Anschluss daran) queer gelesen werden, letztendlich auch von Personen, die sich selbst nicht einer der unter dem Sammelbegriff „queer" subsumierten Gruppen zuordnen, aber – zum Beispiel aus politischen Gründen – einen queeren Ansatz verfolgen. Das heißt jedoch nicht, dass biblische und rabbinische Passagen zu weiblicher und männlicher Homoerotik[7] aus dem Blickfeld eines queeren Forschungsinteresses wegfallen und sich Wissenschaftler_Innen[8] wie ich nicht weiter daran

---

[5] Diese Personen haben das ursprüngliche Schimpfwort gegen sie – englisch „*queer*" bedeutet „seltsam", „sonderbar" – als affirmative Selbstbezeichnung vereinnahmt und verwenden es im Sinne von „positiv pervers". Eine positive Umdeutung von Beschimpfungen wie bei dem Begriff *queer* ist nicht neu, zum Beispiel englisch *Quaker* („Quäker"), französisch *huguenots* („Hugenotten") oder niederländisch *geuzen* (als Selbstbezeichnung niederländischer Freiheitskämpfer im Achtzigjährigen Krieg, die als französisch *gueux*, „Bettler" geschmäht wurden). In der Linguistik heißen solche Wörter im Anschluss an letztgenanntes Beispiel „Geusenwörter". Als Verb wird englisch *to queer* gebraucht für „jemanden irreführen, etwas verderben oder verpfuschen". Substantivisch steht es zum Beispiel für „Falschgeld". Es spielt also mit der gedanklichen Verbindung, dass solche Leute so etwas wie Falschgeld sind, mit dem die *straight world*, die Welt der „richtigen" Frauen und Männer, getäuscht werden soll.

[6] Ken Stone, welcher einen queeren Kommentar zur Bibel herausgegeben hat (vgl. Ken Stone [ed.], *Queer Commentary and the Hebrew Bible* [Sheffield Academic Press: London/New York 2001], Journal for the Study of the Old Testament: Supplement Series 334), thematisiert diesen diskursiven Wechsel. Vgl. Ken Stone, „Homosexuality and the Bible or Queer Reading? A Response to Martti Nissinen," in: *Theology and Sexuality* 14 (2001), 107-118.

[7] Der im Zusammenhang mit Lev 18,22 und Lev 20,13 heute oft fälschlich assoziierte Terminus „Homosexualität" ist an moderne Konzepte der Sexualität gebunden, und auch das Wort „Homoerotik" ist nicht gänzlich frei davon. Um nicht ohne Begriff auskommen zu müssen und mangels eines besseren Terminus schließe ich mich einem namhaften Bibelwissenschaftler an und verwende trotzdem den Begriff „Homoerotik". Vgl. Martti Nissinen, *Homoeroticism in the Biblical World: A Historical Perspective* (Fortress Press: Minneapolis 1998).

[8] Meine Schreibweise ist eine Kombination des Gender Gaps mit dem Binnen-I. Diese Praxis stellt einen Kompromiss zwischen Ansichten der Queer-Theorie und des Feminismus dar. So sollen mit dem Gender Gap (Geschlechterzwischenraum) auch Menschen angesprochen werden, die sich nicht in einem rein binären Männlich/Weiblich-Schema wiederfinden können/wollen. Mit dem Binnen-I wird weiterhin einer nicht sexistischen Schreibweise Rechnung getragen.

abarbeiten, wovon meine jüngste Publikation zu jüdischen gesetzlichen Auslegungen zu weiblicher Homoerotik zeugt.[9]

Queere Lesarten der Hebräischen Bibel und ihrer jüdischen und christlichen Auslegungen und Rezeptionen nehmen nicht normative Sexualitäten ins Blickfeld. Heteronormativität wird dabei unterlaufen. Ziel queerer Auslegungen ist es, unterschiedliche queere Lebensweisen zu fördern und somit unterschiedliche queere Personen zu stärken.[10]

In diesem Artikel thematisieren queere Lesarten der Liebesgebote aus dem biblischen Buch Levitikus Selbstliebe aus queerer Sicht (Abschnitt 1) und fordern den Einbezug von Frauen und diversen queeren Personen sowohl im schöpfungsethischen Diskurs (in Verbindung mit dem Gedanken der Gleichheit aller geschaffenen Menschen) (Abschnitt 2) als auch hinsichtlich der Maxime der Goldenen Regel (Abschnitt 3). Die hier zu besprechende biblische Überlieferung im Zusammenhang mit den Liebesgeboten aus Levitikus und deren weitere Interpretationen im Judentum und Christentum sind nämlich traditionsgemäß von rein androzentrischen Sichtweisen, das heißt von jenen, welche den Mann ins Zentrum des Denkens stellen, geprägt. Bisher hat auch noch kaum jemand die Liebesgebote aus Levitikus queer gelesen.

In diesem Beitrag möchte ich also – im Sinne einer queeren Lektüre – den Blick weg von den für Schwule, aber auch für Lesben et cetera problematischen Bibelstellen im 18. und 20. Kapitel des Buchs Levitikus[11] lenken – hin zu den Liebesgeboten, welche sich dazwischen, im 19. Kapitel desselben biblischen Buchs, befinden. Zu den Liebesgeboten des Heiligkeitsgesetzes[12] zählen das

---

[9] Vgl. Karin Hügel, „Jüdische gesetzliche Auslegungen zu weiblicher Homoerotik," in: *Journal of Ancient Judaism* 10/3 (2019), 416-454 (https://doi.org/10.13109/jaju.2019.10.3.416).

[10] Ähnlich Stone (ed.), *Queer Commentary*, 33.

[11] Die Verbote männlicher Homoerotik haben einen relativ geringen Stellenwert in der Hebräischen Bibel, weil sie nur im Heiligkeitsgesetz in Lev 18,22 und Lev 20,13 und nicht auch im Dekalog und in den anderen beiden großen Rechtssammlungen, im Bundesbuch Exodus 20-22 und im Deuteronomium im 5. Buch Mose 12-26, genannt werden. Außerdem existiert nicht etwa ein eigenes Gesetz bezüglich Sex unter Frauen analog zu den Verboten männlicher Homoerotik Lev 18,22 und Lev 20,13. Spätere jüdisch-rechtliche Anschauungen assoziieren jedoch sexuelle Lust und Heirat zwischen Frauen mit dem „Brauch des Landes Ägypten" in Lev 18,3 aus der einleitenden Ermahnung im 18. Kapitel des Buchs Levitikus. Vgl. Sifra zu Lev 18,3 und Maimonides' *Mischne Tora, Sefer Keduscha, Hilchot Issure Bia* 21,8 bzw. Hügel, „Jüdische gesetzliche Auslegungen zu weiblicher Homoerotik".

[12] Das sogenannte Heiligkeitsgesetz umfasst aus moderner wissenschaftlicher Sicht die Kapitel Levitikus 17-26, in welchen Heiligkeit (קְדֹשׁ) in der Beziehung zwischen G*tt (יהוה) und seinem Volk Israel ein zentraler Begriff ist. Die Schreibweise der Bezeichnungen für

Nächstenliebegebot Lev 19,18 und das Fremdenliebegebot Lev 19,34. Queere Auslegungen dieser häufig zitierten Verse stelle ich hier vor.

Weder die Verbote männlicher Homoerotik Lev 18,22 und Lev 20,13 des Buchs Levitikus noch das Crossdressingverbot Dtn 22,5[13] des Buchs Deuteronomium finden sich etwa als Schriftzitate im Neuen Testament. Das Nächstenliebegebot, welches sich erstmals im Buch Levitikus befindet, wird jedoch mehrere Male und an zentralen Stellen des Neuen Testaments zitiert.[14] Möglicherweise ist nicht allen christlichen Leser_Innen bekannt, dass das Nächstenliebegebot bereits in der Hebräischen Bibel vorhanden ist.

In der Hebräischen Bibel gibt es insgesamt drei Gebote, in welchen G*tt (יהוה) zur Liebe aufruft, nämlich – neben dem Nächstenliebegebot Lev 19,18 und dem Fremdenliebegebot Lev 19,34, deren Besprechung aus queerer Sicht in diesem Beitrag das Thema ist, – auch das „Höre, Israel" (שְׁמַע יִשְׂרָאֵל) in Dtn 6,4-5: „Du sollst G*tt, deinen G*tt, von ganzem Herzen, mit jedem Atemzug und mit all deiner Kraft lieben [וְאָהַבְתָּ אֵת יהוה אֱלֹהֶיךָ בְּכָל־לְבָבְךָ וּבְכָל־נַפְשְׁךָ וּבְכָל־מְאֹדֶךָ]." Diese drei Liebesgebote der Hebräischen Bibel sind drei Dimensionen einer einzigen, tiefen Beziehung: G*tt (יהוה) zu lieben, bedeutet andere Menschen zu lieben, diejenigen, welche wie wir sind und auch diejenigen, welche es nicht sind.[15] Eine Verbindung von Gottes- und Nächstenliebe durch Anführen von Schriftzitaten findet sich jedoch nicht etwa in rabbinischer, sondern nur in

---

Gottesnamen mit dem Stern wie G*tt (יהוה), G*tt (יהוה אֱלֹהִים) et cetera in der Hebräischen Bibel und G*tt (יי), G*tt (הקב״ה), G*tt (מָקוֹם) et cetera in späteren jüdischen Schriften, stammt von mir und ist ebenfalls wie die Schreibweise mit dem Gender Gap von Anschauungen der Queer-Theorie inspiriert. יהוה hat nämlich kein grammatikalisch eindeutig zu bestimmendes Geschlecht; das Körperkonzept dieses Gottesnamens spart die Dimension des sexuellen Geschlechts aus.

[13] Die eigentliche Zielperson des Crossdressingverbots Dtn 22,5 ist der junge, kräftige Mann, welcher keine Frauenkleider anziehen soll. Dass ein solcher Mann nicht seine männliche Vorrangstellung in einer patriarchalen Gesellschaftsordnung verlieren soll, indem er sich nicht wie eine gewöhnliche Frau anzieht, ist eine mögliche, nicht unplausible Interpretation des Crossdressingverbots unter dem Postulat eines hierarchischen Geschlechterverhältnisses zu Ungunsten der Frau. Vom Wunsch eines Manns, Frauenkleider zum eigenen Lustgewinn oder zwecks Erweckung von Begierden anderer Männer tragen zu wollen, ist in Dtn 22,5 jedoch nicht die Rede. Dieses biblische Gesetz könnte außerdem bedeutet haben, dass eine Frau nicht die Waffen eines Manns tragen soll, sodass Frauen nicht den Rang von männlichen Kriegern einnehmen. Vgl. Karin Hügel, *Queere Lesarten der Hebräischen Bibel*, im Erscheinen.

[14] Vgl. Abschnitt „Du sollst deinen Nächsten lieben, wie *du* dich selbst *liebst* bzw. *lieben sollst*."

[15] Vgl. Tamara Cohn Eskenazi, „Another View," in: Tamara Cohn Eskenazi und Andrea L. Weiss (eds.), *The Torah: A Women's Commentary* (URJ Press: New York 2008), 716.

christlicher Literatur.[16] Aus christlicher Sicht erhalten das „Höre, Israel" und das Nächstenliebegebot der Hebräischen Bibel einen besonderen Stellenwert, wenn sie in der synoptischen[17] Tradition des Neuen Testaments als sogenanntes „Doppelgebot der Liebe" (Mk 12,28-34 und Parallelen)[18] als Schriftzitate vorkommen und dabei als die größten Gebote bezeichnet werden. So mögen die Liebesgebote der Hebräischen Bibel heute viel mehr Menschen bekannt und bedeutsam sein, sowohl straighten als auch queeren Personen, als einzelne Gesetze der Thora, wie die Verbote männlicher Homoerotik Lev 18,22 und Lev 20,13 oder das Crossdressingverbot Dtn 22,5.

Nun widme ich mich, wie gesagt, den Liebesgeboten der Hebräischen Bibel, nämlich dem Nächstenliebegebot Lev 19,18 und dem Fremdenliebegebot Lev 19,34, und stelle queere Auslegungen im Anschluss an drei traditionelle Interpretationsvarianten des Nächstenliebegebots aus Levitikus vor.

Die beiden Liebesgebote der Hebräischen Bibel richten sich ursprünglich an männliche, erwachsene israelitische Vollbürger.[19] Im patriarchalen Kontext des Heiligkeitsgesetzes legt sich keine inklusive Übersetzung für diese Liebesgebote nahe. Diese Gesetzestexte wurden aus androzentrischer Sicht verfasst. Frauen werden hier ursprünglich nicht angesprochen.[20] Da das Nächstenliebegebot in direktem Zusammenhang mit dem vorigen Vers steht, wo vom Hassverzicht die Rede ist, führe ich Lev 19,18 zusammen mit Lev 19,17 an:

> Du sollst deinen Bruder (das heißt deinen Volksgenossen) nicht hassen in deinem Herzen [לֹא־תִשְׂנָא אֶת־אָחִיךָ בִּלְבָבֶךָ], sondern deinen Mitbürger ernsthaft zurechtweisen

---

[16] Vgl. David Flusser, „A New Sensitivity in Judaism and the Christian Message," in: *Harvard Theological Review* 61/2 (1968), 107-127, hier 125. In zwei Stellen von Mischna Avot, nämlich in mAv 6,1.6, werden zwar in rabbinischen Texten die Liebe zu „G*tt"/zur „Stätte" (הַמָּקוֹם = rabbinische Gottesbezeichnung) und die Liebe zu den „Geschöpfen"/„Menschen" (הַבְּרִיּוֹת = Nomen, das sich vom Verb ברא [„schaffen"] ableitet) Seite an Seite erwähnt, aber dies sind keine Schriftzitate der Hebräischen Bibel.

[17] Das Wort „Synopse" stammt aus dem Griechischen (σύνοψις) und bedeutet „Zusammenschau". Die Synopse ist eine Zusammenstellung von Paralleltexten der ersten drei Evangelien des Markus, Matthäus und Lukas, welche – im Unterschied zu Johannes – weitgehend textlich übereinstimmen. Vgl. Friedrich Hauck und Gerhard Schwinge, *Theologisches Fach- und Fremdwörterbuch* (Vandenhoeck & Ruprecht: Göttingen 1987, 6., durchg. und erg. Aufl.), 192.

[18] Vgl. Mt 22,34-40; Lk 10,25-28. Vgl. außerdem auch die frühchristliche Schrift Didache 1,2.

[19] Vgl. Michael Ebersohn, *Das Nächstenliebegebot in der Synoptischen Tradition* (N. G. Elwert Verlag: Marburg 1993), Marburger Theologische Studien 37, 39.

[20] Es gibt im Heiligkeitsgesetz zum Beispiel auch keine Verbote weiblicher Homoerotik.

Karin Hügel
Queere Auslegungen der Liebesgebote aus Levitikus

[הוֹכֵחַ תּוֹכִיחַ אֶת־עֲמִיתֶךָ], damit du nicht seinetwegen Schuld auf dich lädst [וְלֹא־תִשָּׂא עָלָיו חֵטְא].[21] (Lev 19,17)
Du sollst nicht Rache üben [לֹא־תִקֹּם] und gegenüber deinen Volksgenossen nicht nachtragend sein [וְלֹא־תִטֹּר אֶת־בְּנֵי עַמֶּךָ], sondern du sollst deinen Nächsten lieben wie dich selbst [וְאָהַבְתָּ לְרֵעֲךָ כָּמוֹךָ][22]. Ich bin G*tt [אֲנִי יהוה]. (Lev 19,18)

Nicht nur im Deutschen ist „Hass" das Gegenteil von „Liebe", auch im Althebräischen ist „hassen" (שׂנא) die Antithese von „lieben" (אהב).[23] In dieser viel zitierten Stelle des Heiligkeitsgesetzes wird das Unterbrechen der Spirale des Hasses und der Gewalt geboten und stattdessen zur Liebe aufgerufen.

Die gängige Übersetzung von Lev 19,17, nicht „im Herzen" zu hassen, könnte die Vorstellung erzeugen, dass ein Gefühl wie Hass in der Hebräischen Bibel – ähnlich wie im europäisch-abendländischen Bereich – im Inneren des Menschen verortet ist. Heutige Gefühlskonzepte unterscheiden sich aber von jenen der Hebräischen Bibel. Emotionen werden in der Hebräischen Bibel nicht als aus dem Menschen entspringend gesehen.[24] Stattdessen werden biblische Figuren von Gefühlen von außen erfasst – wie König Saul vom bösen Geist Gottes.[25] Nicht „im Herzen" zu hassen mag in Lev 19,17 darauf hinweisen, dass Hass keine tiefen Wurzeln in den Betroffenen schlagen soll, sondern dass sie sich von ihm befreien sollen. Das Gebot aus dem Heiligkeitsgesetz setzt – im Unterschied zu Erzähltexten wie jenen im ersten Samuelbuch über Sauls Hassliebe zum jungen schönen David[26] – voraus, dass ein Mensch

---

[21] Die Übersetzungen von Textpassagen der Hebräischen Bibel nach Karl Elliger und Wilhelm Rudolph (eds.), *Biblia Hebraica Stuttgartensia* (Deutsche Bibelgesellschaft: Stuttgart [4]1990) stammen von mir.
[22] Die Verwendung der Präposition לְ in der Formulierung אהב לְ („jemanden lieben") statt dem Akkusativzeichen אֶת־/אֶת in Lev 19,18 und Lev 19,34 gehört zu den Besonderheiten des Späthebräischen, wobei dies im Aramäischen ganz gewöhnlich war. Vgl. Wilhelm Gesenius, Emil Kautzsch und Gotthelf Bergsträsser, *Hebräische Grammatik* (Georg Olms Verlagsbuchhandlung: Hildesheim 1962, reprograph. Nachdr. der 28. vielfach verb. und verm. Aufl. Leipzig 1909), § 117n, 381. Auch Paul Joüon und Takamitsu Muraoka betrachten לְ in diesen Stellen als Hinweis auf den Akkusativ des direkten Objekts. Vgl. Paul Joüon und Takamitsu Muraoka, *A Grammar of Biblical Hebrew* (Editrice Pontificio Istituto Biblico: Roma 2006), Subsidia Biblica 27, 418.
[23] Ebersohn, *Nächstenliebegebot*, 25.
[24] Vgl. Andreas Wagner, „Gefühle, in Sprache geronnen. Die historische Relativität von Gefühlen am Beispiel von ‚Hass'," in: Andreas Wagner, *Emotionen, Gefühle und Sprache im Alten Testament. Vier Studien* (Verlag Hartmut Spenner: Waltrop 2006), 49-73, hier 73.
[25] Vgl. 1 Sam 16,14-16.23; 1 Sam 18,10 und 1 Sam 19,9.
[26] Im Zusammenhang mit König Sauls Hassliebe zum schönen jungen David sind zwei Textpassagen aus den Kapiteln 16 und 18 des ersten Samuelbuchs relevant, wobei die erotische

sich Emotionen tatsächlich widersetzen kann. Möglicherweise kann er das verstandesmäßig tun. Da das Herz in der Hebräischen Bibel auch als der Sitz des Verstandes angenommen wird, könnte לֵבָב[27] in Lev 19,17 auf die Denkfähigkeit des Menschen abzielen. Hass gilt es sozusagen rational zu vermeiden. Deshalb wird als alternative Übersetzung von בִּלְבָבְךָ „mit deinem Verstand" vorgeschlagen.[28] Ebenso unverständlich wie die Möglichkeit, sich starken Emotionen wie Hass widersetzen zu können, mag umgekehrt für viele Lesende heute sein, dass Liebe – wie im Nächstenliebegebot Lev 19,18 – verordnet werden kann. Dieselbe Frage kann letztendlich auch hinsichtlich des Gottesliebegebots Dtn 6,5, dem „Höre, Israel" (שְׁמַע יִשְׂרָאֵל), gestellt werden, in welchem zur Liebe zu G*tt (יהוה) „von ganzem Herzen" (בְּכָל־לְבָב) aufgerufen wird.

Anhand von Lev 19,17 ist das Vorhandensein einer nachexilischen jüdischen Rechtsprechung nicht nachweisbar. In diesem Vers von Levitikus 19 ist nicht etwa von rechtlichen Schritten vor Gericht, sondern nur von einer ernsthaften Zurechtweisung jener israelitischen Mitbürger die Rede, die einen Grund zum Hass geliefert haben. Es bleibt vollkommen unbestimmt, was alles Hass innerhalb der israelitischen bzw. nachexilischen jüdischen Gemeinschaft hervorgerufen haben mochte. Interessant ist die abschließende Bemerkung in Lev 19,17, dass ein Israelit wegen der Hass erzeugenden Handlung eines anderen Israeliten nicht Schuld auf sich laden soll. Das zeugt von einem Schuldverständnis, nach dem nicht nur die Erzeuger von Hass selbst Schuld tragen,

---

Auslegung der zweiten Stelle 1 Sam 18,22, nämlich Sauls *Lust* auf David als Grund für dessen Verheiratung mit Michal, die David zum Schwiegersohn des Königs macht, eine erotische Auslegung der ersten Stelle 1 Sam 16,21-22 ermöglicht, wo von Sauls entfachter *Liebe* zu David die Rede ist. Wegen Sauls Verfluchung Jonathans in 1 Sam 20,30 („Verkehrter Rebell! Weiß ich nicht, dass du dich mit dem Sohn Isais [das heißt mit David], dir selbst und dem Schoß deiner Mutter zur Schande, verbunden hast?") können die früheren Hinweise auf Sauls Hassliebe zu David rückwirkend verstärkt in einem erotischen Sinn verstanden werden. Laut 1 Sam 20,30 muss Saul begriffen haben, dass sein eigenes – ehemals intimes – Verhältnis zu David gestört wurde, indem sein Sohn Jonathan ein sexuelles Verhältnis mit demselben gutaussehenden, aufstrebenden, jungen Mann hat. Hügel, *Queere Lesarten der Hebräischen Bibel*.

[27] לֵבָב bedeutet „Herz". Vgl. Ludwig Koehler und Walter Baumgartner, *Hebräisches und aramäisches Lexikon zum Alten Testament* [HAL] (Brill: Leiden und Boston 2004, 3. neu bearb. Aufl.), 1, 490. Das Wort לֵבָב kann aber auch andere Bedeutungen wie „Verstand" et cetera – ähnlich wie לֵב – haben.

[28] Wagner, „Gefühle, in Sprache geronnen", 72.

sondern sich auch andere Mitbürger mitschuldig machen, wenn sie deren Verhalten nicht zu unterbinden versuchen.[29]

In den beiden Versen Lev 19,17 und Lev 19,18 werden unterschiedliche hebräische Begriffe wie אָח ("Bruder" bzw. "Volksgenosse"), עָמִית ("Mitbürger"), בְּנֵי עַם (Volksgenossen") und רֵעַ ("Nächster")[30] für diejenigen Leute verwendet, unter denen kein Hass, sondern Liebe walten soll. Sie alle meinen Israeliten. Die jüdische Bevölkerung der Diaspora wurde durch diese beiden Gebote zum inneren Zusammenhalt aufgefordert. Rache gilt es zu unterlassen; nachtragendes Verhalten gegenüber den Volksgenossen ebenso. Anlass für zu unterbindende Rachegelüste musste nicht unbedingt eine unmittelbare Schädigung der in Lev 19,18 angesprochenen Person gewesen sein. Es konnten auch Vergehen in der Vergangenheit oder Verbrechen an anderen israelitischen Personen, zu denen ein Naheverhältnis oder eine wie auch immer geartete Verbindung bestand, ausschlaggebend für Rachegefühle gewesen sein.

Während das Nächstenliebegebot Lev 19,18 zur Liebe gegenüber dem israelitischen Volksgenossen aufruft, fordert das Fremdenliebegebot Lev 19,34 darüber hinaus auch die Liebe zum Fremden (גֵּר)[31] ein. Dieser soll wie ein israelitischer Einheimischer (אֶזְרָח)[32] behandelt werden. Ich zitiere das Fremdenliebegebot im Zusammenhang mit dem vorigen Vers Lev 19,33, welcher die Unterdrückung des Schutzbürgers (גֵּר) untersagt:

> Wenn jemand als Schutzbürger bei dir weilt, als Fremder in eurem Land, sollt ihr ihn nicht unterdrücken [וְכִי־יָגוּר אִתְּךָ גֵּר בְּאַרְצְכֶם לֹא תוֹנוּ אֹתוֹ]. (Lev 19,33)

---

[29] Während bei einem Verbot wie jenem männlicher Homoerotik in Lev 20,13 extra die Schuldformel דְּמֵיהֶם בָּם geschrieben steht, nach welcher die Schuld allein auf die in besonderer Weise sexuell agierenden Männer und nicht etwa auf das ganze Volk Israel zurückfallen soll, wird am Anfang von Levitikus 20 die Sippenhaftung thematisiert.

[30] רֵעַ bedeutet im Zusammenhang mit Lev 19,18 „Nächster" und ansonsten auch „Freund", „Liebling", „Gefährte", „Genosse" oder „Anderer". HAL 2, 1169-1170. Es existieren weibliche Formen von רֵעַ, nämlich רֵעָה („Gefährt_In", „Freund_In") oder im Hohelied רַעְיָה („Gefährt_In", „Freund_In" = Geliebte), und auch der sprechende Name Ruth (רוּת), welcher „Gefährt_In", „Freund_In" bedeutet, steht im Zusammenhang mit dem Verb רעה („sich befreunden"). Die griechische substantivierte Form ὁ πλησίον, mit welcher die Septuaginta רֵעַ im Zusammenhang mit Lev 19,18 übersetzt, bedeutet „der Nahestehende", „der Nächste", „der Mitmensch". Walter Bauer, *Griechisch-deutsches Wörterbuch zu den Schriften des Neuen Testaments* (de Gruyter: Berlin und New York 1988, 6. neu bearb. Aufl.), 1352.

[31] גֵּר bedeutet „Schutzbürger", „Fremdling". HAL 1, 193.

[32] אֶזְרָח bedeutet „Einheimischer", „Vollbürger". Ebenda, 28.

Der Fremde, der sich bei euch aufhält, soll wie ein Einheimischer bei euch gelten [כְּאֶזְרָח מִכֶּם יִהְיֶה לָכֶם הַגֵּר הַגָּר אִתְּכֶם], und du sollst ihn lieben wie dich selbst [וְאָהַבְתָּ לוֹ כָּמוֹךָ]; denn ihr seid Fremde in Ägypten gewesen [כִּי־גֵרִים הֱיִיתֶם בְּאֶרֶץ מִצְרָיִם]. Ich bin G*tt, euer G*tt [אֲנִי יהוה אֱלֹהֵיכֶם]. (Lev 19,34)

In Lev 19,34 fällt ein Numeruswechsel auf: Allein der Satz „... du sollst ihn [das heißt den Fremden] lieben wie dich selbst [וְאָהַבְתָּ לוֹ כָּמוֹךָ]" weist – ähnlich wie „... du sollst deinen Nächsten lieben wie dich selbst [וְאָהַבְתָּ לְרֵעֲךָ כָּמוֹךָ]" in Lev 19,18 – eine Anrede im Singular auf. Deshalb wird ein Zusammenhang zwischen dem Fremden- und Nächstenliebegebot und eine Abhängigkeit des Verses Lev 19,34 von Lev 19,18 in bibelwissenschaftlicher Literatur behauptet.[33] Ein Zusammenhang zwischen diesen beiden Versen wurde schon in einem antiken halachischen Midrasch zum Buch Levitikus, nämlich in Sifra[34] Qedoschim („Heilig")[35] 8 (91a) zu Lev 19,34, behauptet:

> Wie Bezug nehmend auf Israel gesagt wurde [כשם שנאמר לישראל]: „... du sollst deinen Nächsten lieben wie dich selbst [ואהבת לרעך כמוך]" [Lev 19,18], so wurde im Bezug auf Fremde gesagt [כך נאמר לגרים]: „... du sollst ihn [das heißt den Fremden] lieben wie dich selbst [ואהבת לו כמוך]" [Lev 19,34].[36] (Sifra Qedoschim 8 [91a] = Sifra 205,1,6 nach der englischen Ausgabe von Neusner)

Aus Sicht dieser alten jüdischen Schrift wurde das biblische Nächstenliebegebot als Aufruf zur Liebe zum Israeliten betrachtet und das Fremdenliebegebot analog dazu als Aufruf zur Liebe zu Fremden (גֵרִים) verstanden.

---

[33] Vgl. Eckart Otto, *Deuteronomium 1-11, Zweiter Teilband: 4,44-11,32* (Herder: Freiburg et al. 2012), Herders Theologischer Kommentar zum Alten Testament, 1039 bzw. Christophe Nihan, „Resident Aliens and Natives in the Holiness Legislation," in: Reinhard Achenbach, Rainer Albertz und Jakob Wöhrle (eds.), *The Foreigner and the Law: Perspectives from the Hebrew Bible and the Ancient Near East* (Harrassowitz Verlag: Wiesbaden 2011), Beihefte zur Zeitschrift für Altorientalische und Biblische Rechtsgeschichte 16, 111-134, hier 121, Fußnote 40.

[34] Sifra (סִפְרָא; „Buch") ist die Bezeichnung für „halakhic commentary on Leviticus" (den „halachischen Kommentar zu Levitikus"). Vgl. Marcus Jastrow, *Dictionary of the Targumim, the Talmud Babli and Yerushalmi, and the Midrashic Literature* (Hendrickson Publishers: Peabody 2006), 1018.

[35] Vgl. Vers Lev 19,2, den ich weiter unten in diesem Abschnitt zitiere.

[36] Eigene Übersetzung aus dem Hebräischen bzw. Aramäischen nach Isaak Hirsch Weiss, *Sifra. Commentar zu Leviticus aus dem Anfange des III. Jahrhunderts* (Jacob Schlossberg's Buchhandlung: Wien 1862). Bezüglich einer englischen Übersetzung vgl. Jacob Neusner, *Sifra: An Analytical Translation* (Scholars Press: Atlanta 1988), 3: *Aharé Mot, Qedoshim, Emor, Behar and Behuqotai*, Brown Judaic Studies 140, 128-129.

Die beiden Verse Lev 19,33 und Lev 19,34 zu richtigem Verhalten Fremden gegenüber mögen ein Gesetz aus dem Bundesbuch Exodus, nämlich Ex 22,20, voraussetzen:[37] „Einen Fremden sollst du nicht unterdrücken und bedrängen [וְגֵר לֹא־תוֹנֶה וְלֹא תִלְחָצֶנּוּ], denn ihr seid Fremde in Ägypten gewesen [כִּי־גֵרִים הֱיִיתֶם בְּאֶרֶץ מִצְרָיִם]." Hier ist nämlich ebenfalls davon die Rede, den Fremden (גֵּר) nicht zu unterdrücken (ינה im Hif'il),[38] und die Begründung ist dabei die gleiche. Auffallend ähnlich ist außerdem folgendes kurzes Gebot Dtn 10,19 aus Deuteronomium 10 (einem Teil der Rahmung der Gesetzessammlung des Deuteronomiums in Deuteronomium 12-26), in welchem dazu aufgefordert wird, den Fremden (גֵּר) zu lieben (אהב):[39] „Ihr sollt den Fremden lieben [וַאֲהַבְתֶּם אֶת־הַגֵּר], denn ihr seid Fremde in Ägypten gewesen [כִּי־גֵרִים הֱיִיתֶם בְּאֶרֶץ מִצְרָיִם]."

Im Fremdenliebegebot Lev 19,34 wird – wie in Ex 22,20 und auch in Dtn 10,19 – an eine Tradition angeknüpft, in welcher an die leidvolle Erfahrung als Fremde in Ägypten erinnert wird. Auf diese Weise wird das Gebot der Zuwendung zu Schutzbürgern (גֵּרִים) in nachexilischer Zeit begründet. Die Erfahrung eines anderen Exils, nämlich jene des babylonischen Exils, dürfte ausschlaggebend gewesen sein, dass Jüd_Innen ein spezifisches Selbstverständnis als Fremde entwickelt hatten.

Aus Levitikus 19 und den anderen Kapiteln des Heiligkeitsgesetzes ist es schwierig, den wirtschaftlichen und gesellschaftlichen Status eines Fremden (גֵּר) schlüssig näher zu bestimmen. Der Fremde (גֵּר) wird in Levitikus 19 neben Lev 19,33-34 nur in Lev 19,9-10 im Zusammenhang mit der Nachlese auf dem Feld und im Weinberg erwähnt. Den Fremden soll es – wie den Armen – ermöglicht werden, Feldfrüchte und abgefallene Trauben nach der Ernte aufzusammeln.[40] Nicht nur in Lev 19,10, sondern auch in Lev 23,22 wird der Fremde (גֵּר) zu denjenigen Personen gezählt, welche sich wirtschaftlich nicht selbst erhalten können und von israelitischen Landbesitzern abhängig sind. Aus anderen Stellen des Heiligkeitsgesetzes erfahren wir aber auch, dass ein Fremder (גֵּר) die Mittel gehabt haben muss, um ein Schlachtopfer

---

[37] Vgl. Karl Elliger, *Leviticus* (J.C.B. Mohr [Paul Siebeck]: Tübingen 1966), Handbuch zum Alten Testament 1,4, 250.
[38] Otto, *Deuteronomium 1-11, Zweiter Teilband: 4,44-11,32*, 1039.
[39] Im Unterschied zu Nihan, „Resident Aliens," 121, welcher Lev 19,34 als Rezeption von Dtn 10,19 versteht, ist es vorstellbar, dass Dtn 10,19 und Lev 19,33-34 auch ohne Kenntnis voneinander in unterschiedlichen Rechtssammlungen überliefert worden sind.
[40] Bezüglich ähnlicher Gesetze im Deuteronomium, nach denen Fremden, Waisen und Witwen die Nachlese auf dem Feld, im Olivenhain und im Weinberg ermöglicht werden soll, vgl. Dtn 24,19-22.

(זֶבַח) oder ein Brandopfer (עֹלָה)[41] „mit einwandfreien, männlichen Exemplaren von Rind, Lamm oder Ziege"[42] darzubringen. In Lev 25,47 wird der Fremde (גֵּר) im Zusammenhang mit der Gesetzgebung des Erlassjahres sogar als reich genug beschrieben, um israelitische Männer als Sklaven zu haben.[43] In der Septuaginta wird גֵּר nicht nur im Zusammenhang mit dem Fremdenliebegebot Lev 19,34, sondern im ganzen Heiligkeitsgesetz mit προσήλυτος („Hinzugekommener") übersetzt. Gemeint ist jemand, der als Fremder an einem Ort angekommen ist,[44] das heißt ein „fremder Ortsansässiger".

Wird das Fremdenliebegebot Lev 19,34 auf rechtliche Belange bezogen,[45] bleibt letztendlich unklar, welche Gesetze deshalb genau für Fremde – wie für Einheimische – im Heiligkeitsgesetz gelten sollten. Das Gesetz Ex 22,20 des Bundesbuchs Exodus, auf das in Lev 19,33-34 zurückgegriffen worden sein mag, steht im Zusammenhang mit dem sozialen Schutzrecht. In Dtn 10,18, dem Vers vor dem Fremdenliebegebot in der Rahmung der deuteronomischen Gesetzessammlung, ist zu lesen, dass G*tt (יהוה) das Recht von Waisen und Witwen durchsetzt und den Fremden (גֵּר) liebt, indem er ihm Speise und Kleidung gibt. Ein ähnliches Bestreben nach sozialer und wirtschaftlicher Gerechtigkeit kann also auch für Lev 19,33-34 angenommen werden.[46]

Die Differenzierung zwischen Einheimischem (אֶזְרָח) und Fremdem (גֵּר) findet sich im Heiligkeitsgesetz zuvor in der abschließenden Paränese von Levitikus 18 in Lev 18,26 und später am Anfang von Levitikus 20 in Lev 20,2. Beides sind Textpassagen, die redaktionelle Ergänzungen darstellen. Die Unterscheidung zwischen Vollbürger (אֶזְרָח) und Schutzbürger (גֵּר) kommt in den Kapiteln Levitikus 18, 19 und 20 des Heiligkeitsgesetzes neben Lev 18,26

---

[41] Vgl. Lev 17,8-9. Laut Num 15,14 soll ein Fremder (גֵּר) auf gleiche Weise wie ein Israelit G*tt (יהוה) ein Feueropfer (אִשֶּׁה) darbringen.

[42] In Lev 22,18-19 werden diese männlichen Tiere im Zusammenhang mit einem Brandopfer (עֹלָה) erwähnt.

[43] Im Kontext der Verfluchung bei Nichteinhaltung der deuteronomischen Gesetze wird in Dtn 28,43-44 ausgesagt, dass der Fremde (גֵּר) sozial aufsteigen wird – im Gegensatz zur israelitischen Bevölkerung, welche immer tiefer sinken wird. Hier wird thematisiert, dass der Fremde (גֵּר) derjenige sein wird, der verleiht. Der Fremde wird „der Kopf", der Israelit aber „der Schwanz" sein.

[44] „One who has arrived at a place as foreigner." Vgl. Takamitsu Muraoka, *A Greek-English Lexicon of the Septuagint* (Peeters: Louvain et al. 2009), 594.

[45] Nihan, „Resident Aliens," 122.

[46] Ebenda, 122.

nur in Lev 19,34 und Lev 20,2 vor.[47] Das Fremdenliebegebot Lev 19,34 könnte daher eine späte rechtliche Ergänzung im Anschluss an Ex 22,20 und Lev 19,18 im Zuge einer redaktionellen Bearbeitung von Levitikus 19 darstellen – vor oder gleichzeitig mit der Einfügung von Lev 20,2-5 in Levitikus 20. Da das Heiligkeitsgesetz in die Perserzeit datiert wird, in welcher nicht das jüdische Volk, sondern das Geschlecht der Achämeniden das Sagen hatte, sind die Nächsten- und Fremdenliebegebote – ähnlich wie die Verbote männlicher Homoerotik Lev 18,22 und Lev 20,13[48] – als Teile spezifischer jüdischer Utopien zu betrachten. Sie könnten ebenfalls der Wunschvorstellung einer antiken Redaktor_In des Heiligkeitsgesetzes entsprochen haben, eine religiöse, rechtliche Weltanschauung zu erschaffen, die nie realisiert worden ist.

Bezüglich des zahlenmäßigen Vorkommens der beiden Liebesgebote der Hebräischen Bibel ist Folgendes zu sagen: Während das Nächstenliebegebot keinerlei Parallelen in der Hebräischen Bibel hat,[49] finden sich Fremdenliebegebote sowohl im Heiligkeitsgesetz in Lev 19,33-34 als auch in der Rahmung der deuteronomischen Gesetzessammlung (Deuteronomium 12-26) in Dtn 10,19. Zusätzlich existierte mit Ex 22,20 bereits ein ähnliches Gesetz im sozialen Schutzrecht des Bundesbuchs Exodus. Der Gedanke der Fremdenliebe war also kein unbedeutender in der Hebräischen Bibel. Wie bereits erwähnt, spielte nach dem babylonischen Exil die eigene Erfahrung des Fremdseins im Judentum eine große Rolle.

Die abschließenden kurzen Sätze „Ich bin G*tt [אֲנִי יהוה]" im Nächstenliebegebot Lev 19,18 und „Ich bin G*tt, euer G*tt [אֲנִי יהוה אֱלֹהֵיכֶם]" im Fremdenliebegebot Lev 19,34 des Heiligkeitsgesetzes verweisen auf einen besonderen religiösen Kontext. Am Anfang des 19. Kapitels des Buchs Levitikus wurde in Lev 19,2 die ganze israelitische Gemeinde dazu aufgerufen: „Ihr sollt heilig sein [קְדֹשִׁים תִּהְיוּ], denn ich, G*tt, euer G*tt, bin heilig [כִּי קָדוֹשׁ אֲנִי יהוה אֱלֹהֵיכֶם]". So stehen, synchron gelesen, die einzelnen, auffallend

---

[47] Außerhalb des Heiligkeitsgesetzes ist in Ez 47,22 davon die Rede, dass ein Fremder (גֵּר) wie ein Einheimischer (אֶזְרָח) unter den Israeliten gelten soll und dieser auch Erbbesitz erhalten können soll.

[48] Die Verbote männlicher Homoerotik mochten der Prävention gedient haben. Sie wurden aus utopischer Sicht verfasst. Die Adressaten mochten durch diese Rhetorik „einen Kopf kürzer" gewesen sein. Es ist aber nicht nachweisbar, dass sie deshalb umgebracht worden sind. Es gab keine direkte Anwendung von Lev 20,13 in biblischen Zeiten. Das Vorhandensein einer nachexilischen jüdischen Rechtsprechung ist anhand von Levitikus 18 und 20 nicht belegbar. Hügel, *Queere Lesarten der Hebräischen Bibel*.

[49] Ebersohn, *Nächstenliebegebot*, 17.

unterschiedlichen[50] Gesetze von Levitikus 19 im Zusammenhang mit der göttlichen Heiligkeit, an welcher die jüdische Gemeinde der Diaspora durch gesetzeskonformes Verhalten teilhaben soll. Der Kontext des Heiligkeitsgesetzes ist also ein ganz anderer im Vergleich zum heutigen Kontext unterschiedlicher queer Lesender, die womöglich ein anderes religiöses Selbstverständnis haben oder sich nicht mehr als religiös bezeichnen.

Eine umfassende Abhandlung der jüdischen und christlichen Rezeptionen des Nächsten- und Fremdenliebegebots aus Levitikus würde den Rahmen meiner Arbeit sprengen. Deshalb fokussiere ich hier nun allein auf Auslegungen von Lev 19,18 und Lev 19,34, welche für queere Personen relevant sind.

Was können die beiden ähnlichen Sätze im Nächsten- und im Fremdenliebegebot „… du sollst deinen Nächsten lieben wie dich selbst [וְאָהַבְתָּ לְרֵעֲךָ כָּמוֹךָ]" und „… du sollst ihn [das heißt den Fremden] lieben wie dich selbst [וְאָהַבְתָּ לוֹ כָּמוֹךָ]" alles bedeuten? Das Wort כָּמוֹךָ in Lev 19,18 und Lev 19,34 wurde im Zuge der jüdisch-christlichen Auslegungsgeschichte unterschiedlich interpretiert. Auch queere Lesarten des Nächsten- und Fremdenliebegebots sind abhängig von folgenden drei unterschiedlichen Übersetzungsvarianten von כָּמוֹךָ, die ich nun in den anschließenden Abschnitten bespreche: „Du sollst deinen Nächsten lieben … [Lev 19,18]" (1) „… wie *du* dich selbst *liebst* (bzw. *lieben sollst*)", (2) „… denn er ist *ein Mensch* wie du" und (3) „… *sodass, was dir verhasst ist, du ihm nicht tun sollst*" (negative Goldene Regel).

Du sollst deinen Nächsten lieben, wie *du* dich selbst *liebst* (bzw. *lieben sollst*)

Meist wird כָּמוֹךָ in Lev 19,18 und Lev 19,34 als adverbiale Bestimmung von אהב („lieben") betrachtet.[51] Auch wird כָּמוֹךָ als Vergleichspartikel in einem verkürzten Satz verstanden, bei dem das gleichbleibende Agens und das Verb eingespart wurden.[52] So kann das Nächstenliebegebot Lev 19,18 וְאָהַבְתָּ לְרֵעֲךָ כָּמוֹךָ auch folgendermaßen übersetzt werden: „Du sollst deinen Nächsten lieben, wie *du* dich selbst *liebst*."[53] Ähnlich hat zum Beispiel der jüdische Philosoph

---

[50] Michael Ebersohn spricht von einer recht bunten Mischung verschiedener Bestimmungen in Levitikus 19. Ebenda.
[51] Ebenda, 25.46.
[52] Vgl. Ernst Jenni, *Die hebräischen Präpositionen* (Kohlhammer: Stuttgart et al. 1994), 2: *Die Präposition Kaph*, 110.
[53] Vgl. die englische Übersetzung „You must love your neighbour as (you love) yourself," in David J. A. Clines (ed.), *The Dictionary of Classical Hebrew* (Sheffield Academic Press: Sheffield 1998), IV, ל-י, 428.

Moses Mendelssohn (1729-1786) den Vers Lev 19,18 in *Sefer netivot ha-schalom* (*„Buch der Pfade des Friedens"*) ins Deutsche übersetzt.[54] Seine Übersetzung des Pentateuchs wird *Targum aschkenasi* genannt. Mendelssohn und seine Mitarbeiter schufen mit dieser Pentateuchedition, die zwischen 1780 und 1782 in Berlin erschienen ist, eines der wirkungsmächtigsten Werke der Haskala (das heißt der jüdischen Aufklärung).

Auch die Septuaginta versteht כָּמוֹךָ im Nächsten- und Fremdenliebegebot des Heiligkeitsgesetzes als adverbiale Bestimmung, wenn sie וְאָהַבְתָּ לְרֵעֲךָ כָּמוֹךָ in Lev 19,18 mit καὶ ἀγαπήσεις τὸν πλησίον σου ὡς σεαυτόν („Du sollst den Nächsten lieben wie dich selbst") und וְאָהַבְתָּ לוֹ כָּמוֹךָ in Lev 19,34 mit καὶ ἀγαπήσεις αὐτὸν [das heißt προσήλυτον] ὡς σεαυτόν („Du sollst ihn [das heißt den Hinzugekommenen, den fremden Ortsansässigen] lieben wie dich selbst") übersetzt.[55] Das Neue Testament, welches das Nächstenliebegebot aus dem Buch Levitikus mehrmals und an zentralen Stellen aufgreift, folgt bei seinen Schriftzitaten der Septuagintaübersetzung von Lev 19,18.[56] Das Nächstenliebegebot gilt auch deshalb als das wichtigste Gebot im Neuen Testament überhaupt, weil es sowohl bei allen Synoptikern (Markus, Matthäus und Lukas) als auch bei Paulus und Jakobus vorkommt.

In dem Maß, wie jemand sich selbst liebt, soll – nach diesem Verständnis des Nächstenliebegebots Lev 19,18 – auch der Nächste geliebt werden. Hier wird die Selbstliebe vorausgesetzt. Wäre es in der Antike aber nicht auch vorstellbar gewesen, dass Selbstliebe fehlen kann? Fehlende Selbstliebe muss nicht allein psychologisch – wie heute oft – als mangelnde Liebesfähigkeit verstanden werden, sondern hätte auch im materiellen Sinn fehlende Mittel bedeuten können. Dies hätte dann sehr wohl ein Thema hinsichtlich der Liebesgebote der Hebräischen Bibel gewesen sein müssen. Ich habe bereits im

---

[54] Vgl. Moses Mendelssohn, *Pentateuchübersetzung in deutscher Umschrift: Das dritte, vierte und fünfte Buch Moses* (Friedrich Frommann Verlag [Günther Holzboog]: Stuttgart-Bad Cannstatt ²1993), Bearbeitung von Werner Weinberg, Gesammelte Schriften. Jubiläumsausgabe 9,2: Schriften zum Judentum III,2, 47.

[55] Die Übersetzungen von Textpassagen der Septuaginta nach Alfred Rahlfs (ed.), *Septuaginta* [LXX], *Duo volumina in uno* (Deutsche Bibelgesellschaft: Stuttgart 2006) stammen von mir.

[56] Vgl. Mk 12,31; Mt 19,19; 22,39; Lk 10,27; Röm 13,9; Gal 5,14; Jak 2,8. In Mk 12,33 kommt ausnahmsweise ὡς ἑαυτόν statt ὡς σεαυτόν vor. Das Nächstenliebegebot wird in Mt 5,43, wo es um den Gegensatz zwischen Nächsten- und Feindesliebe geht, nicht gänzlich in der Septuagintafassung von Lev 19,18 zitiert, da die Worte ὡς σεαυτόν fehlen. Die Fremdenliebegebote Lev 19,34 und Dtn 10,19 und das ihnen ähnliche Gesetz Ex 22,20 werden hingegen im Neuen Testament nicht wörtlich zitiert.

vorigen Abschnitt erwähnt, dass die Erfahrung des Fremdseins der jüdischen Deportierten im babylonischen Exil, welche ihren Landbesitz und ihre Güter verloren hatten, eine große Rolle im antiken Judentum gespielt hat.

Die Gebote zur Nächsten- oder Fremdenliebe könnten aber gleichzeitig auch als Gebote zur Selbstliebe aufgefasst werden. Nicht nur zur Liebe zum Nächsten- und zum Fremden wird darin aufgerufen, sondern auch zur Liebe zu sich selbst. Dann hieße eine Übersetzung von Lev 19,18 folgendermaßen: „Du sollst deinen Nächsten lieben, wie *du* dich selbst *lieben sollst.*" Dabei wird das Augenmerk daraufgelegt, dass die Selbstliebe der Nächstenliebe vorangeht bzw. die Nächstenliebe die Selbstliebe voraussetzt. In eine ähnliche Richtung verweisen heute Einsichten der Individual- und Sozialpsychologie: Nächstenliebe setzt voraus, dass sie von Individuen ausgeht, deren Selbstverhältnisse mit genügend Sicherheit, Vertrauen und im Blick auf die eigenen Unzulänglichkeiten mit ausreichender Geduld und Nachsicht ausgestattet sind. Erst dann ist Nächstenliebe möglich, die nicht mit Selbstverlust oder verzehrender Selbstaufopferung zusammenfällt, die also eine genuine und authentische Form der Zuwendung zum Nächsten erlaubt. Das heißt im Umkehrschluss freilich ebenso, dass die Art und Weise der Nächstenliebe so beschaffen sein muss, dass sie eben solche gefestigten und zugleich barmherzigen Selbstverhältnisse erlaubt und befördert.[57]

Für eine queere Auslegung des Nächstenliebegebots ist der implizite Aspekt des Gebots zur Selbstliebe ebenfalls zu beachten. Die Art und Weise, wie eine Person ihr eigenes Leben angeht, wird auch für ihre Fähigkeit entscheidend sein, sich anderen Menschen gegenüber ethisch zu verhalten. Die Liebe zum Nächsten ist erst dann möglich, wenn die Liebe zu sich selbst gelernt wird.[58] Deshalb aber womöglich das Nächstenliebegebot Lev 19,18 als Gebot zur Selbstakzeptanz zu erklären, könnte bei etlichen queeren und auch nicht queeren Personen Missfallen hervorrufen und als zynisch betrachtet werden. Nicht alle Menschen der Gegenwart können ein selbstbestimmtes Sexualleben führen. Niemandem mangelt es ohne Grund an Selbstannahme. Ein Umfeld homo-, lesbo-, bi-, transphober und rassistischer Gewalt etwa ist für die

---

[57] Vgl. Andreas Schüle, „,Denn er ist wie Du'. Zu Übersetzung und Verständnis des alttestamentlichen Liebesgebots Lev 19,18," in: *Zeitschrift für die alttestamentliche Wissenschaft* 113/4 (2001), 515-534, hier 519.
[58] Vgl. Rebecca T. Alpert, „Do Justice, Love Mercy, Walk Humbly: Reflections on Micah and Gay Ethics," in: Robert E. Goss und Mona West (eds.), *Take Back The Word: A Queer Reading of the Bible* (Pilgrim Press: Cleveland 2000), 170-182, hier 171.

Selbstliebe diverser queerer Personen nicht förderlich. Für queere und nicht queere Personen, denen ein freies Leben unmöglich ist, wird gebotene Selbstliebe kaum nachvollziehbar sein. Selbstliebe sollte gerade unterschiedlichen queeren Leuten durch die Schaffung eines Umfelds leichter gemacht werden, das ihre Lebens- und Liebesweisen fördert. Selbst Menschen, welche in ihrer Gesellschaft die Möglichkeit hätten, ihre Sexualität anders als heterosexistischen und weiteren Normen des geschlechtlichen Zusammenlebens entsprechend auszuleben, mag gebotene Selbstannahme unrealistisch erscheinen. Muss es tatsächlich immer gelingen, bereits ins Unterbewusstsein verdrängte Persönlichkeitsanteile so zu beeinflussen, dass Homo- und Transphobien und weitere Ängste, die aus psychoanalytischer Sicht für Selbsthass und Hass auf andere queere Personen ausschlaggebend sind, nachlassen? Ein liebevoller Umgang diverser queerer Personen mit sich selbst wiederum wirkt sich auf ihren Umgang mit anderen Mitmenschen positiv aus. Zur Zeit der Hebräischen Bibel wurde noch nicht zwischen queeren und straighten Personen unterschieden bzw. wurden sie nicht als solche bezeichnet. Es wird darin auch von keinen Crossdresser_Innen im heutigen Sinn berichtet. Das biblische Nächstenliebegebot auf Personen anzuwenden, von welchen angenommen wird, dass sie sich nicht lieben (können) oder sich nicht kleiden (können), wie sie wollen, stellt eine neue Auslegung aus gegenwärtiger Sicht dar.

Im Zuge einer queeren Debatte wird hingegen heute – dem Wortlaut nach – nicht so sehr die *Liebe* zu sich selbst und zum Mitmenschen eingefordert, sondern es wird dazu aufgerufen, die *Würde* unterschiedlicher queerer Personen zu respektieren. So wird zum Beispiel in Menschenrechtsfragen auf Artikel 1 der Charta der Grundrechte der Europäischen Union verwiesen: „Die Würde des Menschen ist unantastbar. Sie ist zu achten und zu schützen."[59]

Im populärsten jüdischen Traditionstext,[60] in Mischna Avot,[61] dessen Hauptteil aus überlieferten Weisheitssprüchen besteht, welche frühen Meistern

---

[59] Vgl. Jürgen Meyer (ed.), *Charta der Grundrechte der Europäischen Union* (Nomos/facultas. wuv/Helbing & Lichtenhahn: Baden-Baden et al. [4]2014), GRC Art. 1.
[60] Vgl. Günter Stemberger, „Mischna Avot – Frühe Weisheitsschrift, pharisäisches Erbe oder spätrabbinische Bildung?," in: Günter Stemberger, *Judaica Minora* (Mohr Siebeck: Tübingen 2010), 2: *Geschichte und Literatur des rabbinischen Judentums*, Texte und Studien zum Antiken Judentum 138, 317-330, hier 317.
[61] Avot (Aussprüche) „Väter", auch Pirqe Avot („Abschnitte, Kapitel der Väter") ist ein Traktat in Neziqin („Beschädigungen"). Vgl. Günter Stemberger, *Einleitung in Talmud und Midrasch* (C. H. Beck: München [9]2011), 131.

Karin Hügel
Queere Auslegungen der Liebesgebote aus Levitikus

zugeschrieben werden,[62] ist in mAv 2,10[63] auch schon von der Würde (כָּבוֹד) des Menschen die Rede, wenn Rabbi Eliezer (ben Hyrkanos)[64] folgende Behauptung in den Mund gelegt wird: „Die Würde deines Mitmenschen sei dir so wertvoll wie deine eigene [כנפשך עליך חביב [65חבירך 66כבוד ‏יהי]."[67] Diese rabbinische Aussage basiert auf dem Prinzip der Nächstenliebe in Lev 19,18.[68] Es gibt keine innerrabbinischen Parallelen zu Mischna Avot 2,10,[69] sodass es keine weiteren Anhaltspunkte für eine Datierung dieses mischnaischen Ausspruchs gibt.[70] Auch im Zusammenhang mit dieser Weisheit aus Mischna Avot

---

[62] Stemberger, „Mischna Avot – Frühe Weisheitsschrift," 317.
[63] Vgl. bAv 2,10. Es fehlt jedoch eine talmudische Kommentierung des Mischna-Traktats Avot in der Gemara (das heißt in der Erläuterung der Mischna im Talmud). Ebenda, 320.
[64] Die jüdische Tradition ordnet Rabbi Eliezer ben Hyrkanos (mAv 2,8), in der Mischna schlicht Rabbi Eliezer, der älteren Gruppe der zweiten Generation der Tannaiten zu. Er lehrte in Lydda. Seine halachischen Interessen verbinden ihn mit den Pharisäern. Über ihn verhängten die Rabbinen den Bann (pMQ 3,1,81c-d), was die spätere Tradition stark ausgeschmückt hat (bBM 59a). Aus tHul 2,24 – Ḥullin („Profanes") ist ein Traktat in Qodaschim („Heiliges") (Stemberger, *Einleitung*, 132) – kann nicht abgeleitet werden, dass er dem Christentum zugeneigt gewesen sei, auch wenn seine Verhaftung durch die römischen Behörden vielleicht auf einen solchen Verdacht zurückging. Ebenda, 85.
[65] חָבֵר bedeutet unter anderem *fellow-being* („Mitmensch"). Jastrow, *Dictionary*, 421.
[66] כָּבוֹד bedeutet *honor* („Ehre"), *respect* („Respekt"), *dignity* („Würde"). Ebenda, 607.
[67] Eigene Übersetzung von mAv 2,10 aus dem Mischna-Hebräischen nach Michael Krupp (ed.), *Die Mischna. Textkritische Ausgabe mit deutscher Übersetzung und Kommentar*, 4. Ordnung Nesikin (Lee Achim Sefarim: Ein Karem – Jerusalem 2004), 9: *Avot. Väter*, 19. Bezüglich einer anderen deutschen Übersetzung von mAv 2,10 vgl. Dietrich Correns, *Die Mischna: Das grundlegende enzyklopädische Regelwerk rabbinischer Tradition* (matrixverlag: Wiesbaden 2005), 587-588. Marcus Jastrow übersetzt diesen Satz mit „Let thy neighbor's honor be as dear to thee as thine own" („Die Ehre deines Nächsten sei dir so teuer wie deine eigene"), wobei diese Übersetzung mit „Nächster" im Hinblick auf Lev 19,18 entstanden sein könnte. Jastrow, *Dictionary* 418. Bezüglich einer englischen Übersetzung von bAv 2,10 vgl. Isidore Epstein (ed.), *'Abodah Zarah, Horayoth, Shebu'oth, Makkoth, 'Eduyyoth, Aboth* (Soncino Press: London 1935), The Babylonian Talmud, Seder Nezikin IV, 20.
[68] Ebenda, 20.
[69] Vgl. Günter Stemberger, „Die innerrabbinische Überlieferung von Mischna Avot," in: Günter Stemberger, *Judaica Minora* (Mohr Siebeck: Tübingen 2010), 2: *Geschichte und Literatur des rabbinischen Judentums*, Texte und Studien zum Antiken Judentum 138, 331-346.
[70] Der Traktat Avot, wie er uns in heutigen Druckausgaben, aber auch in frühen Mischna-Handschriften, wie Codex Kaufmann oder Parma, vorliegt, ist spät. Teile des Traktats sind einfache Sammlungen von Aussprüchen, andere wurden zu einem unbekannten Zeitpunkt kunstvoll zu literarischen Einheiten komponiert. Wie aus diesen Einheiten und anderem Spruchmaterial im Lauf der Jahrhunderte der Traktat Avot redigiert wurde, liegt noch im Dunkeln. Stemberger, „Mischna Avot – Frühe Weisheitsschrift," 330.

2,10 gilt es zu bedenken, dass ein Mensch sich erst einmal selbst als würdevoll erleben können muss, indem ihm sein Umfeld ein Leben in Würde zugesteht bzw. ermöglicht. Erst dann wird die Rede, seinem Mitmenschen denselben Respekt zu zollen, den er sich selbst gegenüber hat entwickeln können, für ihn einen Sinn ergeben.

Auf der Suche nach einer Anleitung zur Selbstliebe und zum Glück in der Hebräischen Bibel werde ich im Buch der Sprichwörter, in Sprüche 19,8, fündig: „Wer Verstand erwirbt, liebt sich selbst [[71]קֹנֶה־לֵּב אֹהֵב נַפְשׁוֹ], und wer Einsicht bewahrt, findet Glück [שֹׁמֵר תְּבוּנָה לִמְצֹא־טוֹב]." In dieser Bibelstelle ist von לֵב die Rede – ähnlich wie von לְבָב in Lev 19,17. In beiden Versen vermag die Bedeutung dieser Worte zwischen „Herz" und „Verstand" zu oszillieren. Es ist nämlich schwer denkbar, dass nackter Verstand allein Liebe hervorrufen kann. Zwischen den Begriffen „Verstand" (לֵב) und „Einsicht" (תְּבוּנָה)[72] in Sprüche 19,8 ist ein inhaltlicher Zusammenhang naheliegend: Verstand bewirkt Einsicht. Dieser biblische Spruch könnte dahingehend interpretiert werden, dass Vertrauen in die eigenen Einsichten zu Glück führen kann. Das mögen unterschiedliche queere Personen aufgrund ihrer je eigenen Erkenntnisse anders als straighte Personen lesen.

Du sollst deinen Nächsten lieben, denn er ist *ein Mensch* wie du

Alternativ kann כָּמוֹךָ im Nächstenliebegebot des Buchs Levitikus als attributives Prädikat verstanden werden.[73] Dann lautet eine Übersetzung von Lev 19,18 folgendermaßen: „Du sollst deinen Mitmenschen lieben, der wie du ist"[74] bzw. – bei כָּמוֹךָ im Sinne eines kausalen Beisatzes – „Du sollst deinen Nächsten lieben, denn er ist wie du."[75] Das Wort כָּמוֹךָ wird vor allem im Zusammenhang mit dem Nächstenliebegebot Lev 19,18 als Apposition zu

---

[71] Bezüglich weiterer Stellen, in denen נַפְשׁוֹ reflexiv verstanden wird, vgl. die erste Begegnung zwischen David und Jonathan in 1 Sam 18,1.3 und 1 Sam 20,17, wo Jonathan David „bei seiner Liebe zu ihm" schwören lässt.

[72] Das Nomen תְּבוּנָה leitet sich vom Verb בִּין („verstehen", „einsehen") ab. Der Begriff תְּבוּנָה kann also als Parallelwort zu לֵב (im Sinne von „Verstand") aufgefasst werden. Vgl. Magne Sæbø, *Sprüche* (Vandenhoeck & Ruprecht: Göttingen 2012), Das Alte Testament Deutsch 16,1, 247.

[73] Schüle, „‚Denn er ist wie Du'," 520.

[74] Eigene Übersetzung aus dem Englischen nach Joüon und Muraoka, *Grammar*, 453. Vgl. auch Takamitsu Muraoka, „A Syntactic Problem in Lev. xix. 18b," in: *Journal of Semitic Studies* 23/2 (1978), 291-297, hier 295.

[75] Schüle, „‚Denn er ist wie Du'," 531. Das Fehlen der Relativpartikel אֲשֶׁר ist kein Argument gegen die attributive Auffassung von כָּמוֹךָ im Zusammenhang mit Lev 19,18. Ebenda, 526.

לְרֵעֶךָ verstanden.[76] Es ist jedoch schwierig, כָּמוֹךָ – analog zu Lev 19,18 – auch in Lev 19,34 als Beisatz zu verstehen.[77] Der Fremde (גֵּר) unterscheidet sich nämlich grundsätzlich erst einmal von einem Einheimischen (אֶזְרָח), auch wenn nach dem Fremdenliebegebot der Schutzbürger (גֵּר) wie ein Vollbürger (אֶזְרָח) gelten soll.

Bei einer solchen Lesart des Nächstenliebegebots des Heiligkeitsgesetzes stellt sich die Frage, weshalb für den angesprochenen israelitischen Vollbürger womöglich ein Unterschied zwischen *ihm gleichen* und *ihm nicht gleichen* Mitmenschen existiert haben sollte. Wurde er in Lev 19,18 etwa nur zur Liebe zu seinem Nächsten aufgerufen, wenn dieser *ihm gleich* war? Diese Gleichheit wurde von Bibelwissenschaftler_Innen unter anderem im Sinne von gleicher Volkszugehörigkeit interpretiert.[78] Eine solche Interpretation läuft Gefahr, heutigen nationalistischen und fremdenfeindlichen Auslegungen Tür und Tor zu öffnen. Dagegen ist einzuwenden, dass mit dem Fremdenliebegebot Lev 19,34 eine Vorschrift nachträglich in Levitikus 19 eingefügt worden ist, welche zusätzlich zur Liebe zu den *nicht gleichen* Personen, das heißt zu den Fremden (גֵּרִים), aufruft. Gerade wenn das Nächstenliebegebot Lev 19,18 in nachexilischer Zeit (auch) so verstanden wurde, dass die Liebe nur *gleichen* Personen, das heißt allein israelitischen Volksgenossen (bzw. „einheimischen" Juden in der damaligen Diaspora) galt, ist es nicht unplausibel, dass das Fremdenliebegebot Lev 19,34 redaktionell im Zuge der Entstehung des Heiligkeitsgesetzes ergänzt wurde. In nachexilischer Zeit waren mit גֵּרִים Schutzbürger gemeint. Heute werden mit ihnen sogenannte „Gastarbeiter_Innen"[79] oder Flüchtlinge assoziiert.

In der jüdischen Aufklärung, der Haskala, begründete der jüdische Dichter, Sprachwissenschaftler und Exeget Naftali Herz Wessely (1725-1805)[80] die Gleichheit aller Menschen im Zusammenhang mit dem Nächstenliebegebot

---

[76] Bereits Arnold Bogumil Ehrlich behauptet, dass כָּמוֹךָ in Bezug auf לְרֵעֶךָ epexegetisch (das heißt in der Art einer Apposition erklärend) zu verstehen ist. Vgl. Arnold Bogumil Ehrlich, *Randglossen zur Hebräischen Bibel: Textkritisches, Sprachliches und Sachliches* (Hinrichs: Leipzig 1909), 2: *Leviticus, Numeri, Deuteronomium*, 65.
[77] Vgl. Hans-Peter Mathys, *Liebe deinen Nächsten wie dich selbst. Untersuchungen zum alttestamentlichen Gebot der Nächstenliebe (Lev 19,18)* (Universitätsverlag und Vandenhoeck & Ruprecht: Freiburg und Göttingen 1986), Orbis Biblicus et Orientalis 71, 9.
[78] Ehrlich, *Randglossen* 2, 65.
[79] Ebersohn, *Nächstenliebegebot*, 55.
[80] Vgl. Joshua Barzilay, „Wessely, Naphtali Herz," in: Michael Berenbaum und Fred Skolnik (eds.), *Encyclopaedia Judaica* (Macmillan Reference: Detroit ²2007), 21, 19-21.

theologisch, indem er auf die Schöpfung rekurrierte. In seinem hebräischen Kommentar (*Biur*) zum Buch Levitikus, welcher im dritten Band von Mendelssohns Pentateuchedition *Sefer netivot ha-schalom* („Buch der Pfade des Friedens") im Jahr 1781 in Berlin erschienen ist,[81] widerspricht Wessely Mendelssohns deutscher Übersetzung von Lev 19,18 („… liebe deinen Nächsten, so wie du dich selbst liebst"),[82] indem er כָּמוֹךָ im Sinne von „… welcher *ein Mensch* wie du ist" versteht:[83]

> Liebe deinen Nächsten, welcher wie du ist, dir gleich und dir ähnlich, ist doch auch er in dem Ebenbilde Gottes erschaffen, also ist er ein Mensch wie du. Und das erstreckt sich auf alle Menschen, sind die doch alle im Ebenbilde erschaffen.[84]

Der Nächste ist für Wessely ein Mensch (אָדָם), der zum Bilde Gottes geschaffen wurde, wie in Gen 5,1 – und in der Parallele in Gen 1,27 im ersten Schöpfungsbericht – zu lesen ist. Er verweist dabei auf einen rabbinischen Disput in Sifra Qedoschim 4,12 (89b) zu Lev 19,18, in dem darüber gestritten wird, welches das umfassende Prinzip (כְּלָל גָּדוֹל)[85] der Thora sei. In dieser Stelle des halachischen Midrasch zu Levitikus werden sowohl das Nächstenliebegebot Lev 19,18 als auch der erste Satz von Genesis 5 (und damit auch die Gottesebenbildlichkeit des Menschen [אָדָם], die anschließend in Gen 5,1b beschrieben wird)[86] als konkurrierende, umfassende Prinzipien der Thora genannt.

---

[81] Vgl. Moses Mendelssohn, *Der Pentateuch. Das dritte Buch Moses* (Friedrich Frommann Verlag [Günther Holzboog]: Stuttgart-Bad Cannstatt 1990), Bearbeitung von Werner Weinberg, Gesammelte Schriften. Jubiläumsausgabe 17: Hebräische Schriften II,3, 273-275 bzw. Daniel Krochmalnik (ed.), *Moses Mendelssohn, Pentateuchkommentare in deutscher Übersetzung* (Friedrich Frommann Verlag [Günther Holzboog]: Stuttgart-Bad Cannstatt 2009), Übersetzung von Rainer Wenzel, Gesammelte Schriften. Jubiläumsausgabe 9,3: Schriften zum Judentum III,3, 346-351.

[82] In Mendelssohn, *Pentateuchübersetzung* 2, 47, werden Formen von „lieben" in der deutschen Übersetzung von Lev 19,18 eigentlich ohne „e" geschrieben, also „libe", „libst" et cetera. Vgl. auch Abschnitt „Du sollst deinen Nächsten lieben, wie *du* dich *selbst liebst* bzw. *lieben sollst*".

[83] Wesselys hebräischer Kommentar (*Biur*) verfolgte jedoch grundsätzlich den Zweck, Mendelssohns Übersetzung des Pentateuchs ins Deutsche zur jüdischen exegetischen Tradition in Beziehung zu setzen und auf diese Weise zu rechtfertigen. Krochmalnik (ed.), *Mendelssohn*, IX.

[84] Ebenda, 347.

[85] כְּלָל bedeutet *general rule* („allgemeine Regel"), *principle* (Prinzip). Jastrow, *Dictionary*, 644. גָּדוֹל bedeutet „groß". HAL 1, 170.

[86] Nach dem Hinweis auf das Buch der Geschlechterfolge Adams in Gen 5,1 folgt Gottes (אֱלֹהִים) Schöpfung des Menschen (אָדָם) als Ebenbild Gottes (אֱלֹהִים). Die in Gen 5,2 folgende Aussage („Als Mann und Frau schuf er sie …") gab Anlass zu späteren jüdischen Interpretationen, aufgrund der Ebenbildlichkeit des ersten Menschen G*tt (הקב׳ה) selbst als androgyn vorzustellen.

Karin Hügel
Queere Auslegungen der Liebesgebote aus Levitikus

Diese unterschiedlichen Anschauungen werden Rabbi Akiba, einem bedeutenden Lehrer aus der jüngeren Gruppe der zweiten Generation der Tannaiten in der Zeit von Javne,[87] und dessen Schüler Ben Azzai[88] in den Mund gelegt:

A. *Du sollst deinen Nächsten lieben wie dich selbst* [ואהבת לרעך כמוך] [Lev 19,18]:
B. Rabbi Akiba sagt [רבי עקיבא אומר]: „Dies ist das umfassende Prinzip der Thora [זה כלל גדול בתורה]."
C. Ben Azzai sagt [בן עזאי אומר]: „*Dies ist das Buch der Geschlechterfolge Adams* [זה ספר תולדות אדם] [Gen 5,1a] ist das umfassendere Prinzip [זה כלל גדול מזה]."[89] (Sifra Qedoschim 4,12 (89b) = Sifra 200,3,7 nach der englischen Ausgabe von Neusner)

Dieselben Aussagen von Rabbi Akiba und Ben Azzai finden sich später auch im palästinischen Talmud Nedarim, nämlich in pNed 9,4,41c.[90] Es ist etwas verwirrend, dass im Midrasch zu Genesis hingegen das Nächstenliebegebot als das umfassendere Prinzip der Thora bezeichnet wird. In BerR 24,7 findet sich das längste Zitat. Es kommen noch Rabbi Akibas Gedanken zum Verachtetwerden im Zusammenhang mit dem Nächstenliebegebot und die anschließende Behauptung eines weiteren Rabbi, nämlich Rabbi Tanchuma, dazu:

Ben Azzai sagte [בן עזאי אומר]:

Dies ist das Buch der Geschlechterfolge Adams [זה ספר תולדות אדם] [Gen 5,1a] ist das umfassende Prinzip der Thora [כלל גדול בתורה].

Rabbi Akiba sagte [ר' עקיבה א']:

Aber du sollst deinen Nächsten lieben wie dich selbst [ואהבת לרעך כמוך] [Lev 19,18] ist das noch umfassendere Prinzip [כלל גדול ממנו]. Demzufolge darfst du nicht sagen [שלא תאמר]: „Weil ich verachtet worden bin, soll mein Nächster verachtet werden [הואיל ונתבזיתי יתבזה חבירי]."

---

[87] Stemberger, *Einleitung*, 87.
[88] Die jüdische Tradition siedelt Simeon ben Azzai, gewöhnlich einfach Ben Azzai (Abkürzung aus Azarja) in der jüngeren Gruppe der zweiten Generation der Tannaiten an, zu deren berühmtesten Lehrern unter anderem Rabbi Akiba gehört. In bHag 14b gehören Ben Azzai und Rabbi Akiba zu den vier, die in das „Paradies" gingen, das heißt sich in esoterische Spekulation vertieften, was nur Rabbi Akiba unbeschädigt überstand. Ebenda, 90.
[89] Eigene Übersetzung aus dem Hebräischen bzw. Aramäischen nach Weiss, *Sifra*. Bezüglich einer englischen Übersetzung vgl. Neusner, *Sifra* 3, 109.
[90] Vgl. Heinrich W. Guggenheimer (ed.), *Tractates Soṭah and Nedarim* (de Gruyter: Berlin und New York 2005), The Jerusalem Talmud, Third Order: *Našim*, Studia Judaica 31, 668.

Rabbi Tanchuma sagte ['אמר ר' תנחומ]:

Wenn du dich so verhältst, wisse, wen du verachtest, [denn] [אם עשית כן דע למי אתה] [מבזה]: *Nach dem Abbild Gottes machte er ihn* [בדמות אלהים עשה אתו] [Gen 5,1b].[91] (BerR 24,7)

Auch in Rabbi Akibas Aussage zum Nächstenliebegebot geht es letztendlich um das Unterbrechen der Spirale des Hasses und der Gewalt wie im biblischen Gebot Lev 19,18 selbst, indem Verachtung und Herabsetzung, die einer Person in gewalttätigen und erniedrigenden Situationen widerfahren mag, nicht an andere weitergegeben werden sollen. Das Gebot der Nächstenliebe wurde in rabbinischer Zeit für das wichtigste gehalten, weil Vergeltung für Verachtung und für erlittenes Unrecht – aufgrund der Unterdrückung der jüdischen Bevölkerung im römischen Imperium ganz besonders? – unterbunden werden musste. Heute können wahrscheinlich fast alle Menschen aufgrund von – wie auch immer gearteten – persönlichen Erniedrigungen an die Gedanken Rabbi Akibas anschließen. Es legt sich nahe, dass deshalb nicht nur die Bestrafung der Verursacher der Respektlosigkeit zu unterlassen sei, sondern vor allem die Verschiebung der Gewalt auf andere, schwächere Mitglieder der Gesellschaft und der Familie zu unterbinden sei. Diverse queere Menschen sind oft von besonderen Formen von Verachtung betroffen, gegen die sie sich womöglich nicht immer wehren können. So könnte Rabbi Akibas Aussage heutzutage auch als Ansage verstanden werden, dass Leute, ob als Lesben, Schwule, Bisexuelle oder Transgenderpersonen et cetera geoutet oder nicht, wegen ihrer oftmals schwierigen bis ausweglosen Situation in ihrer jeweiligen Gesellschaft nicht in besonders vehemente Fremdenfeindlichkeiten verfallen sollten bzw. anderen Phobien erliegen sollten. Auch sie sollen keine Rassismen und Sexismen verbreiten, sondern zum allgemeinen Wohle aller ihrer Mitmenschen agieren. Ich habe bereits im vorigen Abschnitt thematisiert, dass die Liebe zu sich selbst, zu welcher in den biblischen Nächstenliebegeboten der Hebräischen Bibel und des Neuen Testaments aufgerufen wird, nicht selbstverständlich ist.[92]

---

[91] Eigene Übersetzung aus dem Hebräischen bzw. Aramäischen nach Julius Theodor und Chanoch Albeck (eds.), *Midrash Bereshit Rabba: Critical Edition with Notes and Commentary* (Wahrmann Books: Jerusalem 1965), 1, 236-237. Bezüglich einer englischen Übersetzung vgl. Harry Freedman und Maurice Simon (eds.), *Midrash Rabbah: Translated into English with Notes, Glossary and Indices* (Soncino Press: London [3]1961), Genesis in Two Volumes, 1, 204.

[92] Vgl. Abschnitt „Du sollst deinen Nächsten lieben, wie *du* dich selbst *liebst* bzw. *lieben sollst*".

Im Midrasch zu Genesis 24,7 sind die in Sifra Qedoschim 4,12 (89b) geschilderten Meinungen von Ben Azzai und Rabbi Akiba (das heißt von Rabbinen, welche in der jüdischen Tradition zur jüngeren Gruppe der zweiten Generation der Tannaiten gezählt werden) erweitert worden, indem die Aussage Rabbi Tanchumas,[93] welcher erst in der fünften Generation der Amoräer in Palästina angesiedelt wird, hinzugefügt wurde. Rabbi Tanchuma weist darauf hin, dass die Verachtung eines Mitmenschen, welcher nach Gen 5,1b ein nach dem Abbild Gottes (אֱלֹהִים) geschaffener Mensch (אָדָם) ist, eine Verachtung Gottes (אֱלֹהִים) darstellt. Respektlosigkeit gegenüber Mitmenschen, egal welchen, gilt es zu unterlassen, weil dies einer Respektlosigkeit gegenüber Gott gleichkommt. Nicht Verachtung, sondern Liebe soll einem anderen Menschen erwiesen werden, denn er ist *Gottes Geschöpf* bzw. *ein (geschaffener) Mensch* (אָדָם) wie du.

Im 20. Jahrhundert greift der bedeutendste Vertreter des deutschen liberalen Judentums, Leo Baeck (1873-1956), diese Stelle aus dem Midrasch zu Genesis in seinem Werk *Das Wesen des Judentums* in der Auflage von 1926 auf und behauptet, dass im Nächstenliebegebot Lev 19,18 das jüdische Konzept des Mitmenschen angesprochen werde, der „wie du" sei, „im Eigentlichen dir gleich", sodass wir im anderen den, der „wie wir" ist, ehren sollen.[94] Im Judentum wird die „Ehrfurcht vor dem Göttlichen in allem, was Menschenantlitz trägt",[95] vermittelt.

Wird hingegen aus heutiger, oft nicht religiöser Sicht der Schöpfungsbezug – anders als im Zuge einer theologischen Begründung der Gleichheit aller Menschen wie bei Wessely oder Baeck – weggelassen, könnte das Nächstenliebegebot Lev 19,18 – inklusiv formuliert – folgendermaßen reinterpretiert werden: „Du sollst deine_n Nächste_n lieben, denn sie_er ist *ein Mensch* wie du." Das Fremdenliebegebot Lev 19,34 würde dann analog so lauten: „Du sollst die_den Fremde_n lieben, denn sie_er ist ein *Mensch* wie du." Mit solchen inklusiven Übersetzungen der Liebesgebote aus dem Buch Levitikus sind Frauen und Männer und nicht nur Menschen uneindeutigen Geschlechts gemeint, aber auch Letztere miteinbezogen.[96] Statt dem biblischen Wort

---

[93] Die jüdische Tradition siedelt Rabbi Tanchum(a) bar Abba, genauer Berabbi Abba, Schüler Hunas, welcher systematisch die Haggada sammelte, in der fünften Generation der Amoräer in Palästina an. Stemberger, *Einleitung*, 112.

[94] Vgl. Albert H. Friedlander und Bertold Klappert (eds.), *Das Wesen des Judentums* (Gütersloher Verlagshaus: Gütersloh 1998), Leo Baeck Werke 1, 217.

[95] Ebenda, 216.

[96] Bezüglich meiner etwas anders gearteten Relektüre von Gen 1,27 hinsichtlich der Erschaffung der Menschheit („Und Gott schuf den Menschen zu seinem Bilde, zum Bilde Gottes schuf er

„lieben" (אהב) könnten heutzutage Begriffe wie „respektieren", „würdevoll behandeln" oder „solidarisch handeln" angedacht werden. Zu Beginn meiner Diskussion der Liebesgebote der Hebräischen Bibel musste ich feststellen, dass der patriarchale Kontext des Heiligkeitsgesetzes keinen Einbezug von Frauen beim Nächsten- und Fremdenliebegebot nahelegt. Diese Inklusion gilt es aber heute im Sinne einer feministischen und queeren Neuinterpretation dieser Liebesgebote einzufordern. So können diese biblischen Liebesgebote aus Levitikus in der Gegenwart als Aufruf zu respektvollem Handeln auch und besonders gegenüber Frauen und diversen Minderheiten – wie unterschiedlichen queeren Personen – ausgelegt werden und damit womöglich sogar eine Brücke zum Gedanken der Gleichheit aller Menschen – wie er zum Beispiel in der EU-Grundrechtecharta verbürgt ist[97] – geschaffen werden. Eine israelische Briefmarke aus dem Jahr 1958 zeigt das Liebesgebot von Lev 19,18 in hebräischer Schrift: „ואהבת לרעך כמוך" in Erinnerung an zehn Jahre Allgemeine Erklärung der Menschenrechte von 1948.[98] So wird eine Assoziation zwischen heutigen Menschenrechtsvorstellungen und dem biblischen Vers aus dem Buch Levitikus hergestellt. Die gegenwärtigen Menschenrechte fußen jedoch ursprünglich auf den Ideen der europäischen Aufklärung des 18. Jahrhunderts.

Du sollst deinen Nächsten lieben, *sodass, was dir verhasst ist, du ihm nicht tun sollst* (negative Goldene Regel)

Viele Jahrhunderte nach der Entstehung der hebräischen Versionen des Nächsten- und Fremdenliebegebots ist das Wort כָּמוֹךָ in der aramäischen Übersetzung des Targum Pseudo-Jonathan, dessen Endform nicht vor dem 7. oder 8. Jahrhundert n. Chr. datiert werden kann, schon als interpretationsbedürftig betrachtet worden und deshalb in TPsJ zu Lev 19,18 und zu Lev 19,34 durch

---

ihn; und schuf sie, Mann und Frau und *jede Kombination dazwischen*") vgl. Hügel, „Queere Lesarten. Ruth und Schöpfungsberichte," 191.

[97] In der EU-Grundrechtecharta, welche mit dem Inkrafttreten des Vertrags von Lissabon am 1. Dezember 2009 Rechtskraft erlangt hat, gibt es nach dem allgemeinen Gleichheitsgebot des Artikels 20, der die Gleichheit aller Personen vor dem Gesetz garantiert, spezifische Diskriminierungsverbote in Artikel 21 – unter anderem wegen des Geschlechts (wobei nicht nur Männer und Frauen, sondern auch Transsexuelle und Menschen mit uneindeutigen Geschlechtsmerkmalen erfasst sind) und wegen der sexuellen Ausrichtung (Sexualpartner_Innen sollen frei wählbar sein). Meyer (ed.), *Charta der Grundrechte der Europäischen Union*, GRC Art. 21 Abs. 1.

[98] Vgl. Israel Philatelic Federation, „Human rights," (http://israelphilately.org.il/en/catalog/stamps/3719/HUMAN%20RIGHTS, 28. Juli 2019).

die Einfügung der negativen Goldenen Regel[99] folgendermaßen paraphrasiert worden:[100]

> Du sollst dich nicht rächen [לא תהוון נקמין] und gegenüber den Mitgliedern deines Volkes nicht nachtragend sein [ולא נטרין דבבו לבני עמך], sondern du sollst deinen Mitmenschen lieben [ותרחמיה לחברך], *sodass, was dir verhasst ist, du ihm nicht tun sollst* [דמן אנת סני לך לא תעביד ליה]. Ich bin G*tt [אנא ייי].[101] (TPsJ zu Lev 19,18)

> Der Fremde, der sich bei euch aufhält, soll wie ein Einheimischer bei euch gelten [כיציבא מנכון יהי לכון גיורא דמתגייר עמכון]; und du sollst ihn lieben wie dich selbst [כותך ותרחם ליה]; *sodass, was dir verhasst ist, du ihm nicht tun sollst* [דמה את סני לך לא תעביד ליה]; denn ihr seid Einwohner[102] in Ägypten gewesen [בארעא דמצרים ארום דיירין הויתון]. Ich bin G*tt, euer G*tt [אנא הוא ייי אלהכון].[103] (TPsJ zu Lev 19,34)

Sowohl im Nächsten- als auch im Fremdenliebegebot des Targum Pseudo-Jonathan ist die negative Goldene Regel als Auslegung des hebräischen Begriffs כָּמוֹךָ aus Lev 19,18 bzw. Lev 19,34 eingeflochten worden. Die beiden Liebesgebote galten damals im Ganzen als auslegungsbedürftig.[104] Ich schreibe im Zusammenhang mit TPsJ zu Lev 19,18 von der Liebe zum „Mitmen-

---

[99] Der Begriff „Goldene Regel" ist erst seit dem Anfang des 17. Jahrhunderts nachweisbar und wird zuerst in England als *Golden Rule* im Zusammenhang mit einer Predigt von Thomas Jackson über Mt 7,12 aus dem Jahr 1615 erwähnt. Vgl. Olivier du Roy, „The Golden Rule as the Law of Nature, from Origin to Martin Luther," in: Jacob Neusner und Bruce Chilton (eds.), *The Golden Rule: The Ethics of Reciprocity in World Religions* (Continuum: London und New York 2008), 88-98, hier 93-94. Das Epitheton „goldene" drückt den Wert, die Vortrefflichkeit bzw. den Nutzen der Regel aus. Vgl. Philip S. Alexander, „Jesus and the Golden Rule," in: James H. Charlesworth und Loren L. Johns (eds.), *Hillel and Jesus: Comparative Studies of Two Major Religious Leaders* (Fortress Press: Minneapolis 1997), 363-388, hier 363, Fußnote 1.

[100] Die negative Goldene Regel wird in TPsJ zu Lev 19,18 und in TPsJ zu Lev 19,34 durch Kursivierung hervorgehoben.

[101] Eigene Übersetzung aus dem Aramäischen nach Alexandro Diez Macho, *Biblia Polyglotta Matritensia IV: Targum Palaestinense in Pentateuchum* (CSIC: Madrid 1980), 3: *Leviticus*, 131. Bezüglich einer englischen Übersetzung vgl. Martin McNamara und Robert Hayward, *Targum Neofiti 1: Leviticus*/Michael Maher, *Targum Pseudo-Jonathan: Leviticus* (T & T Clark: Edinburgh 1994), The Aramaic Bible 3, 177.

[102] In Lev 19,34 ist an dieser Stelle von „Fremden" (גֵרִים) die Rede.

[103] Eigene Übersetzung aus dem Aramäischen nach Diez Macho, *Biblia Polyglotta Matritensia IV: Targum Palaestinense in Pentateuchum*, 3: *Leviticus*, 137. Bezüglich einer englischen Übersetzung vgl. McNamara und Hayward, *Targum Neofiti 1: Leviticus*/Maher, *Targum Pseudo-Jonathan: Leviticus*, 179-180.

[104] Mathys, *Liebe deinen Nächsten*, 47.

schen" – und nicht zum „Nächsten" –, weil in der aramäischen Übersetzung חָבֵר[105] – und nicht wie in der Hebräischen Bibel רֵעַ – steht. Im rabbinischen Judentum dürfte die Goldene Regel in ihrer negativen Form bereits aus dem babylonischen Talmud Schabbat bekannt gewesen sein.

Der vielzitierten, rabbinischen Anekdote aus bSchab 31a zufolge behauptete einmal ein Nichtjude, dass er sofort zum Judentum übertreten wolle, wenn ihm jemand die Thora in der Zeit erläutern würde, in der er auf einem Fuß stehend ausharren könne. Diese Begebenheit wird berühmten Rabbinen der ältesten Zeit zugeschrieben, obwohl sie jünger und nicht historisch sein dürfte.[106] Während Schammai[107] den Nichtjuden vertrieb, nahm ihn Hillel[108] als Proselyten an und verwies ihn dabei auf die negative Goldene Regel:

> Ferner eine Begebenheit, welche einen Nichtjuden betrifft, der zu Schammai kam und zu ihm sagte [א״ל שמאי לפני שבא אחד בנכרי מעשה שוב]: „Mache mich zum Juden unter der Bedingung, dass du mich die ganze Thora lehrst, während ich auf einem Bein stehe" [אחת רגל על עומד כשאני כולה התורה כל שתלמדני ע״מ גיירני]. Daraufhin stieß ihn dieser mit einem Maßstock eines Bauhandwerkers [in der Länge einer Elle], den er in seiner Hand hatte, weg [שבידו הבנין באמת[109] דחפו]. Als er [das heißt der Nichtjude] zu Hillel kam, akzeptierte dieser ihn als Proselyten und sprach zu ihm [לו אמר גיירה הלל לפני בא]: „Was dir verhasst ist, das tue deinem Mitmenschen nicht [תעביד לא לחברך סני דעלך]. Das ist die ganze Thora, während der Rest der Kommentar davon ist [הוא פירושה ואידך כולה התורה כל היא זו]. Geh, lerne [sie] [גמור זיל]!"[110] (bSchab 31a)

---

[105] Das Nomen חָבֵר im, abgeleitet vom Verb חבר („sich verbünden" bzw. „sich verbinden"), bedeutet „Gefährte" (HAL 1, 277) bzw. „Mitmensch" (*fellow-being*) (Jastrow, *Dictionary*, 421).

[106] Alexander, „Jesus and the Golden Rule," 368-369.

[107] Schammai, manchmal ebenfalls „der Alte" genannt, zählt zu den wichtigsten Rabbinen der ältesten Zeit. Da sich die hillelitische Richtung durchsetzte, werden die Traditionen Schammais fast nur noch als Kontrast dazu überliefert. Stemberger, *Einleitung*, 81.

[108] Hillel, „der Alte", soll aus Babylonien stammen und nach gewissen (späten) Traditionen aus dem Hause Davids sein. Er lebte zur Zeit des Herodes. Die oft vertretene Meinung, er sei Lehrer Jesu gewesen, ist bildlich zu verstehen. Die Traditionen über sein Leben sind völlig klischeegeprägt, kontrastieren den sanften Hillel mit dem strengen Schammai und haben viel mit der hellenistischen Gelehrtenbiographie gemeinsam. Ebenda, 80.

[109] Das Wort אַמָּה, welches sonst *fore-arm* („Unterarm"), *cubit* („Elle") und *membrum virile* („Penis") bedeutet, weist in bSchab 31a auf ein Werkzeug (*instrument*) hin. Jastrow, *Dictionary*, 75.

[110] Eigene Übersetzung aus dem Hebräischen bzw. Aramäischen nach der Wilnaer Ausgabe des Talmud Bavli. Bezüglich der englischen Übersetzung vgl. Isidore Epstein (ed.), *Shabbath* (Soncino Press: London 1938), The Babylonian Talmud, Seder Mo'ed I, 140.

Im Unterschied zu Schammai war Hillel in dieser Geschichte der Konversion eines Fremden (נָכְרִי)[111] zum Judentum bereit, die Thora in wenigen Worten zu vermitteln und wählte dafür die negative Goldene Regel. Diese sei die ganze Thora; alles andere sei deren Erläuterung (פֵּירוּשׁ).[112] Es mögen nicht alle Lesenden mit einer solchen Aussage einverstanden sein. Es ist paradox, dass Hillel mit einer Maxime antwortet, die nicht in der Thora und auch in der ganzen Hebräischen Bibel nicht zu finden ist.[113] Das Ausschlaggebende wird aber meist übereinstimmend im letzten Satz gefunden, der zum Studium der Thora aufruft.[114]

In Avot de Rabbi Nathan, einem „außerkanonischen" Traktat,[115] wird in Fassung B, Kapitel 26,6-7 in einer weiteren Begebenheit, in welcher ein Eseltreiber die ganze Thora auf einmal gelehrt bekommen möchte, eine recht ähnlich formulierte negative Regel einem anderen Rabbi in den Mund gelegt. Rabbi Akiba, der ein bedeutender Lehrer in der Zeit von Javne war, soll Folgendes gesagt haben:

> Dies ist das Prinzip der Thora [זה הוא כללה של תורה]: Was du hasst, dir [selbst] zu verursachen, das tue nicht deinem Mitmenschen [מה את שנא לגרמך לחברך לא תעביד]! Wenn du willst, dass ein Mensch dich nicht schädige, dann schädige du ihn auch nicht [אם רוצה את שלא יזיקוך אדם ואף את אל תזיקנו]! Wenn du willst, dass ein Mensch nicht das Deinige wegnehme, dann nimm du auch deinem Mitmenschen nichts weg [רוצה את שלא יטול אדם את שלך אף את לא תטול של חברך]![116] (ARN B 26,7)

---

[111] נָכְרִי bedeutet *stranger* („Fremder"), *gentile* („Nichtjude"). Jastrow, *Dictionary*, 912.
[112] פֵּירוּשׁ bedeutet *explanation* („Erläuterung"), *commentary* (Kommentar). Ebenda, 75.
[113] Alexander, „Jesus and the Golden Rule," 374-375.
[114] Vgl. Andreas Nissen, *Gott und der Nächste im antiken Judentum: Untersuchungen zum Doppelgebot der Liebe* (Mohr Siebeck: Tübingen 1974), Wissenschaftliche Untersuchungen zum Neuen Testament 15, 399.
[115] Avot de Rabbi Nathan (= ARN) ist ein „außerkanonischer" Traktat, weil er nicht die Autorität des eigentlichen babylonischen Talmuds besitzt. Er ist in zwei Fassungen (A und B) überliefert. ARN steht eindeutig in einem Abhängigkeitsverhältnis zum Mischna-Traktat Avot, den es zitiert und kommentiert und gleich ihm enthält ARN nur Haggada. Die Endversion von ARN B, der älteren Version, wird im 3. Jahrhundert n. Chr. datiert. Stemberger, *Einleitung*, 248-250.
[116] Eigene Übersetzung aus dem Hebräischen in Anlehnung an Hans-Jürgen Becker (ed.), *Avot de-Rabbi Natan B: Übersetzung aus dem Hebräischen von Hans-Jürgen Becker* (Mohr Siebeck: Tübingen 2016), Texts and Studies in Ancient Judaism 162, 78-79. Bezüglich der hebräischen Ausgabe (Ms. Parma 2785 [= de Rossi 327], Spanien aus dem Jahr 1289) vgl. Hans-Jürgen Becker (ed.), *Avot de-Rabbi Natan: Synoptische Edition beider Versionen* (Mohr Siebeck: Tübingen 2006), Texts and Studies in Ancient Judaism 116, 357. Hinsichtlich des letzten Satzes in ARN B 26,7 vgl. die Parallelstellen ARN B 26,9; 29,17; 30,13; 32,25.

In einem späteren Kapitel heißt es dann in ARN B 29,17 auch noch: „Wenn du nicht willst, dass ein Mensch dir etwas nachsage, dann sage auch du ihm nichts nach [אם רוצה את שלא יאמר אדם אתריך דבר אף את לא תאמר אחריו דבר]."[117] In Avot de Rabbi Nathan, Fassung B wurde also die negative Goldene Regel mit Schädigungen durch Entwenden materieller Güter bzw. durch üble Nachrede in Zusammenhang gebracht. Heute kann die negative Goldene Regel im Zuge einer queeren Lesart alter jüdischer Texte auf vielfältige Weise auch auf andere Handlungen angewendet werden, die zu Situationen führen, in die kein Mensch hineingeraten möchte.

Nicht nur bedeutsamen Rabbinen wie Hillel oder Akiba, sondern auch Jesus von Nazareth wurde die Goldene Regel zugeschrieben. Sie findet sich im Neuen Testament vornehmlich in zwei Stellen, nämlich in Jesu Bergpredigt im Evangelium nach Matthäus 7,12 und in dessen Feldpredigt im Evangelium nach Lukas 6,31. Im Evangelium nach Matthäus schließt die positiv gefasste Goldene Regel in Mt 7,12 den Hauptteil von Jesu Bergpredigt zusammenfassend ab:

> Alles nun, was ihr wollt, dass euch die Leute tun sollen, das tut ihnen auch [Πάντα οὖν ὅσα ἐὰν θέλητε ἵνα ποιῶσιν ὑμῖν οἱ ἄνθρωποι, οὕτως καὶ ὑμεῖς ποιεῖτε αὐτοῖς]! Das ist das Gesetz und die Propheten [οὗτος γάρ ἐστιν ὁ νόμος καὶ οἱ προφῆται].[118] (Mt 7,12)

Hier ist von „Leuten" bzw. „Menschen" (ἄνθρωποι) die Rede, sodass die positive Goldene Regel im Neuen Testament eine universale Reichweite hat.[119] Die Formel „das Gesetz und die Propheten" benennt die Gesamtheit der göttlichen Forderungen[120] und wird von Matthäus auch in Mt 22,40 in Verbindung

---

[117] Eigene Übersetzung aus dem Hebräischen in Anlehnung an Becker (ed.), *Avot de-Rabbi Natan B: Übersetzung*, 88. Bezüglich der hebräischen Ausgabe (Ms. Parma 2785) vgl. Becker (ed.), *Avot de-Rabbi Natan: Synoptische Edition*, 361.

[118] Eigene Übersetzung aus dem Altgriechischen nach Barbara Aland und Kurt Aland (eds.), *Nestle-Aland: Novum Testamentum Graece* (Deutsche Bibelgesellschaft: Stuttgart [28]2014), 18. Auch alle weiteren Übersetzungen aus dem Altgriechischen von Passagen des Neuen Testaments aus dieser Ausgabe stammen von mir.

[119] Vgl. Gerd Theißen, „Die Goldene Regel (Matthäus 7:12/Lukas 6:31). Über den Sitz im Leben ihrer positiven und negativen Form," in: *Biblical Interpretation* 11/3+4 (2003), 386-399, hier 398.

[120] Vgl. in diesem Abschnitt weiter oben zitierte Aussagen, die prominenten jüdischen Gelehrten zugeschrieben werden, nämlich Hillel in bSchab 31a, nach welchem die negative Goldene Regel „die ganze Thora [כל התורה]" sei, und Rabbi Akiba in ARN B 26,7, nach welchem diese „das Prinzip der Thora [כללה של תורה]" sei.

mit dem doppelten Liebesgebot[121] verwendet.[122] Damit ist die Goldene Regel bei Matthäus dem doppelten Liebesgebot als Summe der Forderungen Gottes (θεοῦ) gleichgesetzt.[123]

Bei Lukas findet sich die Goldene Regel in Lk 6,31 innerhalb von Jesusworten in seiner Feldrede, welche die Feindesliebe als Forderung an das Verhalten der Jünger[124] zum Thema haben:[125] „Wie ihr wollt, dass euch die Leute tun sollen, so tut ihnen auch [Καὶ καθὼς θέλετε ἵνα ποιῶσιν ὑμῖν οἱ ἄνθρωποι ποιεῖτε αὐτοῖς ὁμοίως]!" Innerhalb dieses Abschnitts über Feindesliebe und Gewaltverzicht schließt die Goldene Regel den ersten Teil[126] über das Verhalten der Christen nach außen angesichts der zuvor geschilderten Verfolgungssituation[127] ab. Der Aufruf zu Feindesliebe und Gewaltverzicht wird in einer allgemein anerkannten und evidenten Erfahrungsregel begründet: Das Außerordentliche und Anspruchsvolle (Feindesliebe und Gewaltverzicht trotz Verfolgung) gründet in dem direkt Einsichtigen und Bekannten, nämlich in der Goldenen Regel.[128] In Lk 6,32-35 wird anschließend das Verständnis der Goldenen Regel im Sinne eines reinen Prinzips der Gegenseitigkeit kritisiert. Der Neutestamentler Rudolf Bultmann zeigt ebenfalls die gedankliche Schwäche der Goldenen Regel auf, wenn er behauptet, dass sie, für sich allein genommen, die Moral eines naiven Egoismus enthält.[129] Aus der Sicht von

---

[121] Bezüglich des Doppelgebots der Liebe in Mt 22,37.39 vgl. die Septuagintaübersetzungen des „Höre, Israel" LXX Dtn 6,5 und des Nächstenliebegebots LXX Lev 19,18.

[122] Paulus behauptet hingegen in Röm 13,9 und Gal 5,14, dass das ganze Gesetz in einem einzigen Gebot, nämlich im Nächstenliebegebot LXX Lev 19,18 zusammengefasst bzw. erfüllt ist. Das Nächstenliebegebot wird also bei Paulus noch nicht mit der Goldenen Regel in Verbindung gebracht und es stellt sich die Frage, ob Jesus selbst die Goldene Regel überhaupt gepredigt hat.

[123] Vgl. Roman Heiligenthal, „Goldene Regel, II. Neues Testament und frühes Christentum," in: *Theologische Realenzyklopädie* (de Gruyter: Berlin und New York 1984), 13, 573-575, hier 573.

[124] In Lukas, Kapitel 6 wird keine einzige Frau namentlich als Jünger_In erwähnt. Laut Lk 6,13-16 erwählt Jesus lauter männliche Apostel. Eine inklusive Schreibweise mit „Jünger_Innen" legt sich im Zusammenhang mit diesem Abschnitt also ursprünglich nicht nahe, auch wenn es heute – nicht nur aus feministischer Sicht – haarsträubend erscheinen mag, Frauen bei den wesentlichen christlichen Aussagen nicht miteinzubeziehen.

[125] Vgl. Lk 6,27-36.

[126] Vgl. Lk 6,27-31.

[127] Vgl. Lk 6,20-22.

[128] Heiligenthal, „Goldene Regel, II," 573-574.

[129] Vgl. Rudolf Bultmann, *Die Geschichte der synoptischen Tradition* (Vandenhoeck & Ruprecht: Göttingen [10]1995), Forschungen zur Religion und Literatur des Alten und Neuen Testaments 12 = 29, 107.

Lukas wird aber nicht nur zur Liebe zu Freunden aufgerufen, von der anzunehmen ist, dass sie auf Gegenliebe stoßen wird, sondern auch zur Liebe zu Feinden, von der nicht zu erwarten ist, dass sie erwidert wird. Handelt ein Jünger Jesu im Sinne der Feindesliebe, so ist ihm eschatologischer (das heißt endzeitlicher) Lohn verheißen. Damals wurde das Eintreten der Endzeit als baldiges Ereignis erwartet.

Mag die positive Goldene Regel des Neuen Testaments aus einer gemeinsamen Quelle stammen[130] oder nicht, sie ist jedenfalls in unterschiedlichen Kontexten im Matthäus- und im Lukasevangelium eingeflochten worden.[131] Außerdem ergänzt der sogenannte „westliche Text"[132] der Apostelgeschichte in Apg 15,20.29 den notwendigen Grundkatalog von Forderungen an bekehrte Heiden, wie er im Apostedekret niedergelegt ist, um die negative Goldene Regel.[133] So wird für die Heidenchristen[134] die Abkehr von Götzen(dienst)

---

[130] Die sogenannte „Logienquelle", welche in der Bibelwissenschaft mit dem Siglum „Q" abgekürzt wird, ist die von den Evangelisten Matthäus und Lukas unabhängig voneinander benutzte zweite Quelle neben dem Markusevangelium. Ihre Existenz, die nicht durch Handschriften gesichert ist, beruht auf der „Zwei-Quellen-Theorie", welche die Entstehungsgeschichte der synoptischen Evangelien zu erhellen versucht.

[131] Im Unterschied zu Lk 6,31 kommt die Goldene Regel in Mt 7,12 nicht im Zusammenhang mit der Feindesliebe vor, obwohl auch bei Matthäus von der Feindesliebe die Rede ist, nämlich zuvor in Mt 5,43-48.

[132] Die Majuskelhandschrift D (Codex Bezae Cantabrigiensis) aus der Universitätsbibliothek Cambridge, Nn. II,41, gilt als Hauptzeuge des sogenannten „westlichen Texts", obwohl sie entweder in Ägypten oder Nordafrika geschrieben wurde. Sie ist eine griechisch-lateinische Bilingue, in welcher insbesondere Texte des Evangeliums nach Lukas und der Apostelgeschichte durch Zufügungen, Streichungen und Neuformulierungen umgestaltet wurden. Vgl. Kurt Aland und Barbara Aland, *Der Text des Neuen Testaments. Einführung in die wissenschaftlichen Ausgaben sowie in Theorie und Praxis der modernen Textkritik* (Deutsche Bibelgesellschaft: Stuttgart ²1989), 118-119.

[133] Die negative Goldene Regel findet sich sonst auch in der frühchristlichen Schrift der Didache 1,2, wo sie ein Interpretament von ὡς σεαυτόν aus dem zuvor zitierten Nächstenliebegebot LXX Lev 19,18 ist, mit welchem die Selbstliebe zum Vorbild und Maßstab der Nächstenliebe gemacht wird. Vgl. Kurt Niederwimmer, *Die Didache* (Vandenhoeck & Ruprecht: Göttingen ²1993), Kommentar zu den Apostolischen Vätern 1, 92. Bezüglich der negativen Goldenen Regel in einer weiteren frühchristlichen Schrift vgl. das apokryphe Thomasevangelium, Logion 6.

[134] Auch in der Apostelgeschichte, Kapitel 15, welches mit der Diskussion über die Beschneidung von Heidenchristen (also mit einem männerspezifischen Thema) beginnt, kommen im Zuge der lukanischen Darstellung des Apostelkonvents (das war die Zusammenkunft von Paulus und Barnabas mit den Vertretern der Jerusalemer Urgemeinde zur Beratung über die Heidenmission) keine Frauen unter den Aposteln und Ältesten namentlich vor, und es werden keine Frauen explizit adressiert.

(εἴδωλον), Unzucht (πορνεία) und Blut(vergießen) (αἷμα) und die Befolgung der Goldenen Regel zum verbindlichem Maßstab christlicher Lebensführung.[135]

Somit habe ich mit dem babylonischen Talmud Schabbat 31a und zwei neutestamentlichen Stellen aus Jesu Bergpredigt im Evangelium nach Matthäus (Mt 7,12) und aus seiner Feldpredigt im Evangelium nach Lukas (Lk 6,31) die maßgeblichen Schriften zur Goldenen Regel für das Judentum und für das Christentum dargelegt.[136] In der Antike gab es eine breite Streuung an Belegen für die Goldene Regel aus nicht religiösen Quellen.[137] So zählt der römische Philosoph Seneca die Goldene Regel zu jenen Maximen, deren Wahrheitsgehalt ohne Begründung unmittelbar evident ist.[138] Die Goldene Regel wird außerdem unterschiedlichen Philosophen der Sieben Weisen Griechenlands zugeschrieben, nämlich Pittakos von Mytilene[139] oder Thales von Milet.[140] Aber auch auf Aristoteles wird sie zurückgeführt.[141] Erfunden wurde die Goldene Regel also nicht im Judentum oder im Christentum. Die Goldene Regel gibt es nirgendwo in der Hebräischen Bibel, weder in ihrer positiven, noch in ihrer negativen Form. Erst seit hellenistischer Zeit häufen sich aufgrund der Auseinandersetzung mit der griechischen Kultur die Belege für eine Wertschätzung der Goldenen Regel im Judentum. So findet sich die negative Goldene Regel auf Griechisch beispielsweise im – aus protestantischer Sicht – „apokryphen" bzw. – aus katholischer Sicht – „deuterokanonischen" Buch Tobit, nämlich in LXX Tob 4,15,[142] wo sie von Martin Luther folgendermaßen sprichwörtlich übersetzt wurde: „Was du nicht willst, dass man dir tu, das füg auch keinem anderen zu [καὶ ὃ μισεῖς, μηδενὶ ποιήσῃς]." Auf diese Weise

---

[135] Heiligenthal, „Goldene Regel, II," 574.

[136] Ich beschränke meine Darstellung der Goldenen Regel auf die entscheidenden Texte fürs Juden- und Christentum ohne Anspruch auf Vollständigkeit. Bezüglich weiterer Stellen im Judentum und im frühen Christentum vgl. Albrecht Dihle, *Die Goldene Regel: Eine Einführung in die Geschichte der antiken und frühchristlichen Vulgärethik* (Vandenhoeck & Ruprecht: Göttingen 1962), Studienhefte zur Altertumswissenschaft 7, 8-9.82-84,103-109.

[137] Ebenda, 9.

[138] Vgl. Seneca, Brief 94,25.43.

[139] Vgl. Johannes Stobaios 3 p.120 H.

[140] Vgl. Diogenes Laertios 1,36.

[141] Vgl. Diogenes Laertios 5,21.

[142] Die negative Goldene Regel ist nicht in den vier aramäischen Versionen 4Q196-4Q199 (= 4QpapTob[a] ar, 4QTob[b] ar, 4QTob[c] ar und 4QTob[d] ar) oder der einen hebräischen Version 4Q200 (= 4QTob[e]) aus Qumran nachweisbar. Diese Textfunde aus Qumranhöhle 4 belegen semitische Versionen des Buchs Tobit.

hat Tobit, ein Mann aus dem Stamm Naftali, welcher in Assyrien in der Verbannung lebte, seine Mahnungen an seinen Sohn Tobias zusammengefasst.[143]

Der Wert der Goldenen Regel liegt darin, dass sie an die Erfahrungen der Menschen anknüpft und ihnen die Möglichkeit bietet, einen direkten Zugang zum Wertesystem ihrer eigenen Religion zu gewinnen – sei es die jüdische, die christliche oder eine andere Religion.[144] Sowohl jüdische als auch christliche Leser_Innen der Gegenwart müssten sich also aufgrund ihres Glaubensguts ihrer jeweils eigenen Religion in Form der negativen bzw. positiven Goldenen Regel Gedanken machen, wie sie anderen Mitmenschen – inklusive Frauen, diversen queeren Personen und anderen Minderheiten – begegnen sollten. Im Unterschied zur Antike sind jetzt nicht nur die Verhaltensweisen von Männern anderen Männern gegenüber im Zusammenhang mit der Goldenen Regel ein Thema. Aus heutiger feministischer und queerer Sicht stellt sich die Frage, wie mit antiken androzentrischen Texten umgehen, die ursprünglich nicht an Frauen adressiert waren und auch noch keine Unterscheidung zwischen queeren und straighten Personen trafen. Die naheliegende Antwort darauf ist, sie alle hinsichtlich entscheidender jüdischer und christlicher Glaubensaussagen miteinzubeziehen. Indem sich Frauen und Männer sowie unterschiedliche queere Personen aus verschiedenen Kontexten Glaubensaussagen wie die Goldene Regel aneignen, entstehen neue, umfassendere Interpretationsmöglichkeiten antiker Texte. Theoretisch müsste die Beachtung der

---

[143] Die Goldene Regel kommt in der griechischsprachigen Legende über die Entstehung der Septuaginta im Aristeasbrief 207 vor. In der pseudepigraphischen Schrift Testamentum Naphtali 1,6 findet sich die Goldene Regel im Doppelgebot der Gottes- und Nächstenliebe. In der griechischen Version der apokryphen bzw. deuterokanonischen Schrift Jesus Sirach 31(34),15 wird die Paraphrase des biblischen Nächstenliebegebots der hebräischen Version mit der Goldenen Regel umgedeutet. Zuletzt sei hinsichtlich der Goldenen Regel noch auf Philos Schrift Hypothetika hingewiesen, welche bei Euseb, Praeparatio evangelica („Die Vorbereitung auf das Evangelium") 8,7,6 überliefert ist. Dihle, *Goldene Regel*, 82-84.

[144] Die Goldene Regel findet sich neben dem Judentum und dem Christentum quasi in allen fünf Weltreligionen, nämlich auch im Islam, im Hinduismus und im Buddhismus. Außerdem war sie schon im alten Ägypten, im alten Griechenland und in der griechisch-römischen Kultur bekannt. Es gibt sie in Religionen wie dem Zoroastrismus, dem Konfuzianismus, dem Jainismus und dem Bahaismus. Die Goldene Regel eignet sich daher auch als Ausgangspunkt für interreligiösen Dialog. Bezüglich der Goldenen Regel in den Weltreligionen vgl. Jacob Neusner und Bruce Chilton (eds.), *The Golden Rule: The Ethics of Reciprocity in World Religions* (Continuum: London und New York 2008). Bezüglich eines Vergleichs zwischen der Goldenen Regel im Hinduismus und im Christentum vgl. Freek L. Bakker, „Comparing the Golden Rule in Hindu and Christian Religious Texts," in: *Studies in Religion/Sciences Religieuses* 42/1 (2013), 38-58.

Goldenen Regel (sowohl in ihrer positiven als auch in ihrer negativen Form) dazu beitragen, dass alle Menschen, egal welcher Hautfarbe, welchen Geschlechts oder welcher sexuellen Orientierung et cetera, gewaltfrei miteinander leben können. Niemand möchte nämlich am eigenen Leib Gewalt erleiden müssen. Die Goldene Regel setzt jedoch Empathie (nämlich die Bereitschaft und Fähigkeit, sich in andere Menschen hineinzufühlen) und ethisches Reflexionsvermögen voraus. Wenn Menschen selbst nicht von rassistischer, sexistischer oder heterosexistischer Gewalt bzw. Diskriminierung betroffen sind und zusätzlich keinerlei Einfühlungsvermögen und Verstand haben, werden sie kaum im Sinne der biblischen Liebesgebote und der Goldenen Regel Initiativen ergreifen, um nahestehenden oder auch fremden Personen, die von solchen Formen von Gewalt und Diskriminierung betroffen sind, ein besseres Leben zu ermöglichen. Insofern zeigen sich auch die Grenzen der Golden Regel für eine Ethik des guten Miteinanders aller Menschen dieser Welt.

Karin Hügel promoviert an der Universität von Amsterdam mit einer Arbeit über „Queere Lesarten der Hebräischen Bibel". http://www.uva.nl/profile/k.hugel2 karinhuegel@gmx.at

Eleonore Lappin-Eppel

Bet Debora – Frauenperspektiven im Judentum

Zusammenfassung
Angeregt durch den enormen Wandel, den die jüdische Welt durch den Fall der kommunistischen Regime vor allem in Europa erfuhr, gründeten drei Berlinerinnen 1998 *Bet Debora* (Lehrhaus der Debora). Damit schufen sie eine europäische Plattform jüdischer Frauen, die sich mit dem Status der Frauen in den jüdischen Gemeinschaften, aber auch in der allgemeinen Umwelt befasst. Mit Konferenzen und Vorträgen lotet *Bet Debora* Möglichkeiten aus, die Position jüdischer Frauen zu stärken und ihr Wirken in Gegenwart und Vergangenheit sichtbarer zu machen. Ein wichtiges Prinzip von *Bet Debora* ist die Offenheit. An den Konferenzen nehmen Rabbinerinnen, Kantorinnen, Akademikerinnen, Aktivistinnen, Künstlerinnen sowie interessierte Frauen und Männer teil. Wichtig war uns ist der Austausch zwischen jüdischen Frauen aus Ost- und Westeuropa und ihre jeweils unterschiedlichen Auffassungen und Formen jüdischer Erneuerung. Das gemeinsame Lernen sowie das voreinander Lernen stehen hier im Mittelpunkt. Natürlich wendet sich *Bet Debora* auch an jüdische Frauen in Israel und Nordamerika und steht auch Menschen mit anderen Glaubensbekenntnissen offen.

Der Aufsatz beschreibt die Entwicklung von *Bet Debora* und die wichtigsten Themenkreise, die im Lauf der Jahre behandelt wurden. Dazu gehörten die sukzessive Akzeptanz von Rabbinerinnen und Kantorinnen in jüdischen Gemeinden, der Einfluss von Frauen auf Gemeindepolitik, der Umgang mit unterschiedlichen Formen von Familien innerhalb der jüdischen Gemeinschaft, jüdische Erziehung für Frauen und Mädchen, der Status der LGBT-Bewegung in den jüdischen Gemeinden, der Einfluss historischer Ereignisse und Entwicklungen auf die Gegenwart u.v.m.

Schlagwörter: Judentum; Frauen; Europa; Erneuerung; Gleichberechtigung.

Abstract
Motivated by the enormous change that the Jewish world experienced by the fall of the communist regimes, especially in Europe, three women in Berlin founded *Bet Debora* (House of study of Debora) in 1998. Thereby they created a European platform of Jewish women, which deals with the status of women in the Jewish communities as well as their general environment. Through conferences and lectures *Bet Debora*

fathoms the possibilities to strengthen Jewish women and make their present and past activities more visible. An important principle of *Bet Debora* is its openness. The conferences are attended by female rabbis, cantors, academics, activists, artists as well as interested women and men. An important issue is the exchange between Jewish women from Eastern and Western Europe and their different conceptions and forms of Jewish renewal. The focus is on learning together and learning from each other. Of course, *Bet Debora* also addresses Jewish women in Israel and North America and is open to people from other faiths.

This article describes the development of *Bet Debora* and the most important topics dealt with during the past years. This includes the gradual acceptance of female rabbis and cantors in Jewish communities, women's influence on the politics of the communities, the handling of different forms of families within the Jewish community, Jewish education of women and girls, the status of the LGBT-movement in the Jewish communities, the influence of historical events and developments on the present situation etc.

Keywords: Judaism; women; Europe; renewal; equality.

Resumen

Motivado por el enorme cambio que el mundo judío experimentó con la caída de los regímenes comunistas, especialmente en Europa, tres mujeres fundaron Bet Debora en Berlin (Casa de Estudio de Débora) en 1998. Crearon, así, una plafatorma europea de mujeres judías que aborda el estatus de las mujeres en las comunidades judías así como su ambiente. A través de conferencias y charlas, Bet Debora imagina las posibilidades de reforzar a las mujeres judías y hacer sus actividades presentes y pasadas más visibles. Un importante principio de Bet Débora es su apertura. A las conferencias asisten rabinas, cantoras, académicas, activistas, artistas así como mujeres y hombres interesados. Un tema importante es el intercambio entre mujeres judías de la Europa oriental y occidental y sus diferentes concepciones y formas de renovación judía. Se pone el acento en aprender juntas y aprender de cada una. Bet Débora también se dirige a mujeres judías en Israel y Norteamérica y está abierta a personas de otras fes.

Este artículo describe el desarrollo de Bet Débora y los temas más importantes que ha tratado durante los últimos años. Esto implica la aceptación gradual de rabinas y cantoras en las comunidades judías, la influencia de las mujeres en la política de las comunidades, el manejo de distintas formas de familias dentro de la comunidad judía, la educación judía de mujeres y niñas, el estatus del movimiento LGBT en las comunidades judías, la influencia de los eventos históricos y desarrollos de la situación presente, etc.

Palabras clave: Judaísmo; mujeres; Europa; renovación; igualdad.

1998 riefen drei Frauen, Lara Dämmig, Rachel Monika Herweg und Elisa Klapheck, in Berlin *Bet Debora* ins Leben. Neun Jahre nach dem Fall der totalitären Regimes des Ostblocks wollten sie die Position der jüdischen Frauen in den europäischen jüdischen Gemeinden ausloten. Die Jahre seit 1989 hatten einen enormen Wandel für das europäische Judentum gebracht. In den GUS-Staaten lebten hunderttausende Jüdinnen und Juden, die erst jetzt die Möglichkeit erhalten hatten, ihre Religion, ihre Traditionen und ihr kulturelles Erbe zu entdecken und auszuleben. Die verschiedenen jüdischen religiösen Strömungen schickten Vertreter*innen in die Länder des ehemaligen Ostblocks, um in den sich dort neu organisierenden Gemeinden ihre Auffassung von Judentum zu etablieren. Gleichzeitig begannen aber auch die sogenannten *emerging communities*, die auftauchenden Gemeinden des Ostens, ihre eigenen Vorstellungen zu entwickeln und umzusetzen, die eher kulturell als religiös ausgerichtet waren. Die neu entstandene Dynamik im europäischen Judentum bewirkte religiöse Neuerungsprozesse auch in Deutschland und in Österreich, wo sich liberale Gemeinden etablierten, die sich für die Gleichstellung der Frau im Judentum einsetzten. Im 18. und 19. Jahrhundert war Deutschland die Wiege des Reformjudentums gewesen. Doch nach der *Shoah* waren die Vertreter*innen dieser religiösen Strömung entweder geflohen oder von den Nationalsozialisten ermordet worden. Die großen liberalen Zentren waren im angelsächsischen Raum zu finden, wo sie die Mehrheit der jüdischen Gemeinden stellten. Daher waren weltweit die nichtorthodoxen Strömungen zahlenmäßig wesentlich stärker als die orthodoxen. Die ersten liberalen Nachkriegsgemeinden in Deutschland entstanden im Jahr 1994, heute sind es 27.[1] Finanziert wurden sie von der Weltunion für progressives Judentum (*World Union for Progressive Judaism*). 2002 folgte dann die konservative, die *Masorti*-Bewegung, die seit 2006 in Berlin eine Gemeinde hat. Grund für das Interesse aus dem Ausland und die Neugründungen war der Zuzug jüdischer Kontingentflüchtlinge aus der ehemaligen UdSSR. Zwischen 1991 und 2004 wanderten 220.000 Jüdinnen und Juden aus der vormaligen Sowjetunion in Deutschland ein. Dabei handelte es sich um Juden gemäß der sowjetischen Nationalitätenzugehörigkeit.[2] Ein erheblicher Teil dieser Neuankömmlinge hatte keine jüdische Mutter, war also gemäß dem jüdischen Religionsgesetz nicht jüdisch und musste, um als Jude/Jüdin anerkannt zu werden, konvertieren.

---

[1] Vgl. https://www.liberale-juden.de, 21. Dezember 2018.
[2] Bundesamt für Migration und Flüchtlinge (ed.), Sonja Haug/Peter Schimany, *Jüdische Zuwanderer in Deutschland*, Working Papers 2005, 6.

Dazu kam, dass die meisten Zuwanderer und Zuwanderinnen säkular und oft nicht an Religion interessiert waren. Dennoch schlossen sich 83.000 Neuankömmlinge dauerhaft einer jüdischen Gemeinde an.[3] Damit wurde die Existenz des durch die *Shoah* dezimierten und danach von Überalterung gekennzeichneten deutschen Judentums gesichert, Deutschland hatte wieder eine der großen Gemeinden Europas. Gleichzeitig wurden jedoch die alten Strukturen infrage gestellt. Die Gemeinden übernahmen eine enorme Aufgabe, indem sie sich verpflichteten, die jüdischen Neuankömmlinge nicht nur in die jüdische, sondern auch in die deutsche Gesellschaft zu integrieren.[4]

Die Bet-Debora-Tagungen
Vor diesem Hintergrund entstand 1998 *Bet Debora*. Die Gründerinnen wollten erkunden, was dieses Jahrzehnt des stürmischen Wandels den europäischen jüdischen Frauen gebracht hatte. Um sich diesen Überblick zu verschaffen, beschlossen sie, eine internationale Tagung einzuberufen. Ihre ursprünglichen Befürchtungen, es könnte zu wenige Rabbinerinnen und Kantorinnen in Europa geben, erwiesen sich bald als unbegründet, sodass es in der Einladung zur Konferenz bereits selbstbewusst hieß:

> In diesem Jahrzehnt hat eine faszinierende Entwicklung im europäischen jüdischen Leben stattgefunden. Zunehmend üben Frauen wichtige Kultusfunktionen aus. Schon jetzt amtieren Rabbinerinnen in Städten wie London, Paris und Oldenburg, genauso wie in Moskau, Minsk und Budapest. Was bedeutet dies für die jüdische Tradition und Überlieferung? Wie verschieben sich ihre Inhalte, welche Themen treten in den Vordergrund, welche neuen Herausforderungen stellen sich?[5]

Man fragte sich also nicht nur, wo Frauen im religiösen Leben standen, sondern auch, wie man dieses religiöse Leben für Frauen ansprechender machen

---

[3] https://www.dw.com/de/diskussion-um-jüdische-zuwanderer/a-1441580, 20. Dezember 2018.
[4] Wie schwierig dieser Prozess war und welche Spannungen er zwischen deutschen und zugewanderten Juden erzeugte, ist folgendem Artikel zu entnehmen, dessen Aussage die Autorin nicht vollinhaltlich teilt: Edna Brocke, „Jüdisches Leben in der Bundesrepublik Deutschland", in: Eleonore Lappin (ed.), *Jüdische Gemeinden – Kontinuitäten und Brüche* (Philo: Berlin/Wien 2002), 267-281, hier 272-281.
[5] Einladung zur 1. Internationalen *Bet Debora*-Konferenz, 13.–16. Mai 1999, Berlin. Abgedruckt am hinteren Deckblatt von: Lara Dämmig/Rachel Monika Herweg/Elisa Klapheck (eds.), *Bet Debora Journal, Tagung europäischer Rabbinerinnen, Kantorinnen, rabbinisch gelehrter und interessierter Jüdinnen und Juden* (Hentrich & Hentrich: Berlin 2000). (https://www.bet-debora.net/de/aktivitaeten/1-tagung/publikation, 21. Dezember 2018).

könnte. Daraus entstand auch der Name Bet Debora: Das Judentum kennt eine Vielzahl von gelehrten Schulen, die sich um ein Haus, ein Lehrhaus entwickelten und durch immer neue Auslegungen der alten Schriften die jüdische Tradition schufen. Es war dies ein Prozess, der auf alten Auslegungen fußend Neuerungen hervorbrachte. Genau das sollte auch für Frauen erreicht werden: eine Schule, ein Lehrhaus, das eine frauengerechte Tradition entwickelte. Benannt wurde das Lehrhaus nach der biblischen Richterin und militärischen Führerin Debora. Daher verstand sich die ersten Konferenz als „Forum für ‚rabbinisch gelehrte und interessierte' jüdische Frauen in Europa".[6] Um eine neue europäische jüdische Tradition für Frauen zu inspirieren, luden die Initiatorinnen europäische Rabbinerinnen und Kantorinnen ein. Es kamen acht Rabbinerinnen und vier Kantorinnen. Weitere Vortragende waren Akademikerinnen, die sich mit Fragen der jüdischen Religion befassten, und Gemeindeaktivistinnen, die sich vor allem beim Aufbau egalitärer jüdischer Gemeinden engagierten. Das größte Kontingent an Rabbinerinnen kam aus England mit seinen großen, etablierten liberalen Gemeinden und seinem hervorragenden Rabbinerseminar, dem Leo Baeck College in London. Sybil Sheridan, die erste Frau, die im Vereinigten Königreich zur Rabbinerin ordiniert wurde, würdigte Rabbinerin Regina Jonas, die 1935 als weltweit erste Frau zum Rabbinat zugelassen wurde und dieses Amt sowohl in Berlin als auch nach ihrer Deportation in Theresienstadt ausgeübt hatte. Sie wurde 1944 in Auschwitz ermordet. Sheridan bezeichnete es als großes Versäumnis der ersten Rabbinatsstudentinnen nach der Shoah, sich nicht weiter um ihre ermordete Vorgängerin gekümmert zu haben.[7] Dieses Versäumnis holte Elisa Klapheck nach: Im Jahr der Konferenz brachte sie die Dissertation von Rabbinerin Regina Jonas: „Kann die Frau das rabbinische Amt bekleiden? – Eine Streitschrift"[8] heraus. 2003 folgte dann eine Monographie „Regina Jonas: Die weltweit erste Rabbinerin".[9] Im Rahmen der zweiten Bet-Debora-Tagung wurde am 1. Juni 2001 in Berlin eine Gedenktafel für Regina Jonas enthüllt. In Regina Jonas fand Bet Debora ein *role model* für jüdische Feministinnen und eine Vorläuferin, auf deren Werk sie ihre Erneuerungen aufbauen konnten. Regina Jonas war aber auch ein

---

[6] Editorial, in: Dämmig/Herweg/Klapheck (eds.), *Bet Debora Journal 2000*, 4-5, hier 4.
[7] Sybil Sheridan, „Der Geschichte nicht trauen", in: Dämmig/Herweg/Klapheck (eds.), *Bet Debora Journal 2000*, 6-7.
[8] Berlin 1999.
[9] Elisa Klapheck, *Regina Jonas: Die weltweit erste Rabbinerin* (Hentrich & Hentrich: Berlin 2003), Jüdische Miniaturen 4.

Symbol dafür, was durch die Shoah zerstört wurde, an Menschen ebenso wie an Möglichkeiten für jüdische Frauen. Daher tauchte ihr Name auch in folgenden Konferenzen immer wieder auf, wurde ihr Leben und ihr Vergessenwerden immer neu beleuchtet.

Obwohl gerade die erste Tagung im Schatten der Shoah stand, verstand sie sich gleichzeitig als Aufbruch zur feministischen Erneuerung der jüdischen Religion, im Gebet ebenso wie in der Schriftauslegung. Das Bild vom Status der Frauen im Judentum war nicht zufriedenstellend. Selbst die anscheinend so wohl etablierten britischen Rabbinerinnen litten unter der Tatsache, trotz eigener Gemeinden in einer männlich dominierten religiösen jüdischen Welt noch immer marginalisiert zu sein. Daher setzten sie sich ebenso wie die Aktivistinnen für ein wahrhaft inklusives Judentum ein – nicht nur was Frauen betraf. In die Gemeinden gleichberechtigt aufgenommen sollten auch Lesben, Schwule sowie Vaterjuden/jüdinnen und Konvertit*innen werden, die nach wie vor zum Teil abgelehnte Randgruppen waren. Ein weiteres Thema war die Erneuerung jüdischen Lebens in Osteuropa. Obwohl man sich einig war, dass diese Erneuerung in einem erheblichen Maße von Frauen getragen wurde, gab es doch heftige Diskussionen darüber, welcher religiöse Weg der zukunftsträchtigere war: der orthodoxe mit alle seinen Einschränkungen für Frauen, der sich jedoch über Jahrtausende beim Erhalt des Judentums bewährt hatte, oder der nichtorthodoxe, reformfreudige, wo Frauen auf Gleichstellung hoffen konnten. Einigen konnte man sich nicht. Doch es ist ein Erfolg, dass in Bet Debora solche kontroversiellen Diskussionen geführt werden, dass sich Frauen aller Strömungen hier einfinden.[10] Und zwar bis heute.

Die Bet-Debora-Tagungen stießen durchwegs auf Interesse und im Lauf der Jahre entwickelte sich ein Netzwerk von regelmäßigen Teilnehmer*innen aus allen Teilen Europas, aus Nordamerika und aus Israel, wobei das größte Kontingent stets aus Deutschland kommt. Allerdings war nach der ersten Tagung klar, dass der alleinige Fokus auf religiös gebildete Frauen nicht ausreichte, dass auch das thematische Spektrum erweitert werden musste. Trotzdem behielten die Tagungen ihren Namen bei und wenden sich bis heute an „europäische Rabbinerinnen, Kantorinnen, rabbinisch gelehrte und interessierte Jüdinnen und Juden". Doch tatsächlich gehören dem Bet-Debora-Netzwerk und dem Publikum der Tagungen auch Akademiker*innen, Aktivist*innen,

---

[10] Zur ersten internationalen Bet-Debora-Tagung vgl. https:www.bet-debora.net/de/ aktivitaten/1-tagung und https:www.bet-debora.net/contents/uploads/2013/08/1 -tagung-journal-dt.pdf, 21. Dezember 2018.

Künstler*innen sowie Frauen und Männer an, die sich nicht nur für Religion, sondern auch für Kunst und Kultur interessieren. Sie kommen nicht nur aus Interesse an den Vorträgen, Diskussionen und Workshops, sondern auch aus dem Wunsch heraus, einige Tage in Gesellschaft von jüdischen Frauen zu verbringen. Denn viele Mitglieder unseres Netzwerks gehören zu keiner Gemeinde, entweder, weil es an ihrem Wohnort keine gibt, oder weil sie die existierende Gemeinde nicht anspricht. Für sie wurde Bet Debora zur jüdischen Heimat. Andere Teilnehmer*innen holen sich auf den Konferenzen Anregungen, wie sie ihre Ideen in ihren Gemeinden umsetzen können. Daher sind die Gespräche außerhalb der Vortragssäle besonders wichtig. Oft erfuhren die Organisatorinnen später, wie Vorhaben in Folge der Tagung tatsächlich umgesetzt werden konnten. Bei Bet-Debora-Tagungen entstanden aber auch Ideen zu Büchern, wurden akademische Zusammenarbeiten initiiert und Freundschaften geschlossen.

Die zweite Bet-Debora-Tagung von 2000 war dem Thema „Jüdische Familie – Mythos und Realität"[11] gewidmet. Auch bei dieser Tagung wurde den modernen Entwicklungen Rechnung getragen, dass es neben der traditionellen jüdischen Familie, die als Garant für die Weitergabe der jüdischen Tradition und Voraussetzung für das Weiterbestehen des Judentums galt und gilt, neue Formen des Zusammenlebens gibt. Auf der Tagung wurde die Frage behandelt, wie Alleinerziehende, interkonfessionelle Familien, gleichgeschlechtliche Partnerschaften und dergleichen diesen Anforderungen gerecht und akzeptierte Mitglieder der jüdischen Gemeinden werden können. Angesichts des Auseinanderbrechens der familiären Strukturen kam nun vermehrt Gemeinden die Bedeutung als „jüdische Ersatzfamilien" und somit Trägerinnen und Vermittlerinnen der Traditionen zu. So zum Beispiel, wenn jüdische Feste wie Pessach nicht mehr im Rahmen der Familie gefeiert werden können und zu Gemeindefesten werden. Als besonders schwierig erwies sich das fast gleichzeitige Übernehmen und Weitergeben von jüdischen Traditionen für die nach der Shoah in kommunistischen Ländern geborenen Jüdinnen und Juden, die oft erst nach 1989 damit beginnen konnten, sich mit ihrer Herkunft auseinanderzusetzen. Gleichzeitig zeigte die Tagung, dass der „Mythos jüdische Familie" bereits seit der Wende vom 19. zum 20. Jahrhundert in Frage gestellt wurde. Der erleichterte Zugang zur Bildung ermöglichte es Frauen, Lebensentwürfe außerhalb des herkömmlichen Rollenbilds als Hausfrau und Mutter zu verwirklichen. Gemäß der

---

[11] Die jüdische Familie – Mythos und Realität. 2. Tagung europäischer Rabbinerinnen, Kantorinnen, jüdischer Gelehrter und Aktivistinnen, Berlin, 1.–4. Juni 2001.

Thematik kamen bei der Tagung neben Rabbinerinnen Vortragende aus unterschiedlichsten Disziplinen zu Wort: Historikerinnen, Soziologinnen, Pädagoginnen, Künstlerinnen und viele andere. Neu war auch, dass sich Bet Debora nun explizit an ein nichtjüdisches Publikum wandte.[12]

Auch die dritte Tagung, vom 23.–25. Mai 2003, hatte kein religiöses Thema, sondern befasste sich mit der Frage nach „Macht und Verantwortung".[13] Wie in der Einladung zur Tagung festgehalten, war „Macht" ein problematisches Konzept für Europas Jüd*innen, deren Existenz Jahrhunderte lang gerade von Machtlosigkeit geprägt war. Der Macht von jüdischen Frauen wurden darüber hinaus auch innerjüdisch durch das religiös geprägte patriarchalische Gesellschaftssystem Hindernisse entgegengestellt. Daher erstaunt es wenig, dass auch die an der Tagung teilnehmenden Frauen sich nur ungern zu ihrer Macht bekennen wollten, wohl aber mit der Übernahme der Verantwortung viel anfangen konnten, wie Cynthia Kain, die stellvertretende Vorsitzende der Jüdischen Gemeinde zu Berlin, offen zugab. Gabriele Brenner, Vorsitzende der Jüdischen Gemeinde Weiden, meinte, Frauen hätten in den letzten Jahren der starken Einwanderung aus der ehemaligen Sowjetunion viel Verantwortung besonders auf sozialem Gebiet übernommen, aber deshalb noch lange keine Macht. Grund dafür sei, dass Frauen Macht negativ beschreiben und Frauen, die einflussreiche Positionen anstrebten, mit Misstrauen anstatt Unterstützung begegneten. Charlotte Knobloch, damals Vizepräsidentin des Zentralrats der Juden in Deutschland und Vorsitzende der Israelitischen Kultusgemeinde in München, wies auf Strategien zu Machterwerb und -erhalt sowie zum verantwortungsvollen Umgang damit hin, die allerdings nicht spezifisch weiblich waren.

Der Großteil der Tagung kreiste um vermehrten Einfluss und vermehrte Präsenz von Frauen im Gemeindeleben. Ein wichtiger Schlüssel dazu war, wie einhellig festgestellt wurde, jüdische Bildung. Nur religiöse gebildete Frauen konnten Vorbeterinnen, Lehrerinnen, Rabbinerinnen werden und das religiöse Leben aktiv mitgestalten. Eine Einschränkung von Bildungsmöglichkeiten, wie zum Beispiel bei orthodoxen Frauen, die vom Talmudstudium ausgeschlossen waren, schränkte die Ämter ein, die sie innerhalb ihrer Gemeinden ausfüllen konnten. Dennoch gibt es auch im orthodoxen Bereich eine weibliche Bildungsoffensive.

---

[12] Vgl. https://www.bet-debora.net/de/aktivitaten/2-tagung/ und www.bet-debora.net/contents/uploads/2013/08/2.-tagung-journal-dt.pdf, 21. Dezember 2018.

[13] Die hier genannten Texte sind zu finden unter https://www.bet-debora.net/de/publikationen-2/journal-3-in-2003#macht, 4. Januar 2019.

Ein wichtiger Schritt zu Einfluss ist Sichtbarkeit. Seit den 1970er Jahren suchten jüdische Feministinnen vor allem in den USA daher nach Hinweisen auf Frauen in den jüdischen religiösen Texten, um *role models* zu entdecken und um zu beweisen, dass sie immer „vorhanden" waren, Beiträge leisteten, von den männlichen Autoren der heiligen Schriften jedoch „aus der Geschichte geschrieben" wurden.[14] Moshe Shalvi, einer der Herausgeber der *Encyclopedia Judaica*[15] musste nach Fertigstellung des Werks feststellen, dass nur 0,27 Prozent der Wörter darin Frauen gewidmet waren. Er holte das Versäumte nach. Als er und seine Frau Alice an der Tagung teilnahmen, waren sie mit der Herausgabe der *Encyclopedia of Jewish Women* beschäftigt, die 2006 erschien.[16] Katalin Pécsi wiederum wies darauf hin, dass die Unterdrückung jüdischen Lebens unter dem Kommunismus in Ungarn dazu geführt hatte, dass jüdische Frauen in der ungarischen Literatur weitgehend unsichtbar waren. Damit war ein Bogen vom amerikanisch-jüdischen Feminismus der 1970er und 1980er Jahre, der die Frauen in der biblischen und traditionellen Literatur sichtbar machte und daraus neue Inspirationen für weibliche Spiritualität schöpfte, zur postkommunistischen jüdischen Literatur geschlagen. Sichtbarkeit bedeutete auch Deutungsmacht auf dem Gebiet der jüdischen Tradition, des Gemeindelebens und der jüdischen Kultur.

Ein wichtiges Anliegen der Bet-Debora-Tagungen war stets, Frauen aus Osteuropa einzubinden und ihren Beitrag zur Erneuerung jüdischen Lebens kennen zu lernen. An der dritten Tagung nahmen Frauen aus Russland, Armenien, Georgien, Estland, Moldawien, der Tschechischen Republik, Bulgarien und Ungarn als Vortragende teil. Gleichzeitig erweiterte sich auch die EU nach Osten. Diese Entwicklungen waren mit ein Grund dafür, dass die vierte Bet-Debora-Tagung im August 2006 in Budapest stattfand und von der feministischen Organisation *Ester Tàska* (Esters Tasche) organisiert wurde. *Ester Tàska* war ein jüdisch-feministischer Kulturverein, dem vor allem Akademikerinnen – Historikerinnen, Soziologinnen, Museumskuratorinnen und so weiter – angehörten. Der akademische Anspruch dieser Tagung wurde auch daraus deutlich, dass sie in Räumlichkeiten der *Central European University* abgehalten wurde. Thema der Tagung war *Diversities*. Das Thema trug der Tatsache Rechnung,

---

[14] Vgl. Sondra Henry/Emily Taitz, *Written Out of History: A Hidden Legacy of Jewish Women Revealed Through Their Writings and Letters* (Bloch Pub Co: New York 1978).
[15] Jerusalem/New York 1971/72.
[16] Alice und Moshe Shalvi, *Jewish Women: A Comprehensive Historical Encyclopedia*, hg. von Paula Hyman und Dalia Ofer (Shalvi Pub: Jerusalem 2006).

dass jüdische Frauen in einer vielfältigen Gesellschaft lebten, in der sie einen Platz für ihr Judentum finden mussten. Eines der Unterthemen war wieder Macht, hier im Sinne von Ermächtigung, um die Stärkung der Position jüdischer Frauen in den Gemeinden und in der jüdischen sowie in der allgemeinen Gesellschaft. Großer Wert wurde bei der Tagung daher auf die Vernetzung der Teilnehmerinnen gelegt, um gegenseitige Unterstützung und Förderung zu ermöglichen. Die Vorträge und Diskussionen befassten sich mit jüdischen Frauenorganisationen und einzelnen Frauen in Gegenwart und Vergangenheit, die sich für Gleichberechtigung einsetzten – ein Kampf, der noch lange nicht abgeschlossen erschien. Die Tagung zeigte deutlich die Kluft auf, die sich zwischen den Lebensformen, welche jüdische Frauen seit dem 19. Jahrhundert für sich erkämpfen konnten, und dem traditionellen, religiösen Frauenbild auftat. Diese Kluft wurde umso deutlicher, weil die Vorträge gerade die diversen alternativen Lebensentwürfe zeigten. Im Gegensatz zu den früheren Tagungen war hier der Schwerpunkt nicht auf einem innerjüdischen Erneuerungsprozess, sondern auf säkularen Alternativen, die oft auch zu einer Abkehr vom Judentum führten. Angesichts des hohen Grades an Säkularisierung in Osteuropa – Ungarn war ein eindrucksvolles Beispiel dafür – war die Frage nach der Vereinbarung solcher Lebensentwürfe mit jüdischer Erneuerung besonders wichtig.[17]

Die fünfte Tagung wurde von Tania Reytan im Juni 2009 in Sofia, Bulgarien, organisiert. Erstmals gelang es, eine Tagung in Zusammenarbeit mit der lokalen jüdischen Gemeinde auszurichten. Eine weitere Neuerung bestand darin, dass diese Gemeinde eine sefardische war. Diese Tradition wurde vor allem durch sefardische synagogale Musik repräsentiert, was der Tagung einen wunderbaren künstlerischen Zug verlieh. Tania Reytan hatte bereits auf der dritten Tagung die Frage der jüdischen Erneuerung in einer von Globalisierung und Migration geprägten Welt angesprochen, nun war dies Thema der Tagung. Es ging Reytan darum, zu untersuchen, wie angesichts einer sich globalisierenden Kultur die kulturelle Besonderheit einzelner nationaler Kulturen, also kulturelle Diversität erhalten werden kann. Migration bedeutete für sie nicht nur Ortswechsel, sondern auch Veränderungen der Umwelt und der Lebensumstände, wie dies beim Fall des Kommunismus und dem Zerfall des Ostblocks in Osteuropa geschah. Bei der Bewältigung dieser Umwälzungen wollte sie nicht nur die Rolle der Frauen und nicht einmal nur die Rolle der Juden analysiert sehen, sondern den Blick auf allgemeine Reaktionen und Bewältigungsstrategien lenken und diese

---

[17] Vgl. Judith Gázsi/Andrea Pető/Zuzsanna Toranyi (eds.), *Gender, Memory and Judaism* (Balassi Kiadó: Budapest/Herne 2007).

in Beziehung zu jüdischen Entwicklungen setzen. Erstmals wurde auch Israel verstärktes Augenmerk gegeben, indem Beispiele für die Integration von unterschiedlichen Zuwanderungswellen präsentiert wurden. Gleichzeitig wurde kritisch angemerkt, dass das ethnozentrische israelische Selbstverständnis wenig passend für eine globalisierte Welt erschien. Thema waren auch die Auswirkungen der massiven jüdischen Zuwanderung von der ehemaligen Sowjetunion nach Deutschland. Der Wandel des jüdischen Lebens in Europa wurde somit mit allgemeinen Entwicklungen wie Globalisierung und Migration in Beziehung gesetzt und erhielt einen universelleren Rahmen.[18]

Die sechste Bet-Debora-Tagung fand im Februar 2013 in Wien statt. Thema war „Tikkun Olam. Der Beitrag jüdischer Frauen zu einer besseren Welt".[19] Diese Tagung organisierte die Autorin zusammen mit Sandra Lustig aus Hamburg, ein Mitglied des Bet-Debora-Netzwerks. Ziel war dabei, eine Bet-Debora-Tagung zu organisieren, die auch für die Wiener jüdischen Frauen interessant war, die mehrheitlich orthodox-säkular, also wenig offen gegenüber religiöser Erneuerung sind. Wiener Partnerin war die kleine liberale jüdische Gemeinde *Or Chadasch*, die den Anliegen von *Bet Debora* mit großer Sympathie gegenübersteht. Die Tagung wollte Aktivistinnen ansprechen beziehungsweise *role models* für jüdische Frauen vorstellen. Ein Schwerpunkt waren zwei Podiumsdiskussionen mit Zeitzeuginnen, die in Wien geboren wurden und nach der *Shoah* in vorbildlicher Weise zum Wiederaufbau der demokratischen Gesellschaften ihrer Heimatländer beitrugen. Die Mehrheit der Diskutantinnen lebte in Österreich, es gab aber auch Gäste aus Israel und den USA. Mit Ausnahme der Rabbinerin und Philosophin Eveline Goodman-Thau hatten alle Zeitzeuginnen außerhalb der Gemeinden gewirkt. Obwohl sie sich wenig mit der Tradition verbunden fühlten, hatten sie ein ausgeprägtes jüdisches Bewusstsein. Ihre Arbeit für die Gesellschaft hatte mit ihrem Verfolgungsschicksal und der Hoffnung zu tun, Gräuel wie den Nationalsozialismus auf Dauer verhindern zu können. Ein weiteres Panel bot jungen jüdischen Frauen Gelegenheit, ihren Beitrag zu einer besseren Welt vorzustellen. Diese Frauen waren Mitglieder der sefardischen Gemeinden Wiens, die heute etwa die Hälfte der jüdischen Bevölkerung ausmachen. Ihre Familien stammten aus Tadschikistan, Usbekistan oder Georgien und waren jüdisch konservativ und traditionsbewusst. Die jungen Frauen rebellierten gegen diese Traditionen.

---

[18] Vgl. Tania Reytan-Marincheshka (ed.), *Migration, Communication & Home. Jewish Tradition, Change and Gender in a Global World* (LIK Publishing House: Sofia 2011).

[19] Vgl. https://www.bet-debora-net/de/publikationen-2/bet-debora-journal-tikkun-olam, 4. Januar 2019.

Durch Bildung gelang es ihnen, Karrieren in Sozialberufen einzuschlagen. Sie gründeten zum Teil interkonfessionelle Familien, in denen das Judentum weniger bedeutend ist als in ihren Elternhäusern. Dennoch ist *Tikkun Olam*, das Streben nach einer besseren Welt, ein Auftrag, den sie aus der jüdischen Tradition erhielten. Rabbinerin Irit Shilor aus London führte bereits in ihrer Eröffnungsrede aus, dass jüdische Jugendliche in Großbritannien vor allem dann für jüdische Gemeindeprojekte zu gewinnen seien, wenn es sich um soziale Aufgaben handelte. Ob diese außerreligiöse, ethisch motivierte Bindung an das Gemeindeleben von Dauer ist, bleibt jedoch fraglich. Dem standen die Aktivistinnen von jüdischen Frauenvereinen gegenüber, die ein ganz anderes Bild von jüdischem Engagement zeichneten. Auch ihr Wirken war eher sozial als religiös ausgerichtet, bewegte sich aber ausschließlich im jüdischen Raum und hatte nicht zuletzt das Ziel, die jüdische Gemeinschaft zu stärken.[20] Hatte diese Tagung Auswirkungen auf die Wiener jüdischen Frauen? Es gab keinen Aufbruch zu neuen Ufern, aber über die Jahre hinweg ist *Bet Debora* eine Anlaufstelle für feministische Anliegen geblieben.

Nach drei eher säkular ausgerichteten Tagungen – wobei religiöse Themen niemals fehlten –, fand 2015 in Hoddesdon bei London eine Konferenz statt, wo Rabbinerinnen einen großen Teil der Vortragenden stellten. Organisatorinnen in England – unterstützt vom Bet-Debora-Vorstand – waren Rabbinerin Sylvia Rothschild, die bereits an der ersten Berliner Tagung teilgenommen hatte, und Rabbinerin Irit Shilor. Zu den teilnehmenden Rabbinerinnen gehörte auch Elisa Klapheck, Mitbegründerin von *Bet Debora*, die inzwischen die liberale Gemeinde in Frankfurt betreut. Sybil Sheridan, die erste britische Rabbinerin, nahm als junge Pensionistin teil, ebenso wie Rabbinerin Elizabeth Tikvah Sarah und Rabbiner James Baaden, der nur wenige Bet-Debora-Tagungen ausgelassen hatte. Dazu kam noch eine ganze Reihe weiterer Rabbinerinnen aus Großbritannien, Israel und Deutschland. Auch Rabbinerin Regina Jonas war präsent. Gail Reimer, Gründerin und langjährige Leiterin des *Jewish Women's Archive* an der *Brandeis University*, stellte die These auf, dass das Vergessen von Rabbinerin Regina Jonas auch die Einstellung des amerikanischen Judentums gegenüber Europa reflektiert, das als großer jüdischer Friedhof gesehen wird und nicht als möglicher Ausgangspunkt für wichtige Neuerungen wie das weibliche Rabbinat. Wie Reimer betonte, lernte sie selbst erst auf der Bet-Debora-Tagung die Vielfältigkeit

---

[20] Vgl. *Bet Debora* Journal II: *Tikkun Olam* (Hentrich & Hentrich: Berlin 2014).

und Lebendigkeit des europäischen Judentums und seiner Frauen kennen, von denen man in den USA nichts weiß.

Die Fragen nach der Position der Frau im religiösen Leben und nach einer geschlechtssensiblen Erneuerung wurden lebhaft und aus unterschiedlichen Perspektiven diskutiert. Ein weiteres Thema war orthodoxer Religionsunterricht, der die moderne Lebenswirklichkeit jüdischer Frauen reflektiert, die neben Familien auch ein erfolgreiches Berufsleben haben. Welche religiösen *role models* eignen sich für die heutigen jüdischen Mädchen? Eine große Neuerung stellte die Möglichkeit auch für orthodoxe Frauen, Rabbinerinnen zu werden, dar. Dina Brawer, damals noch in Ausbildung, heute Rabbinerin in New York, stellte ihren Lebensweg und ihre Entscheidung dazu vor. Solche Möglichkeiten wurden bei den frühen Konferenzen zwar angedacht, schienen aber noch in großer zeitlicher Ferne zu liegen. Eine weitere Erfolgsstory war der Weg der Mitglieder der LGBT-Gemeinschaft in die jüdischen Gemeinden. Wie hoch der Grad der Akzeptanz heute bereits ist, lässt sich nicht zuletzt am hohen Anteil von lesbischen und schwulen Rabbiner*innen ablesen, die in europäischen liberalen Gemeinden amtieren. Gegen die Gleichstellung der Frauen im religiösen Leben gibt es jedoch noch erhebliche Widerstände. Die Tagung behandelte das Problem der *Agunot*, von Frauen, denen ihre Männer die Scheidung verwehren. Sharon Shenhav, Anwältin aus Jerusalem, setzt sich seit Jahrzehnten beim Rabbinatsgericht für solche Frauen ein. In Hoddesdon wurde ihr Vortrag durch den bewegenden israelischen Film „Gett" von Ronit und Shlomi Elkabetz ergänzt.

Trotz solcher andauernden Diskriminierung von Frauen zeigte die Tagung einen enormen Fortschritt seit der ersten Tagung 1999. Frauen genießen ungleich größere Möglichkeiten der Partizipation und Gestaltung des religiösen Gemeindelebens. Die jüdische Erziehung bedenkt vermehrt moderne Lebensentwürfe, ist auf weiten Strecken koedukativ und nimmt – zumindest in Großbritannien – auf die Bedürfnisse von Mädchen Rücksicht. Die Gemeinden öffnen sich vermehrt früheren Randgruppen. Für die kontinentalen Teilnehmer*innen der Tagung war es eine neue Erfahrung, eine große, jüdische Gemeinschaft kennen zu lernen, die nicht durch die *Shoah* dezimiert wurde und viele der deutschen fortschrittlichen religiösen Traditionen weiterentwickeln konnte.

Bereits im September 2016 fand die bisher letzte Bet-Debora-Tagung statt. Veranstaltungsort war Wrocław, das damals europäische Kulturhauptstadt war. In Wrocław, dem deutschen Breslau, gab es bis zur *Shoah* nach Berlin und Frankfurt die drittgrößte jüdische Gemeinde in Deutschland. Es war Heimatstadt vieler bedeutender jüdischer Frauen. In den ersten Nachkriegsjahren erlebte das polnische Wrocław neuerlich eine kurze kulturelle Blüte, die von polnischen Jüdinnen und Juden getragen wurde. Heute hat Wrocław eine kleine jüdische Gemeinde. Dass Wrocław auch jüdische Kultur zu bieten hat, ist der *Bente-Kahan-Foundation* zu danken, welche die Tagung zusammen mit *Bet Debora* und der Organisation „Czulent", Krakau, organisiert hat.[21] Die jüdische Gemeinde war mit einer wunderbaren *Kabbalat Shabbat* (Schabbat-Eingangs-Feier am Freitagabend), einem Samstagmorgen-Gottesdienst in der Storchen-Synagoge, der einzigen erhaltenen Synagoge der Stadt, und *Hawdala* (Verabschiedung des Schabbat am Samstagabend) im Gemeindezentrum beteiligt.

Thematischer Schwerpunkt der Tagung waren jüdische Frauen in Wrocław/Breslau und in Polen überhaupt. Sehr eindrucksvoll waren die polnischen Teilnehmerinnen einer Podiumsdiskussion, die alle erfolgreiche Akademikerinnen und Kulturschaffende sowie Feministinnen sind. Sie fühlten sich unter der konservativen Regierung als Frauen und als Jüdinnen unter Druck, zeigten jedoch erheblichen Kampfgeist. Überhaupt zeigten die polnischen Künstlerinnen und Akademikerinnen eindrucksvolle Vitalität. Neu war für die meisten ausländischen Teilnehmer*innen die Offenheit, mit der die Zugehörigkeit zum Judentum in Polen gehandhabt wird. Eine jüdische Mutter war nicht nötig, ein jüdischer Vater und der Wunsch, zur jüdischen Gemeinschaft zu gehören, reichte. Dabei konnte diese jüdische Gemeinschaft durchaus kulturell, ethnisch, also eben säkular geprägt sein. Viele junge Pol*innen, die sich heute für die jüdische Erneuerung engagieren, haben nur zufällig von ihren jüdischen Wurzeln erfahren. So zum Beispiel die Mitglieder der Organisation „Czulent", Krakau, welche die Tagung mitorganisierte. Ausgehend von Polen befasste sich die Tagung mit weiblichen Lebenswelten in anderen kommunistischen Ländern wie Rumänien, Bulgarien, Ostdeutschland und Jugoslawien.[22]

Die Bet-Debora-Tagungen reflektieren einerseits die Interessen der Organisatorinnen, werden aber andererseits von den Beiträgen der aktiven Teilnehmer*innen geprägt. Gleichzeitig verstehen sie sich als internationale Plattformen für Gedankenaustausch zwischen Teilnehmer*innen aus unterschiedlichsten Ländern, die ähnliche Anliegen haben. Erfreulich ist, dass sich bei den letzten Konferenzen zahlreiche junge Frauen dem Bet-Debora-Netzwerk angeschlossen haben, was eine weitere dynamische Entwicklung verspricht.

---

[21] Vgl. https://www.bet-debora.net/de/publikationen-2/bet-debora-journal-iv, 21. Dezember 2018.
[22] Vgl. *Bet Debora* Journal III: *Frauenpolitik für ein modernes Judentum* (Hentrich & Hentrich: Berlin 2016).

Veranstaltungen in Berlin

Bet Debora e.V. organisiert nicht nur Tagungen im Ausland, sondern auch Veranstaltungen in Berlin. Ein Fixpunkt seit 2010 ist der „Kulinarische Dialog". Gegründet wurde dieser von Gaby Nonhoff und Talin Bahcivanoglu, die zusammen mit den Teilnehmer*innen Gerichte aus der jüdischen und armenischen Küche zubereiten und dabei über die damit verbundenen Kulturen sprechen. Gleichzeitig erhalten die Teilnehmer*innen Gelegenheit, ihre eigene Herkunft und Traditionen zu reflektieren und darzulegen. Mit wechselnden Köchinnen findet der „Kulinarische Dialog" bis heute statt, zuletzt stellten im November 2019 Ewa Alfred und Najda Sinanyan-Erbas Küche und Kultur aus Osteuropa und Armenien vor.

Daneben veranstaltet *Bet Debora* Vorträge und Diskussionsrunden, die sich mit frauenspezifischen jüdischen Themen befassen. Der Schwerpunkt liegt hier auf dem jüdischen Leben in Deutschland und der Frage, wie man die Gleichheit der Frauen hier fördern kann. Diskutiert wird auch der Status der jüdischen Frauen in der deutschen Gesellschaft. Wiederholt wurden Zeitzeuginnen vorgestellt, die nach der *Shoah* zum Aufbau jüdischen Lebens in Deutschland beigetragen haben. Die Veranstaltungen zeigen, dass die Gleichstellung der Frau in der jüdischen Gemeinschaft seit Langem angestrebt, aber noch nicht erreicht ist. Nach jeder internationalen Tagung wird eine Podiumsdiskussion in Berlin abgehalten, um zentrale Ideen Frauen, die nicht hatten teilnehmen können, zu präsentieren und zur Diskussion zu stellen.

Anlass für Bet-Debora-Veranstaltungen sind auch die jüdischen Festtage *Schawuot* und *Chanukka*. *Schawuot*, das Fest der Offenbarung der Thora, wird in jüdischen Gemeinden mit Lernnächten gefeiert. Dieser Tradition schließt sich *Bet Debora* mit dem Studium von religiösen Texten von und über Frauen an. *Chanukka*, das Fest der Wiedereinweihung des Jerusalemer Tempels, dient einerseits der Diskussion frauenspezifischer Themen, andererseits der Geselligkeit mit Krapfen und Fröhlichkeit.

Mit dem Eintreten für die Gleichberechtigung der Frau und die Erneuerung des Judentums gehört *Bet Debora* zu den fortschrittlichen jüdischen Stimmen. Trotzdem sieht es sich nicht als Teil der liberalen Strömung des Judentums, wo Frauen bereits weitgehende Gleichberechtigung genießen, sondern als über den Gruppierungen stehend und Mitglieder aller Richtungen gleichmäßig ansprechend. Daher hat *Bet Debora* seit 2018 eine Kooperation mit der konservativen Synagoge Fränkelufer, mit der es gemeinsame Bildungsveranstaltungen durchführt. Interkonfessioneller und interkultureller Dialog begleiten *Bet Debora* bei den Tagungen und bei den Veranstaltungen in Berlin. So erschien „Inta – Interreligiöses Forum" von 2014–2016 in Kooperation mit *Bet Debora*. *Bet Debora* kooperiert auch mit anderen zivilgesellschaftlichen Organisationen. So gehört es zu den Organisatorinnen des Gedenkens an die „Fabrik-Aktion" und die Proteste in der Rosenstraße am 27. Februar 1943. Zusammen mit dem Deutschen Juristinnenbund initiierte *Bet Debora* die Anbringung von zwei Gedenktafeln, die an die ersten deutschen Juristinnen erinnerten. 2003 wurde die Gedenktafel an Dr. Margarete Berent (1887 Berlin–1965 New York), die erste Juristin Preußens, enthüllt. 2010 folgte ein Erinnerungszeichen an Dr. Marie Munk (1885 Berlin–1978 Cambridge/Mass.), die 1914 zusammen mit Dr. Margarete Berent und Dr. Margarete Mühsam-Edelheim den „Deutschen Juristinnen-Verein" gegründet hatte.

Die Fülle an Themen kann nur mit Hilfe des starken und über die Jahre gewachsenen Netzwerks behandelt werden. Denn *Bet Debora* ist zwar seit 1998 ein eingetragener Verein in Berlin, hat aber nur neun Mitglieder.[23] Das Kernteam ist der Vorstand von *Bet Debora*, der nach wie vor aus lediglich drei Frauen – Tanja Berg und Lara Dämmig in Berlin, Eleonore Lappin-Eppel in Wien – besteht. Zur Organisation der Konferenzen kommen dann jeweils Partnerorganisationen oder Personen aus dem jeweiligen Veranstaltungsort dazu. Außerdem arbeiten Organisatorinnen früherer Tagungen sowie Mitglieder des europäischen Netzwerks unterstützend mit. Funktionieren kann *Bet Debora* nur dank des jahrelangen Engagements unserer Mitglieder.

Eleonore Lappin-Eppel ist Historikerin und lebt in Wien. Sie ist Vorstandsmitglied von *Bet Debora* und Gründungs- sowie Vorstandsmitglied der jüdischen liberalen Gemeinde *Or Chadasch* in Wien. bet.debora@gmail.com

---

[23] Bet Debora e.V. hat neben dem Vorstand nur neun Vereinsmitglieder. Wichtiger ist jedoch das europäische Netzwerk von *Bet Debora*. Dieses umfasst die Frauen, die regelmäßig über *Bet Debora* informiert werden und an einer oder mehreren Tagungen teilgenommen haben. Die genaue Zahl ist nicht feststellbar, beträgt aber mehrere Hundert.

Ulrike Sallandt

Pentekostalismus und Körper: Religionsästhetische Impulse für die Untersuchung von Körperpraktiken pentekostaler Frömmigkeit

Zusammenfassung
Der Artikel richtet seinen Blick auf Pentekostalismus und Körper. Zuerst will die Autorin einen Einblick in das Phänomen und die aktuelle Forschung dazu geben. Zweitens führt sie das Konzept des Körperwissens der Religionswissenschaftlerin Anne Koch ein. Drittens beschreibt sie pentekostale Gottesdienste, Rituale und Gebete, wobei sie ihre Körperdimension identifiziert, um Bewusstsein für das Potential des Konzepts des Körperwissens für die Forschung über den Pentekostalismus zu wecken.

Schlagwörter: Pentekostalismus; Religion; Ästhetik; Körper; Wissen.

Abstract
The article focuses on Pentecostalism and the body. Firstly, the author intends to give an insight into the phenomenon, considering current research. Secondly, she introduces the concept of body knowledge by Anne Koch, scholar of religion. Thirdly, she describes the Pentecostal services, rituals and prayers, identifying their body dimension in order to raise awareness about the potential of the concept of body knowledge in the research on Pentecostalism.

Keywords: Pentecostalism; religion; aesthetics; body; knowledge.

Resumen
El artículo se centra en el pentecostalismo y el cuerpo. En un primer momento, la autora introduce el fenómeno tomando en consideración la investigación más reciente. En segundo lugar, presenta el concepto "conocimiento del cuerpo" (*Körperwissen*) de la investigadora de la religión Anne Koch. En tercer lugar, describe los servicios, rituales y oraciones pentecostales, identificando la dimensión de su cuerpo para crear conciencia del potencial del concepto "conocimiento del cuerpo" en la investigación del pentecostalismo.

Palabras clave: pentecostalismo; religión; estética; cuerpo; conocimiento.

Ulrike Sallandt
Pentekostalismus und Körper: Religionsästhetische Impulse für die Untersuchung von Körperpraktiken pentekostaler Frömmigkeit

Einführung

Im vorliegenden Beitrag möchte ich zunächst einen kurzen Einblick in die gegenwärtige Situation des Pentekostalismus und der Pentekostalismusforschung geben. Im Anschluss stelle ich das Konzept des Körperwissens von der Religionswissenschaftlerin Prof. Dr. Anne Koch dar, das sich im Übergang von Religionsästhetik und Religionssomatik verorten lässt. Unter Berücksichtigung dieses Ansatzes gebe ich drittens eine idealtypische ‚dichte Beschreibung'[1] pentekostaler Frömmigkeit. Dabei gehe ich insbesondere auf die Körperlichkeit ihrer Ritualpraxis ein. Auf diese Weise nehme ich andere als die kognitiven Inhalte des religiösen Phänomens in den Blick. Ich orientiere mich an der Fragestellung erstens, ob (und inwieweit) eine Untersuchung des Körpers im Kontext pentekostaler Frömmigkeit alternative Konzepte von Wissen (Epistemologien) aufzeigt, und zweitens, ob (und inwiefern) dieses Körperwissen dazu beiträgt, die Eigenständigkeit pentekostaler Kultur und Theologie wissenschaftlich (besser) erfassen zu können. Ich befinde mich mit meinem Vorhaben auf der Grenze von Kultur- und Religionswissenschaften, insbesondere den Teildisziplinen von Ethnologie und Religionsästhetik, das heißt ich beleuchte das Phänomen des Pentekostalismus an dieser Stelle nicht aus dogmen- und theologiegeschichtlicher, geschweige denn aus ekklesiologisch-liturgischer Perspektive protestantischer bzw. römisch-katholischer Theologie.

Pentekostalismus und Pentekostalismusforschung

In den letzten zehn bis fünfzehn Jahren ist die Verbreitung pentekostaler und charismatischer Kirche(n) und Theologie(n) weltweit deutlich angestiegen.[2] Nebst dem schon lange zu beobachtenden Wachstum des pentekostalen und charismatischen Christentums,[3] insbesondere auf der Südhalbkugel, zeigt sich

---

[1] Clifford Geertz, *Dichte Beschreibung. Beiträge zum Verstehen kultureller Systeme* (Suhrkamp: Frankfurt a.M. 1983). Der Begriff geht auf den britischen Philosophen Gilbert Ryle zurück, von dem Geertz sich inspirieren ließ.

[2] Typologisch in der Forschung in drei Phasen unterschieden: der traditionelle Pentekostalismus, das Auftreten und die Verbreitung der charismatischen Bewegung in den 1960er Jahren und die Etablierung des Neopentekostalismus. Da diese Typologie mittlerweile durch das Aufkommen neuer Forschungsschwerpunkte in die Kritik gekommen ist und die Grenzen im Feld des Pentekostalismus fließend sind, nutze ich im vorliegenden Beitrag ausschließlich den Begriff des Pentekostalismus im Sinne eines Oberbegriffs für das ganze Phänomen in seinen diversen Manifestationsformen und Ausdrücken.

[3] 1970 waren es 63 Millionen, 2013 628 Millionen und die Prognose für das Jahr 2025 liegt bei 828 Millionen Mitglieder (https://www.idea.de/detail/newsticker.html?tx_newsticker_pi1[id]=21287, 30. November 2019).

nun seit mehr als einer Dekade im westlichen Kulturkreis ein Interesse, sich wissenschaftlich mit diesem Phänomen auseinanderzusetzen. Dieses Interesse äußert sich auf der einen Seite in einer Vielzahl ethnologisch-kulturwissenschaftlicher Fallstudien, die die Heterogenität und Diversität des Pentekostalismus ausdrücken,[4] auf der anderen Seite anhand neuerer Entstehungs- und Geschichtstheorien, die den Pentekostalismus nicht auf einen Ursprungsort reduzieren, sondern vielmehr von einem komplexen dynamischen Phänomen reden, das sich netzwerkartig in den verschiedenen Kulturkreisen entwickelt hat.[5] Dabei geht es wissenschaftlich insbesondere darum, das ganze Phänomen des Pentekostalismus zu untersuchen, um die unter diesem Begriff erfassten vielfältigen Erfahrungen und diversen Ausdrucksformen in ihrer Breite wahrzunehmen.[6]

Pentekostale Frömmigkeitsstile, die primär körperlich erfahren werden und zum Ausdruck kommen,[7] stellen meines Erachtens große Anforderungen an die wissenschaftliche Forschung. Der Untersuchungsgegenstand erfordert theoretische Methoden, die dem Bruch mit traditionellen epistemologischen Theorien und kolonialen Herrschaftsstrukturen gerecht werden. Gerade in feministischen Studien, insbesondere in der Genderforschung, ermöglicht die Berücksichtigung der Körperlichkeit, des Körperwissens es, die traditionelle Differenz zwischen Körper und Verstand zu überwinden. Darin äußert sich die Kritik an traditionellen Rollenbildern, die sich vor dem Hintergrund des patriarchalischen Dualismus geschichtlich kognitiv festgesetzt haben. Der körperliche Zugang unterläuft diese eindeutige und eindimensionale Festschreibung, löst sich von der binären Denkweise griechischer Philosophie. Damit öffnen sich neue Deutungsräume traditioneller Rollenbilder, die sich durch äußere Zuschreibungen, insbesondere durch Deutungsmachtmissbrauch des männlichen Patriarchats als von Gott gegeben, Geltung verschafft haben.

---

[4] Aktuelle Veröffentlichungen: https://www.glopent.net/iak-pfingstbewegung.aspx/ressourcen/bibliografien, 30. November 2019; http://www.glopent.net/pentecostudies, 29. November 2019.

[5] Vgl. Michael Bergunder, „Der ‚Cultural Turn' und die Erforschung der weltweiten Pfingstbewegung," in: *Evangelische Theologie* 69/4 (2009), 245-269, hier 249, 258.

[6] Giovanni Maltese, Judith Bachmann und Katja Rakow, „Negotiating Evangelicalism and Pentecostalism: Global Entanglements, Identity Politics and the Future of Pentecostal Studies," in: *PentecoStudies* 18/1 (2019), 7-19, hier 17.

[7] Vgl. Michael Wilkinson und Peter Althouse (eds.), *Pentecostals and the Body* (Brill: Leiden 2017), Annual Review of the Sociology of Religion 8.

Demzufolge muss insbesondere aus feministischer Perspektive ein Freiraum geschaffen werden, der erlaubt, „Formen reflexiver Erfahrung" jenseits der klassischen Trennung von Subjekt und Objekt zu denken und somit den Körper in seiner ganzheitlichen Funktion als „Produkt" und „Produzent" wahr- und ernst zu nehmen. Dabei wird deutlich, dass der Körper, anstatt das sozial festgeschriebene (bessere) Geschlecht, die Welt unmittelbar erfassen kann, „weil die dabei verwendeten kognitiven Strukturen aus der Einverleibung der Strukturen der Welt resultieren, in der er [der Körper] handelt; weil die Konstruktionselemente, die er verwendet, um die Welt zu erkennen, von der Welt [Gott] konstruiert wurden".[8] Es geht demnach darum, andere als die äußerlich zugeschriebenen kognitiven Inhalte, die Autorität und Macht bestimmen, sowohl in Bezug auf gesellschaftliche Rollenbilder als auch bezüglich pentekostaler Theologie(n) und Frömmigkeitsstile, zu berücksichtigen.

Pentekostale Glaubensüberzeugungen werden primär nicht in Wort und Schrift ausgedrückt, sondern in körperlicher Bewegung in Gemeinschaft erlebt und erfahren. Körperlich geprägte liturgische Rituale im Gottesdienst schaffen einen konkreten Raum der Begegnung, in dem über erwähnte gesellschaftliche Differenzen und Dissense hinweg die ursprüngliche Einheit der ganzen Lebenswirklichkeit (Schöpfung Gottes) vom Einzelnen empfangen, empfunden und darin sichtbar wird.[9] Äußerliche Ungerechtigkeiten, gesellschaftliche und sozial-politische (Rollen-)Zuschreibung und Marginalisierung, stellen kein Hindernis mehr dar. In der Begegnung mit Gott verlieren kulturell geprägte Genderrollen ihre destruktive unterdrückende Macht. Sie werden im Vollzug des Rituals aufgebrochen bzw. unterlaufen. Biologische und soziale Differenzen vereinen sich, jenseits von Gesellschaft und kultureller Tradition, körperlich.

Die Pentekostalismusforschung hat auf dem europäischen Kontinent in den letzten Jahren deutlich zugenommen. Mit der Gründung des *Interdisziplinären Arbeitskreises Pfingstbewegung* (2004), initiiert von Prof. Dr. Michael Bergunder in Heidelberg, sowie durch das im selben Jahr gegründete Netzwerk *European Research Network on Global Pentecostalism* (GloPent), ist die Anzahl an Literatur über den Pentekostalismus und vor allem auch von

---

[8] Frank Bockrath, Bernhard Boschert und Elk Franke (eds.), *Körperliche Erkenntnis. Formen reflexiver Erfahrung (*transcript: Bielefeld 2008), 12.

[9] Marcus A. Friedrich untersucht den Beitrag von Schauspieltheorien und -techniken für die Pastoralästhetik (vgl. Marcus A. Friedrich, *Liturgische Körper. Der Beitrag von Schauspieltheorien und -techniken für die Pastoralästhetik* [Kohlhammer: Stuttgart 2001], Praktische Theologie heute 54).

pentekostalen Wissenschaftler*innen deutlich angestiegen. Neben den Arbeiten von Prof. Dr. Michael Bergunder selbst,[10] sind insbesondere die Forschungen von Prof. Dr. Giovanni Maltese (Hamburg), der zunächst mit der vergleichenden kritischen Analyse des pentekostalen Erfahrungsbegriffs *Geistererfahrung zwischen Transzendenz und Immanenz* (2013) auf sich aufmerksam machte, zu nennen. Malteses gemeinsam mit Dr. Jörg Haustein herausgegebenes *Handbuch pfingstliche und charismatische Theologie* (2014) versucht, pentekostalen Wissenschaftler*innen eine Stimme im europäischen Kontext zu geben. In seiner Dissertation untersucht Maltese den Pentekostalismus mit Blick auf die Beziehung zwischen *Politik und Gesellschaft in den Philippinen* (2017). Richtungsweisend äußert er sich gemeinsam mit Judith Bachmann und Katja Rakow, dass das Phänomen des Pentekostalismus primär situativ-kontextuell „within the setting of local negotiating and global entanglements"[11] untersucht werden sollte.

In Abgrenzung zu den soziologischen Forschungsprojekten am *Center of the Interdisciplinary Research on Religion and Society* (CIRRUS), mitgegründet von Prof. Dr. Dr. Heinrich Schäfer (Bielefeld), sowie denen von Prof. Dr. Heuser an der Theologischen Fakultät in der Schweiz (Basel), zeigt sich die Untersuchung des Körpers im Pentekostalismus in dem jüngst von Dr. Michael Wilkinson und Dr. Peter Althouse veröffentlichten *Annual Review of the Sociology of Religion: Pentecostals and the Body* (2017). Die darin enthaltenen Beiträge konzentrieren sich anhand von Fallstudien auf die Bedeutung von *body* und *embodiment*. Sie versammeln eine Reihe von interessanten Beobachtungen, die den Körper in seiner wesentlichen Doppelbedeutung als „Produkt" und „Produzent" zeigen.[12]

Im Rahmen der noch jungen Professur *Interkulturelle Theologie und Körperlichkeit* arbeitet Prof. Dr. Claudia Jahnel in einem interdisziplinär angelegten Forschungsprojekt (Transgressive Bodies/Grenzüberschreitende Körper)

---

[10] Vgl. http://rmserv.wt.uni-heidelberg.de/webwebwebwebwebweb10.html/publikationen/uebersicht, 30. November 2019.
[11] Maltese, Bachmann und Rakow, „Negotiating Evangelicalism and Pentecostalism," 15.
[12] Vgl. die Arbeiten der niederländischen Anthropologin Prof. Dr. Birgit Meyer (Utrecht) https://www.zmo.de/forschung/projekte_2008_2013/Nieber_Habitats_Habitus_e.html, 30. November 2019 und der US-amerikanische Anthropologin Prof. Dr. Tanya M. Luhrmann (University of Chicago) in ihrer Studie *When God talks back; Understanding the American Evangelical Relationship with God* (Vintage: New York 2012) über das evangelikale Christentum in den Vereinigten Staaten.

über die Bedeutung des Körpers.[13] In ihrer preisgekrönten Habilitationsschrift *Interkulturelle Theologie und Kulturwissenschaft* (2016) erkennt Jahnel auf der Grundlage ihrer biografischen Erfahrungen im afrikanischen Kulturraum, insbesondere in Texten afrikanischer Theologie, die Bedeutung des Körpers in seiner Spannung „zwischen der Verletzbarkeit, Fragilität, Schutzlosigkeit und Ausgeliefertsein des Körpers […] einerseits, und der Konstruiertheit […], seiner soziokulturellen und politischen Aufladung, Idealisierung, Domestizierung und Erfindung […] andererseits".[14]

Als Beispiel für die Studien und Untersuchungen aus katholischer Perspektive kann der von Prof. Dr. Gunda Werner (Bochum) herausgebrachte Sammelband *Gerettet durch Begeisterung. Reform der katholischen Kirche durch pfingstlich-charismatische Religiosität?* (2017)[15] betrachtet werden, der vor allem Beiträge enthält, die ausgehend von der eigenen dogmatischen Position versuchen, die Auswirkungen der pentekostal-charismatischen Theologie(n) und Ausdrucksformen innerhalb der eigenen Reihen im Kontext Lateinamerikas zu analysieren.

Körper und Körperwissen
Im Folgenden führe ich in den wissenschaftlichen Ansatz der Religionswissenschaftlerin Anne Koch aus Linz ein, den sie ausgehend von ihrer Habilitationsschrift aus dem Jahr 2007 entwickelt hat. Dabei liegt mein Anliegen darin, für das von ihr propagierte Konzept des Körperwissens am Übergang von Religionsästhetik und Religionssomatik zu sensibilisieren und schließlich erste Impulse zu geben, wie es möglich ist, dies für die Untersuchung des Pentekostalismus zu berücksichtigen.

Religionsästhetik und Kognitionswissenschaften
Die Religionsästhetik ist […] eine Teildisziplin der allgemeinen und vergleichenden Religionswissenschaft, die sich der sinnlichen Seite von Religion zuwendet und danach fragt, wie Religion über die Sinne ästhetisch vermittelt, wahrgenommen, verkörpert, symbolisiert und wirksam gemacht wird. Die Religionsästhetik will sich daher der Komplexität sinnlicher Wahrnehmung

---

[13] Vgl. http://www.ev.rub.de/it-jahnel/projekte.html.de, 1. November 2019.
[14] Claudia Jahnel, *Interkulturelle Theologie und Kulturwissenschaft. Untersucht am Beispiel afrikanischer Theologie* (Kohlhammer: Stuttgart 2016), 238.
[15] Vgl. Rezension der Verfasserin https://www.glopent.net/iak-pfingstbewegung.aspx/Members/webmaster/rezensionen/rezension-werner/view, 29. November 2019.

nähern, ohne allein den Körper oder allein die fünf Sinne in ihrer jeweiligen Isolierung voneinander zu betrachten.[16] Im Artikel Religionsästhetik des *Handbuchs religionswissenschaftlicher Grundbegriffe* (HrwG 1988)[17] spricht Alexander Gottfield Baumgarten von einer „sinnlichen Erkenntnis". Unter Berücksichtigung dieser Erkenntnis menschlicher Wahrnehmung erfolge eine Korrektur an einem „nur auf Vernunftschlüsse setzenden Rationalismus"[18] (2). Es gehe demnach um eine Kritik „an einer Schattenseite des Rationalismus: die Vernachlässigung von Sinnlichkeit und damit einhergehende Überbewertung von Wort und Text im Logozentrismus" (ebenda). Damit rückt die *Rezeptionsweise* in den Vordergrund, das heißt der Körper steht außerhalb des „Symbolparadigmas", und dient insbesondere als „Wahrnehmungssystem".[19] Dies, so stellt Anne Koch in ihrem Beitrag heraus, drückt eine ursprüngliche „Kombination und Multiperspektivität" aus, die das innovative, kritische Potential der Religionsästhetik unterstreicht. Sie sei fähig, „konnektive[n] Strukturen" von Kultur und Gesellschaft aufzudecken. Ihren Vorbehalt gegenüber „leitenden Ideologien" trage sie von Anfang in sich (7).

Die Religionsästhetik fragt entsprechend nach dem Zusammenspiel unbewusst ablaufender, affektiver Körperbewegungen, den durch diese Körperbewegungen und -haltungen induzierten Selbstwahrnehmungen und die damit verbundenen interaktiven Sinnkonstruktionen in religiösen Kontexten. Sie fragt daher nicht nur nach den jeweiligen religiösen Deutungen von Körperlichkeit, sondern nach den körperlichen (somatischen) Bedingungen für die Konstruktion religiöser Wirklichkeit. Sie kann entsprechend nicht nur als Erweiterung zu einer Anthropologie des Körpers gelesen, sondern muss vor dem disziplingeschichtlichen Hintergrund der Religionswissenschaft auch als ein erster Versuch eines genuinen Beitrags zum Themenfeld Religion und Körper bzw. Religion und Sinne gewertet werden.[20]

---

[16] Sebastian Schüler, „Der Körper, die Sinne und die Phänomenologie der Wahrnehmung: Vom Embodiment-Paradigma zur Religionsästhetik," in: Gritt Klinkhammer und Eva Tolksdorf (eds.). *Somatisierung des Religiösen. Empirische Studien zum rezenten religiösen Heilungs- und Therapiemarkt* (Universität Bremen: Bremen 2015), 13-46, hier 28.
[17] Hubert Cancik und Hubert Mohr, „Religionsästhetik," in: *Handbuch religionswissenschaftlicher Grundbegriffe* (Kohlhammer: Stuttgart 1988), I, 119-156.
[18] Anne Koch, „Religionsästhetik jenseits der Massendinghaltung," Vortrag am 28. Oktober 2003 an der Universität Göttingen; Zahlenangaben im Text beziehen sich auf die Verschriftlichung des Vortrags (https://www.youtube.com/watch?v=jqF427Ry3YE, 30. März 2020).
[19] Vgl. dazu Anne Koch, *Körperwissen: Grundlegung einer Religionsästhetik* (Habil., München 2007), 113.
[20] Schüler, „Der Körper, die Sinne und die Phänomenologie der Wahrnehmung," 29.

Ulrike Sallandt
Pentekostalismus und Körper: Religionsästhetische Impulse für die Untersuchung von Körperpraktiken pentekostaler Frömmigkeit

Für die Untersuchung von Körper und Körperlichkeit im Kontext des Pentekostalismus gehe ich demnach an dieser Stelle insbesondere auf das Anliegen der Religionsästhetik[21] als Theorie *sinnlicher Erkenntnis* ein, um vor dem Hintergrund der dargelegten Beschreibung pentekostaler Frömmigkeit ihren theologischen Ertrag anzudeuten.[22] Dabei geht es mit Anne Koch um die Frage, „welches Wissen [wir] brauchen […], um ästhetische Vorgänge zu beschreiben?" (7) Neben dem historischen wird ein Wissen benötigt, *wie* Menschen diese Vorgänge wahrnehmen. Wie nehmen beispielsweise die Gläubigen im pentekostalen Heilungsgottesdienst „berührende als heilende Hände" wahr? Diese wesentliche Anbindung helfe der Kognitionswissenschaft, die primär die Wechselbeziehung von Subjekt und Objekt im Blick hat und dabei ohne konkreten kulturellen Bezugspunkt auskommt,[23] dieser Schwäche vorzubeugen und sie aus kultur- und religionswissenschaftlicher Perspektive durch den empirischen Bezug zu vervollständigen. Kulturwissenschaftlich kann Terry Eagleton zufolge „eine gemeinsame Kultur […] nur hergestellt werden, weil unsere Körper im großen und ganzen gleichartig sind".[24] An dieser bindenden Schnittstelle von Körper und Kultur wird Anne Koch zufolge die Herausforderung an die Religionsästhetik deutlich, nämlich der „Transfer von Wahrnehmungs- und Körpertheorien auf kulturelle Sachverhalte" (8). Das bedeutet nicht, dass Religionsästhetik als eine angewandte Kognitionswissenschaft zu verstehen sei, sondern lediglich, dass sie kognitionswissenschaftliche Konzepte für ihr Anliegen nutzen kann beziehungsweise soll. Mit Blick auf die geforderte Transferleistung sind vor allem deren Arbeitsfelder der körperlichen Kognition (*embodied cognition*), situativer Kognition und der Ökologie der Wahrnehmung von Bedeutung, wobei ich an dieser Stelle insbesondere auf ersteres eingehe, da es für das Thema des vorliegenden Beitrags grundlegend

---

[21] Anne Koch differenziert in ihrem Artikel „Religionsästhetik jenseits der Massendinghaltung ein dreifaches Anliegen der Religionsästhetik: a) als Analyse dominanter ästhetischer Codes, b) als Theorie sinnlicher Erkenntnis und c) als integrative Perspektive (3).
[22] Zur Geschichte der Religionsästhetik verweise ich auf Isabel Schwaderer und Katharina Waldner (eds.), *Annäherung an das Unaussprechliche: Ästhetische Erfahrungen in kollektiven religiösen Praktiken* (transcript: Bielefeld 2020): darin insb. auf Katharina Waldner, „Die Ästhetisierung der ‚religiösen Erfahrung' oder Wie sinnlich ist Religion?," 17-54.
[23] Exemplarisch verweise ich auf Humberto R. Maturana und Francisco J. Varela, *Der Baum der Erkenntnis: Die biologischen Wurzeln menschlicher Erkenntnis* (Fischer: Frankfurt a.M. [6]2015), 257-263.
[24] Terry Eagleton, *Was ist Kultur? Eine Einführung* (C.H. Beck: München 2009), 156.

ist.[25] Die körperliche Kognition geht davon aus, dass „sinnliche und motorische Systeme" ursprünglich konstitutiv an allen Erkenntnisprozessen teilhaben. Körperliche Kognition basiert und konstituiert sich demnach auf dem Körper. Im Zuge des *body turns* der 1990er Jahre,[26] der wissenschaftlichen soziologischen Hinwendung zum Körper, hat sich die Aufmerksamkeit auf den Körper in differenzierter Weise entwickelt: erstens als Forschungsobjekt, zweitens als theoretisches Konzept und schließlich, und davon ist an dieser Stelle die Rede, als Erkenntnisinstrument.

> Dieser Trend, der sich hier in der Soziologie des Körpers und der Anthropologie der Sinne abzeichnet und der über das klassische Embodiment-Paradigma hinausweist, ohne dieses Erbe zu vernachlässigen, zeigt sich auch in der Wiederentdeckung des Körpers und der Sinne in der Religionswissenschaft respektive in der Formierung einer Religionsästhetik.[27]

Der körperliche Zustand, seine Veränderung, seine situative Ordnung bzw. Unordnung, wird wahrgenommen und für Wissens- und Erkenntnisprozesse relevant: Der Körperzustand bzw. dessen Wahrnehmung beeinflusst den Gewinn von Erkenntnis beziehungsweise die Interpretation/Deutung des Körperverhaltens! Diese Beziehung ist als produktive, prozessartige Wechselwirkung zwischen Körper und Erkenntnis zu denken und grenzt dieses Konzept der *embodied cognition* von dem der *Embodiment*-Theorien der 1980er Jahre deutlich ab. Die *Embodiment*-Theorien nehmen lediglich eine Außenperspektive auf den Körper ein, wobei sie die produktive Eigendynamik des Körpers

---

[25] Der Beitrag für Religionswissenschaften lässt sich hier vor der erwähnten Situation ihres „unerklärten" Forschungsgegenstandes als sinnvoll erachten. Michael Bergunder setzt sich ausführlich mit dem religionswissenschaftlichen Desiderat einer Definition des Religionsbegriffes auseinander (vgl. Michael Bergunder, „Was ist Religion? Kulturwissenschaftliche Überlegungen zum Gegenstand der Religionswissenschaft," in: *ZfR* 19 [1/2/2011] 3-55). Der kognitionswissenschaftliche Beitrag liegt in der unausweichlichen doppelten Kontingenz von Nachdenken und Beschreiben: „Beides sind Prozesse der Kognition" (Koch, „Religionsästhethik," 10). Eine Theorie der Kognition gilt grundsätzlich als wissenschaftliche Voraussetzung, um überhaupt Argumente und Schlussfolgerungen zu treffen.

[26] Vgl. Robert Gugutzer, „Der *body turn* in der Soziologie: Eine programmatische Einführung," in: Robert Gugutzer (ed.), *Body turn: Perspektiven der Soziologie des Körpers und des Sports* (transcript: Bielefeld 2006), 9-56, hier 9. In der zweiten Hälfte des 20. Jahrhunderts sprach man in den Kulturwissenschaften und der Soziologie bereits vom *cultural turn*, ab den 1980er Jahren vom *spatial turn*.

[27] Schüler, „Der Körper, die Sinne und die Phänomenologie der Wahrnehmung," 28.

nicht dezidiert in den Blick nehmen.[28] Ihre Perspektive bleibt insofern phänomenologisch: Der Körper wird als Träger von bereits vorhandenem Wissen verstanden und nicht als aktiver Mit-Produzent.

Nimmt man dem kognitionswissenschaftlichen Ansatz dieser *embodied cognition* ernst, stellt sich für die Religionsästhetik die Frage, wie man sinnliche Erkenntnis erfasst und wie diese im wissenschaftlichen Diskurs sinnvoll erfasst und ausgearbeitet werden kann. Diese Frage potenziert die religionsästhetische Herausforderung der bereits erwähnten Transferleistung in der Spannung von Theorie und Empirie. Anne Koch stellt sich dieser Herausforderung mit dem Begriff des Körperwissens,[29] der sowohl die Körperlichkeit-an-sich (somatisch) als auch ihre situativ-kulturelle Einbettung des Wissens (sozial) berücksichtigt. Insbesondere anhand der Kognitionspsychologie gelingt es ihr, das Konzept des Körperwissens zu vertiefen und jenseits der simplen positiven Behauptung, dass es Körperwissen gibt beziehungsweise es symboltheoretisch zu verstehen ist, nach der Methode (nach dem Wie?) seines Vollzugs zu fragen. Dabei ist religionswissenschaftlich interessant, Körperwissen einerseits als diskursives Ereignis, andererseits als wissenschaftlich tragfähiges Konzept zu berücksichtigen.

Körperwissen als Diskurs und Konzept
In der vergangenen Dekade zeichnet sich im wissenschaftlichen Diskurs[30] eine erhöhte thematische Beschäftigung mit der „Medialisierung des Körpers" ab. Es geht nicht mehr darum, Wissen über den Körper zu erlangen, sondern vielmehr um „kognitionspyschologisches Wissen […] zur Motorik, afferenten Emotion oder primordialen Wahrnehmung".[31] Das bedeutet, der Körper wird insofern aufgewertet, als er als „Körperwissen thematisiert, medialisiert und abstrahiert wird" und als „eigenständiger Akteur" auftritt.[32] Das Anwachsen

---

[28] Schüler, „Der Körper, die Sinne und die Phänomenologie der Wahrnehmung," 21.

[29] Um Kritik gegenüber diesem Begriff vorzubeugen, entwickelt Anne Koch in ihrer Habilitationsschrift *Körperwissen: Grundlegung einer Religionsästhetik* (München 2007) zunächst einen non-propositionalen Wissensbegriff, den sie in einem zweiten Schritt für das Körperwissen nutzt (vgl. 116-132, hier insbesondere 126-132).

[30] Dies ist nicht nur im wissenschaftlichen Bereich zu beobachten, sondern auch im populärwissenschaftlichen und spirituellen. Letztere werde ich an dieser Stelle nicht berücksichtigen.

[31] Anne Koch, „‚Körperwissen': Modewort oder Grundstein einer Religionssomatik und Religionsästhetik?," in: Oliver Krüger und Nadine Weibel (eds.), *Die Körper der Religionen – Corps en religion* (PANO: Zürich 2015) CULTuREL Religionswissenschaftliche Studien 6, 21-45, hier 25.

[32] Koch, „Körperwissen," 26.

dieses diskursiven Interesses führt unausweichlich zu der Frage, ob und, wenn ja, wie dieses Körperwissen zu operationalisieren ist. Diese Konzeptualisierung des Körperwissens ist von seinem diskursiven Ereignis abzugrenzen und zu unterscheiden, da es sich kritisch (nicht nur deskriptiv) einmischt. Man könnte auch sagen: Der Körper hat (analog zu einer Person) eine eigenständige Meinung:

> Körperwissen bezeichnet in der Folge nicht Wissen über den Körper, sondern durch den Körper erlangtes und vollzogenes Wissen. Sodann ist zu unterscheiden zwischen dem Körperwissen, das um unseren Körper weiß, und dem Körperwissen, das nach neueren Theorien der kognitiven Psychologie Grundlage jedweden Wissens ist, insofern alle Wissensbestände auf der Basis von rezeptiver Formung repräsentiert und wiederholt werden.[33]

Diesen Überlegungen liegt ein veränderter Wissensbegriff zugrunde. Im Kontext sozial-, kultur- und kognitionswissenschaftlicher Diskurse wird Wissen nicht mehr exklusiv symbolhaft verstanden, sondern vielmehr weist es „epistemische Grade" auf. Von „Vermuten, Meinen bis überzeugt Sein und Gründe-Haben" umfasst der Begriff ein Spektrum, das seinen eher pragmatischen Charakter prägt. „Wissen [ist] das, woran man keine Gründe hat, zu zweifeln."[34] Das Wissen als Praxiswissen erscheint in dieser Hinsicht als tendenziell entdeckendes, exploratives Wissen (in Aktion), das weniger auf eine bestimmte Aussage zielt (Proposition), sondern eher eine konkrete subjektive Leistung des Einzelnen impliziert. Während Pierre Bourdieu anhand seiner Habituslehre vor allem die soziale Dimension des Körpers in diesem Zusammenhang stark macht,[35] fordert Catherine Bell darüber hinaus auch die somatische des Körpers, die ich an dieser Stelle stark machen will, zu berücksichtigen.[36] Das bedeutet, es reicht nicht aus, lediglich die soziale Lücke zu schließen, wie auch im Kontext der *Embodiment-Theorien* kritisch zu beobachten ist. Je komplexer ein soziales Gefüge ist, desto wichtiger ist es für wissenschaftliche Erkenntnis, die doppelte Dimension von Körper (somatisch und sozial) – dies verankert im jeweils situativen Kontext – wahrzunehmen.

---

[33] Koch, „Körperwissen," 28f.
[34] Koch, „Körperwissen".
[35] Pierre Bourdieu, „Körperliche Erkenntnis," in: Pierre Bourdieu, *Meditationen: Zur Kritik einer scholastischen Vernunft* (Suhrkamp: Frankfurt 2001).
[36] Catherine Bell, *Ritual Theory, Ritual Practice* (Oxford University Press: New York und Oxford 1992).

Ulrike Sallandt
Pentekostalismus und Körper: Religionsästhetische Impulse für die Untersuchung von Körperpraktiken pentekostaler Frömmigkeit

Dafür müssen Gesetzmäßigkeiten gewonnen werden, anhand derer die ganzheitliche Körperlichkeit erfasst und als Wissen-im-Vollzug epistemologisch gerechtfertigt werden kann. Es handelt sich wissenschaftlich um den Übergang von der Religionsästhetik zur Religionssomatik, die es gemeinsam ermöglichen, den ganzen Körper als „graduelles Kontinuum von implizitem zu explizitem Wissen" in den Blick zu nehmen.[37]

> Körperwissen ist kein rein habitualisiertes Wissen wie bei Bourdieu, und auch kein nur unbewusstes oder selbstreferentielles Wissen um eigene Körperfähigkeiten und (innere) körperliche Vorgänge, sondern ein aktiv erkennendes Organ.[38]

Sichtbar wird diese Behauptung im Zuge generationaler gesellschaftlicher Entwicklung. Judith Butler[39] beobachtet beispielsweise den Generationswechsel, insbesondere mit Blick auf die sozialen Geschlechter. Anhand des Performativitätsbegriffs zeigt sie, dass (Körper-)Wissen nicht propositional ist, das heißt einem expliziten Sinn (einer Generation) unterliegt, sondern vielmehr dynamisch und instabil ist: Konventionen wiederholen sich zwar über Generationen hinweg, verändern sich jedoch zugleich in diesem stetigen Übergang. Dabei verdeutlicht sich die kritische Funktion des Körperwissens als Schutz gegen externe Verfügungsgewalt und Deutungsmacht(-missbrauch). Der Körper bewahrt dem menschlichen Sein seine natürliche Freiheit, die dem sozialkulturellen Geschlecht abgesprochen wird.

Kategorie(n) des Körperwissens
An dieser Stelle ist nicht der Raum, ausführlich auf die Vielfalt an Kategorien des Körperwissens aktueller wissenschaftlicher Diskurse in der Kognitionswissenschaft und Neurologie einzugehen. Grundsätzlich liegt der Unterschied der Theorien darin, dass sie jeweils einen anderen Verstehensbegriff voraussetzen. Im Fall der Simulationstheorie, auf die ich mich im Folgenden beschränke, da für sie die *embodied cognition* von zentraler Bedeutung ist,

---

[37] Koch, „Körperwissen," 32. Wichtig ist dabei, dass auf diese Weise verhindert wird, das Körperwissen neurologisch zu codieren, erneut festzulegen und dadurch zu reduzieren. Dabei schützt die zusätzliche Unterscheidung von implizitem Wissen, in solches, das explizit, und solches, das sich medial/symbolisch nicht äußert, wie beispielsweise in religiöser Metasprache zu beobachten (Beispiel Karl Barth).
[38] Koch, „Körperwissen".
[39] Vgl. Judith Butler, *Bodies That Matter: On the Discursive Limits of "Sex"* (Routledge: New York und London 1993).

wird Verstehen „über Simulation von bereits verkörperten Situationen (wieder)gewonnen".[40] Der Kognitionswissenschaftler Lawrence W. Barsalou[41] hat eine Simulationstheorie des Verstehens entwickelt, um damit unter aderem die Kritik, dass auch diese Theorie nicht ausschließlich auf implizitem und nonpropositionalem Wissen beruhe, zu entkräften. Der Schlüssel seiner Argumentation liegt darin, dass kognitives Wissen und Bedeutungszusammenhänge letztlich ebenfalls auf situativer Wahrnehmung basieren. Der unbestreitbare *modale* Zugang allen Wissens binde jede Art von Erkenntnisprozessen, auch die des vermeintlich reinen Theoriewissens, situativ, das heißt jedes Wissen stehe in untrennbarer Beziehung zu seiner „Erwerbssituation".

> [K]nowledge depends inherently on the brains, bodies, and environmental situations in which it resides, rather than existing independently of them. Different theories emphasize different aspects of physical contexts in the representation of knowledge. Whereas simulation theories focus on roles of modality-specific systems, embodied theories focus on roles of bodily states, and situated theories focus on roles of environmental situations.[42]

Als „embodied theories of knowledge" wendet Barsalou seine Simulationstheorie des Verstehens auch auf das religiöse Feld an.[43] Besonders interessant für den vorliegenden Beitrag ist das Kapitel über religiöse Rituale gegen Ende des Aufsatzes. Barsalou unterscheidet dort in *„once-in-a-lifetime rituals"* einerseits, *„mundane rituals"* andererseits, und ermöglicht damit, differenzierter die Funktion und Bedeutung religiöser Ritualpraxis zu untersuchen. Während die erstgenannten Rituale eine radikale Unterbrechung beziehungsweise eine Umkehr in der Denkweise und Einstellung bedeuten würden (zum Beispiel die Glossolalie im Pentekostalismus), ermöglichten die zweiten, nach einer radikalen Abkehr vom alten Leben, sich auf dem neuen Weg zurechtzufinden (zum Beispiel pentekostale Gebetspraxis). „The

---

[40] Koch, „Körperwissen," 35.
[41] Lawrence W. Barsalou, „Perceptual Symbol System," in: *Behavioral and Brain Science* 22/2 (1999), 577-660.
[42] Lawrence W. Barsalou, „Embodiment in Religious Knowledge," in: *Journal of Religion and Culture* 5/1-2 (2004), 14-57, hier 24.
[43] Barsalou, „Embodiment in Religious Knowledge," 36-48. Bezüglich der christlich-theologischen Ansätze stellt er fest, dass sie „minimize the importance of the physical world. Because these religions focus so heavily on the spiritual, the body and environment become peripheralized. Indeed, the body is so unimportant in Christian Science that if one becomes ill, the only recourse is to spiritual healing, not to medical (physical) healing" (36).

primary function of repeated mundane rituals may be to establish this new conceptual system."[44]

Die Pointe Barsalous liegt meines Erachtens darin, dass sich religiöses Wissen seiner Simulationstheorie zufolge anhand von Körperwissen in der Ritualpraxis, aber auch an religiösen Visionen und Überzeugungen,[45] entdecken lässt: „Verkörpertes Wissen [...] ruft religiöses Wissen aus Vorerfahrungen, religiöser Ästhetik, religiösen Bildern und den Aussagen religiöser Texte ab."[46] Die Grundüberzeugung, dass jedem Wissen von Anfang an ein konkreter Entstehungskontext anhafte, spiegelt sich hier deutlich wider und lässt das Konzept der *embodied cognition* gerade auch für die religiöse Forschung bedeutsam werden. Der Gewinn liegt für die Religionswissenschaft darin, dass (religiöses) Wissen aus seiner theoretischen Zwangsjacke von propositionalem und explizitem Inhalt befreit und der Körper nicht mehr auf einen Träger von Symbol und Metapher reduziert wird. Das Konzept des sich im Vollzug konstituierenden Körperwissens stellt eine zunehmend religionswissenschaftlich, ästhetisch und somatisch anerkannte (methodische) Alternative dar,[47] um komplexe kulturwissenschaftliche Phänomen, insofern auch religiöse, differenziert und interdisziplinär-innovativ zu untersuchen, ohne das Ergebnis der Untersuchung schon im Vorfeld festzulegen.

Beschreibung pentekostaler Ritualpraxis

Die pentekostale Ritualpraxis ist ein solches komplexes Phänomen, das wissenschaftlich interdisziplinäre, insbesondere religionsästhetische und somatische Forschung notwendig macht. Um dem Pentekostalismus in seiner Mehrdeutigkeit gerecht zu werden, bietet sich meines Erachtens an, anhand der dargelegten religionswissenschaftlichen Annäherung zunächst seine Ritualpraxis zu beschreiben, sodann zu analysieren. Eine genauere Untersuchung dieser körperlichen Frömmigkeit ermöglicht es, so meine These, äußere Zuschreibungen, die das Phänomen des Pentekostalismus bzw. Teilaspekte, wie zum Beispiel das Frauenbild, eindeutig festlegen, zu öffnen und für eine befreiende Lesart zu sensibilisieren.

---

[44] Barsalou, „Embodiment in Religious Knowledge," 47.
[45] Auf diese bin ich an dieser Stelle nicht näher eingegangen; vgl. Barsalou, „Embodiment in Religious Knowledge," 36-46.
[46] Koch, „Körperwissen," 33.
[47] Vgl. die Aufsätze in der Zeitschrift Anne Koch (ed.), in: *Verkündigung und Forschung*, Religionswissenschaft. Religionsästhetik 2 (2019).

In dieser Hinsicht stellt der peruanische evangelische Anthropologe Ruben Paredes Alfaro[48] in seiner Studie über die Erneuerung der Liturgien den gewinnbringenden Beitrag der pentekostalen Frömmigkeitsstile heraus. Er erkennt in den stark körperlich geprägten Ritualen die Sprache einer tief in der peruanischen Kultur verwurzelten Festivität, deren bevorzugte körperliche Ausdrucksweisen im Tanz und in der Musik liegen, die soziale Grenzen überwinden. Die Musik, ein elementarer und bedeutender Begleiter im Gottesdienst, schafft eine angenehme Atmosphäre, in der die Gläubigen ihren Alltag hinter sich lassen. Indem sie sich auf den Klang der Musik konzentrieren, mitsingen und mittanzen, betreten sie einen neuen Raum jenseits von Alltag und Gesellschaft. Oft ändert sich die musikalische Begleitung zwischen den einzelnen Phasen des Gottesdienstes. Während zu Beginn die eher lebendigen, aktiven Rhythmen dominieren, bereiten die meditativen Lobpreislieder die Gläubigen für den Empfang des Wortes Gottes vor. Körperlich expressiv, nahezu tänzerisch, drücken die Gläubigen ihre Bereitschaft und Offenheit aus, sich dem Wort Gottes zu öffnen: „[Die Gottesdienstbesucher*innen] erheben ihre Hände zum Himmel, schließen ihre Augen und treten ein in [...] die Aura des Heiligen Geistes."[49] Es scheint, als ob ihre äußerlich ritualisierten Bewegungen sich „verinnerlichen". Diese innere Erfahrung lasse sie nicht mehr nur die körperliche Beziehung untereinander, sondern die ursprüngliche Anbindung an die ganze Schöpfung Gottes „erkennen".

> The key idea is that ritual is a side of social interaction and the embodiment of particular religion. Ritual reinforces religious traditions so that participants carry with them its culture. [...] Emotions as experienced in and among bodies through a process of attunement and entrainment, support religious sentiment in such a way that the religion is "lived" in context.[50]

Für Michael Wilkinson ebnet das Körperkonzept den geeignetsten Weg, sich pentekostaler Wirklichkeit zu nähern. „Der Körper wird dabei nicht nur als Mittler zwischen Ich und Welt verstanden, sondern Ich und Welt sind immer schon körperlich vermittelt, das heißt der Körper ist Teil der sozialen Welt

---

[48] Ruben Paredes Alfaro. *Con permiso para danzar* (CEMAA: Lima 2006).
[49] Ulrike Sallandt, *Der Geist Gottes im Süden Perus: Risiken und Chancen charismatisch – pfingstlicher Verkündigung am Beispiel der AdD* (LIT: Münster 2007), Kirchen in der Weltgesellschaft 2, 50.
[50] Michael Wilkinson, „Pentecostalism, the Body and Embodiment," in: Wilkinson und Althouse (eds.), *Pentecostals and the Body*, 17-35, hier 20.

und diese ist in ihm körperlich angelegt."[51] Demnach erhalte jegliche soziale Interaktion ihre lebendige Energie durch körperliche Gegenwart, Begegnung und Rituale, die das momentane Beziehungs- und Austauschgeschehen des Menschen an das dahinterliegende Ganze binde.[52] In dieser Hinsicht äußert sich auch Peter Althouse in seiner Untersuchung der charismatischen Heilungs- und Gebetspraxis. Ihm zufolge konstituieren sich die Gefühle und Emotionen durch die „dialectic interaction between social agents and structures". Der Mensch erfahre sie „both *in* the body and […] *of* the body and therefore embodied as corporal, subjective and culturally located and consequently enmeshed with gender and power".[53] Körper und Körperlichkeit haben im Vollzug religiöser Rituale und Praxis eine eigenständige Bedeutung. Sie ermöglichen nicht nur einen Übergang zu einer supranaturalen Hinterwelt, in die der/die Gläubige mittels des Rituals flieht. Vielmehr zeigt sich mit Blick auf pentekostale Körperpraktiken, inwiefern Religion in das kulturellsoziale Geschehen eingebettet ist, das von der einen Lebenswirklichkeit getragen wird.[54] Darin liegt auch ihr Transformationspotential. Ohne diese körperliche Lebendigkeit der pentekostalen Rituale in ihrer bindenden Kraft zum Lebensganzen wahrzunehmen und zu erkennen, besteht Wolfgang Vondey zufolge die Gefahr, dass der Pentekostalismus zu einer theoretischen Angelegenheit verkomme. Deshalb analysiert Vondey die materielle Dimension des Pentekostalismus aus eschatologischer Perspektive und kommt zu folgendem Ergebnis:

> Eschatological practices have redefined the materiality of Pentecostal theology in terms of political activism, racial reconciliation, concerns for pacifism, economic justice, and ecological liberation. […] This materiality of eschatological practice is essential for the embodiment of the full gospel; the weakness of eschatology is likely to affect Pentecostal spirituality at the core not in its doctrines but its spirituality.[55]

---

[51] Bockrath, Boschert und Franke, *Körperliche Erkenntnis*, 12.
[52] Bockrath, Boschert und Franke, *Körperliche Erkenntnis*.
[53] Peter Althouse, „Emotional Regimes in the Embodiment of Charismatic Prayer," in: Wilkinson und Althouse (eds.), *Pentecostalism and the Body*, 36-54, hier 37.
[54] Vgl. Peter Althouse, „Emotional Regimes in the Embodiment of Charismatic Prayer," in: Wilkinson und Althouse (eds.), *Pentecostalism and the Body*, 36-54, hier 52.
[55] Wolfgang Vondey, „Embodied Gospel: The Materiality of Pentecostal Theology," in: Wilkinson und Althouse (eds.), *Pentecostals and the Body*, 102-119, hier 113.

Verkündigung erleben

Die Predigt vollzieht sich als ein kommunikatives Erbauungsereignis, bei dem weniger historisch-kritisch mit dem Bibeltext umgegangen wird, sondern die Predigt primär darauf abzielt, die Gottesdienstbesucher*innen affektiv zu berühren, emotional zu erbauen und pastoral-seelsorgerlich zu trösten. Der/die Prediger*in lässt sich vom Heiligen Geist leiten, überzeugt davon, dass Gott ihm/ihr im Geist die richtigen Worte des Evangeliums in den Mund legt. Zwischen Prediger*in und Gottesdienstbesucher*innen kommt es idealerweise zu körperlich-affektiver Bindung, eine Begegnung, die nur im Gottesdienstgeschehen selbst erleb- und erfahrbar wird. Dabei ist der intuitive Wechsel von körperlichem Ausdruck und verbaler Artikulation zu beobachten, der die Hörenden aneinanderbindet. Zum besseren Verständnis hilft an dieser Stelle Helmut Plessners Begriff der Artikulation, mit dem er darauf aufmerksam macht, dass sich Sinn nicht nur verbal ausdrücke, sondern sich in der Vielfalt von diversen Ausdrucksmöglichkeiten konstituiere.[56] Sinn stifte sich auch jenseits von „propositionalisierbaren Medien",[57] das heißt auch in affektiver Bindung, wie sie sich beispielsweise in diesem wechselseitigen Verhältnis zwischen Prediger*in und Gemeinde im pentekostalen Gottesdienstgeschehen ereigne. Theologisch gedeutet: Die „Transzendenz in der Immanenz" offenbart sich als ein besonderer Beziehungsraum im Hier und Jetzt, der vom/von der Prediger*in nicht intendiert wird, sondern vielmehr als sinnhafter Ausdruck der göttlichen Gegenwart und Gemeinschaft gelten kann. Kann man dieser Deutung folgen, erhält der Affekt in pentekostaler Verkündigung insofern eine dynamische Brückenfunktion, als dass er die unmittelbare, sinnstiftende Bindung von Körper und Sprache bewirkt. Für John Bialecki ist diese unmittelbare sinnstiftende Wirkung des Affekts nicht nur bei der pentekostalen Verkündigungspraxis von schöpferischer Bedeutung, sondern zeigt sich tendenziell im Feld des pentekostalen Christentums:

> I'd like to suggest that the way to imagine the relation between embodiment and language in Pentecostal/charismatic Christianity is to think in terms of affect. Here, we will think of affect as the intensities and energies found in particular moment

---

[56] Zur Vertiefung von Plessners Verständnis verweise ich exemplarisch auf Matthias Jung, „‚Making us explicit': Artikulation als Ordnungsprinzip von Erfahrung," in: Magnus Schlette und Matthias Jung (eds.), *Anthropologie der Artikulation. Begriffliche Grundlagen und transdisziplinäre Perspektiven* (Königshausen & Neumann: Würzburg 2005), 103-142.

[57] Katrin Arnold, „Ausdruck und Artikulation: Ein Grenzübergang zwischen Philosophischer Anthropologie und Symbolischem Interaktionismus," in: Schlette und Jung (eds.), *Anthropologie der Artikulation,* 85-102, hier 99.

or object that has consequences on others that it is in contact with that moment. Affect would be defined as the preconscious movements and stillness of the body, the quickenings and slowings, the twitches and pauses, that others respond to often without even being aware of it.[58]

Indem John Bialecki das Vorbewusste des Affekts betont, verdeutlicht er dessen bereits erwähnte unmittelbare Wirkung und grenzt ihn von – zum Teil synonym verwendeten – Begriffen der Emotion und des Gefühls ab.[59] In der Verkündigung konstituiert sich eine besondere „Aura der Faktizität",[60] die nicht auf reflektierten Gefühlszuständen basiert, sondern im Augenblick des Affekts auftaucht. Im Nachklingen der Predigt, in dieser unmittelbaren Gegenwart Gottes, lädt der/die Prediger*in die Gläubigen ein, in den Altarraum zu treten, um den Heiligen Geist zu empfangen.

Gebet erleben (Zungenrede)
Nach pentekostalem Verständnis überbrückt die Zungenrede (*Glossolalie*), das sichtbare Zeichen der Geisttaufe, die Ungereimtheiten dieser Welt und offenbart den ständigen leibhaftigen Übergang zur mystischen Wirklichkeit bzw. den Rückgang an einen Ort vor-allem-Bewusstsein. Im ekstatischen Gebet berichten die Gläubigen, erleben sie, wie sie von der profanen Alltagswelt in die heilige Gegenwart Gottes gelangen. Sie lassen sich körperlich auf dieses außerordentliche und außergewöhnliche Ereignis ein, öffnen sich in ihrem ganzen Sein, um Gott zu begegnen. Unzählige Zeugnisse geben nur annähernd ein Bild davon, was die Menschen in diesem Gebet erleben. Diese prophetische Botschaft des Zungengebets kann demnach nicht primär kognitiv-reflexiv empfangen, geschweige denn rational nachvollzogen werden. Vielmehr ereignet sich die Botschaft für jeden Einzelnen in der unverfügbaren Begegnung mit dem Anderen: dem Anderen in mir, im Mitmenschen und in Gott. Frank

---

[58] Jon Bialecki, „Affect: Intensities and Energies in the Carismatic Language, Embodiment, and Genre of North America Movement," in: Simon Coleman und Rosalind I.J. Hacket (eds.), *The Anthropology of Global Pentecostalism and Evangelicalism* (University Press: New York 2015), 95-108, hier 97.

[59] Unter den Pfingsttheologen herrscht diesbezüglich keine Einigkeit. Vgl. dazu Giovanni Maltese, *Geistererfahrung zwischen Transzendenz und Immanenz: Die Erfahrungsbegriffe in den pfingstlich-charismatischen Theologien von Terry L. Cross und Among Young im Vergleich* (Vandenhoeck & Ruprecht: Göttingen 2013), 61-64.

[60] Clifford Geertz, *Dichte Beschreibung: Beiträge zum Verstehen kultureller Systeme* (Suhrkamp: Frankfurt a.M. 1987), 73.

D. Macchia kommt in seiner Studie „Zungen als Zeichen" im kritischen Vergleich mit dem Sakramentsverständnisses Karl Rahners zu dem Ergebnis, dass die Wunder und Zeichen, insofern auch die Zungenrede, „Gottes freie, eschatologische Präsenz in das ‚Hier und Jetzt' transportieren, um zu bevollmächtigen, zu befreien und zu heilen".[61] Es geht weniger – wie oft angenommen – um die „unmittelbare Begegnung mit Gott", geschweige denn um einen reinen „Emotionalismus, ohne Bezug zu einem objektiven Gnadenmittel."[62] Es ist die Unverfügbarkeit Gottes, die den Menschen sprachlos macht und ihn körperlich befähigt, in Zungen zu reden. In dieser Hinsicht deutet der Pfingsttheologe und Exeget Gordon D. Fee die Zungenrede als Zeichen der körperlichen Schwäche des Menschen, der durch Gottes Wort im wundersamen Wirken des Geistes aufgerichtet werde. „Die Gläubigen, die in Zungen beten, geben das ‚Seufzen' der gesamtem Schöpfung als Echo wider, während wir gemeinsam die endgültige Vollendung der Zukunft erwarten, die Gott in der Auferstehung und der Gabe des Geistes schon begonnen hat."[63] In diesem Seufzer drücke sich die Abhängigkeit des Geschöpfes seinem Schöpfer gegenüber aus, widersetze sich dem Verständnis anhand von grammatikalischen Regeln und sprachlicher Syntax und erscheint nach Meinung von James K. A. Smith auf diese Weise als „Sprache des Widerstandes". Smiths Untersuchung der Zungenrede anhand der Sprachphilosophie führt ihn zu einer Revision der Sprechakttheorie (Austin) mit der Erkenntnis, dass die Zungenrede „einen Forschungsausblick für Sprachphilosophie darstellt", die die Grenzen von Systemen, Kategorien und Zuschreibungen aufzeige.[64] Trotz möglicher Kritik an Smiths Schlussfolgerung, dass „Zungenrede [...] ein Diskurs [sei], der symbolisch für ein tieferes und breiteres Verlangen steht, den besonderen ökonomischen und politischen Strukturen zu widerstehen und sie infrage zu stellen", wird hier die Notwendigkeit deutlich, die pentekostale Frömmigkeits- und Glaubenspraxis unter Berücksichtigung anderer als nur der kognitiven Inhalte zu untersuchen.

---

[61] Frank D. Macchia, „Zungen als Zeichen: Wege zu einem sakramentalen Verständnis pfingstlicher Erfahrung," in: Jörg Haustein und Giovanni Maltese (eds.), *Handbuch pfingstliche und charismatische Theologie* (Vandenhoeck & Ruprecht: Göttingen 2014), 249-266, hier 266.

[62] Macchia, „Zungen als Zeichen," 266.

[63] Gordon D. Fee, „Weg zu einer paulinischen Theologie der Glossolalie," in: Haustein und Maltese (eds.), *Handbuch*, 93-106, hier 104. Das Seufzen geht auf den Bibelvers Röm 8,26 zurück. Paulus drückt damit in der Spannung von sichtbar und unsichtbar die Hoffnung auf das Leben im Geist aus.

[64] James K.A. Smith, „Zungen als ‚Widerstandsdiskurs': Eine philosophische Perspektive," in: Haustein und Maltese (eds.), *Handbuch*, 267-298, hier 291.

Dabei geht es insbesondere um diskursive Untersuchungen des Körpers, des körperlichen Erlebens und Erfahrens. Diese ermöglichen im Sinne von David Perry, nicht nur die äußerlichen, sondern auch die innerlichen Erfahrungen wahr- und ernst zu nehmen.[65]

Zeugnis ablegen
Die affektiv-körperliche Wirkung des im Gottesdienst unmittelbar erlebten Pfingstgeschehens auf die Gläubigen erzählt sich in den narrativen Zeugnissen im Gottesdienst und über ihn hinaus.

> Der Körper ist ein Träger von inkorporierter Geschichte. [...] Der fortwährende Prozess von Produktion und Reproduktion, von Geschichte, die inkorporiert, und Inkorporierung, die aktualisiert wird, ist ein Prozess, der ablaufen kann, ohne je zum Objekt einer spezifischen, sprachlich explizit artikulierten, institutionellen Praxis zu werden.[66]

Menschen erzählen von ihren existenziellen Schicksalen, den konkreten Veränderungen, die ihr Leben in Christus ihnen gebracht hat (Konversionserzählungen).[67] Jenseits der klassischen Phänomenologie wird ein ganz anderes Wissen beim Erzählen körperlich erfahren, das jeder Art verbaler Artikulation vorausgeht. Ganz im Sinne der bereits angesprochenen *Anthropologie der Artikulation* (2005), die zwischen körperlichem Ausdruck und verbaler Artikulation differenziert, öffnet sich dabei ein anderer Erkenntnisbereich. Befreit von den eigenen kulturellen Zeichen- und Symbolsystemen wird es möglich, dem Anderen und den anderen Menschen im Ereignis, im Vollzug der körperlichen Bindung, zu begegnen. Diese „Begegnung ohne Begegnung" mit dem Göttlichen ist nicht in eindeutigen Aussagesätzen mitzuteilen, sondern findet vielmehr ihren Ausdruck in der körperlich nachempfundenen imaginationsreichen Narration. Eindeutige Aussagesätze würden einen „apriorisch gegebenen Erfahrungsgehalt"[68] suggerieren, der der Diversität menschlicher Bekehrungserlebnisse widerspreche.

---

[65] Vgl. David Perry, *Spirit Baptism: The Pentecostal Experience in Theological Focus* (Brill: Boston und London 2017), 72.
[66] Pierre Bourdieu, *Was heißt Sprechen? Zur Ökonomie des sprachlichen Tausches* (New academic press: Budapest ²2015), 15.
[67] Vgl. Volker Krech, „Religiöse Erfahrung und artikulatorische Identitätsbildung in Konversionserzählungen: Wissenschaftsgeschichtliches und Systematisches," in: Schlette und Jung (eds.), *Anthropologie der Artikulation*, 341-370, hier 341.
[68] Vgl. Volker Krech, „Religiöse Erfahrung," in: Schlette und Jung (eds.), *Anthropologie der Artikulation*, 341-370, hier 348.

Unter Berücksichtigung der Konversionsforschung ist mit Blick auf pentekostale Narrationspraxis eher davon auszugehen, dass der Gehalt des Bekehrungserlebnisses in kommunikativen Narrativen der Gläubigen sichtbar wird. Diese sind von körperlich sicht- bzw. hörbaren narrativen Brüchen, von Stottern und Wiederholung der Konvertiten*innen, geprägt, da sich der Gegenstand, von dem sie berichten, dem unmittelbar erzählerischen Fluss entzieht.[69]

> Die Konversionserzählung wird jetzt in einem engeren Zusammenhang mit dem Konversionsprozess selbst gesehen. [...] Mit dieser Perspektive [wird] deutlich, dass die Spannungen, die der Bekehrung zugrunde liegen, in divergierenden sprachlichen Interpretationen des Selbst- *und Weltverhältnisses* bestehen.[70]

Die körperlich geprägte Erzählung selbst erhält dadurch einen höheren Stellenwert, da sie den Moment der subjektiv erlebten Bekehrung narrativ (erneut) vollzieht und insofern selbstkonstruierend zum Ausdruck kommt. Dabei ist die Erzählung weniger von der rationalen Durchdringung des Gegenstandes gekennzeichnet, als von der religiösen Deutung und Sinnsuche des Einzelnen. „Dieses Narrativ bietet also die Grundlage für eine (theologische) Reflexion, die sodann in zukünftige Reflexionen einfließt. [...] Positiv bedeutet das, dass die theologische Reflexion das narrative Moment der Erfahrung nicht vernachlässigen"[71] darf. Ähnlich wie die Verkündigung inszeniert sich die Konversionserzählung in der Wirkung der göttlichen Gegenwart, „sichtbar" in der schöpferischen Bindung von Körper und Sprache in der gottesdienstlich-performativen Praxis.

Reflexion pentekostaler Frömmigkeit

Im abschließenden Kapitel soll es darum gehen, die „dichte Beschreibung" der pentekostalen Frömmigkeitspraxis aus religionswissenschaftlicher, insbesondere aus religionsästhetischer und somatischer Perspektive zu analysieren. Es handelt sich dabei weniger um eine vollständige Analyse beziehungsweise Reflexion, sondern vielmehr darum, anhand von auftauchenden Fragen dafür zu sensibilisieren, dass eine andere religionswissenschaftliche, insbesondere

---

[69] Vgl. Bernd Ulmer, „Konversionserzählungen als rekonstruktive Gattung: Erzählerische Mittel und Strategien bei der Rekonstruktion eines Bekehrungserlebnisses," in: *Zeitschrift für Soziologie* 17 (1988), 19-33, hier 26.
[70] Volker Krech, „Religiöse Erfahrung," in: Schlette und Jung (eds.), *Anthropologie der Artikulation*, 341-370, hier 350.
[71] Giovanni Maltese, *Geistererfahrung*, 64.

Ulrike Sallandt
Pentekostalismus und Körper: Religionsästhetische Impulse für die Untersuchung von Körperpraktiken pentekostaler Frömmigkeit

religionsästhetische und religionssomatische Zugangsweise als die von der eigenen dogmatisch-theologischen Tradition ausgehende, sinnvoll sein kann, um die innerchristliche Diversität in ihrer Eigenlogik wahrzunehmen, von äußeren Zuschreibungen zu befreien und sich auf diese Weise (immer wieder) herausfordern zu lassen.

Schon der bekannte Pfingstforscher Jürgen Hollenweger erkannte in Abgrenzung zur allgemeinen Meinung, es herrsche im pentekostalen Gottesdienst kein liturgischer Ablauf, dass in jedem Gottesdienst „die meisten Elemente der historischen Liturgien" auftreten.[72] Der Unterschied, so Hollenweger, liege allein darin, dass der dreifache Aufbau von *entrance, duration* and *exit* pentekostaler Gottesdienste andersartig angeordnet und insbesondere auf spirituelle Erfahrungen ausgerichtet sei. Beschrieben werden die Gottesdiensterfahrungen als „highly calculated processes intimately connected to the work of self-construction and identity formation". In Auseinandersetzung mit der Kritik, es handle sich um antimoderne und antirationale Erfahrungen, betont Terry Cooper diese „as highly deliberative or contested process linked to the formation of selfhood or identity". Dabei ist der Körper „the primordial object and the tool of cultural action".[73] Die Gottesdienstteilnehmenden empfinden demnach die Gegenwart Gottes im liturgischen Erleben primär körperlich. Sie lernen ihren Körper in der liturgischen Wiederholung besser kennen und werden fähig, sich selbst mit und in ihrem Körper zu inszenieren, ihn zu lesen und zu deuten. Die Eingangsphase des Gottesdienstes bietet den Gläubigen „Raum", sich immer wieder aus dem gegenwärtigen körperlichen Zustand, mit anderen Worten aus dem Alltag, in den von Gott gegebenen aufzumachen. Der/die Gläubige konzentriert sich darauf, jegliche Ablenkungen seines/ihres Alltags hinter sich zu lassen, und eine neue Perspektive, nämlich „a real state of communion with the divine", einzunehmen.[74] Nachdem der/die Gläubige vom Alltag losgelassen hat und sich sozusagen bereit fühlt, sich auf die Gottesdienstfeier einzulassen, strebt er/sie danach, sich immer mehr der Gemeinschaft mit Gott hinzugeben. Gläubige berichten, die Gegenwart des Heiligen Geistes immer mehr an und in ihrem Körper zu spüren. Gefühle aller Art können dabei auftreten, meistens geprägt von körperlichen

---

[72] Jürgen Walter Hollenweger, *Charismatisch-pfingstliches Christentum: Herkunft – Situation – Ökumenische Chancen.* (Vandenhoeck & Ruprecht: Göttingen 1997), 302.

[73] Terry Cooper, „Worship Rituals, Discipline and Charismatic Pentecostal Techniques," in: Wilkinson und Althouse (eds.), *Pentecostals and the Body*, 78.

[74] Cooper, „Worship Rituals," 85.

Begleiterscheinungen (unter anderen Lachen, Weinen, Rufen, Schreien, Tanzen, Singen). Sie lassen die „Zuschauenden" ahnen, was für einen inneren Kampf die/der Gläubige am eigenen Leib spürt. Der Körper zeigt sich dabei als aktiver Träger dieses herausfordernden Grenz-/Übergangsgeschehens von der menschlichen zur göttlichen Gemeinschaft: „The materiality of the human embodiment exceeds one's spiritual aptitudes."[75] Dieses konkrete, körperlich-kulturell anbindende Potential der pentekostal-religiösen Glaubenspraxis wurde aus meiner Sicht lange Zeit vernachlässigt. Die Betonung der Geistdimension, verbunden mit einem defizitären Körperverständnis, hat nicht selten dazu geführt, die pentekostale Frömmigkeit mit einem unbegründeten Dualismus zu stigmatisieren und ins Abseits einer Hinterwelt zu stellen. Für den peruanischen Pfingsttheologen Bernardo Campos wiederholt sich in den pentekostalen Gottesdiensten das Pfingstfest. Nach biblischem Bericht „wurden alle erfüllt von dem Heiligen Geist und fingen an, zu predigen in andern Sprachen, wie der Geist ihnen gab, auszusprechen".[76] Die pentekostale Liturgie diene dazu, dieses schöpferische[n] Erleben im Geist immer wieder am eigenen Körper zu spüren und damit lebendig zu halten.[77] Die darin sich ausdrückende Suche nach Gott ist eine Suche im Geist, erlebt und erfahren am eigenen Körper, der in Beziehung zu anderen und in Beziehung zum ganzen Körper (zur Schöpfung Gottes) getragen wird. Es handelt sich Campos' zufolge um eine dynamische Ekklesiologie, die sich vom persönlichen Geisterlebnis, der inneren Gewissheit der Erlösung und Befreiung in Jesus Christus, ereignet.[78] Dieses persönliche, affektiv erlebte und sinnlich erfahrene Rettungsgeschehen wirkt für den Gläubigen jenseits vom klassischen Verständnis der Soteriologie sinnstiftend. Es widerspricht den endlichen Selbstverständlichkeiten, ist Zeit und Raum enthoben und ereignet sich insofern diachron und asymmetrisch. Sein Gehalt lässt sich nicht begreifen, vielmehr widersteht er der Eindeutigkeit des Begriffs, drückt sich weniger kognitiv aus. Es scheint vielmehr, als ob der Gehalt insbesondere in der Wirkung liegt und den Einzelnen und die Gruppe körperlich berührt. In gewisser Analogie zur Kunst und Theaterwelt prägen Inszenierung und Performativität den liturgischen Aufbau

---

[75] Cooper, „Worship Rituals," 89.
[76] Apg 2,4 übersetzt von Martin Luther.
[77] Vgl. Bernardo Campos, *Experiencias del Espiritu Santo Claves para una interpretacion del pentecostalismo* (CLAI: Quito 1997), 97.
[78] Vgl. Bernardo Campos, „Situación del Pentecostalismos en Peru hacia 2013" (https://de.slideshare.net/ipermaster/situacion-de-los-pentecostalismos-en-el-peru-2013, 01. April 2019).

Ulrike Sallandt
Pentekostalismus und Körper: Religionsästhetische Impulse für die Untersuchung von Körperpraktiken pentekostaler Frömmigkeit

pentekostaler Gottesdienste. Die Gläubigen betreten wie *actors* in körperlich-schöpferischer Wiederholung neue Gestaltungsräume, die Sinnlichkeit und Emotionalität aufwerten. Dabei kann beobachtet werden, dass das unmittelbare Körper-Erleben (transzendente Körpererfahrung), die sinnliche und sinnstiftende Erkenntnis des körperlich Ursprünglichen sich selbst als aktiver Träger von Sinn und Erkenntnis in Szene setzt. Diese Geistatmosphäre im pentekostalen Gottesdienstgeschehen konstituiert sich anhand von sinnlicher und sinnstiftender Erkenntnis. Die Gläubigen erleben durch eine von Wiederholung geprägte Liturgie eine „unmittelbare Körpererfahrung" (siehe oben), erfahren das unmittelbar Körperliche schöpferisch. Die Frage ist, *wie* sie in dieser schöpferischen Wiederholung, auf der Suche nach dem Heiligen Geist, den Empfang, die Gegenwart des Heiligen Geistes fühlen. In welcher Form zeigt sich das implizite, non-propositionale Wissen von neuen Gestaltungsräumen, die der Heilige Geist ihnen öffnet? Wie empfinden die Gläubigen diese Geistatmosphäre auf der Suche nach dem Heiligen Geist? Mit der Simulationstheorie des Verstehens (Barsalou), der zufolge Verstehen durch Nachahmung zustande kommt, und dem Wissen um das non-propositionale Wissen kann das gesamte Ritualgeschehen im pentekostalen Gottesdienst besser nachvollzogen werden. Es ist insofern ver-rückt, als dass es nicht um explizites Wissen geht, sondern in der Pfingstliturgie insbesondere darum, das biblisch bezeugte Pfingstfest, seinen Gründungstag, wie er in der Apostelgeschichte überliefert wird, zu etablieren. Die Intensität des pentekostalen Gottesdienstes liegt mit Barsalou darin begründet, dass die Rituale den Raum schaffen, die neue religiöse Weltsicht zu festigen und das, wofür man sich entschieden hat, immer wieder neu zu erfahren. Seine Unterscheidung der Rituale in „once-in-a-lifetime rituals" einerseits, „mundane rituals" ermöglicht in dieser Hinsicht im pentekostalen Kontext genauer zu untersuchen, wie die Menschen durch die Geisttaufe und Zungenrede eine Grenzerfahrung erleben, und wie diese als religiöse Entscheidung im Weiteren gelebt wird. Bei dieser Untersuchung stehen nicht nur Kultur und Kontext in wechselseitiger Beziehung, das heißt es geht nicht „nur" um den sozialen Habitus einer Person, sondern darum, dass die somatische Dimension des Körpers es als dynamisches Bindeglied der Person ermöglicht, das unsichtbare, implizite Wissen für sich zu entdecken. Der Körper agiert dem Konzept des Körperwissens zufolge wie eine Person, das heißt er ist wie der menschliche Verstand fähig, sich zu erinnern (und zu vergessen) und an seine Erinnerungen anzuknüpfen. Damit lassen sich religiöse Studien allgemein, in diesem Fall pentekostale, vertiefen, da die kulturelle Dimension durch die somatische, das heißt durch die individuelle Erfahrung, ergänzt beziehungsweise vervollständigt wird. Warum empfinden einige Menschen die Musik, den Lobpreis pentekostaler Liturgie attraktiv und fühlen sich emotional davon angesprochen und andere nicht? Welche Rolle spielen dabei körperliche Erfahrungen der eigenen Sozialisation und Biografie, derer die Person sich teilweise gar nicht mehr bewusst ist? Wie lassen sich die Ambivalenzen und Fluktuationen erklären, in denen sich Menschen räumlich beziehungsweise zeitlich angezogen und zugleich abgestoßen fühlen? Diese Fragen weisen darauf hin, dass die somatische Dimension es ermöglicht, Heterogenität religiösen Erlebens zuzulassen und wissenschaftlich zu untersuchen. Im Gegensatz zur sozial(-politischen) Dimension, die Gefahr läuft, menschliche Erfahrungen anhand traditioneller Denkstrukturen begrifflich zu reduzieren, ermöglicht die somatische *ratio* und *emotio* aneinander zu binden und dadurch Einseitigkeit in beide Richtungen zu identifizieren. Loslösung der einen von der anderen Dimension hat wissenschaftlich *per se* eine eindimensionale Untersuchung zur Folge, die grundsätzlich nicht abzulehnen, derer sich die Forschung aber bewusst sein oder werden sollte. Diese Beobachtung ist im Kontext des Pentekostalismus, insbesondere bei der Ausrichtung der neopentekostalen Kirchen, wichtig. Birgit Meyer hat mit dem Begriff „*Sensation*" (engl.) diese Bedeutung von Emotionalität und Affektivität im Pentekostalismus deutlich gemacht.

> Sensational may well be understood as both appealing to the senses and spectacular. Echoing the current craving for sensations and experiences in the framework of religion, Pentecostal/charismatic churches emphasize the importance of sensing the presence and power of the Holy Spirit directly and immediately. As the embodied presence of God, the Holy Spirit is a portable power source. Having such sensations of divine presence does not happen unexpectedly but requires the existence of a particular shared religious aesthetic, through which the Holy Spirit becomes accessible and perceptible.[79]

Sobald Sinnlichkeit und Affektivität instrumentalisiert und von einer Elite politisch für eigene Ziele genutzt werden, Menschen sich entsprechend dafür benutzen lassen, verliere sich die somatische Anbindung an das ganze Geschehen. Die der *ratio* folgenden Autoritäten werden zu Sklaven der *ratio*, ihre Gefolgschaft zu Sklaven der *emotio*. Das religionsästhetische und somatische Konzept des Körperwissens, mit dem auf der Grundlage eines holistischen

---

[79] Birgit Meyer, „Aesthetics of Persuasion: Global Christianity and Pentecostalism's Sensational Forms," in: *South Atlantic Quarterly* 109/4 (2010), 741-763, hier 742.

Ulrike Sallandt
Pentekostalismus und Körper: Religionsästhetische Impulse für die Untersuchung von Körperpraktiken pentekostaler Frömmigkeit

Wissens- und Verstehensbegriffs Emotionen und Affekte neben dem Verstand wertgeschätzt werden, erkennt einen holistischen Zugang zu Erkenntnis und Wissen an und bietet die Möglichkeit, Einseitigkeiten dieser Art aufzudecken. Meyer fordert, ästhetische Konzepte für die Untersuchung des Pentekostalismus wiederzugewinnen.[80]

Die Untersuchung pentekostaler Körperpraktiken auf ihre epistemologische Tragfähigkeit ermöglicht, andere als die kognitiven Inhalte dieses religiösen Phänomens zu berücksichtigen. Wesen und Wirkung pentekostaler Frömmigkeit kommen aus dieser religionsästhetischen Sicht differenzierter in den Blick. Indem Körperwissen und Erkenntnis im Kontext des Pentekostalismus untersucht werden, besteht die Möglichkeit, gesellschaftlich-politische Zuschreibungen, die im Zusammenhang mit diesem Phänomen bzw. im jeweiligen gesellschaftlich-politischen Kontext existieren, kritisch zu überdenken. Dabei geht es nicht darum, kognitive Reflexion und Interpretation abzulehnen, sondern vielmehr darum, sie durch die religionswissenschaftliche Analyse alternativer Wissenskonzepte zu erweitern und zu vertiefen.

Ulrike Sallandt, Dr. theol., seit 2015 Wissenschaftliche Mitarbeiterin am Lehrstuhl der Evangelischen Theologischen Fakultät an der Friedrich-Wilhelm-Universität in Bonn (Post-doc), Master in Philosophie und ordinierte Pfarrerin, lebte und arbeitete von 2002 bis 2014 in Peru, dort Feldforschung für ihre Dissertation über die charismatisch-pfingstliche Theologie. usalland@uni-bonn.de

---

[80] Meyer, „Aesthetics of Persuasion," 758.

Trees van Montfoort

Green theology: The (in)visibility of the non-human world

Last year I published a book on eco-theology: *Groene theologie* ('Green theology').[1] It got the prize for the best Dutch theological book of the year 2019:

> The jury, reviewers from the Dutch daily papers *Trouw* and *Nederlands Dagblad*, calls it **"a hyper-urgent and necessary book"**. It challenges "a far-reaching Christian theological reflection on the relationship between God, creation, nature and man." According to the jury, this book also shows that ecology has everything to do with theology.[2]

The book introduces and designs an eco-theology for the Churches in the Netherlands and Flanders, both Catholic and Protestant. This article is about the main arguments of the book and something of its reception. I argued why a new worldview is necessary in the context of the ecological crisis, reread the Bible from an eco(-feminist) point of view (on Creation, God, and animals, Salvation of the earth). I also discussed the traditional apprehension of and even downright resistance against any form of connecting God and nature, and examined the possibilities of four eco-feminist theologians for the Dutch-speaking countries.

Theology in times of ecological crisis
My main argument is that ecological theology is not a subdiscipline of theology but a rediscovery of theology as such. Theology, in general, is too much focused on God and human beings – or just on human beings – making the rest of the world invisible. Since the end of the Middle Ages, men have become the centre of the world, that is to say, some human beings: male, white, etcetera. Therefore, I use the word "men". With the rise of humanism,

---

[1] Trees van Montfoort, *Groene theologie* (Skandalon: Middelburg 2019). An English translation is in preparation.
[2] https://www.nachtvandetheologie.nl/, 20 November 2019.

the scope narrowed from God and the whole world to men and their societies. Philosophers like Kant and Hegel reinforced existing hierarchical dualisms between humans and nature, spirit and matter, humanities and science. The whole non-human world was made an object to explore and to exploit. This way of thinking is at the root of the ecological crisis. Too much of the ecological activities of the Churches in the Netherlands take for granted this frame of men exploiting the world with technology in search of profit, what Pope Francis calls "the techno-economic paradigm." The only thing that eco-theology seems to offer is some additional motivation to be careful with the resources because they are not endless. I, on the other hand, maintain that theology should be more than an inspiration for ecological practices like solar panels and more than ethics or anthropology. Theology should envision the whole world again. Cosmology should be part of theology again in order to say something new from its own sources about the ecological crisis.

Bible and dogma

The Bible is a book from a patriarchal society that needs a lot of interpretation to be beneficial for women. An ecological reading of the Bible is to some extent much easier because the Bible is much more inclusive about nature than modernity. The Bible could, therefore, function as a mirror for modern people by showing a different worldview: the role of human beings in relation to the earth is, first of all, to be aware that one is a creature among other creatures. It came as a surprise to me that texts about God creating often represent God with female characteristics, as a Spirit, giving birth or as Lady Wisdom. In the New Testament, Jesus is even portrayed as the incarnation of Wisdom. Texts on Christ as creator have a lot of resemblances with hymns of Sofia, Wisdom, a fact that is either completely overlooked or downplayed in a lot of commentaries. Christ and Wisdom are represented as being with God before the creation, as the firstborns of creation, the image of God, executor of God's works... In short: as fully God and fully part of the world. This Wisdom Christology may not be new at all in feminist theology,[3] but it is certainly new for most of my readers. An eco-feminist approach to Christology is important because much of eco-theology with a Protestant or Evangelical bend focuses on the male power of God and Christ. "Christ is the Lord of the whole world," "God

---

[3] See for instance Celia Deane-Drummond, *Eco-Theology* (Darton, Longman and Todd: London, 2008) and Celia Deane-Drummond, "Sophia: The Feminine Face of God as a Metaphor for an Ecotheology," in: *Feminist Theology* 6/16 (Sep/1997), 11-31.

owns the world"... The *logos* of the New Testament is translated as "Word" or "Son," thus associating Christ with a male omnipotent creator who creates out of nothing by commanding from the outside. I found that the Bible pictures God cooperating with the earth (Gen 1:24: "God said 'Let the earth bring forth'"). God is either just male or female and both immanent and transcendent. Christ as the incarnation of Wisdom and savior of the world becomes an important topic, which is also the key for an eco-feminist Christian theology. I propose a re-evaluation of the dogma of the two natures of Christ as a deconstruction of the hierarchical dualisms of God and the earth, spirit and matter, male and female. The incredible dogma splits open in the diversity of creation.

The Bible and this dogma can help us to make the non-human world visible again in theology and to depict nature neither as something hostile nor as a background for the history of God and man, but as the very world of which we are a part and on which we depend, as all cultures seem to acknowledge except the modern Western one.

Resistance against eco-theology

Many of my readers respond well to what I write about the Bible. The chapter on the Bible broadens their horizon, being a real eye-opener for some. Surprisingly, these reactions come from liberal Christians as well as Evangelicals and Orthodox Protestants and Catholics. Only the admirers of Karl Barth are not amused, which is hardly surprising, because they tend to associate a positive approach of nature with paganism and even with national socialist ideology. There is still a great fear in some parts of the Protestants Churches of connecting God and the earth too closely. They contrapose nature and history as if nature is static and captivating and history is about God liberating human beings from nature. This is based on 19th-century biblical theology that saw the religion of Israel as anti-nature.[4]

Eco-feminism

In the fourth chapter of my book, I explicitly treat eco-feminism and show how the insights of eco-feminist theologians worldwide can enrich theology in the context of the Netherlands. I argued that every eco-theology needs to be feminist theology as well as to avoid some pitfalls of eco-theology. The first pitfall is – I already mentioned it – that the traditional image of God does

---

[4] Kune Biezeveld, *Als scherven spreken: Over God in het leven van alledag* (Meinema: Zoetermeer 2008).

not change, God continues to be a male ruler and the scheme of domination is left unquestioned. The second pitfall is that the image of mankind does not change. The question has to be asked: which human beings are included and which are excluded? Who are human beings in the great scheme of things? How does a human being relate to the place where she happens to live? The third pitfall is that eco-theology emphasizes the splendor of the evolving cosmos, leaving aside suffering and evil in all its manifestations.

I selected three eco-feminist theologians: Ivone Gebara (Catholic, Latin American), Catherine Keller (Protestant, North American), and Elizabeth Theokritoff (Orthodox, European).[5] Later I added Sallie McFague, one of the founding mothers of eco-feminist theology. My selection criteria were that they are engaged with the Christian tradition but in very different ways, and that they are systematic theologians. A common thread in all of them is a panentheistic view and an emphasis on relatedness. Panentheistic is neither theistic nor pantheistic, neither God as a being outside of the world nor God as interchangeable with the world, but God in everything and different from everything. Panentheism means immanence and transcendence.

Gebara, Keller and Theokritoff

Brazilian Ivone Gebara teaches the perspective of poor women and a type of anthropology in which human dignity does not compete with God or the earth but is embedded in both. In her epistemology, she shows that ecological and gender perspectives are needed to understand the world and to unmask the leading "religion" of the market economy.

To give an example, she gave me a key to unlock Psalm 8, a hymn so often used to legitimize domination of man over nature, because it says "thou hast made him little less than God, and [...] hast given him dominion over the works of thy hands."[6] In the context of the Western man subduing the earth, women, and the non-Western world, these words of the Psalm have proved to be devastating, whereas the question in the Psalm is: "What is man that thou art mindful of him?" It poses humans (or men?) between heaven and the

---

[5] The most important works for my research were: Ivone Gebara, *Longing for Running Water: Ecofeminism and Liberation* (Fortress Press: Minneapolis 1999), Catherine Keller, *The Face of the Deep: A Theology of Becoming* (Routledge: London 2003), and Elizabeth Theokritoff, *Living in God's Creation: Orthodox Perspectives on Ecology* (St. Vladimir's Seminary Press: New York 2009).

[6] Quotations from the Revised Standard Version of the Bible (RSV).

animals, and hears the power of God in the voices of little children. Humans are embedded in the glory of God that is "in all the earth" and reveals itself in full power in the powerless. This interpretation makes full use of the contradictions and empty spaces in the Psalm.

This kind of reading a text is derived from Catherine Keller, the second of my three eco-feminist theologians. Her book *Face of the Deep* offered a new, creative method of theology. She probes all kinds of texts – biblical, theological, and novels – to deconstruct the doctrine of *creatio ex nihilo* ('creation out of nothing'). She unravels how the doctrine came into being, and maps the consequences for women and the creation. Under the surface, she detects the undertows and gaps in the texts for constructive theology. Creation as a process is not just a concept but also a method for theologizing. When she perceives that differences are unfolding on the surface of the deep, she is following Deleuze. Keller rejects the concept of salvation history and uses postmodern philosophy and metaphors derived from science, for instance, God as a "strange attractor". It is hardly surprising that most of my readers have great difficulties in understanding the theology of Keller, due to her postmodern method and her idiosyncratic writing. I could not make it easier. Although Keller makes hard reading, her method is extremely insightful and fruitful, also for the inter-church dialogue.

The third eco-feminist theologian is Elizabeth Theokritoff, who is British and a member of the Greek Orthodox Church. Although Eastern Orthodox Churches have the image of being stagnant, conservative, and patriarchal, they have kept alive a theology that is not as discolored by the Enlightenment as Western theology. Their theology is definitely less anthropocentric. Theokritoff derives a nondualist worldview from the Church Fathers. God is not a being but Being itself, like in premodern western theology. The leading concept is not salvation history but God's being in the world, Christ, and liturgy. There is no competition between God and the world as we find so often in Protestant theology. God and the world are also quite different, unlike in the theologies of Gebara and Keller. The old practice of asceticism is read as positive self-restriction, necessary in our context of ecological crisis. Because asceticism is related to liturgy, as an expression of God's glory in the world, it is not world-denying.

The Dutch context
Celebrating and self-restriction are good partners, also in the Dutch context. I hope I have made that convincing with the example of my own practice, which I described in the last chapter: a church service on sustainability in

Boxtel, in the south of the Netherlands. As members of the church, we brought vegetables and fruits from the gardens in the neighborhood, mourned about pollution, climate change and the disappearance of animals and plants, confessed our sins, joined in the praise of all creatures, heard about God letting the earth bring forth, and shared the figs and grapes of the church garden. And by doing all of this we shared hope.

Trees van Montfoort is an independent theological researcher, journalist, and minister of the Protestant Church. She studied Catholic as well as Protestant theology in Utrecht and Leiden. She worked for several national radio broadcasting companies. She published and edited books and articles on theological topics, in the last years with an emphasis on eco-feminism. See: www.VanMontfoortCommunicatie.nl

EUROPEAN SOCIETY OF WOMEN IN THEOLOGICAL RESEARCH

EUROPÄISCHE GESELLSCHAFT FÜR THEOLOGISCHE FORSCHUNG VON FRAUEN

ASSOCIACÍON EUROPEA DE MUJERES EN LA INVESTIGACIÓN TEOLÓGICA

President – Präsidentin – Presidenta
Dr.[in] Gertraud Ladner, Innsbruck, Austria

Vice-President – Vize-Präsidentin – Vicepresidenta
Prof.[in] Dr.[in] Jone Salomonsen, Oslo, Norway

Secretary – Sekretärin – Secretaria
Prof.[in] Dr.[in] Agnethe Siquans, Vienna, Austria

Vice-Secretary – Vize-Sekretärin – Vicesecretaria
Sofia Nikitaki, Leuven, Belgium

Treasurer – Schatzmeisterin – Tesorera
Lcda. Ágata Jané Sainz, Barcelona, Spain

Vice-Treasurer – Vize-Schatzmeisterin – Vicetesorera
Dr.[in] Luise Metzler, Bielefeld, Germany

Networking
Prof.[in] Dr.[in] Małgorzata Grzywacz, Poznań, Poland

Journal – Jahrbuch – Revista
Clara Carbonell Ortiz, Madrid, Spain
Dr.[in] Anne-Claire Mulder, Groningen, Netherlands
Prof.[in] Dr.[in] Agnethe Siquans, Vienna, Austria

Website of the ESWTR
http://www.eswtr.org

ESWTR Journal – advisory board

Accepted:
- Prof. dr Elzbieta Adamiak, Univ. Koblenz/Landau, GER.
- Sr. dr Jadranka Rebeka Anić, Inst. für Sozialwissenschaften Ivo Pilar, Split, KRO.
- Prof. dr Kristin De Troyer, Univ. Salzburg, AUT.
- Prof. dr Annemie Dillen, Kath. University Leuven, BE.
- Dr Montserrat Escribano Cárcel, Univ. de Valencia, ESP.
- Dr Teresa Forcades i Vila, OSB, Barcelona, ESP.
- Prof. dr Judith Gruber, Kath. University Leuven, BE.
- Emer. Prof. dr Maaike de Haardt, Radboud Universiteit Nijmegen, NL.
- Prof. dr Judith Hartenstein, Univ. Koblenz/Landau, GER.
- Prof. dr Maria Häusl, TU-Dresden, GER.
- Prof. dr Susanne Scholz, Southern Methodist University, Texas, USA.
- Prof. dr Nicola Slee, The Queens Foundation Birmingham, UK/VU Amsterdam, NL.
- Prof. dr Teresa Maria Leal de Assunção Martinho Toldy, Univ. Fernando Pessoa, Porto, PT.
- Prof. dr Angelika Walser, Univ. Salzurg, AUT.
- Prof. dr Heleen Zorgdrager, Protestant Theological University, NL.